The Politics of New African Resource Discoveries in the Post-Curse Era

The Politics of New African Resource Discoveries in the Post-Curse Era

Edited by Angela Zivo Gapa

LEXINGTON BOOKS
Lanham • Boulder • New York • London

Published by Lexington Books
An imprint of The Rowman & Littlefield Publishing Group, Inc.
4501 Forbes Boulevard, Suite 200, Lanham, Maryland 20706
www.rowman.com

86-90 Paul Street, London EC2A 4NE

British Library Cataloguing in Publication Information Available

Library of Congress Cataloging-in-Publication Data

Names: Gapa, Angela Zivo, editor, author.
Title: The politics of new African resource discoveries in the post-curse era / edited by
    Angela Zivo Gapa.
Description: Lanham : Lexington Books, 2024. | Includes bibliographical references
    and index.
Identifiers: LCCN 2024015197 (print) | LCCN 2024015198 (ebook) |
    ISBN 9781666952018 (cloth) | ISBN 9781666952025 (ebook)
Subjects: LCSH: Natural resources—Government policy—Africa, Sub-Saharan. |
    Resource curse—Africa, Sub-Saharan. | Mineral industries—Africa, Sub-Saharan.
    | Petroleum industry and trade—Africa, Sub-Saharan. | Gas industry—Africa,
    Sub-Saharan.
Classification: LCC HC800.Z65 P66 2024 (print) | LCC HC800.Z65 (ebook) | DDC
    333.80967—dc23/eng/20240403
LC record available at https://lccn.loc.gov/2024015197
LC ebook record available at https://lccn.loc.gov/2024015198

Contents

Preface

In the realm of global development and politics, few phenomena have garnered the scholarly and policy attention that the "resource curse" has. For decades, researchers have delved into the complexities of how abundant, point-source, non-renewable natural resources often lead to economic stagnation, political instability, and conflict, especially when compared to their resource-poor counterparts. Nowhere have these effects been more consequential than in Africa.

Thirty years since the term was first coined, it is undeniable that our understanding of the African resource curse has evolved. The past African decade has witnessed new mineral, oil, and natural gas discoveries unfolding alongside heightened global demand, advancements in green technology, and democratized access to information. Africa finds itself at a pivotal juncture in its twenty-first-century development trajectory: positioned as a key participant in the global commodities market due to its wealth in mineral and hydrocarbon resources. It is fast gaining recognition as the new frontier for critical resource exploration in light of the clean technology revolution. A sizable amount of the world's strategic subterranean resource reserves are found on the continent, including vital industrial minerals like cobalt and lithium and precious metals like gold and platinum, essential to developing the electric vehicle and renewable energy industries. Furthermore, Africa holds immense potential in the domain of rare earth mineral exploration.

Amid these changes, there is a growing awareness both among African citizens and African governments of the ramifications of the resource curse, fueling optimism that it can be addressed. This renewed optimism is reinforced within the literature that as societies and states democratize, their ability to buffer the resource curse is improved, as was the case of Botswana and South Africa. In addition, the democratization of knowledge, facilitated by the internet and digital technologies, further expands the availability of educational resources about the resource curse. This heightened transparency empowers citizens to hold their governments accountable.

The compendium of chapters in this book thus examines the questions: *Are we in a post-resource-curse era? Have newly resource-rich African countries learned lessons from the mistakes of their traditionally resource-rich counterparts and altered the incentive structures in their resource sectors and beyond to facilitate economic growth? And, considering the increase in knowledge access surrounding the resource curse, will new natural resource discoveries hold greater economic promise for poverty alleviation for citizens? Or does the global political economy continue to constrain resource development in low-income countries despite citizen feedback?*

This book emerges from a collective endeavor to tackle these pressing questions within the context of Africa—a continent ostensibly rich in natural resources, yet often marginalized globally, and plagued by persistent socio-economic and political challenges. Through a series of African case studies, we aim to unravel how African states with jackpot endowments have sought to mitigate or adapt to the resource curse through citizen feedback mechanisms, institutional restructuring, or alternative approaches. By examining the resource curse through the lens of recent resource discoveries, we shed light on the evolving landscape of resource governance and its implications for African states, economies, and societies, especially those whose institutional frameworks were not originally designed to manage substantial resource wealth. We hope to contribute to a more nuanced understanding of the phenomenon by bridging this gap.

Ultimately, this book is a testament to the collective efforts of scholars and practitioners committed to unearthing the complexities of African resource governance, informing policies that promote African agency in the global resource political economy, and advancing the well-being of both established and emerging resource-rich African societies.

Acknowledgments

I wish to extend the deepest gratitude to my parents Pheneas and Otilia Gapa for your encouragement, belief in me, and keen interest in my academic achievements; my family, Cherub, Tatenda, Tadiwa, Vimbai, Ruvarashe, Tinashe, Kunashe, Kuzivakwashe, Joy, Everjoice, Shungu, Tashinga, Onai, Lucky, and Grace, for your love and support; my chosen family, Mercy, Varaidzo, Belinda, Buhle, Gamu, Lusayo, Margaret, Moono, Carolina, Joyce, Lee, Atupele, Rumbi, Bianca, Blessing, Florence, Doris, Mutale, Grace, Prisca, Michael, Lorraine, and Mbuya Mushipe for being my support system; my mentors, John and Sherrow, for challenging me intellectually; to all the contributing authors to this volume for your diligence and hard work, to California State University, Chico, the University of the Witwatersrand, the University of Botswana, the International Political Science Association, and the African Studies Association for the resources which allow me to engage in research I'm passionate about; to my students for inspiring me; and to Ryan, for your love and moral support.

PART I

Introduction and Overview

Introduction

Africa's Resource Renaissance: New Discoveries in a Post-Curse Era

Angela Zivo Gapa

Three decades since the term "resource curse" was coined by Richard Auty, there is renewed academic and policy interest in the role of natural resources in African economies. New economically viable hydrocarbon deposits have been identified in Kenya, Uganda, and Ghana, marking the emergence of a new generation of resource-rich African nations. Furthermore, Tanzania and Mozambique are developing offshore liquefied natural gas deposits, reshaping the geopolitical dynamics and political economy of East Africa. The global demand for natural gas demand has peaked as a more environmentally friendly alternative to oil due to its lower greenhouse gas potential. Mozambique's natural gas windfall saw a liquefied natural gas investment worth twenty billion dollars (Szymczak 2023). The combined gold output of Ghana, Burkina Faso, Mali, and the Republic of Guinea (Conakry) reached 10.8 million ounces in 2023. Ghana, as the top gold producer in Africa and an important exporter in the world market, has seen its production bolstered principally by the improved productivity at the Bibiani mine (Signé and Johnson 2021).

In the Sahel region, recently dubbed the "coup belt," there is a strategic leveraging of gold and uranium wealth to engage alternative partners like Russia. This move aims to develop natural resources to reduce dependence on French neo-colonialism (Mensah and Aning 2022). Simultaneously, Zimbabwe seeks to break free from years of global isolation by focusing on its lithium industry. With the discovery of the largest lithium reserves and mines in Africa, Zimbabwe now ranks prominently among the leading lithium-producing and -supplying countries, following in the footsteps of Chile, Australia, China, Argentina, and Brazil. The surging global demand for lithium, driven by the increasing production of electric vehicles crucial for a zero-carbon emission energy transition, has attracted a surge of potential lithium mining investors, particularly from China. Zimbabwe holds some of the world's most significant hard-rock lithium deposits, attracting seven hundred million dollars in investment from several Chinese firms (Goodenough, Deady, and Shaw 2021). The Democratic Republic of the Congo produces over 70 percent of world's cobalt used in rechargeable batteries, super alloys, and catalysts, and in medical applications such as orthopedic implants and radiotherapy (Roberts and Gunn 2014).

Perhaps the most significant potential in African resource politics over the next few decades is the development of rare earth minerals. Rare earth minerals, also known as rare earth elements, are a group of seventeen chemical elements in the periodic table, consisting of fifteen lanthanides (elements with atomic numbers fifty-seven through seventy-one) and scandium and yttrium (Voncken 2016). Rare earth elements have become crucial in developing green energy technologies such as batteries for electric vehicles, solar panels, and wind turbines. Additionally, they play a strategic role in advanced technologies, including laser systems, jet engines, and sonar devices. Africa provides an alternative to China and the Middle East as a reservoir for these resources and has made many bonanza discoveries in the past decade. Burundi has one of the world's highest-grade rare earth deposits and is Africa's only producing rare earth mine. Burundi, Malawi, South Africa, Mozambique, Zambia, Kenya, Tanzania, and Namibia are the principal reserves for these newly strategic resources used in battery technology. To counter China's dominance in that rare earth space, the United States and the European Union are looking for alternative sources of battery metals. These vast amounts of natural resources, including minerals, oil, and gas, have the potential to contribute to Africa's economic development significantly. Hence, Africa's resource politics has evolved in scope beyond that of familiar resource-cursed countries like Nigeria, Democratic Republic of the Congo, Angola, and Sudan.

The resource curse has been the lens through which resource development in Africa has been viewed for decades. It typically manifests in nations abundant in point-source non-renewable natural resources (Petkov 2018). Such countries often experience lower rates of economic development, an elevated likelihood of violent conflict, or a greater inclination toward authoritarianism compared to their counterparts with fewer natural resources. The resource curse arises from the arbitrary global distribution of strategic natural resources like oil and minerals, making some countries notably more resource rich. Despite their global scarcity, these resources hold immense value as internationally traded commodities crucial for the economic growth of both developing and developed nations. The substantial rent generated from possessing these resources significantly fuels political and economic competition. Moreover, in the absence of a global governing authority, states' relative power and behavior in the international system often wield more influence over the political and economic outcomes of countries than regional and international governance institutions or international law (Gapa 2020). Beyond the conventional strategic and geopolitical perspective on resource competition, academic debates emphasize the political and economic vulnerabilities inherent in states dependent on such resources.

Nowhere are these vulnerabilities more felt than in sub-Saharan Africa. African natural resources are among the most abundant but, historically, have not contributed to the economic development and democratization of the continent, leaving most resource-rich countries in a poverty trap. In Africa, there has been a steady rise in the export of natural resources, outpacing the overall growth of total merchandise exports and manufactured goods. According to the World Trade Organization (2010), during the period between 1998 and 2008, the export of natural resources experienced a growth rate higher than 20 percent. This is in contrast to the annual growth rate for total merchandise exports and manufactured goods which was 12 percent and 10 percent, respectively.

It is important to note that Africa has not been excluded from profiting from the earnings derived from the global natural resources sector. By 2019, the total value of the continent's natural resource exports was just under US$406 billion, comprising 73 percent of the continent's total exports (Al Jazeera 2022). This ratio is notably higher when compared to the allocation of natural resources in exports from other regions, notably North America (20 percent), South and Central America (47 percent), Europe (14 percent), and Asia (14 percent). Across all these regions, the fuel component of natural resources dominated the export. Furthermore, Africa's aspiration to maximize profits from the natural resources sector has spurred countless explorations throughout the continent (Purtill and Littleboy 2023).

With the increase in knowledge about the resource curse from citizens and African governments, there is renewed optimism that states can benefit from their natural resources. Evidence from the literature bolsters the optimism that as institutions democratize, they can help buffer the resource curse, as in countries like Botswana and South Africa. The democratization of knowledge access, facilitated by the internet and digital technologies, thus increases the availability of educational resources on natural resource exploration, distribution, and management. This increased transparency empowers citizens to hold their governments accountable.

But *are we in a post-resource curse era? Have newly resource-rich African countries learned lessons from the mistakes of their traditionally resource-rich counterparts and altered the incentive structures in their resource industries? Considering the increase in knowledge access surrounding the resource curse, will new natural resource discoveries hold greater economic promise for poverty alleviation for citizens? Or does the global political economy continue to constrain resource development in low-income African countries despite evolving domestic politics?*

The chapters in this book examine these questions through African case studies on the new politics of natural resources, focusing on how African governments have managed jackpot resource discoveries in the post–resource curse era. This book will fill a void in the literature on the resource curse, which until now has focused on the effects of natural resources on political and economic development and the role institutions play in addressing the resource curse while failing to account for the dynamic ways in which African societies can shape elite incentives and vice versa. Through the lens of both newly resource-rich and traditionally resource-rich African countries, this volume will specifically look at whether the collective knowledge we have gathered about the resource curse in the past thirty years has helped to mitigate its effects on emerging resource-exporting nations in Africa and those with recent resource discoveries.

This chapter begins by surveying the current literature on the resource curse, including the discussion on how institutions play an intermediary role in determining which countries experience it. It concludes by describing the structure of the book.

WHAT WE CURRENTLY KNOW ABOUT THE THREE RESOURCE CURSES IN AFRICA

The resource curse explains the varying fortunes of countries based on their resource wealth, with resource-rich countries faring much worse than their resource-poor counterparts. The curse typically manifests in three main ways. The first is observed in the adverse effects natural resource exports have on a country's economy, hereby known as the curse of underdevelopment. The second is observed in how resource abundance creates the institutional foundations for authoritarianism. Thirdly, the resource curse is observed in how countries abundant in strategic natural resources tend to be more prone to violent conflict (Gapa 2013). This section will explore the manifestation of these three resource curses.

The Curse of Underdevelopment

The first of the three resource curses is the curse of underdevelopment. Substantial empirical evidence indicates that natural resources, especially point-source and non-renewable resources, paradoxically tend to hinder rather than promote economic growth. Countries with abundant and heavy reliance on extractive resource exports tend to exhibit lower economic growth rates than those dependent on their manufacturing and service economic sectors. In addition, resource-rich countries have generally failed to translate the fortunes from their natural resource wealth into concrete financial and economic developmental planning (Gapa 2013).

Sachs and Warner (1995) first identified an inverse relationship between natural resource abundance and economic growth. Their worldwide study provided empirical backing for the existence of the natural resource curse while controlling for various growth variables, including initial income levels, trade policies, average investment, and bureaucratic efficiency. Later, Weinthal and Luong (2006) observed that, from 1965 to 1998, members of the Organization of Petroleum Exporting Countries (OPEC) universally experienced low or negative annual growth rates despite the surge in world commodity prices. These countries experienced increased debts, compelling them to allocate a significant portion of their gross domestic product (GDP) to debt servicing.

The adverse impacts of natural resources extend beyond the economic realm, affecting human development. According to Chen et al. (2023), poor resource governance can impede growth and induce economic distortions, ultimately influencing the Human Development Index. Citizens in resource-rich nations often face higher levels of poverty, child mortality, and income inequality, and tend to have more authoritarian political systems. In addition, wealth from natural resources disproportionately impacts women. Oil-rich countries tend to have fewer women in the workforce. This stems from the fact that sectors typically more accessible to women, such as export-oriented manufacturing, face lower prospects of success in resource-rich countries due to the prevalence of Dutch disease (see the following discussion) (NRGI 2015).

In contrast, resource-poor and resource-diverse countries, exemplified by the Asian tigers, have stood out as global success stories over the past few decades (Weinthal and Luong 2006). A study conducted on sixty-five resource-rich nations for the period between 1970 and 1998 revealed that only four achieved long-term investment exceeding 25 percent of GDP on average—similar to various industrial resource-poor countries—and per capita gross national product growth exceeding 4 percent per year on average during the same period (Gylfason 2001). These exceptional cases were

Botswana, Indonesia, Malaysia, and Thailand. The latter three achieved success through economic diversification and industrialization, while Botswana, rich in diamonds, achieved comparable success without significant diversification. From 1960 to 1976, leading hard-rock mineral exporters in the developing world had average per capita GDP growth rates of 1.9 percent, nearly half the rate of the control group of resource-poor states (Gylfason 2001). Similarly, Shahbaz et al. (2019) investigated the impact of natural resource abundance and dependence on economic growth across thirty-five countries from 1980 to 2015. They observed that while natural resource abundance fosters economic growth in the presence of trade openness and financial development, natural resource dependence hampered economic activities, leading to negative economic growth. Additionally, they noted that countries facing currency overvaluation suffered negative economic consequences, influenced by both resource abundance and dependence.

The conventional interpretation of the resource curse attributes it to the "Dutch disease," named after the impact of sudden windfall from natural gas on the Dutch economy during the 1970s. The Dutch economy witnessed a surge in the production and export of natural gas, leading to increased revenues from gas exports and causing the Dutch guilder to appreciate against other global currencies. Inadvertently, this increased the prices of exports of Dutch manufactured goods, making them less competitive on the global market and resulting in the overall economy stagnating. The Dutch disease is prevalent in African oil exporters. With the accumulation of crude oil revenues in Nigeria's economy, exporting other labor-intensive agricultural commodities, like peanuts and cocoa, became unprofitable. The agricultural sector thus lost its appeal to investors, leading to a decline in production and hurting the peasant farmers who had produced them. Thus, as Collier (2007) argued, the Dutch disease damaged the growth process by crowding out export activities that otherwise would have the potential to proliferate and generate sectoral reallocation of productive resources in response to favorable price shocks. The booming oil and mineral sectors distorted the growth patterns of agricultural and manufacturing sectors that drove long-lasting economic growth (Yates 1996). Resultantly, in resource-rich countries, there is a temptation for governments to maintain artificially high exchange rates for their national currencies to increase the currency's purchasing power. As a result, other more labor-intensive sectors within the economy suffer.

Another contributing factor to the underdevelopment curse is revenue volatility. Nations heavily dependent on resource exports find that the sharp fluctuations in global market prices translate into domestic economic instability, rendering government incomes and foreign exchange supplies unpredictable and making private investment excessively risky (Ross 1999). Similarly, in countries that export oil and minerals, the fluctuation and unpredictability of revenue impede planning, lead to increased deficits and elevated spending, and often result in a rise in national debt. When oil or mineral prices experience an upsurge, countries become more creditworthy to international lenders like the International Monetary Fund, thereby amplifying the debt burden on resource-rich nations (Shaxson 2005).

In Africa, the political economy of natural resources is typically characterized by rent-seeking. Rent-seeking occurs when individuals or organizations seek to generate income by capturing economic rents through manipulating and exploiting the political economy instead of earning money through legitimate economic transactions and creating additional wealth (Khan 2010). Thus, a rent-seeker attains economic profits without contributing to any economic production. In countries that export resources, rent-seeking manifests through the imposition of regulations affecting consumers and businesses, facilitating the capture of monopoly privileges. This phenomenon is particularly prevalent in "rentier" states, referring to countries whose primary revenue source is external to the domestic economic system. In these nations, external rent situations dominate, with the government being the primary beneficiary of such external rent within the economy. Rentier state theory thus posits that resource abundance causes weak and predatory state institutions (Waldner and Smith 2015).

One consequence of this rentier system is the tendency for the state to relax constraints on foreign exchange. In a rentier economy, foreign exchange is readily available, enabling the state to import goods more affordably. This leads to the displacement of domestically produced goods, especially in agriculture and manufacturing, which struggle to compete with foreign products produced on a larger scale. Another outcome is the government's ability to undertake significant capital-intensive development projects. This is facilitated by the availability of foreign exchange from external rents, allowing the state to acquire foreign technology and create a superficial appearance of modernization without bolstering the economy's actual "goods-producing" capacity (Yates 1996; Waldner and Smith 2015).

As a result, resource-exporting countries often prioritize revenue satisfaction rather than maximization. Substantial rents tend to make state officials myopic and risk-averse, as Ross (1999) noted. Upon receiving significant rents from natural resources, resource-exporting governments often shy away from adopting wealth-generating policies, relying on the assured rents they receive. Instead, there is a tendency for governments to develop an unwarranted sense of optimism about future revenues, allocating a significant portion to maintaining the status quo at the expense of sustained development and democratic principles (Yates 1996; Waldner and Smith 2015).

The Curse of Authoritarianism

The second aspect of the resource curse is the curse of authoritarianism. Nations exporting non-renewable natural resources tend to exhibit undemocratic tendencies and greater authoritarianism when compared to their resource-poor counterparts. In addition, citizens in resource-rich countries struggle to exert pressure on their governments for democratic reforms. Examples of oil- and mineral-rich countries that have endured authoritarianism in Africa and the Middle East include Iraq under Saddam Hussein, Nigeria under Ibrahim Babangida, and Zaire (now the Democratic Republic of Congo) under Mobutu Sese Seko. The presence of oil wealth extends the tenure of authoritarian leaders. Besides oil, there exists a similar effect with kimberlite diamonds, unlike alluvial diamonds and other mineral types which often diminish the duration of authoritarian leaders and parties (Andersen and Aslaksen 2013). However, Smith (2005) contends that it may be more apt to describe oil as promoting "pro-regime stability" rather than being "anti-democratic," as it can contribute to the survival of both autocracies and democracies. Wolfers and Zitzewitz (2009) concludes that oil windfalls generally result in extended terms for elected local officials. In addition, he indicates that the increased incumbency advantage brought on by oil is often associated with a decline in the quality of candidates.

Several mechanisms illuminate how natural resources hinder political development, leading to authoritarianism. The first mechanism is the rentier effect, which fiscally severs the government from its citizens by exempting populations in resource-rich nations from taxation. In such states, establishing a tax system would yield only a small fraction of the revenue obtained from resource rent. Consequently, the absence of representative institutions like taxation reduces government accountability. The rentier effect also allocates most resource revenues to creating and sustaining clientelistic and patronage networks. Those favoring prolonged political incumbency use resource-generated revenues to appease clients, thus gaining political support. This poses a significant obstacle to the forces of democratization (Berman 1997). Moreover, in rentier states, investments in security forces are prioritized to suppress the population and safeguard political incumbents from potential challengers to their positions, significantly stifling the political voice of the citizens (Ross 1999).

The second mechanism that explains the effects of resources on democracy is the modernization effect. When a country undergoes modernization, it influences various facets of life, generating positive feedback and reinforcing transformations within political institutions. This leads to increased specialization in occupations, urbanization, higher levels of education, extended life expectancy, improved human development indicators, and elevated primary economic growth rates. Moreover, modernization fosters increased mass political participation, ultimately strengthening democratic political institutions. In contrast, resource-rich nations often spend less on education than their resource-poor counterparts, thereby constraining democratic development (Gylfason 2001).

Natural resources provide the foundation for personal rule and neopatrimonialism (Englebert 2000). Neopatrimonialism is characterized by personalizing power and utilizing state resources for personal gain. In such a system, governments use their positions of power to distribute resources to those loyal to them at the expense of rational-legal procedures. Here, resource regimes collect and distribute rents as patronage instead of developing infrastructure and institutional capacities for broad-based markets. Furthermore, political appointments depend on loyalty and kinship; transactions are personalized, and political office is treated as an extension of presidential personal property and a source of private gain. Hence, in such a system a clear sense of a public interest transcending private ones does not exist (Leonard and Strauss 2003).

Due to its resonance with pre-colonial political culture, many countries in sub-Saharan Africa have neopatrimonialistic institutions (Bratton 1994). Prior to colonial influence, African states were characterized by high levels of centralization and hierarchy. Typically, the chief was the singular custodian of natural resources, overseeing their access and distribution through patron-client relationships. In Africa, where kinship networks and other primary reciprocities governed communities, informal institutions held more significance than formal ones. Rational-legal authority resultantly gained less traction in modern African settings than in other regions that have transitioned to more efficient forms of governance. Africa has retained its hierarchical, patriarchal, community-centered orientation resonant with pre-colonial political culture (Hyden 2006). This manifests in how natural resources have helped fuel personalistic rule. One extreme example is that of Mobutu Sese Seko's Zaire (now Democratic Republic of Congo). In his thirty years in power, Mobutu succeeded in generating huge amounts of wealth for himself and his clients, while 99 percent of that country's population faced a disintegrating economy. To survive, Mobutu only needed to maintain diamond, gold, copper, cobalt, and other minerals and collect foreign aid to protect his state and perpetuate his rule (Dunning 2005). Thus, natural resources were used to sustain a kleptocratic government.

The Curse of Violent Conflict

The third dimension of the resource curse revolves around the observed empirical connection between natural resources and an increased likelihood of violent conflict. According to Klare (2001), conflict tends to concentrate in regions abundant with valuable natural resources such as petroleum, natural gas, and diamonds. These areas are often strategically important and draw attention in the military planning of dominant world powers like the United States and China. Globally, various violent conflicts have been both funded by and prolonged due to access to natural resources. Conflict is more prone to erupt due to the discovery of oil in economically disadvantaged regions compared to the national average (Østby et al. 2009) and inhabited by marginalized ethnic groups (Basedau and Richter 2014; Hunziker and Cederman 2012). Additionally, the risk of conflict increases when oil is situated in areas with a highly concentrated ethnic group (Morelli and Rohner 2015) and when ethnic minority entrepreneurs leverage it to foster collective resistance against the central government (Aspinall 2007). However, while oil is a strategic resource in interstate conflicts, especially involving superpowers like the United States, civil conflicts are frequently associated with alluvial diamonds, alluvial gemstones, other non-fuel minerals and contraband good like coca leaves (Ross 2015). Consequently, areas where prolonged conflicts occur in regions rich in alluvial diamonds, these are labeled as "conflict diamonds," or more commonly "blood diamonds." Diamonds extracted amid post-colonial civil wars in Angola, Ivory Coast, Sierra Leone, Liberia, Guinea, and Guinea-Bissau have all been categorized as such (Gilmore et al. 2005).

Two conflicting theories explain the connection between resource wealth and violent conflict: greed and grievance theories. As Collier and Hoeffler (2005) proposed, the greed theory contends that wealth derived from primary commodities increases the likelihood of the onset of civil war. This is driven by the motivation of greedy rebels to take up arms, prolong fighting, or intervene militarily, either directly or by supporting internal warring factions, to gain or maintain control over valuable resources. On the other hand, the "grievance" theory suggests that perceived deprivation in producing regions and among social groups, or the indirect negative economic impacts of resource wealth, creates grievances that trigger violent uprisings. In such scenarios, resource wealth fuels civil war by incentivizing people in resource-rich areas to seek greater autonomy in controlling natural resources or establishing a separate state. This is particularly evident when the distribution affects ethnically or geographically distinct regions that are typically disenfranchised. This rationale has been a driving force behind secessionist movements in regions rich in natural resources, such as Cabinda in Angola (rich in oil), Biafra in Nigeria (rich in oil), and southern Sudan (abundant in natural gas).

Violent conflict in regions abundant with resources typically manifests after a significant downturn in economic growth and a weakening of state institutions. Ross (2002) observed that civil wars in the Democratic Republic of the Congo, Sierra Leone, and Liberia were all preceded by a rapid decline in GDP per capita and the presence of corrupt institutions. Furthermore, resource reliance overwhelms the state's budgetary processes and encourages incumbents to use funds for patronage. Consequently, states lack accountability to their citizens and fail to invest in the necessary security apparatus to maintain stability within the country. Instead, they prioritize building up security forces to protect their regimes rather than the citizens.

Finally, Ross (2002) argues that resource abundance provides an opportunity for rebel financing. When Angola's National Union for the Total Independence of Angola (UNITA) lost its financial backing from the United States at the end of the Cold War and the apartheid era in South Africa, it turned to its diamond revenue to support military expenses. Resources like diamonds and oil produce high rents and are usually done in a specific location, making looting and extortion feasible. The sale of war booty can also foster violent conflict in resource-rich states. In 1997, in Congo-Brazzaville, the private militia of President Sassou-Nguesso was funded by the sale of war booty and the rights to future exploitation rights to the country's oil reserves (Englebert and James 2004).

Institutions and the Resource Curse

The occurrence of the resource curse is closely tied to the quality of a nation's institutions. Adherents of the institutionalist perspective believe that, with the proper institutional framework, non-renewable resources can enhance a country's economic and human development (Boschini, Petterson, and Roine 2007). In nations with effective institutions, the presence of resource wealth attracts entrepreneurs to engage in production. Conversely, entrepreneurs diverge from production in countries with fragile institutions and toward unsustainable rent-seeking activities. Here, natural resources can incentivize politicians to dismantle effectively operating institutions regulating the utilization of natural resources, all in an effort to secure access to the associated revenues (Ross 2003). The varying growth outcomes among resource-exporting countries primarily stem from how rents are distributed through a country's institutional framework.

Mehlum, Moene, and Torvik (2005) distinguish between "producer-friendly" institutions, where rent-seeking activities complement economic production, and "grabber-friendly" institutions, where rent-seeking competes with production. Grabber-friendly institutions aim to benefit from specialization in unproductive environments marked by weak rule of law, dysfunctional bureaucracy, and corruption. Such institutions divert entrepreneurial resources from production, leading to negative economic growth. Similarly, Robinson, Torvik, and Verdier (2006) contend that depending on the quality of institutions, politicians favor certain policies over others in response to incentives created by resource booms. Low-quality institutions encourage poor policy choices, enabling politicians to engage in inefficient redistribution to influence election outcomes.

In contrast, high-quality institutions make such political strategies less appealing. Scholars emphasizing the role of institutions in the resource curse express optimism about escaping it, believing that with appropriate laws and structural adjustments, resource-rich countries can overcome the curse. They advocate for establishing savings funds, policies promoting economic diversification to reduce resource dependence, and income redistribution to benefit resource-rich countries positively from their resource endowments (Alayli 2005).

Rosser (2006) argues that the nature of institutions in resource-exporting countries is shaped by enduring social patterns and dynamics, especially where natural resource dominance in the economy occurred after state formation. In such cases, resource endowments become integrated into ongoing development processes and a network of identities. Watts (2004) develops this idea in his study of Nigeria, examining how petro-capitalism generates forms of rule and political authority, creating "governable spaces" from the contextual realities in which it operates (Watts 2004). Therefore, the counter-argument to the resource curse posits that the distinction between countries benefiting from resources and those that do not is determined by the institutional context into which natural resources are introduced.

The development of institutional frameworks has not remained unaffected by the influence of natural resources. According to Basedau (2005), contentious colonial legacies and reliance on resource revenues undermine state institutions, thus formulating suboptimal economic policies. In the historical context of African nations abundant in natural resources, political institutions and property rights were established to extract valuable resources for the benefit of the metropole efficiently. During the African colonial era, institutions were biased toward empowering the colonial elite to extract minerals or cultivate cash crops. Consequently, secure property rights were only granted to the politically and socially influential colonial elite.

The quality of institutions is influenced by the dependence on economic rents derived from natural resources. Ross (2003) contends that revenues from natural resources can hinder a government's ability to address social conflicts in two ways: by impeding the effectiveness of the state bureaucracy and by weakening the state's territorial control monopoly. He argues that a state's strength lies in its ability to tax its citizens, and abundant natural resources can undermine this capacity as the state has less incentive to establish tax infrastructure due to the ease of obtaining economic rents. Additionally, if a country possesses valuable resources that can be informally mined, such as coltan, tanzanite, and alluvial diamonds, the state's control over law and order in the extraction region may be compromised. These "lootable" minerals attract rural miners who often resort to extralegal and sometimes violent measures to establish claims and settle disputes. The high value-to-weight ratios of these resources compromise their taxability, facilitating smuggling. Furthermore, as argued by Basedau (2005), they contribute to high levels of corruption within the government and beyond. In certain cases, this combination of weak institutions, corrupt governance, compromised authority, and resilient criminal organizations can escalate to the emergence of rebel movements.

Contrastingly, in the case of Botswana, the abundance of resources, particularly diamonds, has not negatively impacted economic development, peace, security, or democracy. Diamond wealth has not incentivized the economic elite to establish neopatrimonialistic networks or discouraged taxation. Property rights have been efficiently allocated, and the state maintains significant control over resource extraction. This chapter builds upon Acemoglu, Johnson, and Robinson's (2001) assertion that despite initial economic and geographic disadvantages during the colonial period, Botswana achieved rapid development due to its high-quality institutions. This raises questions about why Botswana's institutions have remained robust and why diamond wealth has not led to undesirable behavior in Botswana as it has in other sub-Saharan African countries rich in natural resources.

Are We in a Post–Resource Curse Era?

It has been thirty years since the term "resource curse" was first coined by Richard Auty. As outlined earlier, this phenomenon, which manifests as various economic, political, and social distortions, has been the subject of immense scrutiny and debate among development specialists and scholars. It is, therefore, imperative to ascertain whether the global landscape has transcended the grips of the resource curse and if resource-rich countries have successfully adapted to the challenges it poses, heralding a post–resource curse era.

Over the past three decades, many countries have made conscious efforts to navigate their development trajectories away from the pitfalls of the resource curse. Some focused on addressing symptoms of the curse, specifically through attempts to diversify their economies and improve their management of natural resources. Zambia stands out as a prime example of a country whose government has made strides to diversify its mineral-led economy. According to the Seventh National Development Plan of Zambia (2017–2021), the key sectors toward economic diversification included agriculture, manufacturing, tourism, and energy sectors. Given the potential for increased agricultural output and the importance of agriculture to the Zambian labor force, the government prioritized agriculture during the past decade to drive diversi-fied growth. In order to add value to agricultural produce, the government, through the Industrial Development Corporation, increased investments in pineapple processing in the North-Western Province, fruit processing in the Eastern Province, and cashew nut processing in the Western Province. Furthermore, in Muchinga Province, an out-grower scheme for palm oil trees was rolled out to five hundred households covering 380 hectares under the Industrial Development Corporation. On the other hand, travel and tourism is Zambia's fastest-growing national economic sector, contributing nearly two million US dollars to the national economy and over three hundred thousand jobs to the Zambian economy in 2018 while posting a 6.3 percent increase in its GDP, making it the fastest and most bullish economic sector in the country. Similarly, plans are underway for massive renewable energy sources such as solar farms, geothermal plants, mini hydro grids, and wind farms to relieve strain on the national electricity grid (Banda 2022).

However, many countries continue to grapple with the effects of the resource curse and remain susceptible to its emerging and further dependence on their extractive industries. The disparity in outcomes is largely a product of the political and economic institutions in the countries as well as their supportive political culture. Countries rely on their state's capacity to imple-ment effective policies and reforms remain key to its success. Furthermore, African resource exporters remain dependent on trends in the global political economy and the geopolitical preferences of more powerful nations.

The landscape of resource politics has been shifting in Africa in the past decade due to new resource discoveries. In the fast-globalizing world, natural resource endowments pose many opportunities for resource-rich countries, and the allocation of their natural resource wealth can either be state-based or market-based. State-based resource allocation strategies typically fall under the auspice of resource nationalism. Resource national-ism is a state-led resource management approach aimed at consolidating state control over subterranean resources and the harmonization of this with national development plans. This is unlike resource liberalism, which denotes a more market-based approach to resource wealth allocation (Wilson 2011). According to Caramento, Saunders, and Larmer (2023), Africa has experienced two primary waves of resource nationalism: the 1960s to 1970s and the late 2000s. The initial phase coincided with the continent's inde-pendence and was characterized by post-colonial governments' efforts to enhance national ownership and control of mining and petroleum resources. Strategies included nationalizing mining companies, establishing state-run resource marketing bodies, and participating in global initiatives like the Intergovernmental Council of Copper Exporting Countries to impact mineral supply and pricing. However, much of this framework was dismantled in the

1980s and 1990s in favor of resource liberalism, due to a revitalization of neoliberal ideals championed by the Reagan and Thatcher administrations, prompting an era of privatization and deregulation under structural adjustment programs. The second wave of resource nationalism, which emerged in the late 2000s, focused more on boosting mineral revenues via new fiscal measures, enhancing regulatory frameworks through capacity development, and fostering economic linkages between mining and other economic sectors (Caramento, Saunders, and Larmier 2023). African countries that have attempted large-scale resource nationalism include Tanzania, the Democratic Republic of Congo, Zambia, and Ghana (Hall 2021).

In Africa, another shift is ensuing, with a rise in artisanal and small-scale informal mining. The drivers of artisanal mining in Africa are multifaceted. The search for better opportunities by rural peasants living in agriculturally depleted areas makes informal mining very attractive and lucrative, given the high commodity prices of the minerals and their high global demand. Peasant labor processes in Africa and other parts of the developing world have slowly been shifting from agriculture to informal mineral extraction and best explain the contemporary changes in rural, mineral-rich tracts throughout Africa. As a result, peasant mining practices are placing the politics of poverty within broader debates on resource politics (Lahiri-Dutt 2018). Yet another factor driving artisanal mining is the lack of regulation in these artisanal spaces. The lack of environmental oversight, legal mining titles, and adherence to occupational health and safety standards allow informal mining to thrive (Lahiri-Dutt 2018).

The development of green technology is yet another aspect of the post–resource curse era. Over the past fifteen years, the commodities market has been roiled by a supercycle that first sent oil, gas, and mineral prices soaring, followed by a drastic decline. In addition, resource companies and exporters face a new disruptive era. Technological innovation—including artificial intelligence; the adoption of robotics, internet technology, and data analytics; macroeconomic trends; and changing consumer behavior—is altering the way the production and consumption of non-renewable natural resources (Woetzel et al. 2017). On the demand side, energy consumption is becoming more efficient as people use less energy daily and energy-efficient technologies become more integrated in homes, businesses, and transportation. Furthermore, technological advancements are enabling the reduction of the cost of renewable energies, such as solar and wind energy, handing them a more significant role in the global economy's energy mix. On the supply side, resource producers are increasingly deploying a range of technologies, placing mines and wells that were once inaccessible within reach, boosting the efficiency of extraction processes, pivoting to predictive maintenance, and using sophisticated data analysis to identify, extract, and manage new resources (Woetzel et al. 2017).

The final marker of the post–resource curse era is the rise of information technology, bringing several changes, including greater accessibility of information on the resource curse and the rise of social media and online political influencers. The globalization of information has been instrumental in increasing transparency and accountability in resource-rich countries by enabling the rapid dissemination of information and exposing corruption and mismanagement of resource revenues. Social media has been a vehicle for activism and mobilization, amplifying the voices of marginalized communities. Social media has also had significant market influence as it influences consumption patterns. However, social media can also be a conduit for propaganda and misinformation. Take the Democratic Republic of Congo as an example. According to Milain Fayulu, a Congolese technology entrepreneur and political science scholar, "Over 21 million Congolese are online, and out of that number over 98% access social media primarily through their cell phones which means one out of five Congolese are connected online . . . debates are raging online, political parties hire a number of influencers and the truth is fake news travels faster than the truth so different types of factions are trying to harness it in different shapes or forms" (Voice of America 2022). Hence, if used irresponsibly and unethically, social media can exacerbate social and political conflicts, especially in high-stake, resource-rich areas, potentially leading to instability.

STRUCTURE OF THE BOOK

Part I of this book contains the introduction "Africa's Resource Renaissance: New Discoveries in a Post-Curse Era," which provides a comprehensive survey of the resource curse phenomenon, outlines the fast-evolving global landscape of resource politics, and situates the book's core themes. Gapa examines the scope and significance of the volume of chapters in the book and provides a structure of the remaining book.

Part II of this book surveys the experiences of newly resource-rich African countries that have been endowed with jackpot natural resources within the past decade including Uganda, Tanzania, Burundi, Ghana, Mozambique, Kenya, and Cameroon.

Chapter 1, entitled "Uganda's Oil Discovery: The Double-Edged Sword of Development and Resource Curse," examines the potential implications of Uganda's recent discovery of oil in its Lake Albert region and considers its potential impact on Uganda's authoritarian electoral politics. In this chapter, Kodero explores domestic civil society resistance to the government's oil management via environmental and native rights activists in light of community displacement and disempowerment in frontier areas, and the global resistance to oil discoveries in light of the green energy movement. Kodero argues that instead of increasing good governance and democratic processes, the discovery of oil in Uganda will solidify the grasp of the quasi-democratic ruling National Resistance Movement in Ugandan politics as the reigning elites thwart the country's institutions and resources for their advantage. In addition, he posits that Ugandan oil industry will catalyze regional integration under the East African Community.

Chapter 2, entitled "Beyond Resource Curse: How Tanzania Avoided the Resource Curse in the Natural Gas Sector," explores Tanzania's mixed experiences with its jackpot mineral and oil and natural gas discoveries. Walwa argues that while the mining sector in Tanzania has been marred by various issues, notably lack of transparency and violation of local communities' land and economic rights, Tanzania has done increasingly well to avoid the resource curse in the natural gas sector. The natural gas laws have placed natural gas under the national oil company, which allowed the country to maintain a stake in the natural gas sector, enabling it to leverage the operation of the natural gas sector toward prioritizing production for domestic needs. This helped to address the two problems in the country: unemployment and energy deficit. However, Walwa argues that legal reforms should back the new law on the natural gas extractive industry to create strong oversight institutions capable of checks on the operations and conduct of actors involved in the governance of the natural gas extractive sector.

Chapter 3, entitled "The Political Economy of Mining Resources in Burundi," explores newly resource-rich Burundi which, despite being one of the poorest countries in the word, has recently been endowed with bonanza mineral resources in the form of gold, nickel, copper, cobalt, tantalum, tin, tungsten ore, and, most importantly, rare earth minerals. In this chapter, Ndoricimpa and Achandi examine Burundi's natural resource management value chain, specifically exploring how prospecting contracts and licenses are awarded, how taxes are collected, and how mining operations are regulated and monitored. In doing so, the authors uncover the nature of gendered engagement in mineral exploitation and of rent-seeking and rent-seizing opportunities created by elites in the resource sector, thus questioning the efficacy of Burundi's institutions in facilitating economic growth.

Chapter 4, entitled "Ghana's Petroleum Management Regime: Challenges and Opportunities," examines Ghana's attempt at democratic oil governance in light of its recent discovery. Aboagye and Ogbe explore Ghana's robust legislative and regulatory frameworks for oil management. While it is generally expected that a country that is relatively well governed would have a good resource governance regime, and that the country would ultimately benefit developmentally from resource exploitation, Aboagye and Ogbe challenge this orientation and call for a critical scrutiny of Ghana's oil governance regime. This chapter examines the nature and effectiveness of Ghana's oil governance regime to demonstrate that certain policy and regulatory shortcomings can be blamed for having contributed to the country's limited gains. In addition, they propose an innovative way of increasing citizen participation in petroleum revenue management: the use of spatial crowdsourcing technology.

Chapter 5, entitled "Gas Curse or Gas Compliment? The Politics of Mozambique's Jackpot Natural Gas Discoveries," analyzes Mozambique's recent exploration into natural gas, purporting to offer a much-needed source of money to alleviate poverty and inequality. Gapa and Hamandishe examine the policy reactions of the Mozambican government and civil society organizations to natural gas discoveries and explore institutional frameworks established by the Mozambican government to assure openness, accountability, and community engagement in resource governance, as well as the obstacles and limits of these efforts in light of the jihadist the insurgency in Cabo Delgado. Gapa and Hamandishe argue that Mozambique's experience exemplifies the difficulties of resource governance and the necessity for inclusive and participatory policies that prioritize the well-being of local populations and the environment.

Chapter 6, entitled "The Political Economy of Oil Discovery in Turkana, Kenya: Prospects and Challenges," is an inquiry into the exploration and discovery of windfall oil in Turkana, Kenya. Chacha, Nyangena, and Imbiakha argue that this discovery has exposed serious political challenges as oil discovery is unfamiliar territory in Kenya. While the sector largely engages with foreign actors, this discovery has opened up opportunities for other stakeholders including the Kenyan diaspora and an often-neglected enclave minority ethnic group, the Turkana. In addition, increasingly enlightened citizens who have recently been in contact with devolution modes of governance and modern education are exposing how enhancements in knowledge access have influenced local political leadership on legitimacy and corporate social responsibility in Kenya's oil management.

Chapter 7, entitled "Cameroon's Extractive Revival: The New Policy on Mineral Exploitation," endeavors to spotlight Cameroon's recent mining policy and the hurdles it confronts in achieving its anticipated outcomes. The mining policy, announced in December 2023, outlines the legal framework for Cameroon's mining sector, covering various aspects such as reconnaissance, exploration, mining, transportation, and marketing of mineral resources in order to integrate SONAMINES, the new mining entity, into Cameroon's regulatory framework. In the chapter, Mekongo-Mballa, Oumba, and Gapa critique the revised legislation's aims at enhancing profitability, ensuring state revenue, and fostering an environment conducive to investment and sustainable mining practices, juxtaposed with its institutional potential to significantly contribute toward creating national wealth.

Part III of this book focuses on the new ways in which traditionally resource-rich economies—Zimbabwe, Sudan, Zambia, and Nigeria—have adjusted to the global political economy of their resource exports in an era where there is more citizen awareness and information access has been democratized.

In chapter 8, entitled "A Political Settlement Analysis of Extractive Governance Practices in Zimbabwe," Sithole argues that despite the democratization of information access on natural resources, critical power actors in Zimbabwe's liberation struggle protracted colonial governance practices and used extractive resource governance to further their interests and accumulate power. Using anonymized interviews, Sithole discovers that despite new resource discoveries particularly lithium in the past decade, reforms in Zimbabwe's resource exploitation have been skewed toward state control, hindering efforts to redistribute resources and address inequalities in mining communities.

In chapter 9, entitled "'Why Should We Pay Tax?': Fiscal Policy and Tax Morale in Sudan (1999–2019)," Resti and Nour explore how the Sudanese regime has dealt with increasing pressures from the citizenry for robust resource management since its separation from the South. This transition, which came as an unprecedented shock for Sudanese public finances, initially promised to transition Sudan from a rentier state toward a post–resource curse economy. However, Resti and Nour, using evidence from anonymized interviews, argue that new resource discoveries, such as gold, are yet to take over long-gone oil revenues and explores the factors that are constraining the latest endeavors to mobilize resource revenue.

Chapter 10, entitled "Political Power versus Economic Power? The Case of Zambia's Mining Sector," explores the impediments to sustained development in Zambia's mineral sector. Through an analysis of the state of artisanal and small-scale mining in the rural Zambia, as well as Zambia's new mineral resource development policy, mining sector policy reforms, and the local political-economic contexts, Lange argues that the best way for Zambia to salvage its mineral resources is through streamlining political power away from the central government and empowering key local stakeholders in Zambia's mining industry.

Chapter 11, entitled "New Resource Discoveries, Old Patterns of Accumulation, Politics, and Development in Nigeria," argues that despite new resource discoveries that generate income for the state, old patterns of capital accumulation in the interest of a few elites, violent politics to control the state, and unequal and disjointed development prevail within Nigeria's resource economy. Sha argues that resource discoveries in Nigeria have rein-forced old patterns of resource accumulation. Moreover, recent discoveries of oil in Gombe State, as well as solid minerals such as gold, lead, and sapphire, have intensified violent competition for political power between the Nigerian government and local indigenous communities in resource-rich regions over the allocation of oil and mineral resource rents. Sha posits that there is need for new collective action politics to advocate for the creation of political institutions capable of implementing reforms and building resource-based economies on the ethos of good governance and democracy.

Part IV of the book includes the conclusion: "Resource Futures: African Strategies for a New Era in Resource Politics." Here, Gapa examines points for the future of natural resource governance in Africa, including the oppor-tunities toward increased African agency in navigating the value chains of resource discoveries in Africa.

REFERENCES

Alayli, Mohammed Ali. 2005. *Resource Rich Countries and Weak Institutions: The Resource Curse Effect*. Berkeley, CA: University of California.

Al Jazeera. 2022. "Mapping Africa's Natural Resources." https://www.aljazeera.com/news/2018/2/20/mapping-africas-natural-resources#, accessed December 21, 2023.

Acemoglu, Daron, Simon Johnson, and James A. Robinson, 2001. "The Colonial Origins of Comparative Development: An Empirical Investigation." *American Economic Review*, 91(5): 1369–401.

Andersen, J. J., and S. Aslaksen. 2013. "Oil and Political Survival." *Journal of Development Economics*, 100(1): 89–106.

Aspinall, E., 2007. "The Construction of Grievance." *Journal of Conflict Resolution*, 51(6): 950–72.

Banda, W. 2022. "Economic Diversification: The Case of the Zambian Mining Sector." Zambia Institute for Policy Analysis and Research; Committee on National Economy, Trade and Labour Matters.

Basedau, M., 2005. "Context Matters—Rethinking the Resource Curse in Sub-Saharan Africa." GIGA Working Paper No 1, German Institute of Global and Area Studies, Hamburg.

Basedau, M., and T. Richter, T. 2014. "Why Do Some Oil Exporters Experience Civil War but Others Do Not? Investigating the Conditional Effects of Oil." *European Political Science Review*, 6(4): 549–74.

Berman, S. 1997. "Civil Society and Political Institutionalization." *American Behavioral Scientist*, 40(5): 562–74.

Boschini, Anne D., Jan Petterson, and Jesper Roine. 2007. "Resource Curse or Not: A Question of Appropriability." *Scandinavian Journal of Economics*, 109(3): 593–617.

Bratton, M. 1994. "Civil Society and Political Transition in Africa." IDR Reports 11(6).

Caramento, A., R. G. Saunders, and M. Larmer. 2023. "The Return of Resource Nationalism to Southern Africa—Introduction." *Journal of Southern African Studies*, 49(3): 339–57.

Chen, Y., A. Khurshid, A. Rauf, H. Yang, and A. C. Calin. 2023. "Natural Resource Endowment and Human Development: Contemporary Role of Governance." *Resources Policy*, 81: 103334.

Collier, Paul, and Anke Hoeffler. 2005. "Resource Rents, Governance and Conflict." *Journal of Conflict Resolution*, 49(4): 625–33.

Collier, Paul. 2007. *The Bottom Billion: Why the Poorest Countries are Failing and What Can be Done about It*. New York, NY: Oxford University Press.

Dunning, Thad. 2005. "Resource Dependence, Economic Performance and Political Stability." *Journal of Conflict Resolution*, 49(4): 451–82.

Englebert, Pierre. 2000. *State Legitimacy and Development in Africa*. Boulder, London: Lynne Reinner Publishers.

Englebert, Pierre, and Ron James. 2004. "Primary Commodities and War: Congo-Brazzaville's Ambivalent Resource Curse." *Comparative Politics*, 37(1): 61–81.

Gapa, Angela. 2013. "Escaping the Resource Curse: The Sources of Institutional Quality in Botswana." Doctoral Dissertation, Florida International University

Gapa, Angela. 2020. "Natural Resources and African Economies: Turning Liability to Asset." In *The Palgrave Handbook of African Political Economy*, edited by Samuel Ojo Oloruntoba and Toyin Falola, 679–97. Berlin: Springer.

Gilmore, E., N. P. Gleditsch, P. Lujala, and J. K. Rød. 2005. "Conflict Diamonds: A New Dataset." *Conflict Management and Peace Science*, 22(3): 257–72.

Goodenough, K., E. Deady, and R. Shaw. 2021. "Lithium Resources, and their Potential to Support Battery Supply Chains, in Africa." British Geological Survey, Natural Environment Research Council Technical Report.

Gylfason, T. 2001. "Natural Resources and Economic Growth: What Is the Connection?" CESifo Working Paper, CESifo Group, Munich.

Hall, Matthew. 2021. "Mapping the Rise of Resource Nationalism in Africa." https://www.mining-technology.com/features/mapping-the-rise-of-resource-nationalism-in-africa/?cf-view, accessed January 31, 2024.

Hunziker, P. M., and L. E. Cederman. 2012. "No Extraction Without Representation: Petroleum Production and Ethnonationalist Conflict." In APSA 2012 Annual Meeting Paper.

Hyden, G., 2006. Between State and Community: Challenges to Redesigning Governance in Africa. In *Working Conference on "Designing Constitutional Arrangements for Democratic Governance in Africa: Challenges and Possibilities,"* 30–31.

Khan, Z. R., C. A. Midega, T. J. Bruce, A. M. Hooper, and J. A. Pickett. 2010. "Exploiting Phytochemicals for Developing a 'Push–Pull' Crop Protection Strategy for Cereal Farmers in Africa." *Journal of Experimental Botany*, 61(15): 4185–96.

Klare, Michael T. 2001. "The New Geography of Conflict." *Foreign Affairs*, 80(3): 49–61.

Lahiri-Dutt, K. 2018. "Extractive Peasants: Reframing Informal Artisanal and Small-Scale Mining Debates." *Third World Quarterly*, 39(8): 1561–82.

Leonard, David K., and Scott Strauss. 2003. *Africa's Stalled Development: International Causes and Cures*. Boulder, CO: Lynne Reinner Publishers.

Mehlum, H., K. Moene, and R. Torvik. 2005. "Crime-Induced Poverty Traps." *Journal of Development Economics*, 77(2): 325–40.

Mensah, A. N. A., and K. Aning. 2022. "Russia Resurgent? Untangling the Role and Meaning of Moscow's Proxies in West Africa and the Sahel." *The Strategic Review for Southern Africa*, 44(1).

Morelli, M., and Rohner, D. 2015. "Resource Concentration and Civil Wars." *Journal of Development Economics*, 117: 32–47.

Natural Resource Governance Institute (NRGI). 2015. *The Resource Curse: The Political and Economic Challenges of Natural Resource Wealth*. New York.

Østby, G., R. Nordås, and J. K. Rød. 2009. "Regional Inequalities and Civil Conflict in Sub-Saharan Africa." *International Studies Quarterly*, 53(2): 301–24.

Petkov, B. 2018. "Natural Resource Abundance: Is It a Blessing or Is It a Curse?" *Journal of Economic Development*, 43(3): 25–56.

Purtill, J. A., and A. K. Littleboy. 2023. "More and Better Mine Rehabilitation— Lessons from Queensland." World Mining Congress.

Roberts, S., and G. Gunn. 2014. "Cobalt." In *Critical Metals Handbook*, edited by G. Gunn, 122–49. Hoboken, NJ: Wiley.

Robinson, James, Ragnar Torvik, and Thierry Verdier. 2006. "Political Foundations of the Resource Curse." *Journal of Development Economics*, 79(2): 447–68.

Ross, Michael. 1999. "The Political Economy of the Resource Curse." *World Politics*, 51(2): 297–322.

Ross, Michael. 2002. "Natural Resources and Civil War: An Overview with Some Policy Options." In *Governance of Natural Resources Conference, December 9–10, 2002*. Paris: World Bank and Agence Francaise du Developpement.

Ross, M. 2003. "The Natural Resource Curse: How Wealth Can Make You Poor." In *Natural Resources and Violent Conflict: Options and Actions*, edited by Ian Bannon and Paul Collier, 17–42. Washington, DC: World Bank.

Ross, M. L. 2015. "What Have We Learned about the Resource Curse?" *Annual Review of Political Science*, 18: 239–59.

Rosser, A. 2006. "The Political Economy of the Resource Curse: A Literature Survey (Vol. 268)." Institute of Development Studies, University of Sussex.

Sachs, Jeffrey D., and Andrew M. Warner. 1995. "Natural Resource Abundance and Economic Growth." NBER Working Paper 5398, National Bureau of Economic Research, Cambridge, MA.

Signé, L., and C. Johnson. 2021. "Africa's Mining Potential: Trends, Opportunities, Challenges and Strategies." Policy Paper May 2021, Policy Center for the New South, Salé, Morocco.

Shahbaz, M., M. A. Destek, I. Okumus, and A. Sinha. 2019. "An Empirical Note on Comparison between Resource Abundance and Resource Dependence in Resource Abundant Countries." *Resources Policy*, (60): 47–55.

Shaxson, Nicholas. 2005. "New Approaches to Volatility: Dealing with the Resource Curse in Sub-Saharan Africa." *International Affairs*, 81(2): 311–24.

Smith, B. 2005. "Life of the Party: The Origins of Regime Breakdown and Persistence under Single-Party Rule." *World Politics*, 57(3): 421–51.

Szymczak, P. D. 2023. "Location, Location—Tanzania, Mozambique Soon to Join Club of Global LNG Suppliers to India, China, Southeast Asia." *Journal of Petroleum Technology*, 75(05): 40–46.

Voice of America. 2022. "African Social Media Influencers Cash In on Politics." https://www.voaafrica.com/a/african-social-media-influencers-cash-in-on-politics /6580471.html, accessed January 31, 2024.

Voncken, J. H. L. 2016. *The Rare Earth Elements: An Introduction.* Cham, Switzerland: Springer International Publishing.

Waldner, D., and B. B. Smith. 2015. "Rentier States and State Transformations." In *The Oxford Handbook of Transformations of the State*, edited by S. Leibfried, E. Huber, M. Lange, J. D. Levy, F. Nullmeier, and J. D. Stephens. New York: Oxford University Press.

Watts, M. 2004. "Resource Curse? Governmentality, Oil and Power in the Niger Delta, Nigeria." *Geopolitics*, 9(1): 50–80.

Weinthal, E., and P. J. Luong. 2006. "Combating the Resource Curse: An Alternative Solution to Managing Mineral Wealth." *Perspectives on Politics*, 4(1): 35–53.

Wilson, J. D. 2011. "Resource Nationalism or Resource Liberalism? Explaining Australia's Approach to Chinese Investment in Its Minerals Sector." *Australian Journal of International Affairs*, 65(3): 283–304.

Woetzel, L., R. Sellschop, M. Chui, S. Ramaswamy, S. Nyquist, H. Robinson, O. Roelofsen, M. Rogers, and R. Ross. 2017. "How Technology Is Reshaping Supply and Demand for Natural Resources." McKinsey Global Institute report.

Wolfers, J. and Zitzewitz, E. 2009. "Using Markets to Inform Policy: The Case of the Iraq War." *Economica*, 76(302): 225–50.

World Trade Organization. 2010. "World Trade Report 2010: Trade in Natural Resources." Geneva.

Yates, Douglas A. 1996. *The Rentier State in Africa: Oil Rent Dependency and Neocolonialism in the Republic of Gabon.* Trenton, NJ: Africa World Press.

PART II

The Politics of Jackpot Resources in Newly Resource-Rich States

Chapter 1

Uganda's Oil Discovery

The Double-Edged Sword of Development and Resource Curse

Cliff Ubba Kodero

Uganda looks set to become the "El Dorado" of African energy, a viable, and perhaps, the "hottest inland exploration frontier" of the global energy industry (Pećinar 2020). Uganda's oilfields are in the Lake Albert region, known as "Mwitanzinge" by the native Banyoro (people of Bunyoro Kingdom) until it was renamed by the British explorer Samuel Baker in 1864 (El-Sheekh and Elsaied 2023: 24). The oilfields will be the largest onshore mines in sub-Saharan Africa discovered in the last twenty years and will decidedly shape the future of Uganda. This chapter places the conversation of the Ugandan oil find around the political economy of the resource curse. It explores the potential implications of Uganda's recent discovery of oil in Lake Albert in related issues such as rent-seeking, democratization, exclusion, dispossession, democratization, and development.

The resource curse theory suggests that countries rich in non-renewable natural resources often experience negative economic and political consequences, such as increased corruption, authoritarianism, and slower economic growth (Auty 1993). However, recent scholarship suggests that the real damage of natural resources is the harm they inflict on those countries' developmental potential (Ziyadov and Shaffer 2012; Schubert, Engel, and Macamo 2020). Consequently, the question of the resource curse is often relevant to countries with deeper institutional problems (Collier 2010; LeVan 2014: 139). The discovery of oil in Uganda presents a double-edged sword, potentially alleviating poverty and stimulating economic development while risking adverse outcomes associated with the resource curse (Patey 2017; Kodero

2020). This chapter investigates how the oil discovery may affect Uganda's and East Africa's political economy. Specifically, it problematizes the potential impact of oil on Uganda's authoritarian electoral system, as oil revenue often diminishes governments' dependence on taxes, which can entrench or increase authoritarianism (Cheeseman and Fisher 2021: 46). Lastly, the chapter explores the rationale for resistance to oil mining from environmental and native rights activists, as it could lead to displacement and disempowerment of communities in frontier areas.

This chapter makes three critical arguments to add to the conversation about the resource curse from the perspective of the neopatrimonial theory that shapes and moves governance in Uganda. First, while discovering oil in Uganda might increase the country's total gross domestic product (GDP), it will likely not improve other socio-economic and developmental indicators such as its Human Development Index (HDI). Oil economies tend to be extractive and non-inclusive, associated with destructive processes that often curtail rather than embed development into disempowered and underprivileged communities.

The second argument is that instead of increasing good governance and democratic processes, the discovery of oil in Uganda will solidify the grasp of the ruling National Resistance Movement (NRM) in Ugandan politics. Uganda might erode its minimal gains under a quasi-democratic system as the reigning elites thwart the country's institutions and resources for their advantage.

Third, the Ugandan oil industry can catalyze regional integration under the East African Community (EAC). Still, it has instead led to mistrust, realignment, and betrayal of key actors, including Tanzania and Kenya (Opondo 2019: 248). Therefore, rather than strengthening regional cooperation, Ugandan oil could break Uganda's allyship with Kenya, potentially breaking over a century of close economic ties.

THEORETICAL AND CONCEPTUAL FRAMEWORK

This chapter utilizes neopatrimonialism theory to understand the resource curse and the Ugandan newly found oil. First developed by Eisenstadt (1973), neopatrimonialism theory has gained prominence in African political scholarship since the 1980s. It offers valuable insights into the continent's complex governance, power, and resource management dynamics. McFerson (2010: 343) labeled it as a "self-sustaining dynamic [where] lack of accountability enables elite appropriation of resources which in turn raises the monetary value of political control and finances continued repression." While the resource curse theory suggests that countries with invaluable resources often face economic and political challenges, this chapter indicates that Uganda's situation cannot be solely attributable to resource dependence. Instead, the neopatrimonial nature of politics in Uganda plays a significant role in shaping the outcomes.

Neopatrimonialism, as a theoretical framework, builds upon Weber's concept of patrimonialism, wherein political and administrative power relations are primarily based on personal relationships rather than formal institutions (Cheeseman, Bertrand, and Husaini 2019; Roessler 2016: 17). Loyalty, rewards, and clientelism are key features in a neopatrimonial system that creates patron-client networks that extend from powerful individuals or regimes down to the grassroots level, with reciprocal obligations at each level (Clapham 1986).

"Neo" in patrimonialism signifies the coexistence of bureaucratic state elements within a framework dominated by personalized relationships. Formal institutions may exist on paper in such systems, but they often function as private property rather than serving the public interest (Bruhns 2013). The personal ruler, usually male, holds considerable authority and secures loyalty through ethnic, regional, class, or family ties. The system relies on a web of clients, each with its sub-clients, creating a hierarchical power structure. Successful neopatrimonial rulers co-opt significant elites and groups, resulting in the "fusion of elites" and the establishment of factionalism (Bayart 2009; Sklar 1979). However, this often leaves out potential clients seeking to destabilize the system (Wrong 2010; Bratton and Van de Walle 1994).

Neopatrimonial states frequently lead to personal rule, characterized by arbitrary decision-making, a lack of rule of law, and ostentatious displays of wealth. The client-patron relationship remains intact despite the regime changes (Englebert and Dunn 2013). The neopatrimonial system poses significant challenges to governance. Instead of struggling over impersonal institutions, ideologies, public policies, or class interests, political culture in such systems revolves around rivalries and power struggles among influential individuals. Charismatic leaders rely on clientelism to legitimize their rule, often resorting to arbitrary oppressive measures (Soest 2022; Eriksen 2011). Factional competition and regime changes do little to sever the client-patron nature of the state system.

However, not all scholars agree with neopatrimonialism as a challenge to development. Pitcher, Moran, and Johnston (2009: 126) have argued that neopatrimonialism does not capture the complexity of power in Africa. There must be a careful distinction between regimes, which refers to the "means by which positions of power are filled in a state and the degree to which citizens are allowed to participate in the process." Indeed, some more stable African countries, such as Botswana, have patrimonial monarchial roots as the source of their authority. Therefore, there is a need for disaggregation of explanations to account for huge variations within neopatrimonial impacts within states and regions.

In other words, a continuum of neopatrimonialism exists in understanding African politics. Mkandawire (2015: 563) argued that while neopatrimonialism holds some value in its description of social practices of the states and political elites in Africa, "the concept has no predictive value with respect to economic policy and performance." A new group of scholars championing a heterodox view on African development proposes that some of these neopatrimonial characteristics of African countries may be employable for economic development. They argue that African states can develop if they pursue policies aimed at galvanizing rents, which they describe as "excess incomes" existing in imperfect markets (Kelsall et al. 2010). For example, Rwanda and Ethiopia exhibit a transformation described as "developmental patrimonialism" that checks patrimonial politics' destructive attributes by drawing a strategic vision for industrialization (Booth and Golooba-Mutebi 2011: 2).

The resource curse theory, which asserts that countries rich in natural resources tend to experience negative economic and political consequences, intersects with neopatrimonialism. Neopatrimonial states are especially susceptible to the resource curse due to their personalist rule and the concentration of power in the hands of a few individuals. As resources become a source of wealth and patronage, they further entrench neopatrimonial dynamics. Hence, Uganda typifies this phenomenon, offering an excellent case study of the intersection between natural resources, development, and neopatrimonialism. The case of Uganda exemplifies how neopatrimonialism can shape the practice of power and politics, influencing the outcomes of resource-dependent states (Hickey & Izama 2017). The interplay between neopatrimonialism, cultural norms, and rational responses to political constraints underscores the complexity of African governance. Acknowledging the role of neopatrimonialism is essential for crafting effective policies and strategies that address the challenges and opportunities in these contexts.

BACKGROUND AND CONTEXT OF UGANDAN OIL

Uganda struck oil in 2006 in the country's Lake Albert, which also serves as the border with the expansive Democratic Republic of Congo (Sandner 2018). Uganda possesses approximately 1.4 million barrels of recorded oil reserves (Nakayi and Witte 2019: 223). The French firm TotalEnergies and China National Offshore Corporation (CNOOC) holds licenses for developing these resources. Oil production in Uganda was to commence in 2022 (Langer, Ukiwo, and Mbabazi 2020). Projections indicate that Uganda's oil production could reach two hundred thousand to 250,000 barrels, potentially positioning Uganda as a middle-level producer. Uganda's oil resources, in terms of scale, do not have a transformative impact on the global oil industry or the African oil landscape.

The history of oil in Uganda predates its official discovery in 2006. Local communities had long been aware of oil seepages along the Lake Albert area. British explorers made the first formal references to oil in the region in the late 1890s. In 1925, surveyors working for colonial administrators mapped out indications of oil in the country. In 1938, a South African company conducted its first exploration well (Vokes 2012: 304). Following independence in 1962, political instability in the country discouraged investment in oil prospects. The insecurity halted exploration activities (Nuwagaba and Lukumba-Muhiya 2021). Uganda's oil was also expensive to extract due to the cost of transporting it over a thousand kilometers to the nearest port of Mombasa, as it is a landlocked country (Patey 2015a: 9).

Interest in oil resumed in the 1980s, with a World Bank survey generating new data and mapping sedimentary sub-basins. The Milton Obote regime passed the first draft of the Petroleum Act in 1985. It established the petroleum unit within the Geological Survey and Mines Department. When Yoweri Museveni came to power in 1986, he suspended negotiations with oil companies. Museveni aimed to develop capacity by endowing Ugandan professionals with stronger bargaining power. He sent Ugandan officials to study oil management in India, Norway, and the United States for that task. The Museveni regime later passed a Conduct of Exploration Act in 1993, which regulated upstream exploration of oil (Wolf and Potluri 2018: 5). The oil became commercial in 2006 when Australian wildcatting company Hardsman Cutters, Anglo-Canadian Heritage Oil, and British and Irish Tullow Oil began to drill oil wells (Van Alstine et al. 2014: 51).

President Yoweri Museveni has made oil a cornerstone of his development agenda, with oil revenue sharing expected to be critical in Uganda's journey toward achieving middle-income status. However, the discovery of oil in historically marginalized areas has sparked discussions on the distribution of resources. Disputes over the allocation of benefits from oil wealth often become entangled with long-standing issues of inclusion/exclusion, social identity crises, and complex land relationships (Scurfield and Bagabo 2022). For example, the Bunyoro kingdom rejects the claims made by the Uganda Wildlife Authority over sections of oil-rich lands. The monarchy in Bunyoro believes they have the rightful ownership over the land (Olanya 2015: 53).

Uganda implemented a neoliberal approach to resource management aimed at addressing development deficits influenced by the social norms promoted by non-governmental organizations (see Kodero's review 2020b). These organizations emphasize corporate social responsibility initiatives applied by relevant companies such as Tullow Oil and TotalEnergies (Smith and Van

Alstine 2018). In frontier states such as Uganda, neoliberalism morphs and adopts a posture of "re-regulation" (Smith and Van Alstine 2018: 237). Here, the state's role facilitates and improves private accumulation. The phenomena manifests through activities such as granting exploration licenses to multinational corporations with exclusive rights of exploitation for a given period, the acquisition of customary lands for private ownership, and a culture of dispossession such as land grabbing and speculation by local actors connected to the ruling regime (Smith and Van Alstine 2018).

WILL OIL LEAD TO DEVELOPMENT IN UGANDA?

This chapter's first argument is that while oil may trigger some developmental gains, it will unlikely make Uganda an "Emirate-style" middle-income country. However, despite the Lake Albertine oil find, Uganda may build up on its growth trajectory. The needs of the expanding Ugandan society may consume the gains from oil. Conversely, the population boom may be useful for Uganda's growth if facilitated and supported by incentives made available by the state and society. Already, Ugandans are apprehensive about whether oil will be the panacea of their country's development (Neiman 2023). Life expectancy in Uganda is 62.85 years, and more than 25 percent of Ugandans are illiterate (World Health Organization 2023).

While the middle class has increased in the last thirty years, poverty is still rampant. Northern Ugandans in the frontier grapple with hunger (Owori 2020). A 2022 World Bank survey reported that Ugandan households have difficulty accessing essential goods and food. Most respondents pointed to a lack of money and increased prices (Atamanov et al. 2024). While the possibility of oil has Ugandans excited about better prospects, the ongoing delays of the oil project and the retrogressive economic system make the people anxious. A phenomenon that some have described as a culture of "not-yet-ness" (Nakayi and Witte 2019: 223).

One challenge with oil economies is that they tend to be exclusive rather than inclusive. Studies suggest the Ugandan oil industry will create approximately eleven thousand to fifteen thousand jobs, mostly temporary and low-skilled, in oil infrastructure, such as oil pipelines, transport networks, roads, and warehouses (Agiresaasi 2017). The government has set up colleges such as the accredited Uganda Petroleum Institute at Kigumba, which serves as a national research, training, and consultancy center in petroleum exploration, recovery and refinement, and resource utilization. Four other technical institutes offer skills necessary for the oil market (Mugisha 2022). Yet the nature of oil economies is that the high-paying jobs are skill-intensive and more technologically based, requiring expansive resumes. From a position of job creation, oil will not be ideal for most Ugandans. Jobs will be created if the Ugandan government invests the oil funds in other job-creating ventures that align with the decarbonization strategic shift.

Ugandan oil is anticipated to contribute an average net present value of about two billion dollars, equivalent to 10 percent of GDP for at least twenty-six years (Lakuma 2020). The number translates to about thirty-eight dollars per capita yearly over the next thirty-three years (Wolf and Potluri 2018). Despite significant progress since the end of its internal conflicts, Uganda still ranks 159 out of 189 countries on the HDI. Uganda has a population growth of 3 percent per annum, with the Uganda Bureau of Statistics indicating that the population will double in twenty-three years and reach 85.8 million people by 2044, a staggering number that increases public expenditure, consequently diminishing the viability of returns from oil to improve quality of life (National Population Council et al. 2022).

There are fears that power relations triumph over technical concerns in Uganda, becoming the most important predictors of eventual developmental outcomes. Oil revenue will total about two billion dollars over the thirty years, which will not allow Ugandans to stop working or substantially increase their GDP per capita, which was $883.89 in 2021 (International Monetary Fund 2021). Realizing the income challenge, Uganda has adopted the Norwegian model of an oil wealth fund. The Norwegian model recommends that oil be placed on a petroleum fund to be used to invest in a sovereign wealth fund. The sovereign wealth fund is meant to invest the revenues abroad to mitigate the challenges of the Dutch disease, which refers to the negative effects of an inflated domestic currency often arising from natural resources such as oil. But as will be indicated later, some of the challenges of this model include gaps in management, volatility of the political system, lack of isolation from political cronyism, and inadequate clarity of institutions and their roles (Polus and Tycholiz 2017: 190). And these governance models, assuming the present regime still reigns, will not change under the oil management.

Issues of environmental choices in oil have increasingly become consequential for Uganda. There have been questions about whether the oil boom has come too late when the world, especially the more industrialized economies, is transitioning toward greener energy. The global picture is increasingly becoming anti–fossil fuel (Atuhaire 2022). A McKinsey 2022 analysis suggested that more than one million jobs in Africa could be vulnerable as global economies transition away from oil and gas and international consumption patterns shift in favor of lower carbon-intensity production (Leke, Gaius-Obaseki, and Onyekweli 2022).

The environmental challenges pose a two-pronged challenge. First, it questions the profitability of the oil venture. Uganda's oil infrastructure, including airports, roads, and pipelines, are primarily funded by debt (Atuhaire 2022).

These investments have cost the Ugandan public, with public debt increasing from 26 percent in 2012/2013 to 37 percent or $9.4 billion in 2016/2017. The government further plans to increase public expenditure. These debts are not pegged on future oil earnings, but the government's position is that the future oil earnings will play a role in managing accumulated debt, which will decline as oil revenues come in (Wolf and Potluri 2018). However, the feasibility of the whole project needs to be clarified, as the second point illustrates. Environmental concerns have generated negative press for the project, sending investors away and consequently jeopardizing its profitability (see Huxham et al. 2020). Critics have pointed out that drilling oil pipelines threatens biodiversity and endangers the water sources of the Nile (Lee and Abenaitwe 2021).

In September 2022, the European Parliament passed a resolution to compel Uganda, Tanzania, and TotalEnergies to delay the development of the East Africa Crude Oil Pipeline (EACOP). The resolution cites violations of human rights in Uganda and Tanzania linked to investments in fossil-based fuels (Oxfam 2022). Over half of the banks that historically financed Total's projects have backed out. More oil and gas companies are positioning themselves as champions against fossil fuel–induced climate change. The European Commission has blatantly indicated that they do "not support the financing of oil projects in Africa" (Moisan 2022).

The Ugandan government dismisses claims of negative environmental consequences of the oil find. Proscovia Nabbanja, the chief executive of Uganda National Oil Company, argued that Uganda is dealing with "energy poverty"; therefore, conversations about green transitioning are "premature" at this stage. In essence, the oil project should go on to protect Uganda from severe energy shortfalls (Atuhaire 2022). In terms of suspending the project for one year, the Ugandan Deputy National Assembly speaker stated: "These are projects which the parliament of Uganda approved, the parliament of a sovereign country, and anything to do with challenging their approval is an affront to the independence of this house, and we cannot take it lightly" (*Le Monde* with AFP 2022).

Yet the French government has supported Total, signaling how resource-based economic arrangements may also perpetuate dependency relationships between the Global South and northern economies. In a 2021 letter, France's President Macron described EACOP as a "major opportunity" for Uganda and France to "expand their cooperation" (Moisan 2022). It is difficult to discern if Paris' position mirrors the European Commission's.

In summary, Uganda's oil resources are unlikely to lead to a transformation into a wealthy nation. There are concerns about project delays and a regressive economic system. In addition, the potential exclusivity of the oil industry's job market questions the overall impact of oil revenue, given

Uganda's rapidly growing population. Despite these concerns, the Ugandan government remains committed to the project, citing the need to address energy poverty.

POLITICAL ECONOMY OF DISTRUST
OF THE STATE AND EXCLUSION

This chapter's second argument is that oil is subverting democratic gains in Uganda while entrenching political exclusion. Political dysfunction could widen as revenues from the oil industry widen fissures between local and national elites. Although the oil deals that President Museveni made with the oil corporations were favorable to Uganda, there is an overlap between political interests and policy. Many Ugandans view the oil industry as a tool for the ruling NRM to tap new resources of campaign financing for national elections and staying power in government (International Crisis Group Rep. 2017). These political challenges will only increase as many Ugandans, especially Albertine natives, feel left out of oil benefits.

Developing a sound and well-functioning oil government regime has recently become the country's most important public policy. The government of Uganda and other stakeholders, including the parliament, local businesspeople, civil society, and non-governmental organizations, have been hard-pressed to ensure that the Ugandan oil find does not lead to a "resource curse." Mbabazi and Muhangi (2020: 42) analyzed the formal institutions of Uganda that have been established to manage, oversee, and regulate Uganda's oil exploration. They argue that while Uganda has attempted to embrace sound resource management principles, serious challenges remain. These challenges do not lie in applying technical approaches, as Uganda has enough human resources and capacity. They must lie in the political context. Mbambazi & Muhangi (2018) indicated that Uganda has not complied with the best resource management practices as there is too much space and leeway for abuse and misappropriation of funds. A particular focus is the interplay between corruption, oil, and democracy. There are valid fears that the industry will intensify authoritarianism and catalyze corruption.

Uganda has a long history of extractive political culture. It is a hybrid state where an authoritarian patronage system underpins a performative democracy under the leadership of President Museveni, who has led the NRM since 1986 (Van Alstine et al. 2014). Although Uganda reintroduced a multiparty election in 2006, there has never been a peaceful power transfer. Before that, Uganda was under a "no-party" system for the first ten years of Museveni's rule. Since the re-introduction of multipartyism, elections have been mired in allegations of bribery, intimidation, and ballot stuffing (Polus and Tycholiz

2017). In 2021, during the last presidential polls, Museveni was elected for a historic sixth term. It looks increasingly like the promise of oil and its benefits will entice Museveni not to let go of power peacefully.

Even with a "no-party" government policy and evidence of intimidation of opposition politicians, the World Bank and Western governments held Museveni's regime up as an example of good governance. However, the removal of term limits has tarnished NRM's reputation. In 2006, Uganda held its first multiparty elections in twenty-six years. Human Rights Watch reported violations by the government, electoral malpractice, and other practices that maligned free and fair voting (Roth 2022). Moses Khisa (2021) has argued that Museveni did not win the 2006 elections against closest rival Kizza Besigye. The Supreme Court of Uganda decided against overturning the election outcome even though they wanted to due to "external pressure." The Supreme Court was usurped in this context. Similar sentiments were shared over the subsequent elections that involved Besigye in 2011 and 2016. In 2021, popular musician Robert Kyagulanyi, known by his stage name Bobi Wine, ran against Museveni. The Electoral Commission declared Museveni the winner in January 2021 (Okiror 2021). The process of election rigging was followed by a series of manipulative exercises and legal maneuvers to remove the presidential term and hand Museveni life presidency.

In many regards, Uganda's resource management challenge emanates from the central government's outstanding institutional and legitimacy issues. Jjuuko (2021) commented that not so many years ago, Uganda emerged from a protracted conflict and regional disparities in development. The Albertine region has suffered immense conflict, including armed struggles that have slowed growth, disrupted development, and alienated citizens from true citizenship. Particular attention could help alleviate potential crises that could emerge from resource curses. Yet this is not what is happening. The Ugandan oil and gas sector is shrouded in secrecy, with minimal engagement of the local and cultural groups. The existing cultural institutions, such as the King of Bunyoro kingdom, Omukama (King) Solomon Iguru, the twenty-seventh, have been sidelined in the process. Increased militarization of the Lake Albertine region through the increased personnel of Uganda police and Uganda People Defense Forces in the oil mining areas may inflame the natives over social grievances (Patey 2015b).

In the post-independence era, many citizens of smaller kingdoms have felt more loyal to their legitimate leaders than to the central governments in Kampala. Much of this power tussle occurs between land reforms and state power (Taylor 2021). Many citizens of the kingdoms feel marginalized by state agencies, whom they associate with the loss of land and control (Tumusiime, Mawejje, and Byakagaba 2016). Ugandan oil has also reignited a power struggle between the central government and regional kingdoms.

The Bunyoro Kitara Kingdom, where most of the oil is located, demands an equitable share of oil revenue for the domain. According to Uganda's Public Finance Act, the central government should grant 1 percentage point for the royalty to the gazette cultural and traditional institutions. Ugandan law also states that 6 percent of the total royalty revenues will be shared among local governments "located with the petroleum exploration and production areas" (Scurfield and Bagabo 2022). However, many residents have been confused about what this means. Following the first suggestion, gazette kingdoms in Uganda should receive 1 percent of the total oil royalties. The Bunyoro Kitara Kingdom is the kingdom from which the oil comes. They feel differently about getting the same share with other kingdoms.

Rent-seeking refers to unproductive and exploitative activities that bring personal benefits to individuals but negative outcomes for society (Congleton and Hillman 2015). Rent-seeking may take many forms, including bribery, corruption, smuggling, and black market selling. Uganda's political history is shaped by rent-seeking, and evidence suggests that even as Museveni's regime continues to advocate for best practices, its political survival depends on how much rent it can generate for the ruling elites. As Pendergast, Clarke, and Van Kooten (2011) suggested, the discovery of oil will not guarantee that Uganda will come out of poverty since oil deals with petroleum companies seem dubious and organized around speculative land deals. The ruling NRM captures institutions of power. In other words, Ogwang, Vanclay, and van den Assem (2019: 99) suggested that instead of empowering the local communities, the presence of natural resources is "disempowering and makes people more vulnerable to the activities and manipulations of speculators, entrepreneurs, and local leaders." Forces of neopatrimonialism have captured the institutional mechanisms of the state enacted by personally vested bureaucrats.

Thus, Uganda's challenge is the nexus of new resource-dependent countries suffering from poor governance and weak institutions, exacerbating existing social fissures. Consequent outcomes of unfilled expectations develop grievances that can lead to violence (Collier 2008). But the challenge is often rent distribution. Competition over rents often incentivizes political elites to organize around existing institutions to challenge the rent-collecting elites. Oil generates massive rents, making the extractive industry sector a key locus for political contestation (Ogwang, Vanclay, and van den Assem 2019).

The Ugandan oil curse may not be a protracted civil war akin to the Liberian and Sierra Leone's ghastly civil wars of the 1990s because of the state capacity and monopolization of violence in Uganda under the army. The NRM party decentralized power by increasing the number of districts in the country. They wanted to safeguard themselves from accusations of being elitist. However, these expanded districts had limited control and limited autonomous decision-making capacity. By increasing the number of districts, Museveni strengthened his grasp of grassroots politics without the cost of secession tendencies that may have evolved (Titeca and Wiegratz 2018: 112). However, the conflict could be a degenerative, socially and economically dysfunctional political and economic system that slowly transfers power from the local Albertine people to the elites located in Kampala but controlled by Nyankole-speaking groups of Western Uganda. In a slow political-economic death, elements of resistance such as autochthony, economic base, and cultural forces get supplanted by coercive mechanisms of the state as controlled by dominant elites.

The evidence suggests this is already happening before the first oil export pumps out (Gikandi 2022). More than seven hundred people from thirteen villages in Hoima District were displaced by the land taken from them for the Kabale Industrial Park, which will be used for Hoima International Airport, an oil refinery, and other oil-related activities. Human Rights Watch suggests that thousands of people's lives in Uganda will lose their homes, exacerbating the climate crisis already afflicting East Africa. More than one hundred thousand people will lose their homes; a climate of hostility, fraud, and corruption will be created; and people will have been dispossessed from their land. For example, the oil pipeline project has faced compensation delays and relocation problems to further arid areas. The Human Rights Watch report, titled "Our Trust Is Broken," published in July 2023, indicated that many people are worse off than before. The report draws from more than ninety interviews with seventy-five displaced families from the Albertine districts. It documents the devastating impacts on the livelihoods of Ugandan families from the land acquisition process for the oil industry, especially the EACOP pipeline (Horne 2023).

The conventional wisdom on African development studies holds that the African regimes, harboring neopatrimonial and corrupt practices, hinder reforms that negate sustainable economic growth necessary for the continent to alleviate widespread poverty (Kelsall 2013). Tim Kelsall argues the government is more likely to be able to use rents for development if its politics have a top-down structure. Top-down or centralized rent management does not guarantee development or rent use, but bottom-up or decentralized rent-seeking makes it more difficult (Kelsall et al. 2010: 19). In developmental patrimonialism, the neopatrimonial society achieves development when it has a centralized authority over significant rents and a long investment horizon in productive areas such as value addition and industry. The state is development-oriented, though it is neopatrimonial with a working relationship between the state and the business class. It is unclear if this is the model that Uganda seeks to replicate. Rwanda and Ethiopia have been sobriquets of these developmental agendas. But neither Rwanda nor Uganda are oil states.

Within the context of the political discourse, oil states have little interest in developing sound institutions because more independent institutions demand higher accountability. Weak institutions are chiefly responsible for the lack of growth and development in many of the old rich countries in the global south. Uganda has no resources to strengthen its institutions. Still, the evidence suggests that rather than support strengthening institutions, the government of Uganda controls all revenue sharing. President Museveni continues to hold a firm grip on the executive wing of the government. It plans to send 7 percent of all the oil revenue to the oil- and gas-producing areas. The revenue-sharing goals of the Ugandan government suggest that revenue sharing favors a mix of the derivation principle and those like interfiscal transfer formulas. Yet the pipeline's construction has had human costs reverberating into Uganda's political and economic scene.

Uganda's governmental position is that the "oil curse" is attributable not to the discovery of abundant natural resources but to the nature of institutional arrangements that guide the exploitation and management of natural resource deposits and revenues. Diamond & Mosbacher (2013) submit that the quality of institutions is the independent variable that explains the consequences of resources in the economy. Institutions are "constraints devised by humans that structure political, economic, and social interactions. In Uganda, the constitution vests the ownership and control of petroleum in the government on behalf of the people" (Article 244 of the 1995 constitution of Uganda). The government holds the people of Uganda's trust in all minable resources such as minerals and petroleum. In 2009, Ugandan President Yoweri Museveni said,

> There is a lot of nonsense that the oil will be a curse. No way! The oil of Uganda cannot be a curse. Oil became a curse when you got useless leaders, and I can assure you that we don't approach that description even by a thousandth of a mile . . . the oil is a blessing for Uganda, and money from it will be used for development. (IOL 2006; Langer et al. 2020)

Museveni's analysis points to the competence of the Ugandan government in handling the oil resource and, therefore, shielding the society from a resource curse. However, the legal regime for natural resources is less mature than other countries in the region. In Egypt, for example, international agreements or investment contracts come into effect only after parliamentary approval or ratification. This is the same case with Liberia. In Uganda, however, the minister of energy negotiates and enters into agreements without parliamentary oversight. The decision-making process hampers the parliament of Uganda. On the other hand, the minister is part of the executive branch, which means the executive, headed by the president, presides over oil tendering and politically interferes with decisions they do not like. In the past, President Museveni had stated, "In the case of petroleum and gas, I direct that no agreement should ever be signed without my express written approval of that arrangement" (Reuters 2010).

The second argument centers on the impact of Uganda's oil industry on democracy and politics. It contends that oil undermines democracy, leading to political exclusion. Suspicion surrounds President Museveni's "Uganda-first" favorable oil deals, seen as a tool for the ruling NRM to secure campaign funds and hold onto power. While Uganda has tried to establish sound oil governance, challenges arise from the political context rather than technical issues (Wolf 2020). Uganda's history features an authoritarian democracy facade, and oil wealth may further motivate Museveni's grip on power. Regional disparities and disputes over oil revenue distribution within provincial kingdoms add complexity. Rent-seeking and social challenges loom, raising concerns about oil's consequences.

EAST AFRICAN REGIONAL POLITICAL ECONOMY AND OIL

The third argument for this chapter is that Uganda's oil discovery has implicated the regional East African political economy. It has indeed affected regional political and economic calculus, catapulting Uganda into a more central actor than previously while isolating Nairobi's leadership.

The effects of the oil found in Uganda are twofold. First, it has re-engineered an ongoing rivalry of regional influence between Tanzania and Kenya over Kampala. These two countries are the most influential and the largest economies in the EAC. The Ugandan oil find was bound to raise contestations over what would be the biggest beneficiary. The contentious area of interest was on the export route for crude oil. The oil infrastructure would have been lucrative and raised the profiles of Kenya's Mombasa and Lamu ports over Dar-es-salaam and Bagamoyo ports. Secondly, the two battled over capital-intensive investments to facilitate Ugandan oil mining. Another area of battle was loyalty. Uganda has stronger trade ties with Kenya, considering that Britain ruled the two as a colony and they never had a direct military confrontation with each other.

In contrast, Tanzania has fought a war with Uganda. Uganda saw the Tanzanian occupation of their country during the Second Milton Obote regime as an infringement of sovereignty, a quasi-colonial takeover. It generated a lot of resentment, including Uganda's rejection of East Africa's *lingua franca*, Kiswahili.

Regardless of previous feelings toward each other's countries, President Museveni and Tanzanian counterpart Samia Suluhu Hassan signed an agreement to construct the EACOP, estimated to be worth $3.55 billion, connecting the Albertine ravines to the port of Tanga (Further Africa 2021). The sixty-billion-barrels-per-day oil refinery, which has been central to Museveni's vision for the industry, and the thirteen-hundred-kilometer crude oil export pipeline needed to transport the oil through Tanzania to the Indian Ocean are colossal capital projects that will necessitate a close alliance between the state and the international capital markets (Smith and Van Alstine 2018: 236). The enclave nature of resource extraction also means that the oil mining process excludes and restricts communities close to the resource extraction site from accessing land and resources needed for their livelihoods.

The government plans to develop a refinery with a capacity of sixty thousand barrels per day and the associated downstream infrastructure to add value to the oil and gas process. Consequently, the two governments will construct a 1,145-kilometer heated crude oil pipeline to transport crude oil from Uganda to the port of Tanga with partial financing from upstream companies (Mbabazi and Muhagi 2018). The pipeline will be the world's longest and largest heated pipeline upon completion. It will join two oil fields—the Kingfisher Field, operated by the CNOOC, and the Tilenga Field, run by a subsidiary of TotalEnergies based in South Africa (Golubski, Holtz, and White 2021). President Suluhu noted that the deals would create over one hundred thousand jobs, with Uganda exporting around sixty thousand barrels daily and over three billion dollars in earnings. According to the agreement, the oil companies must award at least 30 percent of project-related contracts to Ugandan suppliers.

Resource nationalism is a factor in oil-extracting and other resource-extracting economies, as countries prefer autonomy when exporting oil. But Uganda cannot afford to since it is landlocked. Cannon and Mogaka (2022) reported that cross-border development of oil fields remains an exception rather than a norm. While Uganda discovered minable crude in 2006, Kenya did the same six years later in 2012. Kenya and Uganda are on the verge of becoming oil exporters. Yet geographical constraints have hindered and generated a set of calculations that have hampered profitability. Kenya's oil reserves are islands hundreds of kilometers from the Indian Ocean, the only exit point for oil exports. The two countries needed to share resources to increase the profitability of their oil pipelines. The Kenya-Uganda Crude Oil Pipeline (UKCOP) aimed to link both the Kenyan and Ugandan oilfields through a channel that would end in the historical city of Lamu at the Indian Ocean. The benefits included cost sharing, increased revenues from voluminous exports, and related development.

There were three proposals for importing Ugandan oil to the Indian Ocean. A Japanese company, Toyota Tsusho Corporation, was asked to designate the most feasible pipeline route. Toyota Tsusho, under pressure from the Kenyan government, argued for the northern route, also called UKCOP. The first was the UKCOP proposed in 2014. It was to transport Uganda and Kenya's oil to the Indian Ocean for export. It would begin in Hoima city in Western Uganda at the shores of Lake Albert and cross over the Ugandan landscape into northwestern Kenya near Lokichar in Turkana country. The oil would get to the coast through a pipeline to a new port constructed at Lamu. South Sudan would be part of the new oil pipeline. With the South Sudanese having higher-quality oil, there would be a significant increase in revenue through quality and reduced cost. Chatham House reported that UKCOP to Lamu would cost nearly five billion dollars over 1,476 kilometers. The Kenyan government would charge Uganda $12.60 per barrel for oil exports. Had it been successful, it would have made East Africa a viable oil exporter with more significant revenue and development potential. However, it is also true that it would have benefited the Kenyan developmental project at the expense of a resource they did not own.

The second route was a more conservative and fiscally attainable southern route from Hoima through the Rift Valley, transit in Nairobi, and end at the port in Mombasa. It would use already existing pipelines and railway infrastructure. Yet, despite significant promises and deals signed by leadership from Nairobi and Kampala, UKCOP floundered on regional rivalries and clashing interests of political elites from Kenya, Uganda, and Tanzania. In the end, President Museveni decided to bypass the Kenyan deal and terminate their earlier agreements, putting a wrench in the works for Kenyan President Uhuru Kenyatta's plans, as well as jeopardy the feasibility of Kenya's Vision 2030 cornerstone project labeled Lamu Port and Lamu-Southern Sudan Transport corridor. The Lamu Port and Lamu-Southern Sudan Transport Corridor intended to economically elevate northern Kenya's frontiers by introducing the region as an alternative logistical hub to support the clogged Busia/Malaba-Nairobi-Mombasa corridor (Goldsmith 2021).

Kenya then decided to proceed with their plans by building their pipeline alone, even in the face of reduced profitability. In 2018, the Kenyan government decided to export oil by road. According to Cannon and Mogaka (2022), the Ugandan decision to abandon the UKCOP revealed further tensions within the EAC. It also demonstrated a deep-seated political rivalry between Kenya and Tanzania that thwarts harmonious relationships in the EAC, further endangering the possibility of a more united polity. As to Uganda, it reveals that the dangers of the resource curse are not limited to the state level. The discovery of oil may set up a chain of reactions that may impair already stable political and economic alliances. Because Uganda was worried about its exploitable insecurities as a landlocked state, it figured out the calculated trap that Kenya advanced its economic plans using resources far from its borders.

Tullow Oil, a key actor in the Ugandan oil negotiations, favored the Kenyan northern route. But in secret, they worried about the increase caused and expressed concerns over security in the frontiers of the north. Islamic militants like Al-Shabab had recently attacked coastal cities in Kenya, including the site of the new port. They also worried about the cost of new infrastructure. They politely advocated for a southern Kenyan route. The CNOOC remained neutral. However, TotalEnergies favored the southern way that passed through the Tanzanian port of Tanga. Kenyans felt betrayed as the Ugandan administration favored the Tanzania route advocated by Total. Uganda abandoned the Kenyan government's hope of sharing oil benefits by choosing to go with Tanzania. But this is not new. Uganda had previously bolted out of a critical infrastructural project with Kenya. The East African Standard Gauge Railway was supposed to integrate the whole region by connecting the hinterland with Mombasa Port. Kenya built the first phase of the railway from Mombasa to Nairobi and later completed the second phase, which ended in Naivasha. China turned off funding after Uganda failed to meet the requisite financial metrics to fund the project. The final part would have connected Naivasha to Malaba before snaking into Uganda. Beijing realized that the standard gauge railways were not viable without the connection to Uganda, whose participation was crucial for connecting Rwanda, South Sudan, and the Democratic Republic of Congo (Barigaba 2023).

The failure of Kenya's diplomatic game plan on Ugandan oil (and other transboundary infrastructure) resulted from several reasons. First, security concerns over rampant terrorist and banditry activities in the northern regions of Kenya could have endangered profitability. The security concern was a worthwhile risk that the Ugandan policymakers and other oil stakeholders weighed upon. In the past decade, the Al-Shabab Islamic terror group based in Somalia has conducted terrorist attacks in Kenya, mostly in the regions where the oil pipeline would have gone through. The Armed Conflict Location and Event Data Project (2023) reported nearly one hundred episodes of politically motivated violence activities in Kenya in June 2023 alone. That month, Al-Shabaab contributed to over 50 percent of the total fatalities. It is also true that Kenya's political milieu can be contentious. In a more mature democracy, elections are always close and contested.

In the past election, William Ruto won the presidency by a slim majority of 50.5 percent, translating to more than one hundred thousand votes (Kimeu 2022). These close-call elections sometimes lead to post-election violence that can upset investors and hinterland countries that rely on Kenya's logistic infrastructure. Uganda relies heavily on imports via Mombasa, hauled overland, and in 2007 and 2008, Uganda was cut off due to the post-election violence in Kenya. Lastly, as Cannon and Mogaka (2022) have reported, Kenya's eminent domain laws are entrenched and respected but also manipulated by land speculators. For Uganda, land acquisition would have been costly and lengthy had they gone with the Kenyan pipeline. However, the most important reason is that both Uganda and Tanzania feel that there is a need to de-horn Kenya's domination of the East African political economy, and the Ugandan oil pipeline is a great starting point.

CONCLUSION

This chapter made three critical arguments to add to the conversation about the resource curse from the perspective of the neopatrimonial theory that shapes and moves governance in Uganda. Formal institutions and informal practices intersect and interact constantly in a hybrid, quasi-democracy, or anocratic regime, creating uncertainty regimes (Cammack et al. 2007; Walter 2023: 13). When natural resources of consequential effects appear, the system can unravel. Studies indicate that oil revenue often lessens governments' need for taxes, entrenching or increasing authoritarianism. Relatedly, taxing the middle class encourages consensus building between the taxed, usually the middle and political classes, and the central government. Democracies are more likely to arise and mature when the public rather than natural resources finance the treasury. As Cheeseman (2019: 51) has suggested, oil states are bonded to "proceeds of oil wealth." From the beginning, Uganda's politics was shaped by the elite's rivalry over resources.

First, while discovering oil in Uganda might increase the country's total GDP, it will likely not improve other socio-economic and developmental indicators in the East African nation, such as its HDI. Oil economies tend to be extractive and non-inclusive, associated with creative destructive processes that often curtail rather than embed development into disempowered and underprivileged communities.

The second argument is that instead of increasing good governance and democratic processes, the discovery of oil in Uganda will solidify the grasp of the ruling NRM in Ugandan politics. Uganda might erode its minimal gains under a quasi-democratic system as the reigning elites thwart the country's institutions and resources for their advantage.

Third, the Ugandan oil industry had the potential to be a catalyst of East African integration under the EAC. Still, it has instead led to mistrust, realignment, and betrayal of key actors, including Tanzania and Kenya (Opondo 2019: 248). Therefore, rather than strengthening regional cooperation, Ugandan oil could break Uganda's allyship with Kenya, potentially breaking over a century of close economic ties. In conclusion, this chapter has presented three compelling arguments that shed light on the intricate dynamics of the resource curse in Uganda, particularly within the framework of neopatrimonial theory.

REFERENCES

Agiresaasi, Apophia. 2017. "Will Oil Make Ugandans Rich?" *Global Press Journal,* September 18. https://globalpressjournal.com/africa/uganda/will-oil-make -ugandans-rich/.

Armed Conflict Location & Event Data Project. 2023. "Kenya Situation Update: July 2023: Al-Shabaab Attacks Surge Ahead of Somalia-Kenya Border Reopening." July 17. https://acleddata.com/2023/07/07/kenya-situation-update-july-2023-al -shabaab-attacks-surge-ahead-of-somalia-kenya-border-reopening/.

Atamanov, Aziz, Frederic Pierre Francois Cochinard Hugue, John Ilukor, Audrey Kemigisha, Talip Kilic, Andrew Mupere, and Giulia Ponzini. 2024. "Monitoring Impacts of COVID-19 and Other Shocks on Households in Uganda." Brief 186934, World Bank, Washington, DC.

Atuhaire, Patience. 2022. "Why Uganda Is Investing in Oil Despite Pressures to Go Green." *BBC News,* February 9. https://www.bbc.com/news/world-africa -60301755.

Auty, Richard M. 1993. *Sustaining Development in Mineral Economies: The Resource Curse Thesis.* London, UK: Routledge.

Barigaba, Julius. 2023. "Uganda, Tanzania SGR Line Clear as Kenya Derailed." *The East African,* January 14. https://www.theeastafrican.co.ke/tea/business/uganda -tanzania-sgr-line-clear-as-kenya-derailed-4086104.

Bayart, Jean-François. 2009. *The State in Africa: The Politics of the Belly.* Cambridge, UK: Polity.

Booth, David, and Frederick Golooba-Mutebi. 2011. "Developmental Patrimonialism? The Case of Rwanda." https://cdn.odi.org/media/documents/appp-wp16 -developmental-patrimonialism-the-case-of-rwanda-david-booth-frederic_Np9JXni .pdf, accessed June 25, 2024.

Bratton, Michael, and Nicolas van de Walle. 1994. "Neopatrimonial Regimes and Political Transitions in Africa." *World Politics,* 46(4): 453–89.

Bruhns, Hinnerk. 2013. "Weber's Patrimonial Domination and Its Interpretations." In *Neopatrimonialism in Africa and Beyond,* edited by Daniel Bach and Mamadou Gazibo. London: Taylor & Francis.

Cammack, Diana, F. Golooba-Mutebi, F. Kanyongolo, and T. O'Neil. 2007. "Neopatrimonial Politics, Decentralisation, and Local Government: Uganda and Malawi." https://gsdrc.org/document-library/neopatrimonial-politics-decentralisation- and-local-government-uganda-and-malawi/.

Cannon, Brendon J., and Stephen Mogaka. 2022. "Rivalry in East Africa: The Case of the Uganda-Kenya Crude Oil Pipeline and the East Africa Crude Oil Pipeline." *The Extractive Industries and Society*, 11: 101102.

Cheeseman, Nic, and Jonathan Fisher. 2021. *Authoritarian Africa Repression, Resistance, and the Power of Ideas*. New York: Oxford University Press.

Cheeseman, Nic, Eloïse Bertrand, and Sa'eed Husaini. 2019. *A Dictionary of African Politics*. Oxford, UK: Oxford University Press.

Clapham, Christopher. 1986. *Third World Politics: An Introduction*. Madison, WI: University of Wisconsin Press.

Collier, Paul. 2010. *Plundered Planet: Why We Must—and How We Can—Manage Nature for Global Prosperity*. Oxford, UK: Oxford University Press.

Collier, Paul. 2008. *The Bottom Billion: Why the Poorest Countries Are Failing and What Can Be Done About It*. Oxford: Oxford University Press.

Congleton, Roger D., and Arye L. Hillman. 2015. *Companion to the Political Economy of Rent-Seeking*. Cheltenham, UK: Edward Elgar.

Diamond, Larry, and Jack Mosbacher. 2013. "Petroleum to the People: Africa's Coming Resource Curse—and How to Avoid It" *Foreign Affairs* Vol. 92(5).

Eisenstadt, Shmuel Noah. 1973. *Traditional Patrimonialism and Modern Neopatrimonialism*. Beverly Hills, CA: Sage.

El-Sheekh, Mostafa, and Hosam Easa Elsaied. 2023. *Lakes of Africa: Microbial Diversity and Sustainability*. Amsterdam, Netherlands: Elsevier.

Englebert, Pierre, and Kevin Dunn. 2013. *Inside African Politics*. Boulder, CO: Lynne Rienner Publishers, Inc.

Eriksen, Stein Sundstol. 2011. "'State Failure' in Theory and Practice: The Idea of the State and the Contradictions of State Formation." *Review of International Studies*, 37(1): 229–47.

Gikandi, Halima. 2022. "Land Issues at the Heart of Uganda's Oil Showdown." *The World from PRX*, November 29. https://theworld.org/stories/2022-11-29/land -issues-heart-uganda-s-oil-showdown.

Goldsmith, Paul. 2021. "The Death of Lapsset and Kenya's Poverty of Imagination." *The Elephant*, April 19. https://www.theelephant.info/ideas/2020/11/06/the-death -of-lapsset-and-kenyas-poverty-of-imagination/.

Golubski, Christina, Leo Holtz, and Tamara White. 2021. "Africa in the News: Uganda Oil Pipeline, (Fewer) Locusts in East Africa, and Political Updates." *Brookings*, April 17. https://www.brookings.edu/articles/africa-in-the-news-uganda-oil -pipeline-fewer-locusts-in-east-africa-and-political-updates/.

Hickey, Sam, and Angelo Izama. 2017. "The Politics of Governing Oil in Uganda: Going Against the Grain?" *African Affairs*, 116(463).

Horne, Felix. 2023. "Our Trust Is Broken." *Human Rights Watch*, July 10. https: //www.hrw.org/report/2023/07/10/our-trust-broken/loss-land-and-livelihoods-oil -development-uganda.

Huxham, Matthew, Muhammed Anwar, Eoin Strutt, and David Nelson. 2020. "Understanding the Impact of a Low Carbon Transition on Uganda's Planned Oil Industry." Climate Policy Initiative. https://www.climatepolicyinitiative.org/wp

-content/uploads/2020/12/Understanding-the-impact-of-a-low-carbon-transition -on-Uganda-December-2-2020.pdf, accessed June 25, 2024.

International Crisis Group Rep. 2017. *"Museveni for Life?" Uganda's Slow Slide into Crisis.* Nairobi, Kenya: ICC Group.

IOL. "Uganda Announces Oil Discovery." Independent Online, October 9, 2006. https: //www.iol.co.za/news/africa/uganda-announces-oil-discovery-296822, accessed June 25, 2024.

International Monetary Fund. 2021. "Uganda." https://www.imf.org/external/ datamapper/profile/UGA.

Jjuuko, Dennis. 2021. "Mind the Gap: Policy, Righting Wrongs and Circumventing Oil Curses in Uganda's Albertine Region." Peace Research Institute Oslo, May 20. https://www.prio.org/publications/13358.

Kelsall, Tim. 2013. *Business, Politics, And the State in Africa Challenging the Orthodoxies on Growth and Transformation.* London, UK: Zed Books.

Kelsall, Tim, David Booth, Diana Cammack, and Frederick Golooba-Mutebi. 2010. "Developmental Patrimonialism? Questioning the Orthodoxy on Political Governance and Economic Progress in Africa." ODI Working Paper, ODI, London. https://odi.org/en/publications/developmental-patrimonialism-questioning-the -orthodoxy-on-political-governance-and-economic-progress-in-africa/, accessed June 25, 2024.

Khisa, Moses. 2021. "Contextualizing the Bobi Wine Factor in Uganda's 2021 Elections (with S. Wilkins & R. Vokes)." *African Affairs* 120 (481): 629–43.

Kimeu, Caroline. 2022. "William Ruto Declared Winner of Kenya Presidential Election amid Dispute." *The Guardian.* https://www.theguardian.com/world/2022/ aug/15/william-ruto-declared-winner-of-kenya-presidential-election-amid-dispute, accessed August 15, 2023.

Kodero, Cliff Ubba. 2020a. "Review—Authoritarian Africa: Repression, Resistance, and the Power of Ideas." E-international relations, August 30, 2020. https://www .e-ir.info/2020/08/30/review-authoritarian-africa-repression-resistance-and-the -power-of-ideas/.

Kodero, Cliff Ubba. 2020b. "Uganda: The Dynamics of Neoliberal Transformation." *African Studies Quarterly*, 19(1).

Lakuma, Corti Paul. 2020. "Oil Wealth in Uganda: Analysis of the Macroeconomic Policy Framework." In *Oil Wealth and Development in Uganda and Beyond Prospects, Opportunities and Challenges*, edited by Arnim Langer, Ukoha Ukiwo, and Pamela Mbabazi, 127–48. Leuven: Leuven University Press.

Langer, Arnim, Ukoha Ukiwo, and Pamela Mbabazi. 2020. *Oil Wealth and Development in Uganda and Beyond: Prospects, Opportunities, and Challenges.* Leuven, Belgium: Leuven University Press.

Le Monde with AFP. 2022. "Uganda Furious EU Parliament Called to Postpone Oil Megaprojects." *Le Monde*, September 16. https://www.lemonde.fr/en/le-monde -africa/article/2022/09/16/uganda-furious-eu-parliament-called-to-postpone-oil -megaprojects_5997181_124.html, accessed September 16, 2023.

Lee, Megan S., and Cliff Abenaitwe. 2021. "Uganda's First Oil: What Is at Stake?" *Water Journalists Africa*. https://waterjournalistsafrica.com/2021/02/ugandas-first -oil-what-is-at-stake/, accessed February 16, 2024.

Leke, Acha, Peter Gaius-Obaseki, and Oliver Onyekweli. 2022. "The Future of African Oil and Gas: Positioning for the Energy Transition." McKinsey & Company. https: //www.mckinsey.com/industries/oil-and-gas/our-insights/the-future-of-african-oil -and-gas-positioning-for-the-energy-transition, accessed June 8, 2023.

LeVan, A. Carl. 2014. *Dictators and Democracy in African Development: Nigeria's Political Economy of Good Governance*. Cambridge, UK: Cambridge University Press.

Mbabazi, Pamela, and Martin Muhangi. 2020. "Uganda's Oil Governance Institutions: Fit for Purpose?" In *Oil Wealth and Development in Uganda and Beyond Prospects, Opportunities, and Challenges*, edited by Arnin Langer, Ukoha Ukiwo, and Pamela Mbabazi. Leuven, Belgium: Leuven University Press.

Mbabazi, Pamela, and Martin Muhangi. 2018. "Uganda's Oil Governance Institutions: Fit for Purpose?" CRPD Working Paper 60, Centre for Research on Peace and Development, KU Leuven.

McFerson, Hazel M. 2010. "Extractive Industries and African Democracy: Can the 'Resource Curse' Be Exorcised?" *International Studies Perspectives*, 11(4): 335–53.

Mkandawire, Thandika. 2015. "Neopatrimonialism and the Political Economy of Economic Performance in Africa: Critical Reflections." *World Politics*, 67(3): 563–612.

Moisan, Dorothée. 2022. "Uganda Oil Project Casts Shadow Over Total's Eco-Friendly Image." *The Guardian*, April 19. https://www.theguardian.com/environment/2022/ apr/19/uganda-oil-project-casts-shadow-over-totals-eco-friendly-image.

Mugisha, Doreen. 2022. "Employment in the Oil and Gas Sector." PwC. https://www .pwc.com/ug/en/press-room/employment-in-the-oil-and-gas-sector.html, accessed December 13, 2023.

Nakayi, Rose, and Annika Witte. 2019. "Making Cultural Heritage Claims on Profitable Land: The Case of the Ngassa Wells in Uganda's Oil Region." *Africa Spectrum*, 54(3): 222–43.

National Population Council, Clare Kyomuhendo, and David Atombire Adumbire, 2022. "The State of Uganda Population Report 2022." Kampala.

Neiman, Sophie. 2023. "Fear and Oil in Uganda." *The New York Review of Books*, January 6. https://www.nybooks.com/articles/2023/01/19/fear-and-oil-in-uganda -sophie-neiman/.

Nuwagaba, Innocent, and Tshombe Lukamba-Muhiya. 2021. "The Impact of the Oil and Gas Exploitation Projects on the Environment in Western Uganda." *African Renaissance*, 199–216.

Ogwang, Tom, Frank Vanclay, and Arjan van den Assem. 2019. "Rent-Seeking Practices, Local Resource Curse, and Social Conflict in Uganda's Emerging Oil Economy." *Land*, 8(4): 53.

Okiror, Samuel. 2021. "Uganda Opposition Leader Bobi Wine Calls on Court to Nullify Election Result." *The Guardian*. https://www.theguardian.com/world/2021

/feb/01/uganda-opposition-leader-bobi-wine-calls-on-court-to-nullify-election
-result, accessed February 1, 2024.

Olanya, David Ross. 2015. "Will Uganda Succumb to the Resource Curse? Critical Reflections." *Extractive Industries and Society*, 2(1): 46–55.

Opondo, Paul. 2019. "Politics of Oil in Eastern Africa: Does It Present Another Geopolitical Pivot?" In *Contemporary Africa and the Foreseeable World Order*, edited by Francis Onditi, Gilad Ben-Nun, Cristina D'Alessandro, Zach Levey, and Abu Bakarr Bah. Lanham, MD: Lexington Books.

Owori, Moses. 2020. "Poverty in Uganda: National and Regional Data and Trends." *Development Initiatives*. https://devinit.org/data/datasets/poverty-uganda-national
-and-regional-data-and-trends/, accessed October 1, 2023

Oxfam. 2022. "Reactive: European Parliament Resolution on Violations of Human Rights in Uganda and Tanzania Linked to the Investments in Fossil Fuels Projects." https://uganda.oxfam.org/latest/press-release/reactive-european-parliament
-resolution-violations-human-rights-uganda-and, accessed September 20, 2023.

Patey, Luke. 2017. *A Belated Boom: Uganda, Kenya, South Sudan, and Prospects and Risks for Oil in East Africa.* Oxford, UK: Oxford Institute for Energy Studies.

Patey, Luke. 2015a. "Oil in Uganda: Hard Bargaining and Complex Politics in East Africa." OIES Working Paper 60, Oxford Institute for Energy Studies, Oxford.

Patey, Luke. 2015b. *Uganda's Oil Sector.* Oxford, UK: Oxford Institute for Energy Studies.

Pendergast, Shannon M., Judith A. Clarke, and G. Cornelis Van Kooten. 2011. "Corruption, Development and the Curse of Natural Resources." *Canadian Journal of Political Science*, 44(2): 411–37.

Pećinar, Aleksandra. 2020. "African Oil in Bunyoro-Kitara." https://www.meer.com/en/61439-african-oil-in-bunyoro-kitara, accessed March 7, 2024.

Pitcher, Anne, Mary H. Moran, and Michael Johnston. 2009. "Rethinking Patrimonialism and Neopatrimonialism in Africa." *African Studies Review*, 52(1): 125–56.

Polus, Andrzej, and Wojciech J. Tycholiz. 2017. "The Norwegian Model of Oil Extraction and Revenues Management in Uganda." *African Studies Review*, 60(3): 181–201.

Reuters. 2010. "Ugandan President to Approve All Oil, Gas Deals." https://www.reuters.com/article/markets/oil/ugandan-president-to-approve-all-oil-gas-deals-idUSLDE67I0XZ/, accessed July 16, 2024.

Roessler, Philip G. 2016. *Ethnic Politics and State Power in Africa: The Logic of the Coup-Civil War Trap.* Cambridge, UK: Cambridge University Press.

Roth, Kenneth. 2022. "World Report 2022: Rights Trends in Uganda." Human Rights Watch. https://www.hrw.org/world-report/2022/country-chapters/uganda, accessed January 13, 2024.

Sandner, Philipp. 2018. "The Great Lakes, Africa's Contested Waters." https://www.dw.com/en/contested-waters-conflict-on-africas-great-lakes/a-45245425, accessed August 27, 2023.

Schubert, Jon, Ulf Engel, and Elísio Salvado Macamo. 2020. *Extractive Industries and Changing State Dynamics in Africa: Beyond the Resource Curse.* London: Routledge.

Scurfield, Thomas, and Paul Bagabo. 2022. "Uganda's Local Governments Need Clarity on Oil Revenue Sharing." *Natural Resource Governance Institute.* https://resourcegovernance.org/articles/ugandas-local-governments-need-clarity-oil-revenue-sharing, accessed August 23, 2023.

Sklar, Richard L. 1979. "The Nature of Class Domination in Africa." *The Journal of Modern African Studies*, 17(4): 531–52.

Smith, Laura, and James Van Alstine. 2018. "Neoliberal Oil Development in Uganda: Centralization, Accumulation and Exclusion." In *The Dynamics of Neoliberal Transformation*, edited by Jörg Wiegratz, Giuliano Martiniello, and Elisa Greco, 234–48. London: Zed Books.

Soest, Christian von. 2022. "Neopatrimonialism: A Critical Assessment." In *Handbook on Governance and Development*, edited by Wil Hout and Jane Hutchison. Cheltenham, UK: Edward Elgar Publishing.

Taylor, Liam. 2021. "How Land Reform Became Uganda's Most Controversial Problem." *Foreign Policy*, October 15. https://foreignpolicy.com/2021/10/15/uganda-buganda-kingdom-land-reform-debate-museveni-colonialism-indigenous-power/.

Titeca, Kristof, and Jorg Wiegratz. 2018. "More Is Less? Decentralization and Regime Control in Neoliberal Uganda." In *Uganda: The Dynamics of Neoliberal Transformation*, edited by Giuliano Martiniello and Elisa Greco. London, UK: Zed Books.

Tumusiime, David, Joseph Mawejje, and Patrick Byakagaba. 2016. "Discovery of Oil: Community Perceptions and Expectations in Uganda's Albertine Region." *Journal of Sustainable Development*, 9(6): 1.

Van Alstine, James, Jacob Manyindo, Laura Smith, Jami Dixon, and Ivan Amaniga Ruhanga. 2014. "Resource Governance Dynamics: The Challenge of 'New Oil' in Uganda." *Resources Policy*, 40: 48–58.

Vokes, Richard. 2012. "The Politics of Oil in Uganda." *African Affairs*, 111(443): 303–14.

Walter, Barbara F. 2023. *How Civil Wars Start: And How to Stop Them.* New York: Crown.

Wolf, Sebastian. 2020. "Uganda's Oil: How Much, When, and How Will It Be Governed." In *Mining for Change: Natural Resources and Industry in Africa*, edited by Vishal Aditya Potluri. Oxford: Oxford Press.

Wolf, Sebastian, and Vishal Aditya Potluri. 2018. "Uganda's Oil: How Much, When, and How Will It Be Governed?" United Nations University, December. https://www.wider.unu.edu/sites/default/files/Publications/Working-paper/PDF/wp2018-179.pdf.

World Health Organization. 2023. "Health Data Overview for the Republic of Uganda." https://data.who.int/countries/800.

Wrong, Michela. 2010. *It's Our Turn to Eat: The Story of a Kenyan Whistleblower.* London, UK: Fourth Estate.

Ziyadov, Taleh, and Brenda Shaffer. 2012. *Beyond the Resource Curse.* Philadelphia: University of Pennsylvania Press.

Chapter 2

Beyond the Resource Curse

How Tanzania Avoided the Resource Curse in the Natural Gas Sector

William John Walwa

The discovery and initial exploitation of natural gas in the Swahili coastal regions of Tanzania has increased hope to transform the agriculturally dominated and donor-dependent economy of the country "into an industrializing Middle-Income Country (MIC) by 2025" (Kamat 2017: 304). The discovery has made Tanzania one of Africa's new natural gas economies (Henstridge 2020). Natural gas has broadened Tanzania's extractive sector, which was initially dependent on mining precious metals such as gold, diamond, and tanzanite.

Tanzania's developments in the extractive sector cannot be understood separately from the government's economic and political reforms from the mid-1980s. The government amended the post-independence socialist policies in order to attract foreign investments. Economic liberalization allowed Tanzania's extractive sector to attract significant foreign investment, particularly in the mining sector (Polus and Tycholiz 2019; Walwa 2016). Tanzania has since then become one of Africa's largest exporters of gold (Curtis and Lissu 2008; Ericsson and Löf 2018).

Yet Tanzania's experience with the mining extractive sector has garnered mixed feelings from the population. On one hand, the sector's contribution to the economy has been hailed. Accordingly, the sector's contribution to the gross domestic product (GDP) increased from 1.1 percent in 1989 to 2.3 percent in 2000 (Kitula 2004); it reached 7.3 percent in 2022. The government hopes to increase the GDP contribution of the sector to 15 percent in 2025 (*Citizen* 2022b). On the other hand, the mining sector is marred by several concerns, particularly tax evasion by the mining companies (Curtis and Lissu 2008; Lange and Kolstad 2012) and the violation of community members' environmental, economic, and land rights (Kitula 2004; Walwa 2016). There are complaints that Tanzania is not getting an equitable share of economic benefits from the mining sector. In effect, the government has made several critical legal amendments to address concerns in the mining sector. But many of the sentiments remain, so much so that tensions between mining companies and community members have been recurrent. In some mines, such as North Mara, cases of death caused by tensions between mining companies and community members have been reported several times (Walwa 2016).

In this case, Tanzania's experience with the mining sector best fits the resource curse thesis explanation that while discovering natural resources can be considered a blessing, this has not always been the case, particularly in Africa. The experience in several African countries has shown that natural resource discovery and exploitation can become a curse (Collier and Hoeffler 1998; Fearon and Laitin 2003; Fearon 2004; Ross 2013; Robinson, Torvik, and Verdier 2006; Holder 2006). The central argument of the resource curse thesis is that natural resources "make countries perform worse economically than they would otherwise be, and lead them to be more autocratic, civil war-prone and worse off politically" (Marrison 2013: 1122). This could be said about Tanzania, where the boom of the large-scale mining sector never brought the projected economic and social transformation of local communities in the mineral-rich regions, such as Geita, Mwanza, Mara, and Simiyu. Communities in these regions have remained poor despite sitting on top of gold and diamond wealth (Roe 2016).

However, the resource curse thesis has several limitations, including failing to explain how adopting governance in countries like Tanzania allowed them to avoid the resource curse in the recently discovered natural gas sector. As such, this chapter is informed by the concept of governance. It conceives governance as a decisive factor for the resource curse to occur. Governance is defined as smooth government transition, civic liberty, transparency, and government accountability. Relatedly, governance is described as the existence of checks and balances in the government, political stability, effectiveness of the anti-corruption laws and the effectiveness of the rule of law to amend gaps in the law on the extractive industry (Iimi 2007).

Moreover, governance is defined here as the presence of effective institutions that allow the government to be in check (Sebudubudu and Mooketsane 2016). Tellingly, bad institutions block the sustainable growth of the extractive sector (van der Ploeg 2011; Mehlum, Moene, and Torvik 2006). Sound institutions prevent the politicians in power from using the natural resource wealth to finance political ambitions to continue staying in office (Robinson, Torvik, and Verdier 2006).

Contrary to the resource curse's limited understanding of natural resources in Africa, this chapter's central question is: *How has Tanzania sought to avoid the resource curse in the natural gas sector?* In other words, *what has Tanzania learned from the mining sector to avoid replicating a resource curse in the natural gas sector?* The current chapter examines three aspects of Tanzania's natural gas sector to answer this question. First, it analyzes how the legal frameworks on natural gas and oil have attempted to avoid the resource curse. Secondly, it examines how the sector prioritized domestic economic demands for natural gas. Finally, it examines how the sector has sought to secure social license to operate.

In the context of Tanzania, the chapter uses governance as a lens to determine how the principles adopted from the 1990s helped avoid the resource curse in the natural gas industry. Botswana is often cited as an exemplary case in Africa, which translated its natural resources into human capital and infrastructural development (Iimi 2007; Sebudubudu and Mooketsane 2016; van der Ploeg 2011; Mehlum, Moene, and Torvik 2006). Governance promoted checks and balances, eventually allowing Botswana to have a responsive, accountable, and democratic government. Upholding democracy inculcates a culture of seeking the consent of people in decisions regarding natural resources (Sebudubudu and Mooketsane 2016). Democracy allowed Botswana to transition from one government to another, a factor that prevented leaders in power from misusing natural resources because doing so risks being exposed and held accountable. The people's and non-state actors' voices can be heard when there is governance (Iimi 2007).

The chapter is divided into three sections. The first section examines the evolution and shift of the extractive sector in Tanzania, from mining to natural gas. The following section addresses the core focus of the chapter regarding how Tanzania has sought to avoid the resource curse in the natural gas and oil sector. The last part is the conclusion.

EXTRACTIVE SECTOR IN TANZANIA: FROM BOOM IN THE MINING SECTOR TO NATURAL GAS

The period of the mid-1980s was a critical juncture in terms of understanding Tanzania's extractive sector. During this period, Tanzania embarked on economic and political reforms, which saw the transition from socialist to neoliberal economic policies. The Investment (Promotion and Protection) Act was enacted in 1990 to provide a legal roadmap for attracting and protecting foreign investments in different sectors of the economy. However, external factors, such as the Bretton Woods Institutions' Structural Adjustment Program, compelled Tanzania and other countries in the Global South to liberalize their economies. The negative economic impacts of the 1970s oil crisis and the 1978–1979 Uganda–Tanzania War made it difficult for Tanzania to continue embracing its socialist policies (Kanaan 2000).

The post-independence Arusha Declaration of 1967 nationalized all major means of production, including minerals and land. As such, state-owned enterprises, including the State Mining Corporation and the national oil company known as Tanzania Petroleum Development Corporation (TPDC), were established to oversee the mining and the natural gas sectors, respectively. The State Mining Corporation and TPDC continue to exist but no longer enjoy the monopoly over the ownership and operation of the mining, natural gas, and oil sectors.

Tanzania's economic reforms registered positive results in the extractive industry and witnessed a boom in the mining sector. The incoming investors allowed the country to increase mineral production by 51 percent in 1991. This made the country rank the third largest gold producer in Africa, behind South Africa and Ghana. The large-scale gold mines in the country are located in the gold-rich regions in the northwestern part of the country, namely, Mwanza, Shinyanga, Geita, Mara, and Simiyu (Kitula 2004).

Even so, the mining sector's contribution to the GDP remains marginal. As of the end of 2023, the overall GDP contribution of the mining sector was less than 10 percent (Citizen 2022b; Malanga 2023). One of the reasons for this limited contribution is the unfavorable agreements signed between the government and foreign investors. Tanzania's mining contracts allowed the investors 100 percent ownership over the mines. In this respect, since the government has no stakes in the mines, the investors have been exporting the bulk of all processed and unprocessed minerals away from Tanzania (Kitula 2004). Some jobs and other economic opportunities in the mining sector are being transferred abroad. The investors did not invest in developing processors for mineral processing within the country. This was because the mining laws did not provide any legal requirements for mining companies to process the minerals locally. Thus the role of the government was rendered to that of collecting tax and royalties from the mining investors.

It should be noted that several government attempts to amend the legal mistakes in the mining laws to increase public participation in the sector were made. The amendments should be understood in the context of governance. The increase of civic liberty, transparency, and accountability exposed weaknesses in the mining law. This put pressure on the government to amend the law. The most significant amendment was made in 2017. Notably, the government introduced new stringent laws that compelled the licensed mining companies to transfer 16 percent of non-dilutable free interest shares to the government through the Treasury Registrar (United Republic of Tanzania 2017a). In effect, some companies, including the former Acacia Mining

Company, transferred shares to the government, forming a joint venture company called Twiga (Mwakaje and Nyang'anyi 2023). While this government move should be applauded, it will not help the country economically as the lifespan of many ongoing gold mines is ending. Others, for example, the Gold Pride Mine in Nzega District, Tabora Region, have been closed down. Yet these amendments are expected to help the country benefit from prospective mining contracts and the natural gas sector, which is in the infant stage.

Thus, while striving to rectify mistakes in the mining sector, a new extractive natural gas sector has emerged, and there are prospects for the discovery of oil. Natural gas was first discovered in Tanzania in 1974 at Songo Songo in the Lindi Region. However, production started in 2004, about thirty years after the discovery. This was due to the high cost of production and the limited interest of investors to begin the extraction of natural gas. The mid-1980s economic liberalization in the country increased the interest of investors to embark on further exploitation and discovery (Melyoki and Kessy 2020; Lange and Wyndham 2021). Specifically, discoveries have since then taken place in the southern part of the country, in Mtwara, Lindi, and Pwani Regions. As of 2017, the natural gas discovered was estimated at about sixty trillion cubic feet (Polus and Tycholiz 2019). This windfall is expected to be the most significant investment in the history of Tanzania, and it attracted about ten active multinational companies, including Pan Africa Energy, Wentworth (formerly M&P), Ophir, British Gas, and ExxonMobil and Statoil (now known as Equinor) (Melyoki and Kessy 2020).

Only a few offshore natural gas discoveries at Mnazi Bay (about 0.3 trillion cubic feet) in the Mtwara Region and Songo Songo (about 0.7 trillion cubic feet) in the Lindi Region have started production. Of the natural gas produced at Mnazi Bay and Songo Songo, most is being used for electricity production in homes in parts of the capital, Dar es Salaam. As such, most deep-sea reserves remain unexploited. The government is currently negotiating with investors to build a liquefied natural gas plant (LNG) in Lindi Region (Peace Research Institute Oslo 2016).

HOW TANZANIA AVOIDED THE RESOURCE CURSE IN THE NATURAL GAS SECTOR

In order to respond to the question regarding how Tanzania has sought to avoid the resource curse in the natural gas and oil sector, this section seeks to determine the following. First, it analyzes how the legal framework on natural gas has addressed concerns regarding accountability and transparency in the natural gas sector. Secondly, it examines how the sector has prioritized domestic demands for natural gas and job creation. Finally, it examines how the sector's operation sought social license to operate. Each of the aspects is discussed in separate sections.

Addressing the Resource Curse through Legal and Policy Frameworks

Avoiding the resource curse requires adopting a transparent legal framework that ensures the democratic participation of community members in the governance of natural resource wealth. This can only happen when there is governance, which creates an effective rule of law, strong institutions, and transparency in the governance of natural resources. Botswana is an exemplary case in Africa for creating sound institutions, anti-corruption laws, transparency, and effective legal frameworks, which enabled diamond mining to contribute almost 40 percent of the country's GDP from extracting and exporting diamonds (van der Ploeg 2011). Effective anti-corruption laws ensured checks and balances in the government, reducing Botswana's mismanagement of natural resources (Iimi 2007). On the contrary, non-transparent legal frameworks imply that politicians in power can tamper with the natural resources law for their own economic and political ends. In Africa, the presence of natural resources has often tempted political leaders to change the existing law to reap personal benefits from valuable natural resources. The same could be said that the absence of strong legal frameworks has often exposed the extractive industry in Africa to rampant corruption and elite capture (Fabricius 2017; Jingu 2017).

One of the common governance-related problems in the legal frameworks on natural resources in Africa is that they do not provide for transparency, democratic participation, and permanent sovereignty of community members over their natural resources. In Nigeria, for instance, the deficit in the law has paved the way for grand corrupt practices involving collusion between investors and local elites to underreport and steal the proceeds from natural resources (Okada and Shinkuma 2022). Likewise, the absence of a legal framework that provides transparency in the governance of natural resources has made it difficult for Nigeria and some other countries in the sub-Saharan African region to gain substantial economic benefits from the extractive sector (Sala-i-Martin and Subramanian 2003).

Tanzania faced similar governance deficits in the law governing the mining sector. Revealingly, Tanzania's mining concession agreements were never discussed and approved by representative bodies of the people, notably the National Assembly. This resulted from the fact that the mining laws had placed the minerals in the hands of the government. The law never legally required the government to submit the mining contracts to the National Assembly for review. Similarly, the law never established independent oversight institutional mechanisms to scrutinize the mining contracts and operations of the mining companies. In fact, the contracts were developed behind closed doors inside public offices and, as a result, did not adequately provide legal accountability and transparency mechanisms for institutions involved in the governance of natural resources (Luoga 2016).

Tanzania was fortunate in that when developing the legal framework on natural gas and oil, it had the wisdom to learn from the challenges experienced in the mining sector. It can also be said that Tanzania had an advantage in developing legal frameworks on the natural gas industry when the country had adopted governance principles, which require transparency and democratic participation of people in decision-making. The government of Tanzania wanted to avoid repeating the mistakes made in the mining sector in the burgeoning natural gas sector and planned to implement the Norwegian model of sharing benefits from the natural resources. The Norwegian model has established effective fiscal policies, including an oil fund to cater to the needs of future generations. It places natural resources under the state and splits the administration responsibilities between three different agencies of the government: the state oil company, an oil authority, and the government (Polus and Tycholiz 2017).

In 2012, the government of Tanzania constituted a committee of experts to review the legal status of natural gas and oil and hence provide a legal direction for the country to adopt, referring to other gas and oil exporters. These series of meetings culminated in the enactment of three new laws: the Petroleum Act (2015), the Oil and Natural Gas Revenue Management Act (2015), and the Extractive Industries (Transparency and Accountability) Act (2015) (United Republic of Tanzania 2015a; 2015b; 2015c). The Oil and Natural Gas Revenue Management Act (2015) established the Oil and Gas Fund. This holding and saving account is established to safeguard future generations' economic interests. This act enables the government to invest the benefits of natural gas and oil into human capital development, providing supplementary financial savings for future generations. Companies involved in the extractive industry must file and disclose their records accurately and ensure the effective participation of local people in the extractive industry. The Tanzania Extractive Industries (Transparency and Accountability) Act (2015) established an institutional setup to ensure transparency and accountability. It established an independent committee of fifteen members and a chairperson tasked with developing a national framework for transparency and accountability of companies in the extractive industry. The committee has oversight power to make sure that the benefits from natural gas and oil are validated transparently and wisely utilized to benefit the current and future generations.

The Petroleum Act (2015) bestows upon the national oil company, TPDC, exclusive rights over the downstream and midstream natural gas and oil value chain. While this legal breakthrough helps promote domestic investments and equitable benefits from the natural gas industry, it has been criticized for sloping efficient investment in the natural gas sector (Henstridge 2020). Companies intending to engage in the natural gas and oil industry can only operate in Tanzania after entering into agreements with the national oil company. This provision is one of the reasons that has helped Tanzania prioritize domestic needs for natural gas before exporting externally. In practice, the country maintains a stake in the oil and natural gas sector. As a shareholder, the government has the power to influence the operation of the natural gas extractive industry (Luoga 2016).

In 2017, Tanzania revolutionized the governance of the extractive sector by enacting two important pieces of legislation: The Natural Wealth and Resources (Permanent Sovereignty) Act 2017 ("Sovereignty Act") (United Republic of Tanzania 2017a) and the Natural Wealth and Resources (Review and Re-Negotiation of Unconscionable Terms) Act (United Republic of Tanzania 2017b). The Sovereignty Act empowers the National Assembly to approve any natural resources contracts. The Review and Re-Negotiation Act demands the re-negotiation of existing or prospective terms of natural resources contracts and the review of the terms that subject the country to foreign arbitrations. This provision entrusts the adjudication of any disputes related to natural resource extraction to a Tanzanian body. It helps to legitimize local litigation measures dealing with disputes in the extractive industry. Some experts and investors have criticized these two new pieces of legislation for scaring investors and contravening international investment regimes (Mwakaje and Nyang'anyi 2023). However, the laws make provisions for greater transparency in the operation of the extractive industry.

This chapter argues that to achieve the intended results, Tanzania's new legal regimes on natural gas should be backed by legal reforms that empower oversight institutions within the government. Tanzania's transition to liberal democracy and governance in the 1990s has worked well in different ways to increase transparency and the voices of the public. However, this transition occurred without constitutional review or amendment, leaving the executive branch of government very powerful. The 1977 Constitution still has centralized power under the executive body, headed by the president (Makulilo 2008; Bamwenda 2018; Cheeseman, Matfess, and Amani 2021). This centralization has produced weak oversight institutions. As a result, the National Assembly, political parties, civil societies, controller auditor general, and judiciary cannot hold the executive branch accountable (Cheeseman, Matfess, and Amani 2021). Thus, this is to say that the achievements made in the governance space are vulnerable to political manipulation because they are still sitting on an authoritarian constitution. There is a danger that these achievements can be eroded when an authoritarian leader takes control of the government.

The presence of strong oversight institutions facilitates monitoring whether the government is adhering to the legal requirements to maintain oil and natural gas funds for future generations. Experience from the mining sector revealed the centralization of power to be a source of corruption involving officials in the executive branch. In addition, the centralization of power weakened the capacity of the government to hold mining companies accountable. Thus, without reforms in the oversight institutions, it is likely that there will be a repeat of the mismanagement that was the case in the mining sector.

Prioritizing Domestic Needs for Natural Gas and Job Creation

With one of the fastest growing populations in the world, Tanzania is facing twin problems: energy deficit and unemployment. According to the 2022 national census of Tanzania, the current population of Tanzania is about sixty-one million persons, with an annual growth rate of 3.2 percent (United Republic of Tanzania 2022a). In this case, Tanzania needs to build a strong economy accommodating the youthful population. The natural gas sector is considered to have the potential to help deal with unemployment and energy deficit. The mining sector has not had a significant contribution in the creation of jobs because it is not labor-intensive and mining contracts did not oblige companies to invest in building processing industries that would then allow the minerals to be processed and packaged within the country (Kessy, Melyoki, and Nyamrunda 2017; Melyoki and Kessy 2020).

In the natural gas sector, the government has been saluted for attempting to ensure that the sector contributes meaningfully in dealing with problems of unemployment and energy scarcity. Specifically, before exporting natural gas, the country prioritized the domestic needs for electricity. Of interest, the government constructed a 532-kilometer natural gas pipeline from Mtwara to Dar es Salaam. The construction, which started in 2012, was completed in 2015.

When the government started using natural gas from 2004 to produce electricity, the share of natural gas to the national electricity grid surpassed that of hydropower. Natural gas currently contributes more than fifty-six of the country's 1,602 megawatts presently produced. (United Republic of Tanzania 2022b; United Republic of Tanzania 2020). If utilized to its fullest capacity, the pipeline from Mtwara is expected to generate nearly thirty-nine hundred megawatts. However, to meet the increasing demand for electricity in the country, Tanzania needs to raise the amount of electricity produced to at least ten thousand megawatts (United Republic of Tanzania 2020). There is, therefore, a need to increase the use of natural gas to meet this energy demand.

Water dams have been the traditional source of electricity in Tanzania. However, hydroelectric power is becoming unreliable as a result of climate change causing irregular water supply to the dams. Accordingly, while the electricity demand has been increasing significantly, the amount of electricity produced by dams does not match this demand. In effect, the water shortage in the dams has often resulted in power rationing during prolonged dry seasons. It is estimated that the demand for electricity in the country is increasing at a rate of 15 percent annually (TanzaniaInvest 2021). Tanzania's natural gas discovery, therefore, provided a necessary relief from energy scarcity issues brought about by sporadic rainfall.

Tanzania has been one of the success stories in implementing the rural electrification program. This has been possible because of the presence of natural gas that has added a significant amount of electricity to the national grid. The 2022 national census indicated that of the 70 percent of the population in Tanzania residing in rural areas, 69.8 percent have access to electricity, a 20 percent increase from 49.3 percent in 2016. The amount of rural electrification in Tanzania is 20 percent above Africa's average electrification rate, which was reported to be 48.4 percent in 2022 (UN Development Programme 2022). In this case, the presence of natural gas means that the government can continue expanding access to electricity in rural settings to reach the country's 75 percent target of access to electricity by 2025. In addition, using natural gas facilitates increased access to energy and electricity in the country, which implies that most of the population across the country will feel the economic impacts of the natural gas sector (Mwalongo 2022).

Promoting the domestic use of natural gas can stimulate the growth of other sectors of the economy, especially the agricultural sector, which employs the highest number of people in the country. The agricultural sector in Tanzania failed to modernize, partly because of energy deficits and limited financial resources. The challenge of transporting food from the villages to the market in the urban setting was addressed mainly through investments in road networks that connect all regions in the country (Mdoe 2022). Yet there is little investment in the processing and storing of the food produced in rural settings due to challenges related to the reliable electricity supply (Nkwabi et al. 2019).

The reliable availability of energy generated by natural gas has stimulated hope for developing the industrial sector and provides prospects for mitigating climate change. However, Tanzania's industrial base remains weak, partly because of limited foreign investment. TPDC has initiated programs to supply natural gas to industries and homes in Dar es Salaam, Pwani, and Mtwara, notably Dangote Cement. As of 2020, more than one thousand homes and four hundred vehicles in Dar es Salaam had been supplied with natural gas. The use of natural gas for the generation of electricity and domestic and industrial usage has allowed the country to save a total of over fifteen billion US dollars (Zachalia 2020).

Another milestone is the collaboration between the government and investors to build an LNG plant within Tanzania (Lange and Wyndham 2021). The project, whose value is estimated at thirty billion US dollars, promises to be a game changer in the economic development of Tanzania. After successful negotiation, the preliminary host-government agreement between the government and the investors, Shell and Equinor, was signed in June 2022 (*Citizen* 2022a). Indeed, through the Ministry of Energy, the government announced in May 2023 that the negotiations had concluded. The parties to the LNG project are currently drafting the agreements (*Citizen* 2023).

The LNG project significantly impacts the national GDP and share of Tanzania's exports. The 2022 independent report commissioned by Stanbic Bank Tanzania revealed that the LNG project is likely to add seven billion US dollars annually to the GDP of Tanzania. This is an addition of about 20 percent of the current GDP of Tanzania. Similarly, the LNG project is expected to allow the country to earn nearly two billion US dollars in revenues annually (*Citizen* 2022a). This revenue amount is approximately 10 percent of the current annual budget of Tanzania.

Yet several challenges need to be resolved. One of these challenges is the natural gas sector's failure to reduce electricity prices. When the natural gas pipeline construction started, there were hopes that it would help relieve the country from high electricity prices. Instead, the prices of electricity have been increasing. The current price of electricity per kilowatt in Tanzania is roughly 0.09 US dollars, well above that of several countries like Zimbabwe and Zambia, which do not have natural gas power-generating plants. The failure of natural gas to change electricity prices has been one reason discouraging further government investments in natural gas power-generating plants. During the past five years, the government of Tanzania cited high prices of natural gas–generated electricity as one of the reasons to invest in constructing a new hydropower generation dam. This dam, which has been named Julius Nyerere Hydro Electric Power Plant, is expected to produce about 2,115 megawatts. The construction started in 2019 and is expected to be completed in 2024 (Christopher 2023).

Securing Social License to Operate

Natural gas in Tanzania has been discovered in regions (Mtwara, Lindi, and Pwani) that have historically suffered from economic and political marginalization, igniting regionalism (Kamat 2017). Certainly, a local population from Lindi and Mtwara Regions often refer to themselves as "Wakusini" (Southerners), to connote an area that has been forgotten (Peace Research

Institute Oslo 2016). The literature on "greed and grievance" in natural resources has established evidence showing that economic variables, such as concerns around economic inequalities, have strong explanatory power of grievance and hence rebellion (Collier and Hoeffler 1998; 2004). In this case, if not well managed, feelings of marginalization can be manipulated for political, economic, and religious ends. This can create conflicts and violence, contributing to a resource curse in Tanzania. Experience in several African countries, for instance, the Democratic Republic of the Congo, has shown that natural resource-rich areas have been a source of violent conflicts and other forms of social unrest (Baregu 2011).

Natural resources can fuel conflicts and insurgency in different ways: disagreements on the distribution of natural resources benefits, motivations to use natural resources to fund insurgence wars, and the triggering of already existing conflicts. Also, natural resources can hinder achieving post-conflict peace (Rustad and Binningsbø 2012). Of late, the natural resource–rich area of northern Mozambique has become a war zone area. The presence of natural resources triggered already existing problems. Economic marginalization has been driving youth to join extremist and terrorist groups. This was confirmed by the UN Development Programme (2017) research titled "Journey to Extremism in Africa," which interviewed recruits of extremist and terrorist groups. Economic grave dances and promises for jobs are pushing groups of youth from economically marginalized areas to join extremist groups. A recent example of an economically and politically marginalized area that has fallen into the hands of extremist groups is northern Mozambique (Morier-Genoud 2020). Like Mtwara, northern Mozambique has rich natural resources, including natural gas. Since the Mtwara Region borders and interacts closely with northern Mozambique, there are likely chances for extremist activities to penetrate Mtwara.

Companies have to secure a "social license to operate" in order for the investments in natural resources to be accepted by community members. Having a legal agreement to own natural resources is one thing, but having social license to operate is another. For corporations to operate smoothly, they must seek to secure legal and social licenses. The concept of social license to operate stresses that natural resource producers must seek permission, consult with local communities, and facilitate dialogue to legitimize their operations in a local community. Local communities should be stakeholders in the production and management of natural gas. This concept relates to other norms in the extractive sector, such as free, prior, and informed consent, and is a useful lens to understand the interface between the extractive sector and resource curse (Meesters and Behagel 2017).

Tanzania presently has struggled to secure social license in the extractive sector. The most common concerns of communities hosting natural resource investments in Tanzania include low compensation of land taken by corporations and limited contribution of the sector to the community's livelihoods. As such, this has been a source of contention between mining companies and community members staying near the large-scale mines (Kessy, Melyoki, and Nyamrunda 2017).

The discovery of natural gas brought hope to economically marginalized populations in the southern part of the country. This hope was stirred by political statements that natural gas would end the economic hardships of community members. Ardently, politicians from the ruling party promised that natural gas would make Mtwara the "Dubai" or "Singapore" of Africa (Kamat 2017; Heilman and Jingu 2016). Yet the hope of seeing "Dubai" or "Singapore" in Mtwara was unrealized. Instead, there is a sense of exclusion, humiliation, and anger among community members, what the literature describes as "accumulation by dispossession and displacement" (Kamat 2017).

When natural gas discovery was confirmed in Mtwara, the government expressed interest in using this resource to increase power generation in Tanzania by ten thousand megawatts by 2025. Subsequently, in May 2013, the government, through the Ministry of Energy and Minerals, announced plans to construct a 532-kilometer natural gas pipeline to transport natural gas from Mtwara to Dar es Salaam for power generation. However, the government failed to consult the community members and largely ignored democratic principles of free, prior, and informed consent (Heilman and Jingu 2016; Kamat 2017). Instead, excessive use of force by security forces was used to suppress community members in natural resource–rich areas in Mtwara. As a result, community members continue to believe that their natural gas is not benefiting Mtwara (Kessy, Melyoki, and Nyamrunda 2017).

Community members in Mtwara have spoken openly, threatening to withdraw from Tanzania if the government insists on proceeding with the construction of the natural gas pipeline project. They oppose the governmental decree to harness resources in Mtwara without developing the area or its people. Angry mobs of community members in Mtwara rioted for several days in May 2013 to oppose the government's decision. Local politicians and community leaders engineered the riots, and rioters burned public buildings, homes of public officials and police, and other government property, such as vehicles (Kamat 2017; Lange and Wyndham 2021; Melyoki and Kessy 2020).

Despite the riots and resentment from the community, the government proceeded to construct the natural gas pipeline. In his speech responding to the riots, the fourth president of Tanzania, Jakaya Kikwete, insisted that the natural gas belonged to all people in Tanzania, and the government would use this resource to benefit all Tanzanians (Kamat 2017). However, the level of resentment remains high. According to Thobias and Kseniia (2017), people felt suppressed to articulate their concerns because of the fear of a repeat of the May 2013 clash between the security forces and community members, in which about twelve people lost their lives.

It should be noted that the resentment of community members is aimed at the government, not investors. The investors, for example, had promised free electricity to the community members around the natural gas–producing areas. This promise did not materialize as the government disrupted this, stating that electrification was the responsibility of Tanzania Electric Supply Company (Kamat 2017). There were also concerns regarding the payment of low compensation to community members whose land was taken away by the investors. This was the case in Madimba and Msimbati wards in Mtwara, where members believe that their compensation dwarfed in comparison to the compensation paid by other investors, such as the Dangote Cement Factory in Mtwara (Kessy, Melyoki, and Nyamrunda 2017).

On their part, natural gas companies in Mtwara, for example, Shell and Equinor, have implemented several programs to meet their corporate social responsibilities. Such programs include business training for groups of youth, vocational training skills, construction of schools, and empowering community members to participate in the natural gas business chain. Conversely, community members were still concerned that the youths who received vocational training were granted employment by the natural gas companies (Kessy, Melyoki, and Nyamrunda 2017; Melyoki and Kessy 2020).

On the other hand, Lindi, which started exploiting natural gas to generate electricity in 2004, has had a positive experience securing social license to operate. This is partly because of the socio-economic investments that the investor has implemented in the host community. The investor, Pan African Energy, has implemented a number of corporate social responsibility projects in Lindi. Some of these projects included helping communities meet electricity and water connection costs and constructing dispensaries, schools, and laboratories. All these activities stimulated socio-economic development in the community surrounding the natural gas–producing areas (Kessy, Melyoki, and Nyamrunda 2017). In addition, in Lindi, the villages hosting the natural gas investment received preferential treatment of the share of natural gas levies collected by the district government. Specifically, villages have received 20 percent of the corporate social responsibility share of local taxes paid to the district councils. This money is then invested in promoting development programs for community members in the villages hosting the natural gas investment. For example, the money is being used to roof the grass-thatched houses of marginalized community members (Melyoki and Kessy 2020). The divergent experience in Lindi and Mtwara thus speaks to the importance of community consultation and cooperation in developing natural gas in Tanzania (Mwanyoka, Mdemu, and Wernstedt 2021).

CONCLUSION

Economic reforms from the mid-1980s positively impacted the development of Tanzania's extractive sector. Indeed, Tanzania saw a boom in the mining sector thanks to the economic reforms. However, the mining sector has been marred by various issues, notably lack of transparency and violation of local communities' land and economic rights. In addition, the mining sector has had little impact on job creation and contribution to GDP. This was because the concession agreements signed did not oblige the mining companies to process and package the minerals within the country. Also, the mining laws of Tanzania did not oblige the government to establish a mining fund that could be invested for future generations. As a result, Tanzania's mining sector experienced a curse.

Since then, Tanzania has discovered natural gas and learned from the mistakes of its mineral sector. Hence this chapter's central question: how has Tanzania sought to avoid the resource curse in the natural gas sector? The chapter uncovered that Tanzania has done increasingly well to avoid the resource curse in the natural gas sector. The natural gas laws have placed natural gas under the national oil company, TPDC, which allowed the country to maintain stake in the natural gas sector, enabling it to leverage the operation of the natural gas sector toward prioritizing production for domestic needs. This helped to address the two problems in the country: unemployment and energy deficit. Indeed, the completion of the construction of a 532-kilometer natural gas pipeline from Mtwara to Dar es Salaam has made natural gas contribute over 50 percent of the electricity produced in the country. In effect, the government's rural electrification program was made possible due to the availability of electricity from natural gas. Tanzania expects to reap significant economic benefits from the thirty-billion-dollar LNG project whose negotiation has been completed. The LNG project, constructed in Tanzania, will be the most important investment in the country's history.

Tanzania has arguably developed one of the best legal regimes on natural gas. The new law addressed concerns over the absence of transparency in the extractive industry in the country. It compelled companies in the natural gas and oil industry to file and disclose their accounts and ensure the participation of local people in the sector. Likewise, the new law obliged the government to establish an oil and natural gas fund for future generations. Equally, the law empowered people to review natural resource contracts through the National Assembly. It remains the best legal regime on natural gas and oil in East Africa despite being criticized for scaring investors and delaying investments in natural resources.

However, the new law on the natural gas extractive industry should be backed by legal reforms to create strong oversight institutions capable of checks on the operations and conduct of actors involved in the governance of the natural gas extractive sector. The current Constitution of Tanzania has produced weak oversight institutions, which cannot hold the executive branch accountable.

It should be noted that learning from mistakes in the mineral sector should be understood in the context of adopting and promoting governance, which empowers the public to expose problems in the mining law. Political leaders that have been in power at different times responded to the pressure from the public by amending the mineral laws and later developed arguably one of the best laws on natural gas.

On the other hand, it is worth highlighting that Tanzania needs to do better in securing social license to operate in the natural gas extractive sector in Mtwara. Natural gas in Tanzania was discovered in historically economically vulnerable areas. Mtwara borders northern Mozambique, where the current insurgency exacerbates vulnerabilities as communities from the two areas have strong social, cultural, and ethnic ties (Morier-Genoud 2020). As such, the influence of the extremist elements from Mozambique can easily penetrate Mtwara. Violent conflicts in northern Mozambique have already resulted in the closure of the Tanzania-Mozambique border in some districts in Mtwara (*Zitamar News* 2023; Walwa 2022).

Community members in Mtwara have maintained negative perceptions of the government, which they accuse of using force and coercion to take away their natural gas. Upon natural gas discovery, political leaders created unrealistic hopes in Mtwara, exaggerating the prospects of it becoming the Singapore or Dubai of Africa. As such, the people felt betrayed when they saw the government implementing a pipeline project from Mtwara to Dar es Salaam.

Thus, dealing with the grievances of community members in Mtwara requires investing in local-level sustainable job creation programs that will help heal the wounds caused by the government's past mistakes. The government's statements that natural gas is meant to benefit all of Tanzania are the wounds caused by past government mistakes. The use of force to fight off aggrieved, marginalized community members will hardly help to provide sustainable solutions.

To address these concerns, the government needs to do more to provide sustainable resources for marginalized communities, such as free electrification for villages around the natural gas–producing areas. Also, there should be more investments in the local human capital to allow the community members to benefit from employment opportunities in the natural gas sector.

REFERENCES

Bamwenda, Emilia. 2018. "The Symptoms of the Shift Towards an Authoritarian State in Tanzania's President John Pombe Magufuli's Rule." *Politeja*, 6(56): 123–50.

Baregu, Mwesiga L. 2011. *Understanding Obstacles to Peace: Actors, Interests, and Strategies in Africa's Great Lakes Region.* Kampala: Fountain Publishers.

Cheeseman, Nic, Hilary Matfess, and Alitalali Amani. 2021. "Tanzania: The Roots of Repression." *Journal of Democracy*, 32(2): 77–89.

Christopher, Josephine. 2023. "Power Generation at Julius Nyerere Dam to Kick Off Soon." *Citizen*, February 2.

Citizen. 2023. "Energy Companies Conclude Talks with Tanzania on LNG." May 30.

Citizen. 2022a. "LNG Can Boost Tanzania's GDP by Over Sh16 Trillion a Year." October 17.

Citizen. 2022b. "Mining Sector Hits 7.3 Percent of Tanzania's GD." October 8.

Collier, Paul, and Anke Hoeffler. 2004. "Greed and Grievance in Civil War." *Oxford Economic Papers*, 56(4): 563–95.

Collier, Paul, and Anke Hoeffler. 1998. "On Economic Causes of War." *Oxford Economic Papers*, 50(4): 563–73.

Curtis, Mark, and Tundu Lissu. 2008. *A Golden Opportunity? How Tanzania Is Failing to Benefit from Gold Mining.* Dar es Salaam: Christian Council of Tanzania and National Council of Muslims in Tanzania and Tanzania Episcopal Conference.

Ericsson, Magnus, and Olof Löf. 2018. "Mining's Contribution to National Economies between 1996 and 2016." *Mineral Economics*, 32(June): 223–50.

Fabricius, Peter. 2017. "African Leaders Take the Blame for the Continent's Resource Curse." *Institute for Security Studies.* https://issafrica.org/iss-today/african-leaders-take-the-blame-for-the-continents-resource-curse, accessed August 15, 2023.

Fearon, James D. 2004. "Why Do Some Civil Wars Last so Much Longer Than Others?" *Journal of Peace Research*, 41(3): 275–301.

Fearon, James D., and David D. Laitin. 2003. "Ethnicity, Insurgency, and Civil Wars." *American Political Science Review*, 97(1): 75–90.

Heilman, Bruce, and John Jingu. 2016. "The Natural Gas Conflict Trap: Insights from Mtwara Gas-Related Violence." In *The Political Economy of Change in Tanzania: Contestations over Identity, the Constitution and Resources*, edited by Rwekaza Mukandala Rwekaza, 284–97. Dar es Salaam, Tanzania: University of Dar es Salaam Press.

Henstridge, Mark. 2020. "Gas in Tanzania: Adapting New Realities." In *Mining for Change: Natural Resources and Industry in Africa*, edited by John Page and Finn Tarp, 232–55, Helsinki, Finland: UN University World Institute for Development Economics Research.

Holder, Roland. 2006. "The Curse of Natural Resources in Fractionalized Countries." *European Economic Review*, 50(60): 1367–86.

Iimi, Atsushi. 2007. "Escaping from the Resource Curse: Evidence from Botswana and the Rest of the World." *IMF Staff Papers*, 54(4): 663–99.

Jingu, John K. 2017. "State Capture in Tanzania: The Case of the Mining Sector." PhD dissertation, University of Dar es Salaam.

Kamat, Vinay R. 2017. "Powering the Nation: Natural Gas Development and Distributive Justice in Tanzania." *Human Organization*, 76(4): 304–14.

Kanaan, Oussama. 2000. "Tanzania's Experience with Trade Liberalization." *Finance and Development*, 37(2).

Kessy, Flora, Lemayon Melyoki, and Godfrey Nyamrunda. 2017. *The Social License to Operate in Tanzania: Case Studies of the Petroleum and Mining Sectors*. Dar es Salaam: The Institute of African Leadership for Sustainable Development.

Kitula, Angelo G. N. 2004. "The Environmental and Socio-economic Impacts of Mining on Local Livelihoods in Tanzania: A Case Study of Geita District." *Journal of Cleaner Production*, 14(3–4): 405–14.

Lange, Siri, and Ivar Kolstad. 2012. "Corporate Community Involvement and Local Institutions: Two Case Studies from the Mining Industry in Tanzania." *Journal of African Business*, 13(2): 134–44.

Lange, Siri, and Victoria Wyndham. 2021. "Gender, Regulation, and Corporate Social Responsibility in the Extractive Sector: The Case of Equinor's Social Investments in Tanzania." *Women's Studies International Forum*, 84(102434).

Luoga, Frolens D. A. M. 2016. "Challenges in Setting Up Legal Frameworks for Natural Resource Governance in East African Countries." *The African Review*, 43(2): 1–16.

Makulilo, Alexander Bonephace. 2008. *Tanzania: A De Facto One Party State?* Riga, Latvia: VDM Verlag.

Malanga, Nelson Alex. 2023. "How Government Plans to Boost Mining's GDP Contribution to 10 Percent before 2025." *Citizen*, May 24.

Marrison, Kevin M. 2013. "Whither the Resource Curse." *Perspectives on Politics*, 11(4): 1117–25.

Mdoe, Giza. 2022. "Tanzania Road Infrastructure Fueling Development Opportunities." *The Exchange*. https://theexchange.africa/countries/tanzania-transport-infrastructure-president-samia/, accessed October 19, 2023.

Meesters, Evelien Marieke, and Jelle Hendrik Behagel. 2017. "The Social Licence to Operate: Ambiguities and the neutralization of harm in Mongolia." *Resource Policy*, 53: 274–82.

Mehlum, Halvor, Karl Moene, and Ragnar Torvik. 2006. "Institutions and the Resource Curse." *The Economic Journal*, 116(508): 1–20.

Melyoki, Lemayon L., and Flora Kessy. 2020. "Why Companies Fail to Earn the Social License to Operate? Insights from the Extractive Sector in Tanzania." *The Journal of Rural and Community Development*, 15(2): 29–54.

Morier-Genoud, Eric. 2020. "The Jihadi Insurgency in Mozambique: Origins, Nature and Beginning." *Journal of Eastern African Studies*, 14(3): 396–412.

Mwakaje, Saudin J., and Tarangwa Nyang'anyi. 2023. "Reclaiming Sovereignty over Natural Wealth and Resources in Tanzania: Legal and Regulatory Implications on Investments." *ICSID Review*.

Mwalongo, Samuel. 2022. "Rural Electrification: Tanzania's Unrivalled Success." *Daily News*. https://dailynews.co.tz/rural-electrification-tanzanias-unrivalled-success/, accessed October 28, 2023.

Mwanyoka, Idd, Makarius Mdemu, and Kris Wernstedt. 2021. "The Reality of Local Community Participation in the Natural Gas Sector in Southeastern Tanzania." *The Extractive Industries and Society*, 8(1): 303–15.

Nkwabi, Jesca M., Leodger B. Mboya, Jenifer Mhoja Nkwabi, and Joyce Mhoja Nkwabi. 2019. "A Review of the Challenges Affecting the Agro-processing Sector in Tanzania." *Asian Journal of Sustainable Business Research*, 1(2): 68–77.

Okada, Keisuke, and Takayoshi Shinkuma. 2022. "Transparency and Natural Resources in Sub-Saharan Africa." *Resource Policy*, 76: 1–32.

Peace Research Institute Oslo. 2016. "Perceptions of Justice and Violent Mobilization: Explaining Petroleum Related Riots in Southern Tanzania." *Conflict Trends*, 6.

Polus, Andrzej, and Wojciech Tycholiz. 2019. "David versus Goliath: Tanzania's Efforts to Stand Up to Foreign Gas Corporations." *Africa Spectrum*, 54(1): 61–72.

Polus, Andrzej, and Wojciech J. Tycholiz. 2017. "The Norwegian Model of Oil Extraction and Revenues Management in Uganda." *Africa Studies Review*, 60(3): 181–201.

Robinson, James A., Ragnar Torvik, and Thierry Verdier. 2006. "Political Foundations of Resource Curse." *Journal of Development Economics*, 79(2): 447–68.

Roe, Alan R. 2016. "Tanzania—From Mining to Oil and Natural Gas." WIDER Working Paper 79, UN University World Institute for Development Economics Research, Helsinki, Finland.

Ross, M. 2013. "How Do Natural Resources Influence Civil Wars? Evidence from Thirteen Cases." *International Organization*, 58(1): 35–67.

Rustad, Siri Aas, and Helga Malmin Binningsbø. 2012. "A Price Worth Fighting For? Natural Resources and Conflict Recurrence." *Journal of Peace Research*, 49(4): 531–46.

Sala-i-Martin, Xavier, and Arvind Subramanian. 2003. "Addressing the Natural Resource Curse: An illustration from Nigeria." IMF Working Paper 03/139, International Monetary Fund, Washington, DC.

Sebudubudu, David, and Keneilwe Mooketsane. 2016. "Why Botswana Is a Deviant Case to the Natural Resource Curse." *The African Review*, 43(2): 84–96.

TanzaniaInvest. 2021. "Tanzania Power." https://www.tanzaniainvest.com/power, accessed August 20, 2023.

Thobias, Mwesiga, and Mikova Kseniia. 2017. "Mtwara Gas Project Conflict: Causes of Arising and Ways of Atabilization." *Social Sciences*, 6(3): 73–84.

UN Development Programme. 2017. "Journey to Extremism in Africa: Drivers, Incentives, and Tipping point for Recruitment." https://journey-to-extremism.undp.org/enter/v1, accessed August 21, 2023.

UN Development Programme. 2022. "Light is Life: Electrifying the Last Mile." https://stories.undp.org/light-is-life, accessed August 29, 2023.

United Republic of Tanzania. 2022a. "Administrative Units Population Distribution Report." National Bureau of Statistics, Dodoma.

United Republic of Tanzania. 2022b. "The Project for Domestic Natural Gas Production and Supply System in Tanzania." Ministry of Energy, Dodoma.

United Republic of Tanzania. 2020. "Power System Masterplan 2020 Update." Ministry of Energy, Dodoma.

United Republic of Tanzania. 2017a. "Natural Wealth and Resources (Permanent Sovereignty) Act ('Sovereignty Act')." Dodoma.

United Republic of Tanzania. 2017b. "Natural Wealth and Resources (Review and Re-Negotiation of Unconscionable Terms) Act." Dodoma.

United Republic of Tanzania. 2015a. "Tanzania Extractive Industries (Transparency and Accountability) Act." Dodoma.

United Republic of Tanzania. 2015b. "Tanzania Petroleum Act." Dodoma.

United Republic of Tanzania. 2015c. "The Oil and Natural Gas Revenue Management Act." Dodoma.

van der Ploeg, Frederick. 2011. "Natural Resources: Curse or Blessing?" *Journal of Economic Literature*, 49(2): 366–420.

Walwa, William J. 2022. "Beyond Violence: Understanding Social Cohesion and Peace Attributes on the Tanzania-Mozambique Border." *The African Review*.

Walwa, William John. 2016. "Large-scale Mining and the Right to a Clean, Healthy and Safe Environment in Tanzania." *The African Review*, 43(2): 97–123.

Zachalia, Alfred. 2020. "Use of Natural Gas Saves Tanzania $15.6 Billion." *Citizen*, December 24.

Zitamar News. 2023. "Key Tanzania-Mozambique Border Crossing Remains Closed." May 10.

Chapter 3

The Political Economy of Mining Resources in Burundi

Arcade Ndoricimpa and Esther Leah Achandi

Since gaining independence in 1962, Burundi has faced numerous persistent civil conflicts that have impeded its economic development. It ranks among the poorest countries in the world, with approximately 50 percent of the population living below the poverty line. At 261 US dollars per capita gross national income (2015), Burundi ranks among the poorest countries in the world, placing it toward the bottom of global rankings.

Paradoxically, Burundi is rich in mineral resources. Its soil contains abundant gold, nickel, copper, cobalt, and the 3T minerals—tantalum, tin, and tungsten ore—which dominate its mining industry. Burundi boasts two hundred million tons of nickel reserves, which is approximated to be 6 percent of global reserves (International Monetary Fund 2012). Nickel production is currently anticipated on the heels of an agreement between the government and East African Region Project Group, a foreign company. Outside the formal mining sector, Burundi has significant small-scale artisanal mining operations.

Burundi also has one of the world's richest deposits of rare earth minerals, a group of seventeen metals including lanthanides, yttrium, and scandium. They are essential components of digital and low-carbon technologies due to their magnetic and luminescent properties and, therefore, play a significant role in the development of renewable energy technology. In addition, rare earth metals have numerous national defense applications, making them strategically important globally (Goodenough, Wall, and Merriman 2018). The extraction of rare earth minerals in Burundi culminated in the 2017 exploration agreement between the Government of Burundi and British multinational Rainbow Rare Earths.

As minerals gain a lot of attention in Burundi, it is important to assess to what extent the country has put in place safeguards to protect against the "resource curse." In this chapter, we examine Burundi's natural resource management value chain and seek to understand how the regulation and monitoring of mining operations in Burundi can help the country escape the anticipated resource curse. In addition, we endeavor to illuminate informal and artisanal mining governance in Burundi and the challenges related to the collection of taxes and royalties, mineral export misreporting, and the management of revenues from natural resources in Burundi. Finally, we suggest ways for Burundi to avoid the resource curse phenomenon.

The presence of sub-soil natural resource reserves in Burundi provides an opportunity to escape poverty and set the country on a more sustainable path to economic development. Therefore, the chapter's main objective is to suggest policy interventions to transform Burundi's natural resource potential into sustainable development, especially during the lead-up to the 2030 targets of the Sustainable Development Goals.

BURUNDI'S RECENT ECONOMIC PERFORMANCE

Burundi is a small country in East Africa that has suffered six episodes of civil conflicts since its independence in 1962. While conflicts in Burundi have been ethnic in nature, their causes are complex (Ndikumana 2000). Although the last conflict in 2015 was fueled by widespread opposition to a controversial third term of the late President Pierre Nkurunziza, in general, conflicts in Burundi were caused by fights between political elites from the two major groups, the Hutus and Tutsis, utilizing ethnicity for their personal interests, to capture the state and its spoils (Ngaruko and Nkurunziza 2000; Brachet and Wolpe 2005). As Nkurunziza (2022) points out, political violence was perpetuated through the years by the failure of the state and political elites to address the root causes of violence since the early years of independence. A better summary of the causes of conflicts in Burundi is given by Ngaruko and Nkurunziza (2000), who say that "conflicts in Burundi have resulted from a combination of poverty, governance policies of exclusion and the fight for the control of the country's limited resources."

This political instability brought on by the civil conflict has hampered Burundi's economic growth and development, which have remained low through the years. After more than a decade of civil war, which ended in 2005, economic growth performance began to recover in the post-conflict period but remained low compared to other post-conflict countries like Mozambique, Rwanda, and Sierra Leone. Between 2005 and 2014, Burundi's recorded average growth rate was 4.1 percent but declined to 0.6 percent over the most recent period of 2015 to 2022 due to prolonged civil unrest following a controversial 2015 bid by President Pierre Nkurunziza to run for a third term. According to Ndoricimpa and Ndayikeza (2023), several factors can explain the sluggish growth in the post-conflict period, which include, among others, high corruption and poor governance, coupled with the loss of confidence in the domestic economy by both internal and foreign investors. As a result, a discouraging business environment prevailed as the country failed to attract substantial foreign direct investment. Overall, foreign direct investment amounted only to 0.6 percent of gross domestic product (GDP) over the period between 2005 and 2022. Burundi's GDP per capita currently stands at 262 US dollars and is one the lowest in the world. GDP per capita took a downward trend with the 1993 civil war and failed to recover in the post-conflict period, recording a negative average growth rate of GDP per capita of –0.78 percent between 2005 and 2022 (Ndoricimpa and Ndayikeza 2023). Although absolute poverty has been reduced, more than 50 percent of Burundi's population still live below the poverty line, particularly in rural areas.

Additionally, gendered poverty remains an issue of concern, as Muchiri and Nzisabira (2020) observe that among the poor are many women who play the role of primary caretakers. Furthermore, poverty in itself is also a challenge to gender equity, with evidence that it negatively affects the probability of supporting women's rights (Ndikumana 2015). The country recently adopted a national development plan for the period ranging from 2018 to 2027, with a growth rate target of 10.7 percent in 2027, and intends to rely on promoting the mining sector to optimize its contribution to the country's growth and socio-economic development (African Development Bank 2019).

THE MINERAL RESOURCE LANDSCAPE IN BURUNDI

The primary minerals mined and exported in Burundi are gold and the 3Ts (tin, tantalum, and tungsten, from the minerals cassiterite, tantalite, and wolframite). From 2017, rare earths were also extracted and exported. Gold is mined mainly from two provinces, Muyinga and Cibitoke; the 3Ts are found in six provinces (i.e., Cibitoke, Kayanza, Muyinga, Ngozi, Ruyigi, and Kirundo), while the rare earths are mostly found in Bujumbura. The rare earths in Burundi are of exceptional quality, characterized by high in situ grades of bastnaesite and monazite with levels ranging from 47 percent to 67 percent, with an average grade of 55 percent (Perks and Hayes 2016).[1] Burundi also has considerable nickel reserves in Rutana province.

Burundi has a wide potential for mining resources, which, unfortunately, is still poorly exploited. The main causes include the lack of infrastructure;

lack of equipment for prospection and exploitation; lack of transparency concerning mineral availability, production, and sale; rent-seeking behavior from elites; and misnegotiated mining contracts by local officials who lack sufficient information about international prices of minerals and the clear usefulness of exported minerals (Perks and Hayes 2016).

Although the mining sector in Burundi has recently become increasingly industrialized with the arrival of a few multinational companies, it remains dominated by artisanal small-scale miners. Currently, gold in Burundi is generally exploited by mining cooperatives that do artisanal exploitation. Artisanal mining in Burundi is characterized by weak government oversight, and mineral production remains problematic. Women and girls constitute significant proportions of the artisanal and small-scale mining workforce in the Great Lakes Region, where Burundi is located, with even higher percentages reported as engaged in gold mining (Danielsen and Hinton 2022). Between 2003 and 2020, mineral production in Burundi has been erratic, averaging 1.9 tons of gold per year. While gold production was over two tons in 2012 and 2013, it fell significantly from 644 kilograms in 2014 to 396 kilograms in 2016. Perks and Hayes (2016) assert that the increased taxes introduced in 2014 were the major cause of this drop, disincentivizing the mining cooperatives. It should be noted that there is no traceability system in place for gold, and as such, reported production volumes should be interpreted with caution (Midende 2010).

Regarding the 3Ts minerals, there are three sources of data on their production in Burundi (i.e., official export statistics, mine-level production data from the iTSCi system, and anecdotal reports from miners [Perks and Hayes 2016]). Production grew and peaked in 2012 at around 940 tons. From 2013, however, the production of the 3Ts fell off dramatically and reached 185.3 tons in 2016. The reason for this drastic decline in production was the 2013 mineral code, which made mining licenses for formal mining cooperatives very expensive and cost more than thirteen thousand US dollars from an artisanal mining permit fee of fifty-two hundred US dollars in the 1976 code. Consequently, several cooperatives started operating illegally in 2014. However, a decree was issued in June 2015 that cut mining license fees by two-thirds (Gouvernement du Burundi 2015). This caused a recovery in 3T production in 2017 and 2018. However, production levels remained low and further fell in 2019 and 2020, with no production reported for tantalum and tungsten for those two years. The 2013 mining code replaced the 1976 mining code, which contained several imperfections and shortcomings and required profound changes. While the revision was motivated by the existing difficulties in managing artisanal mining with fraudulent practices, which the 1976 code did not have provisions for, Burundi wanted also to have a mining code that respected international practices and that aimed at ensuring the accountability of mining operating companies, transparency, respect for human rights, and respect for environmental standards, as well as a mining code that would combat the illegal exploitation of mining resources. The 2015 decree provided the mining regulations; it set out the terms and conditions for the application of the 2013 mining code of Burundi. It also regulated related matters not expressly provided for, defined, or regulated by the provisions of the 2013 mining code (Gouvernement du Burundi 2015).

The production of Burundi's rare earths started in 2017, totaling 660 tons in 2017 and 2018. Regarding nickel, as mentioned, the reserves in Burundi are approximated to be more than two hundred million tons, reportedly around 6 percent of the world's nickel reserves. The Government of Burundi signed a mining exploitation agreement with Burundi Mining Metallurgy (BMM) International in 2014. As Observatoire de l'Action Gouvernementale (2019) indicates, nickel mining activities were to be carried out in three phases. In the "pilot plant phase" from 2015 to 2016, two thousand tons were to be extracted per year. In the "demonstration phase" spanning from 2016 to 2017, ore processing technology was to be tested on a large scale and mined at one hundred thousand tons per year. The last phase, known as the "factory phase," was slated to begin in 2018 with an estimated production of five hundred thousand tons of ore annually. However, the energy requirements to carry out the nickel production as planned were never met. As a result, until 2022, nickel mining operations by BMM International never went beyond the "pilot plant phase."

Consequently, the mining permit granted to the BMM International Company in 2014 for exploiting nickel and associated ores was revoked in March 2022. No data is available on how much nickel was produced since 2014 and how much revenues accrued from it. A new mining exploitation agreement was signed between the Government of Burundi and the East African Region Group, which expressed a desire to invest in the mining sector to exploit nickel and associated ores.

REGULATIONS AND MONITORING OF MINING OPERATIONS IN BURUNDI

Mining-related activities (i.e., mineral exploration, exploitation, and exports in Burundi) are regulated by various codes, laws, and ministerial decrees. They highlight the regulatory framework of the mining sector in Burundi by emphasizing the conditions or requirements of contract and license awards in mineral exploration and exploitation, as well as the level of tax rate and royalties to be paid by the holders of mineral exploitation licenses. The Ministry of Hydraulic, Energy, and Mines is in charge of executing the mining code.

Mining sector regulation in Burundi began in 1976 with the establishment of the Mining and Petroleum Code by Decree No. 1/138 of July 17, 1976. The Mining and the Petroleum Code of 1976 was revised in 2013 with the adoption of a new Mining Code Decree No. 1/21 of October 15, 2013. The 2013 code opened doors to private investment in the mining sector by removing several legal hurdles, simplifying procedures, and strengthening investor protection. While the 1976 mining code did not specify the tax regime related to mining operations, the 2013 code fixed an ad valorem tax of 4 percent for base metals, 5 percent for precious metals, 7 percent for precious stones, and 2 percent for other minerals, for mining exploitation license holders. For artisanal mine operators and authorized mineral traders, the ad valorem tax was 3 percent for base metals, 2 percent for precious metals, 2 percent for precious stones, and 1.5 percent for other minerals (Gouvernement du Burundi 2013).

In 2021, the Government of Burundi realized the need to revise the mining code for the country to benefit from its minerals. In the previous code, for example, of the two thousand tons of rare earths exported over four years by the Rainbow Mining Company, the government did not get anything on its 10 percent allocation of shares (Ndirariha 2023). The new mining code (Law No. 1/19 of August 4, 2023) came into effect in August 2023, thus altering the stipulations on government shares in partnerships with industrial mining multinational companies. This change saw government shares leap from 10 percent to at least 16 percent, with a provision for a further 5 percent increase each time the exploitation mining permit is renewed. Another significant change effected in the 2023 code is that it introduced the possibility of sharing the responsibility of mineral production between the state and the mining companies. However, the 2023 mining code did not change the ad valorem tax. It remains fixed at 4 percent for base metals, 5 percent for precious metals, 7 percent for precious stones, 4 percent for semi-precious stones, and 2 percent for other minerals for industrial mining. For artisanal mining and small-scale mining, the ad valorem tax is 3 percent for base metals, 1 percent for precious metals, 2 percent for precious stones, 3 percent for semi-precious stones, and 1.5 percent for other minerals (Gouvernement du Burundi 2023).

Another significant change in the 2023 mining code was to ban government officials, army and police officers, civil servants in charge of managing the mining and quarrying sector, magistrates, and people in the provincial, municipal, and zonal administration from getting involved in mining activities. The government instituted these safeguards to mitigate the potential for bribery, rent-seeking behavior, and corruption risks that have historically been associated with the mining industry (Dell'Anno and Maddah 2022). Zúñiga (2019) asserts that the mining industry is susceptible to corruption risks due to its technical complexity, interactions between the private and public sectors, and the substantial revenues it generates. Similarly, Randhawa and Rogers (2021) point out that mining projects involve various multinational parties in complex supply chains, which increases bribery and corruption risks. Grease payments are also expected in the mining sector in various developing countries with unnecessarily long bureaucratic procedures to avoid delays in issuing mining exploration and exploitation permits and other administrative documents or to facilitate timely clearance through customs (Petermann, Guzmán, and Tilton 2007). The mining code, however, does not pay sufficient attention to the regulation of gender aspects nor give provisions targeted toward issues of child labor.

INFORMALITY AND ARTISANAL MINING GOVERNANCE IN BURUNDI

Artisanal and small-scale exploitation dominates mining in Burundi and is often undertaken by individuals, small groups, or family members in an informal setting. In 2015, 55 percent of artisanal small-scale mining (ASM) operations were informal (Matthysen 2015). When not regulated, ASM is usually associated with social and environmental problems such as child labor, crime and conflict, mercury pollution, and soil erosion (Verbrugge and Besmanos 2016). ASM was not regulated before the 2013 mining code. As part of the government's efforts to formalize the mining sector activities, with the 2013 mining code, ASM is carried out by mining cooperatives. These mining cooperatives are formal structures issued with artisanal mining permits. Elite capture since the creation of mining cooperatives has been a problem where, at times, presidents of such cooperatives were affiliate government officials, army and police officers, or members of the local administration, using their positions in society to enrich themselves. This exploitation was at the expense of the miners, the "supposed to be members of the cooperative" who are thus reduced to mere employees of the presidents of the cooperatives. The banning in the 2023 mining codes of such activities was effectively enacted to address these inequities.

In their positions as employees, gendered inequalities cannot be ruled out, especially in participation in activities and subsequent remuneration. Indeed, minerals can be interpreted as a resource curse for local communities as they experience increased social and other inequalities, including gender inequalities (Ogwang, Vanclay, and van den Assem 2019). Osei and Yeboah (2023) note that ASM can be carried out by men, women, youth, and children. Women engage across both actual mining and support services such as water transportation, which, though taxing in terms of effort, is an important livelihood strategy that comes with higher remuneration than traditional agricultural activities (Jenkins 2014). Children work in various activities such as transporting water, actual mining, washing minerals, and retail activities, with many children working in mines after school or during holidays. However, mining has been blamed for rising school dropout rates (Potter and Lupilya 2016). Therefore, children's engagement in mining and its detriment to their opportunities for human capital development is of great concern (Owusu, Afrifa, and Obeng 2022).

According to the 2023 mining code, cooperatives can only sell their mining products at *comptoirs* with governmental licenses to buy and export minerals. However, this process has not been immune to state capture, as to get authorization to trade gold, one typically needs connections to powerful and influential elite individuals (Matthysen 2015). Mining cooperatives only authorize the presidents of the cooperatives to transport mining products to *comptoirs* to be sold. This creates a problem where there is little transparency in knowledge surrounding the quantities sold and the profits obtained by each sale, as the prices are only known by the presidents of the cooperatives. In this case, transparency regarding revenue sharing becomes significantly compromised. The power dynamics in this setting also crowd out possibilities of fair distribution in the revenues that trickle down to vulnerable actors such as women and children who support mining operations. Indeed, within the sector, Matthysen (2015) observes that 64 percent of miners do not believe that they can get fair remuneration since they are reduced to being price-takers. Women and children working in the sector are even more likely to be exposed to exploitation and unfair pay because of their traditionally subordinate position in Burundian society and the much more precarious nature of their engagement compared to men (Muchiri and Nzisabira 2020), both of which can affect their bargaining power. Social issues around ASM also arise with the degradation of social norms and moral standards reported. By engaging in the sector, women and children are more prone to forms of violence (Rustad, Østby, and Nordås 2016).

Gold is currently Burundi's largest export commodity, contributing approximately 28 percent of total export earnings over the recent period between 2016 and 2022. It is important to note that, in the national statistics, gold exports start in 2016, while in international statistics, Burundi's gold exports appear from the early 1990s (Banque de la République du Burundi 2022; UN Conference on Trade and Development 2022). This inconsistency demonstrates the informality characterizing artisanal small-scale gold mining activities before the 2013 mining code and indicates the lack of government oversight. Harbrecht and Volk (2017) reported that informal small-scale mining activities with limited output for the national economy dominate the Burundian mining sector. By failing to register mining production, the country loses foreign exchange earnings from export and tax revenues and cannot enforce labor and other regulatory standards within the sub-sector.

The gold produced by small-scale artisanal miners is sold to *comptoirs*, which then export it. According to Midende (2010), two types of trading *comptoirs* exist: those under the Burundian law, authorized to buy only gold exploited from Burundi, and *comptoirs in transit* that could only buy gold from neighboring countries. *Comptoirs in transit* were, however, not subject to the 4 percent ad valorem tax. In addition, they were not obliged to surrender the foreign exchange from their export receipts (Ndoricimpa 2023). Ostensibly, *comptoirs in transit* were a creation of the elite gold traders to channel locally produced gold to export destinations and avoid taxes. Midende (2010) estimated that 90 percent of gold exploited from Burundi was exported by *comptoirs in transit*. Consequently, the government of Burundi lost a considerable amount of resources in tax revenues and foreign exchange, which were not surrendered.

It should be added that reported corruption and illegal taxes paid to local state agents undermined efforts of formalizing artisanal and small-scale mining activities. As Matthysen (2015) indicates, high corruption is reported in artisanal and small-scale gold mining in Burundi and is an incentive to remain informal. This was confirmed by Perks and Hayes (2016), who argued that gold miners and traders in Burundi were called upon to make informal payments to a wide range of actors. Consequently, mining cooperatives underreported their production to the government to lower their risks of extortion. Indeed, the magnitude of bribes demanded by officials is a function of expected sales from the reported mineral production. The higher the reported mineral production, the higher the bribes demanded. The expected illegal taxes paid to local state agents lead cooperatives to underreport their production. Correspondingly, mining cooperatives also underreport their production to avoid tax liabilities. Bockstael (2014) explains how informality in African artisanal and small-scale mining persists. As artisanal miners cannot pay the required mining fees, they bribe the local state agents to continue their activities, who cannot refuse as they are presented with an opportunity to supplement their meager salaries. In this case, corruption and illegal taxation become a locally grounded formalization of artisanal and small-scale mining.

MINERAL EXPORT MISREPORTING IN BURUNDI: THE CASE OF GOLD

Looking at the statistics of the gold trade between Burundi and its partners, a huge gap exists between the amount of gold exports declared by Burundi and the amount of gold imports from Burundi declared by the trade partners. Export misreporting is an old phenomenon done for two motives: to circumvent exchange controls and to avoid taxes (UN Conference on Trade and Development 2016).

The main market destinations for gold exports from Burundi are Belgium, Switzerland, and the United Arab Emirates. According to UN Comtrade data for the period from 1993 to 1996, the bulk of gold from Burundi was exported to Belgium (83.4 percent) and the rest went to Switzerland (16.1 percent). Between 1999 and 2003, Belgium was the sole destination of gold from Burundi. However, from 2004 to 2006, Switzerland became the main destination, accounting for 67.8 percent of total gold exports. The remaining exports went to the United Arab Emirates (22.2 percent) and Belgium (3.7 percent). Since 2007, 92.5 percent of Burundi's gold has gone to the United Arab Emirates and the remaining 4.4 percent to Belgium. Table 3.1 shows the discrepancies in the reported gold export by Burundi and the reported gold import from Burundi by the rest of the world over the recent period (2011–2022), both in volume and values. The table highlights huge gaps in the reported gold trade, indicating gold export misreporting. Apart from 2011, where an overreporting of gold exports was noticed, gold exports were underreported for the rest of the period, with underreporting reaching, on average, almost two tons per year between 2012 and 2021. The gaps in the reported gold trade volumes translate of course in the reported gold trade values, where export underreporting reached seventy-five million US dollars on average.

Table 3.1. Discrepancy in the Reported Volume and Values in Gold Trade between Burundi and the World

	Reported Gold Trade (in Volume in Kilograms)			Reported Gold Trade (in Millions of US Dollars)		
Period	Reported X	Reported M	Gap	Reported X (fob)	Reported M (cif)	Gap
2011	1,152.0	392.0	−760.0	59.0	19.6	−39.4
2012	2,135.0	2,950.0	815.0	105.2	152.4	47.2
2013	2,915.0	5,144.7	2,229.7	119.8	224.2	104.4
2014	672.0	5,214.1	4,542.1	24.4	209.5	185.1
2015	390.0	4,558.8	4,168.8	13.8	164.3	150.5
2016	396.0	2,841.1	2,445.1	15.3	107.1	91.8
2017	954.2	1,930.0	975.8	36.8	74.4	37.6
2018	1,898.8	3,157.8	1,259.0	56.5	118.7	62.2
2019	1,598.6	3,529.9	1,931.3	66.9	152.4	85.5
2020	863.0	1,866.2	1,003.2	46.0	92.0	46.1
2021	669.6	1,244.1	574.5	40.6	56.7	16.1
2022	913.9	941.6	27.7	51.9	53.5	1.6

Source: Authors, using data from UN Comtrade database.

Table 3.2 shows gold export misreporting as disaggregated by trade partners. Notably, for 2011, 2012, 2017, 2018, and 2019, Burundi reported exporting gold to Belgium, Kenya, China, Romania, India, and Türkiye, who did not report importing gold from Burundi. Similarly, some countries (Uganda in 2018, 2019, 2020; India and Sweden in 2019) reported having imported gold from Burundi, but Burundi did not report exporting gold to these countries, indicating some potential gold smuggling activity from Burundi to these countries.

Table 3.2. Discrepancy in the Reported Volume and Values in Gold Trade between Burundi and Its Partners

Period	Partners	Reported Gold Trade (in Volume in Kilograms)			Reported Gold Trade (Millions of US Dollars)		
		Reported X	Reported M	Gap	Reported X (fob)	Reported M (cif)	Gap
2011	Belgium	16.0	NR	*	0.72	NR	*
2011	Kenya	5.0	NR	*	0.21	NR	*
2011	UAE	1,131.0	392.0	−739.0	58.12	19.62	−38.49
2012	UAE	782.0	2,950.0	2,168.0	39.30	152.35	113.06
2012	Areas, nes	1,353.0	NR	*	65.90	NR	*
2013	Kenya	1.0	NR	*	0.07	NR	*
2013	Lebanon	1.0	5.0	4.0	0.06	0.19	0.13
2013	UAE	2,913.0	5,139.7	2,226.7	119.69	224.04	104.35
2014	UAE	672.0	5,214.1	4,542.1	24.35	209.45	185.10
2015	UAE	390.0	4,558.8	4,168.8	13.75	164.25	150.50
2016	UAE	396.0	2,841.1	2,445.1	15.29	107.11	91.83
2017	China	1.0	NR	*	0.04	NR	*
2017	Romania	8.0	NR	*	0.31	NR	*
2017	UAE	945.2	1,930.0	984.8	36.40	74.39	37.99
2018	China	3.0	NR	*	0.11	NR	*
2018	India	6.0	NR	*	0.21	NR	*
2018	UAE	1,887.8	3,057.8	1,170.0	56.14	114.68	58.55
2018	Türkiye	2.0	NR	*	0.06	NR	*
2018	Uganda	NR	100.0	*	NR	4.06	4.06
2019	UAE	1,588.6	3,318.3	1,729.7	66.48	143.31	76.83
2019	Türkiye	10.0	10.0	0.0	0.40	0.38	−0.01
2019	India	NR	6.0	*	NR	0.22	*
2019	Sweden	NR	0.6	*	NR	0.01	*
2019	Uganda	NR	195.0	*	NR	8.46	*
2020	UAE	863.0	1,436.2	573.2	45.97	72.61	26.64
2020	Uganda	NR	430.0	*	NR	19.43	19.43
2021	UAE	669.6	1,244.1	574.5	40.57	56.68	16.11
2022	UAE	913.9	937.6	23.7	51.90	53.28	1.38
2022	India	NR	4.0	*	NR	0.20	*

Note: nes = not elsewhere specified; NR = Not Reported; UAE = United Arab Emirates.
Source: Authors, using data from UNCOMTRADE database.

For the cases where both sides report gold trade, it can be noticed that the underreporting of gold exports was recurrent. The United Arab Emirates remained Burundi's main gold trade partner in the recent period. However, the export underreporting was substantial. For example, in 2012, there was an underreporting of 2.1 tons of gold exported to the United Arab Emirates; in 2014 and 2015, gold export underreporting reached more than four tons. Over the period 2011 to 2022, the cumulative gold export underreporting is 20.6 tons (see table 3.2). It is important to note that Burundi is losing a considerable amount of money through the practice of mineral export underreporting.

CHALLENGES IN REVENUES IN COLLECTION FROM MINERAL RESOURCES IN BURUNDI

In Burundi, revenues from mineral resources are mainly in the form of mineral taxes and mineral export proceeds. Regarding taxes, in addition to common law taxation, such as income tax and value-added tax, there are also mining taxes applicable to operators in the mining sector engaged in prospecting, mining research, and the exploitation of mines and quarries. These include "fixed duties" paid when obtaining or renewing the required documents; "surface royalties," which are annual taxes paid in proportion to the surface area explored or exploited; "ad valorem taxes" based on the value, weight, or volume of production; as well as an annual contribution paid for the rehabilitation of mining and quarrying sites.

ASM operators in Burundi express dissatisfaction with the imposed tax rates and fees that they deem to be very high and the lack of transparency and tax fairness, which led them to resort to illegal exploitation and tax evasion (Observatoire de l'Action Gouvernementale 2019). For instance, artisanal gold mining permit fees increased from BIF eight million in 1976 to five thousand dollars (equivalent to BIF nine million) in 2015. For precious stones, exploitation permit fees increased from BIF 0.5 million in 1976 to five thousand dollars (equivalent to BIF nine million) in 2015; for semi-precious stones, they increased from BIF 0.5 million in 1976 to two thousand dollars (equivalent to BIF 3.6 million) in 2015; for tantalum ore, fees increased from BIF 0.2 million in 1976 to $ 1500 (equivalent to BIF 2.7 million) in 2015, and from BIF 0.1 million in 1976 to one thousand dollars (equivalent to BIF 1.8 million) in 2015 for tin and tungsten ores. Similarly, the permit fees for *comptoirs* to trade in minerals have also increased from 1976 to 2015. For gold, fees increased from BIF sixteen million to BIF sixty-three million (equivalent to thirty-five thousand dollars); for tantalum and tin, they increased from BIF 0.3 million to BIF eighteen million (equivalent to ten thousand dollars); for tungsten, fees increased from BIF 0.1 million to eighteen million (equivalent to ten thousand dollars). Reportedly, the sharp increase in mineral tax and royalty rates in 2015 compared to 1976 levels has discouraged operators in the mining sector, especially those operating in artisanal mining. As the Observatoire de l'Action Gouvernementale (2019) notes, several mining cooperatives failed to pay for their permits or their renewal and resorted to illegal and clandestine exploitation. Clandestine exploitation is mainly nocturnal, sometimes with recourse to the corruption of administrative officials and the environmental police. Mineral *comptoirs* have also resorted to the illegal trading of minerals.

Despite increased tax and royalty rates, taxes and royalties collected have been low. While minerals represent more than half of total exports, the resulting taxes and royalties are minimal. For instance, in 2019, taxes and fees represented only 3.4 percent of total exports. A number of challenges hamper the process of collecting revenues from mineral resources in Burundi. These include a lack of better coordination and collaboration between the Burundian Office of Mines and Quarries (Office Burundais des Mines et Carrières [OBM]) and the Burundian Revenue Authority (Office Burundais des Recettes [OBR]) in charge of collecting taxes and royalties from the mining sector. As it stands, the collection of mineral revenues is organized in such a way that OBM establishes the amounts to be paid, and OBR collects them (Perks and Hayes 2016). Of course, there is tax evasion, and there are arrears in payment of mining taxes and royalties. Still, the tax collector, OBR, does not have control of the database on the taxpayer (i.e., mining cooperatives, mining trading *comptoirs*, industrial mining companies and subcontractors of mining companies, and the taxable base). In addition, it does not have control over the orders or authorizations of payments issued by the taxing office, OBM, for better follow-up and recovery of payments. Clarity of the system's provisions is also lacking and relies on the self-declaration by taxpayers of taxes and royalties to be paid. The declared mineral production and export by mining cooperatives and *comptoirs* are inevitably bound to be false, manifesting as discrepancies in the declarations and other mining data as recorded by the OBR, Banque de la République du Burundi (BRB), and OBM. Additionally, the presence and persistence of informality pose a challenge to revenue collection, resulting in further revenue losses.

Another challenge in revenue collection from mineral resources in Burundi is related to the surrendering of foreign currencies from mineral exports. Indeed, the low level of repatriation of foreign exchange earnings from mineral export in Burundi is alarming, as can be seen in table 3.3. While the law requires exporters to repatriate all foreign exchange form export earnings, some exporters do not surrender any foreign exchange from their mineral export proceeds. On average, about 70 percent of foreign exchange

Table 3.3. Mineral Export Proceeds Not Repatriated in 2018

Exporters	Quantity (Kilograms)	Export Value (US Dollars)	Repatriated Amount (US Dollars)	Amount Not Repatriated (US Dollars)	Amount Not Repatriated (Percent)
Gold Exporters					
AMEX	836.25	27,204,592.00	2,461,025.00	24,743,567.00	90.95
AVANISH	1.40	54,953.00	-	54,953.00	100.0
HANNAN MINERALS	4.00	155,260.00	-	155,260.00	100.0
GHADDIR GOLD	190.23	7,429,584.00	7,099,233.74	330,350.26	4.45
GOLDEN GOLD	17.25	647,109.00	118,000.00	529,109.00	81.77
TANGANYIKA MINING BURUNDI	1.61	59,756.00	58,156.00	1,600.00	2.68
OREX	436.20	17,219,403.00	300.00	17,219,103.00	99.9
TITANES RESOURCES	3.12	113,936.62	-	113,936.62	100.0
3Ts Exporters					
BME	1,144,763.40	18,174,172.82	17,828,452.83	345,719.99	1.90
EEMC	42,300.00	74,117.00	-	74,117.00	100.00
HRMR	8,456.30	380,392.00	119,970.00	260,422.00	68.46
SECOMIB	12,480.00	81,782.38	116,228.17	-	-
RMR	33,633.50	620,718.94	1,132,269.56	-	-
VOLTACO	7,252.50	65,272.50	105,500.00	-	-
Rare Earths Exporters					
RAINBOW MINING BURUNDI	750,969.50	1,741,827.85	1,556,293.04	185,534.81	10.65

Source: Authors, using information from Observatoire de l'Action Gouvernementale (2019).

earnings from gold export in 2018 was not repatriated. Incidentally, some exporters repatriate more foreign exchange than what would be expected from their reported mineral export volumes. Indeed, exporters can sneak cash that had been hidden overseas back into a country, disguised as export earnings to avoid money laundering scrutiny (UN Conference on Trade and Development 2016). It can also be noted from table 3.3 that some reported mineral export volumes are significantly low, and one can suspect some underreporting. The low level of foreign exchange repatriation is one of the causes of the economic crisis Burundi has been going through due to the low level of foreign reserves. Over the period between 2015 and 2022, the level of foreign exchange reserves has remained extremely low, with an average of 1.5 months of import cover per year.

ANTICIPATING A RESOURCE CURSE? IMPROVING BURUNDI'S INSTITUTIONS TO AVOID IT

There exist two types of resource curse: political resource curse and economic resource curse. The political resource curse suggests that countries with abundant natural resources are prone to the deterioration in the level of democracy and increased conflicts. Indeed, natural resource abundance has been linked to authoritarianism, which supports the expansion of corruption, patronage, and repression, and increases the risk of conflict (Prichard, Salardi, and Segal 2018). The resource curse is a paradoxical situation in which countries with abundant natural resources underperform economically, generating negative developmental outcomes (Sachs and Warner 2001).

It is most likely that there is no political resource curse in Burundi; existing evidence indicates that conflicts in Burundi had other causes linked with ethnic divisions, not to do with mineral resources (see, for example, Ndikumana 2000; Ngaruko and Nkurunziza 2000; Nkurunziza 2022). Kok, Lotze, and Jaarsveld (2009) confirm that minerals were not major factors in conflicts in Burundi. However, recurring political violence in Burundi has hampered the development of the mining sector as some minerals remained unexplored and unexploited. Indeed, the development of the African mining sector depends on foreign investment, which can only be attracted when political stability exists. As Mathebula (2023) points out, improved political stability signals a good climate that can attract investment and develop infrastructure essential for mining activities, leading to increased mineral extraction. A scenario to avoid is political instability coupled with increased mineral extraction, as generated revenue from minerals could spark worse political upheavals (Mathebula 2023). It can also be argued that political violence and wars encourage artisanal mining. It is well-documented that artisanal mining has been an important funding source for armed groups across Africa (Brugger and Zongo 2023). It is, therefore, possible that armed groups during the civil war in Burundi used artisanal gold mining as a funding source for their activities. Another possible link is the presence of mineral resources and presidential terms extension in Africa as elites view leaving the presidential seat as losing potential mineral rents. In 2015, President Nkurunziza decided to go for a controversial third presidential term, which caused widespread opposition and many months of unrest. Could it be possible that the decision was sparked by nickel mining, which had just started after decades in waiting? A nickel mining permit was granted to the BMM International Company in 2014.

Undeniably, Burundi has not yet benefited from its rich sub-soil as it still has one of the lowest levels of development in the world. Until recently, gold and 3Ts mining in Burundi was characterized by anarchy, dominated by ASM with no or less government oversight, benefiting few individuals at the expense of the country's development. As new minerals (i.e. rare earths and nickel) have been discovered and started being exploited, to avoid economic resource curse, improving institutions will be key. This is more critical at this stage, given evidence that with economic resources, rent-seeking activities can lead to speculative behavior, competition for limited social services, land grabbing, land scarcity, land fragmentation, food insecurity, corruption, and polarization (Ogwang, Vanclay, and van den Assem 2019). To avoid an economic resource curse, Burundi must develop a good governance culture. Indeed, institutional quality is the main conduit through which natural resource abundance affects economic development (Schmoll and Swenson 2023). Institutional political factors such as state effectiveness, political accountability, property rights, and the rule of law must be improved and sustained. As the World Governance Indicators database indicates, Burundi, like many other African countries, has been trailing on a number of governance indicators as far as institutional quality is concerned. Over the recent period 2015 to 2022, the average score for the six governance indicators is given as -1.51 for voice and accountability, -1.63 for political stability and absence of violence, -1.35 for government effectiveness, -0.93 for regulatory quality, -1.37 for rule of law, and -1.44 for corruption control (Kaufmann and Kraay 2023). The governance indicators score ranges from -2.5 (weak governance performance) to 2.5 (strong governance performance). Burundi should, therefore, strive to improve its governance institutions to prevent the easy capture of mining resource rents, patronage, illicit enrichment, and unaccountable government spending, a key mechanism of the resource curse (Goes 2022).

Additionally, in the run-up to 2030 (Sustainable Development Goals target year), Burundi still scores low on gender equality indicators (World Bank 2023). Emerging sectors, such as the mining sector, can be vehicles for gender equality by adopting more gender-transformative policies. Indeed, subsequent policy reforms must pay attention to the gender inequalities in the mining sub-sector further to guide the country toward a more equitable development path.

CONCLUSION

Burundi is a country rich in subterranean mineral resources, including gold, rare earth minerals, nickel, copper, cobalt, tantalum, tin, and tungsten ores. Although Burundi is rich in mineral resources, it has yet to be able to benefit from its minerals, and as such, it is still ranked among the poorest countries in the world. Burundi's mining sector is hampered by several challenges related to poor governance. The production of gold, tin, tungsten, and tantalum is dominated by small-scale exploitation characterized by weak government oversight, resulting in underreporting of mineral production and export. The country has thus lost considerable amounts of money through evaded taxes and unrepatriated foreign exchange. Burundi recently adopted a national development plan for the period ranging from 2018 to 2027 and is banking on the development of the mining sector to reach its target of rapid and sustained economic growth and economic development. However, governance in the mining sector should be improved by promoting transparency in mining operations, starting from granting the mining licenses, facilitated by establishing monitoring mechanisms at each link of the production chain. In addition, for transparency, data at each link should be provided and made accessible. Transparency is also needed in how revenue from mineral resources is managed. This would make the investment from foreign capital more attractive as Burundi has signed mineral exploitation agreements with various foreign multinational companies. It is, therefore, vital to adopt precise measures to avoid the hidden transfer of profits through the transfer pricing mechanism to avoid taxes.

NOTE

1. The other largest rare earth mine in terms of grade is in South Africa (Steenkampskraal mine), but its average grade is only 14.4 percent.

REFERENCES

African Development Bank. 2019. "Country Strategy Paper 2019–2023 (CSP 2019–2023)." Country Economics Department, ECCE and East Africa Regional Development and Business Delivery Office.

Banque de la République du Burundi. 2022. "Rapport Annuel de la Banque de la République du Burundi." Bujumbura, Burundi.

Bockstael, Steven Van. 2014. "The Persistence of Informality: Perspectives on the Future of Artisanal Mining in Liberia." *Futures*, 62: 10–20.

Brachet, J., and H. Wolpe. 2005. "Conflict-Sensitive Development Assistance: The Case of Burundi." Conflict Prevention & Reconstruction Social Development Paper 27, World Bank, Washington, DC.

Brugger, F., and T. Zongo. 2023. "Salafist Violence and Artisanal Mining: Evidence from Burkina Faso." *Journal of Rural Studies*, 100: 103029.

Danielsen, K., and J. Hinton. 2022. "A Social Relations of Gender Analysis of Artisanal and Small-Scale Mining in Africa's Great Lakes Region." In *The (In)Visibility of Women and Mining: The Gendering of Artisanal and Small-scale Mining in Sub-Saharan Africa*, edited by B. Rutherford and D. Buss. New York, NY: Taylor & Francis.

Dell'Anno, R., and M. Maddah. 2022. "Natural Resources, Rent Seeking and Economic Development. An Analysis of the Resource Curse Hypothesis for Iran." *Macroeconomics and Finance in Emerging Market Economies*, 15(1): 47–65.

Goes, Iasmin. 2022. "Electoral Politics, Fiscal Policy, and the Resource Curse." *Studies in Comparative International Development*, 57(4): 525–76.

Goodenough, Kathryn M., F. Wall, and D. Merriman. 2018. "The Rare Earth Elements: Demand, Global Resources, and Challenges for Resourcing Future Generations." *Natural Resources Research*, 27: 201–16.

Gouvernement du Burundi. 2023. "Loi N°1/19 du 04 Aout 2023 portant modification de la loi N°1/21 du 15 Octobre 2013 portant code minier du Burundi." République du Burundi, Bujumbura.

Gouvernement du Burundi. 2015. "Décret N°100/193 du 16 Juin 2015 portant règlement minier du Burundi." République du Burundi, Bujumbura.

Gouvernement du Burundi. 2013. "Loi N°1/21 du 15 Octobre 2013 portant code minier du Burundi." République du Burundi, Bujumbura.

Harbrecht, J., and A. Volk. 2017. "Good Governance in the Mining Sector of Burundi." Fact Sheet, Bundesanstalt für Geowissenschaften und Rohstoffe, Hannover, Germany.

International Monetary Fund. 2012. "Burundi: Poverty Reduction Strategy Paper II." IMF Country Report 12/224, Washington, DC.

Jenkins, K. 2014. "Women, Mining and Development: An Emerging Research Agenda." *The Extractive Industries and Society*, 1: 329–39.

Kaufmann, D., and A. Kraay. 2023. "Worldwide Governance Indicators, 2023 (Update)." www.govindicators.org.

Kok, A., W. Lotze, and Salomé Van Jaarsveld. 2009. "Natural Resources, the Environment and Conflict." The African Centre for the Constructive Resolution of Disputes, Durban, South Africa.

Mathebula, Ndzalama C. 2023. "Assessing the Political Risks in the Mining Sector of Burundi." *African Renaissance*, 20(3): 109–26.

Matthysen, K. 2015. "Review of the Burundian Artisanal Gold Mining Sector." International Peace Information Service, Antwerp, Belgium.

Midende, G. 2010. "Les exploitations minières artisanales du Burundi." *L'Afrique des Grands Lacs*, 45–66.

Muchiri, S. W., and S. C. Nzisabira. 2020. "Gender, Poverty Reduction and Social Work: A View from Burundi." *Southern African Journal of Social Work & Social Development*, 32(2): 1–16.

Ndikumana, A. 2015. "Gender Equality in Burundi: Why Does Support Not Extend to Women's Right to Inherit Land?" Afrobarometer, Bujumbura, Burundi.

Ndikumana, L. 2000. "Towards a Solution to Violence in Burundi: A Case for Political and Economic Liberalization." *Journal of Modern African Studies*, 38(3).

Ndirariha, Noble. 2023. "Revision Code Minier: Innovations." *Yaga Burundi*, June 23. https://www.yaga-burundi.com/2023/revision-code-minier-innovations/, accessed December 18, 2023.

Ndoricimpa, A. 2023. "Illicit Capital Movement through Trade Misinvoicing in Burundi: A Disaggregated Approach." *Journal of Money Laundering Control*, 27(3).

Ndoricimpa, Arcade, and Michel Armel Ndayikeza. 2023. "Economic Costs of Civil Conflicts: The Case of Burundi." *Defence and Peace Economics*, 6: 1–24.

Ngaruko, F., and J. D. Nkurunziza. 2000. "An Economic Interpretation of Conflict in Burundi." *Journal of African Economies*, 9(3): 370–409.

Nkurunziza, J. D. 2022. "The Origin and Persistence of State Fragility in Burundi." In *State Fragility: Case Studies and Comparisons*, edited by N. Bizhan. New York, NY: Taylor & Francis.

Observatoire de l'Action Gouvernementale. 2019. *Les entreprises minières et le Fisc au Burundi. Aperçu sur le système de recouvrement des recettes fiscales minières*. Bujumbura, Burundi.

Ogwang, T., F. Vanclay, and A. van den Assem. 2019. "Rent-Seeking Practices, Local Resource Curse, and Social Conflict in Uganda's Emerging Oil Economy." *Land*, 8(4): 53.

Osei, L., and T. Yeboah. 2023. "Imagining a Future from the Pit: Future Aspirations of Young Artisanal-Small Scale Miners in Rural Northern Ghana." *Cogent Social Sciences*, 9(1).

Owusu, Seth A., Richard Donkor Afrifa, and F. Antwi Obeng. 2022. "Effect of Illegal Small-Scale Mining on Basic Education of Children in Rural Communities in Ghana: Perspectives for Future Development." *African Geographical Review*, 41(3): 336–49.

Perks, Rachel, and Karen Hayes. 2016. "Transparency in Revenues from Artisanal and Small-Scale Mining of Tin, Tantalum, Tungsten and Gold in Burundi." World Bank, Washington, DC.

Petermann, Andrea, J. Ignacio Guzmán, and John E. Tilton. 2007. "Mining and Corruption." *Resources Policy*, 32(3): 91–103.

Potter, C., and Alexander C. Lupilya. 2016. "'You Have Hands, Make Use of Them!' Child Labor in Artisanal and Small-scale Mining in Tanzania." *Journal of International Development*, 28(7): 1013–28.

Prichard, W., P. Salardi, and P. Segal. 2018. "Taxation, Non-tax revenue, and Democracy: New Evidence Using New Cross-Country Data." *World Development*, 109: 295–312.

Randhawa, A., and L. Rogers. 2021. "Examining the ABC Risks as the Mining & Metals Sector Gains Critical Momentum." *White & Case*. https://www.whitecase.com/insight-our-thinking/examining-abc-risks-mining-metals-sector-gains-critical-momentum, accessed September 30, 2023.

Rustad, S. Aas, G. Østby, and R. Nordås. 2016. "Artisanal Mining, Conflict, and Sexual Violence in Eastern DRC." *The Extractive Industries and Society*, 3(2): 475–84.

Sach.s, Jeffrey D., and Andrew M. Warner. 2001. "The Curse of Natural Resources." *European Economic Review*, 45(4–6): 827–38.

Schmoll, M., and G. Swenson. 2023. "Avoiding the Political Resource Curse: Evidence from a Most-Likely Case." *Studies in Comparative International Development*, 59: 27–55.

UN Conference on Trade and Development. 2022. "UN Comtrade Database." https://comtradeplus.un.org/, accessed October 3, 2023.

UN Conference on Trade and Development. 2016. "Trade Misinvoicing in Primary Commodities in Developing Countries: The Cases of Chile, Côte d'Ivoire, Nigeria, South Africa and Zambia,." UNCTAD/SUC/2016/2, Geneva.

Verbrugge, B., and B. Besmanos. 2016. "Formalizing Artisanal and Small-Scale Mining: Whither the Workforce?" *Resources Policy*, 47: 134–41.

World Bank. 2023. "Gender Equality Indicators." https://genderdata.worldbank.org/indicators/, accessed December 3, 2023.

Zúñiga, N. 2019. "Corruption Risk Mitigation in the Mining Sector." Transparency International, Berlin.

Chapter 4

Ghana's Petroleum Management Regime

Challenges and Opportunities

Michael Ohene Aboagye and Michael Ogbe

Ghana discovered oil in commercial quantities in 2007. This discovery and subsequent commercial production of petroleum by mainly foreign-owned firms were met with high hopes and aspirations. Ghana's emergence as a significant player in the global oil industry has provided the country with substantial revenue potential (Abraham 2019; Adam 2017; Ogbe 2022a; Sefa-Nyarko, Okafor-Yarwood, and Boadu 2021; Stephens 2019). The management of petroleum revenues, however, presents a complex set of challenges and opportunities (Edjekumhene et al. 2018; Graham et al. 2019; Lujala et al. 2020; Stephens 2019).

Guided by the experiences of oil-producing countries like Nigeria and Angola, which the so-called resource curse has plagued, Ghana has had an opportunity to build a robust legislative and regulatory framework to ensure effective management of its nascent oil and gas industry. Apart from the need to avert the resource curse, the general call for effective governance of Ghana's oil wealth is informed by the country's modest performance in managing other resources, such as gold and timber (Osei-Kojo 2023). As Quartey and Abbey (2018) note, Ghana's performance in managing revenues from the extractive sector has been unimpressive. Besides the country's poor performance in using revenues from this sector to finance its development agenda, there are worrying developments of visible deterioration in the social and economic infrastructure in some of the most prominent mining communities in Ghana, such as Obuasi and Prestea (Quartey and Abbe 2018). These concerns fueled fears of Ghana's oil discovery potentially becoming another episode of natural resource mismanagement for the country (Osei-Kojo 2023). Oil and gas rents can constitute a significant budgetary instrument that can be used to foster long-term socio-economic development (Ackah et al. 2020a). Conversely, this money can be misused to pursue the parochial interests of the ruling elite, such as extending their political power (Ackah et al. 2020a). In response, the government of Ghana, together with local and international policy actors, engaged in debates on policy issues that sought to enhance the governance of the oil resource for the benefit of all Ghanaians. Some of the issues discussed in this policy engagement included local content, environment, health and safety, energy security, and capacity building (Osei-Kojo 2023).

Ghana has a relatively strong democratic record and is regarded as having generally strong oil governance legislation. While it is expected that a relatively well-governed country would have a good resource governance regime, such a country is also expected to ultimately benefit developmentally from resource exploitation. In Ghana's case, despite the country's relatively vibrant institutions, the impact of oil exploitation has been limited. As Ackah et al. (2020b) note, the challenge often stems from the poor implementation of the laws that govern resource management. Some of the laws have discretionary provisions, which afford the relevant individual and institutional actors room to operate in a manner that undermines the national interest. Therefore, good governance of natural resources requires more than creating a robust legislative and regulatory framework; it also requires strong implementation. A robust governance framework that supports strong implementation is believed to guarantee the translation of oil rents into sustainable development (Ackah et al. 2020b). Apart from the abuse of discretionary provisions, there have been clear instances of non-compliance with certain key provisions of the legislative instruments. A case in point, cited by Quartey and Abbey (2018), is the issue of revenue reporting.

The Petroleum Revenue Management Act (PRMA), a piece of legislation that provides a framework for a responsible management of Ghana's petroleum revenue, stipulates that all revenue-reporting agencies must apply the same reporting standards; however, a report by the Ghana Extractive Industries Transparency Initiative indicated that there was no standard format for reporting crude oil lifting for the year 2014 (Quartey and Abbey 2018). Again, Quartey and Abbey (2018) contend that though the PRMA entreats the Investment Advisory Committee—a body mandated to advise Ghana's finance minister and monitor performance of the management of the Ghana Petroleum Funds (the Ghana Stabilization Fund and the Ghana Heritage Fund)—to provide a benchmark on the returns from petroleum revenues, for the year 2015, no such benchmark existed. Moreover, there have been concerns about the huge discrepancies in amounts stated for royalty, carried interest, and participating interests in the reporting of petroleum revenues (Quartey and Abbey 2018). Quartey and Abbey (2018) note that there are concerns about the lack of transparency in issuing licenses to firms interested in undertaking exploration exercises, as well as the non-compliance of Ghana's local content laws by some oil companies.

This chapter explores the intricate web of Ghana's petroleum management regime, addressing both the challenges and opportunities that petroleum revenue management in Ghana presents. Our central argument is that Ghana's petroleum management regime is robust in theory but not in practice. The chapter proceeds as follows. After this introduction, the chapter provides a background to contextualize Ghana's oil economy. Following this, we provide an outline of the major legislation that governs Ghana's petroleum industry, underlining the fact that the country's petroleum management regime is admittedly robust, albeit not in practice. Following this, we demonstrate that the management of the country's petroleum industry faces challenges, using the case of the country's poor management of the petroleum revenue. We then zero in on the challenges facing Ghana's petroleum revenue management. We argue that these challenges can be mitigated by enhancing citizens' participation in revenue management. Finally, we propose an innovative way of increasing citizen participation in petroleum revenue management, using spatial crowdsourcing technology. The chapter then ends with a short conclusion.

BACKGROUND TO GHANA'S PETROLEUM ECONOMY

Ghana became an oil-producing country in December 2010 following the discovery of an estimated six hundred million barrels of light crude oil by the Government of Ghana and a consortium of global energy firms and the EO Group, an indigenous petroleum company, in 2007 (Oppong 2020; Acheampong and Stevens 2022). This discovery was greeted with hope and optimism, as Ghanaians were positive that the petroleum revenue would greatly boost the country's economy. To drive home the zeitgeist of that moment, it is apposite to quote the then president of Ghana, John Kufuor: "Even without oil, we are doing so well. . . . With oil as a shot in the arm, we're going to fly" (BBC News 2007). The president added, "We're going to really zoom, accelerate, and if everything works, which I pray will happen positively, you come back in five years, and you'll see that Ghana truly is the African tiger in economic terms for [sic] development." Subsequent developments have, however, tempered the national euphoria as policymakers, civil society groups, and analysts raise concerns about the challenges of managing Ghana's oil and gas resources.

The discovery and extraction of oil have historically been a source of significant economic potential for many nations: petroleum revenue can play a pivotal role in the economic development of countries endowed with significant oil reserves (Adams et al. 2019; Nweze and Edame 2016). Among other things, the discovery and extraction of oil generate revenue, job creation, and infrastructure development; however, the management of petroleum revenue presents a multifaceted challenge that requires a delicate balance between short-term economic gains and long-term sustainability (Doh, Budhwar, and Wood 2021; Laimon et al. 2022). Many oil-rich countries have historically faced a paradoxical scenario known as the "resource curse" (Acosta 2013; Cameron and Stanley 2017; Ghose et al. 2018; Kolstad and Søreide 2009; Larsen 2006). This phenomenon describes the situation where nations abundant in natural resources, including oil, often experience suboptimal economic outcomes, increased corruption, heightened inequality, and political instability. Notable countries that have experienced the resource curse include Venezuela, Iraq, Nigeria, and Angola. The case of Nigeria is particularly poignant. Despite being one of the largest oil producers in Africa, its heavy reliance on petroleum revenues has led to economic volatility, corruption, and political instability (Mähler 2010; Nweze and Edame 2016). Mismanagement of petroleum revenues, lack of diversification, and a weak governance framework have hindered Nigeria's overall development and contributed to high levels of poverty and inequality (Obi 2010; Olayungbo 2019; Shobande and Enemona 2021).

In the case of Angola, decades of civil war and corruption have hindered the equitable distribution of oil wealth. Most of the population live in poverty, while a small elite benefits from the petroleum revenues (Ghose et al. 2018; Ovadia 2018; Rodríguez et al. 2014). Nevertheless, there are successful cases of countries that have managed their oil wealth effectively. Norway is a classic example. Norway's effective management of petroleum revenues through the Government Pension Fund Global showcases the potential benefits of saving and investing for the future (Cameron and Stanley 2017). Transparent governance, strong institutions, and a commitment to sustainable practices have allowed Norway to transform petroleum wealth into intergenerational wealth (Cameron and Stanley 2017; Chandler 2020; Hunter 2014). Ghana, aware of these cases, took steps to avert the resource curse. Norway and other successful cases served as examples for Ghana.

The country's strong democratic credentials largely informed the optimism that greeted Ghana's discovery of oil in commercial quantities, in addition to the fact that discovery happened at a time of great awareness about the resource curse; however, other analysts (like Gyimah-Boadi and Prempeh 2012) have raised concerns about the resilience of Ghana's democracy to withstand the perils of the resource curse, as empirical studies suggest that oil can have a corrosive effect on democracy. In the words of Paul Collier (2007: 42), "the heart of the resource curse is that resource rents make democracy malfunction." Collier (2007) further notes that while one may think that the discipline offered by democracy would be useful in managing the rents generated by resources, it invariably turns out not to be the case. Nonetheless, the concerns raised by scholars who analyze the potential impact of oil rents on Ghana's democracy (like Gyimah-Boadi and Prempeh 2012) are usually moderated by their own expressions of some amount of optimism, as many observers still find hope in Ghana's democratic developments.

As Gyimah-Boadi and Prempeh (2012) note, many of the institutions and processes established by Ghana's 1992 constitution enjoy widespread public support and legitimacy. Among these institutions and processes are regularly scheduled elections, independent media, and independent constitutional bodies such as the Electoral Commission and the Commission on Human Rights and Administrative Justice (Gyimah-Boadi and Prempeh 2012). "The ballot box, the court of public opinion, and the courts of law have gained popular and elite acceptance as the legitimate avenues for settling differences between contending political factions" in Ghana (Gyimah-Boadi and Prempeh 2012: 95). For instance, in the 2008 and 2020 presidential elections, the New Patriotic Party and the National Democratic Congress, respectively, petitioned the Supreme Court to challenge the validity of the results and the subsequent declaration of Professor Attah-Mills and Mr. Akufo-Addo as the winners of the elections by the Electoral Commission. In both instances, the Supreme Court did not rule in favor of the party that made the petition, but both parties respected the court's ruling. The New Patriotic Party and the National Democratic Congress are the two biggest political parties in Ghana.

Analysts also point to the presence of a relatively strong opposition in parliament, enhancing legislative deliberations and ensuring that government actions do not escape scrutiny (Gyimah-Boadi and Prempeh 2012). Despite Collier's (2007) grim assertion, these key democratic dividends were considered an advantage for Ghana in the early days of its oil discovery. In keeping with this optimistic outlook, some important pieces of legislation were enacted to govern the management of the newly found resource. Historically, petroleum exploration in Ghana began in 1896 based on wildcatting or the chasing of seepages (Stephens and Dzikunu 2022). In 1970, a small-scale oil discovery was made in Saltpond in the Central Region of Ghana, which drilled its first offshore well (Stephens and Dzikunu 2022). Ghana started production from the Saltpond Field in 1978.

At the start of petroleum exploration in Ghana, the country did not have specific legislation for its petroleum industry (Stephens and Dzikunu 2022). As Stephens and Dzikunu (2022) note, Ghana's upstream petroleum industry was subsumed under the general legislation governing the country's mining industry. Following unfavorable developments in the global energy landscape, the country enacted its first pieces of legislation to inject vibrancy into its exploration efforts. To this end, the Ghana National Petroleum Corporation Act 1983 (PNDCL 64) was enacted to establish the Ghana National Petroleum Corporation, the national oil company, to undertake the exploration, development, production, and disposal of petroleum (Stephens and Dzikunu 2022). The Petroleum (Exploration and Production) Act 1983 (PNDCL 68) was also enacted in the same year to provide legislation on operations. It was, however, replaced by the Petroleum (Exploration and Production) Act 1984 (Stephens and Dzikunu 2022). Similarly, the Petroleum Income Tax Act 1986 (PNDCL 185) was enacted to govern taxation in the industry. Still, it was also replaced the following year by the Petroleum Income Tax Act 1987 (PNDCL 188) (Stephens and Dzikunu 2022). Therefore, when the country struck oil in commercial quantities in 2007, these pieces of legislation, though inadequate, were available to govern the industry.

As the world continues to grapple with the transition to cleaner and more sustainable energy sources (Dominković et al. 2018; Nong, Wang, and Al-Amin 2020; Quitzow et al. 2019; Sáez-Martínez et al. 2016), the role of petroleum revenues remains pivotal, albeit in a changing context. In this context, understanding the challenges and opportunities inherent in petroleum revenue management becomes even more critical in Ghana's case. Overall, this chapter contributes to the discourse on energy economics, public policy, and sustainable development by shedding light on the intricate dynamics that shape the management of Ghana's petroleum industry. Ultimately, it underscores the need for holistic strategies that address short-term economic gains in favor of long-term socio-economic stability.

GHANA'S PETROLEUM GOVERNANCE REGIME

This section outlines the major legislation that governs Ghana's petroleum industry, underscoring the fact that the country's petroleum management framework is truly robust on paper. Following the discovery of oil in commercial quantities in Ghana in 2007, the government enacted new pieces of legislation to govern the management of this newly found resource, as the existing legislation was inadequate. These included the Petroleum Revenue Management Act 2011 (Act 815), later amended to the Petroleum Revenue Management (Amendment) Act 2015 (Act 893), the Petroleum Commission Act 2011 (Act 821), the Income Tax Act 2015 (Act 896), the Petroleum Act 2016 (Act 919), and the Revenue Administration Act 2016, among others. The PRMA sets the framework to regulate the allocation and management of revenues obtained from petroleum production in Ghana

(Ackah et al. 2020a). The PRMA details the quantum of petroleum revenues that should be allocated to the various funds created under the governance regime (such as the Annual Budget Funding Amount), the Ghana National Petroleum Corporation, and the two Ghana Petroleum Funds (which are the Heritage Fund and the Stabilization Fund) (Ackah et al. 2020a). The Ghana Stabilization and Heritage Funds were created to ensure revenue accrued from petroleum is used prudently. A percentage of the petroleum revenue is allocated to these two funds to promote intergenerational equity and fiscal stability (Asenso and Ackah 2022). Section 9(2) of the PRMA sets out the purpose of the Ghana Stabilization Fund as thus: to cushion the impact on or sustain public expenditure capacity during periods of unanticipated petroleum revenue shortfalls. Section 10(2) of the PRMA outlines the object of the Ghana Heritage Fund, which is to provide an endowment to support the development of future generations when the petroleum reserves have been depleted and to receive excess petroleum revenue. In addition to allocating revenues to the Ghana Petroleum Funds, the PRMA stipulates what activities or projects the revenues put in the funds could be used for (Ackah et al. 2020a).

The government of Ghana made arrangements to ensure a high level of local content and local participation in the management of the oil and gas resources. Moreover, the government created a mechanism to ensure part of the petroleum revenue is allocated to the Annual Budget Funding Amount to promote efforts to diversify the economy. Additionally, the Public Interest and Accountability Committee (PIAC) was established under section 51 of the PRMA to, among other things, monitor and evaluate compliance with the law. The PIAC is also mandated to provide space and a platform for the public to debate whether spending prospects, management, and use of petroleum revenues conform to development priorities.

The Petroleum Commission Act 2011 (Act 821) establishes the Petroleum Commission as the upstream regulator (Ackah et al. 2020a). The Petroleum Commission is tasked with regulating and managing the utilization of petroleum products and coordinating policies concerning them (Quartey and Abbey 2018). Among other things, the commission is responsible for promoting planned, well-executed, sustainable, and cost-efficient petroleum activities to achieve optimal levels of resource exploitation for citizens' overall benefit and welfare. Moreover, the commission is responsible for ensuring compliance with health, safety, and environmental standards in petroleum activities in accordance with applicable laws, regulations, and agreements.

Additionally, the commission is tasked with promoting local content and local participation in petroleum activities as prescribed in the local content and local participation regulations (Quartey and Abbey 2018). To this end, the Petroleum (Local Content and Local Participation) Regulations 2013 (L.I. 2204) were promulgated in November 2013 to, among other things, promote the maximization of value-added and job creation using local expertise, goods and services, businesses, and financing in the petroleum industry value chain and their retention in Ghana. Section 49 of the Legislative Instrument defines local content as the quantum or percentage of locally produced materials, personnel, financing, goods, and services rendered in the petroleum industry value chain, which can be measured in monetary terms. Local participation refers to the level of Ghanaian ownership in the oil and gas industry (Ghana Petroleum Commission 2022). To qualify as a Ghanaian or indigenous company, a company must have at least 51 percent of its equity owned by a Ghanaian, with 80 percent executive and senior management positions and 100 percent non-management and other positions occupied by Ghanaians (Ghana Petroleum Commission 2022). Among other things, local content development seeks to maximize the patronage of Ghanaian goods and services and increase the employment of Ghanaian professionals by ensuring the localization of job opportunities.

Additionally, it seeks to facilitate technology and skills transfer to Ghanaians through training, research, and development. Moreover, local participation encourages Ghanaians to have equity ownership and management participation in upstream petroleum activities. Local content development also seeks to develop local capacities, resulting in increased capabilities and competitiveness of indigenous Ghanaian companies and individuals (Ghana Petroleum Commission 2022).

Section 10(2) of the Petroleum Commission Act 2011 (Act 821) protects the Commission from the influence of the minister of energy. The section states specifically that the directions given by the minister of energy shall not adversely affect or interfere with the performance of the functions and exercise of the powers of the commission under the act. A seven-member board governs the commission. The governing board is made up of a chairperson, the chief executive officer of the commission, one representative of the Environment Protection Agency who must not be below the rank of a director, one representative of the Institution of Geoscientists, and three other persons, one of whom must at least be a woman.

As amended, Division 1 of Part VI of the Income Tax Act 2015 (Act 896) covers petroleum operations. The Income Tax Act 2015 (Act 896) coexists with the Petroleum Income Tax Act 1987. In the event of any inconsistencies between the two pieces of legislation, the former takes precedence (Stephens and Dzikunu 2022). Section 63(1) of the Income Tax Act 2015 (Act 896) imposes a tax on the income of a person involved in petroleum operations in Ghana. The Petroleum (Exploration and Production) Act 2016 (Act 919) repealed the Petroleum Act 1984 and set out detailed rules that govern petroleum operations in the country (Stephens and Dzikunu 2022). Section 2 of the act states that petroleum existing in its natural state in, under, or upon any land in Ghana; rivers, streams, water courses throughout Ghana; the exclusive economic zone; and any area covered by the territorial sea or continental shelf is the property of the Republic of Ghana and is vested in the president on behalf of and in trust for the people of Ghana. Among other things, the Petroleum (Exploration and Production) Act 2016 (Act 919) promotes the prudent exploitation of petroleum.

Section 26 of the Petroleum (Exploration and Production) Act 2016 (Act 919) states, inter alia, that any organization that is engaged in the exploitation of petroleum in Ghana shall develop and produce petroleum in a manner that will ensure the maximum long-term recovery of the petroleum. The section further adds that the organization shall ensure that its development and production of petroleum in the country is conducted in accordance with best international practice and sound economic principles and in a manner that will ensure that waste of petroleum or loss of reservoir energy is avoided. The act also promotes the employment and training of Ghanaian citizens and the use of Ghanaian goods and services. Section 60(2) of the act enjoins individuals and organizations involved in petroleum activities in Ghana to employ Ghanaian citizens in categories and functions as prescribed. Again, Section 60(4) of the act prescribes that a person carrying out petroleum activities shall, in consultation with the Ghana Petroleum Commission, prepare and implement plans and programs to train Ghanaian citizens in all aspects of petroleum activities. Additionally, Section 64 of the act establishes a Local Content Fund, which seeks to provide financial resources for Ghanaian citizens and companies engaged in petroleum activities in the country. Money from the fund shall be used to support the education, training, research, and development of petroleum activities for Ghanaian citizens, companies, and institutions of learning. Also, the fund shall be used to provide loans on a competitive basis to Ghanaian small and medium-scale enterprises to support their participation in petroleum activities. Sections 81, 82, 83, and 84 of the act lay out principles for protecting the environment and liability for pollution damage. The Revenue Administration Act 2016 (Act 915) replaced the Petroleum Income Tax Act 1987 (PNDCL 188). The act provides for the administration and collection of tax revenue.

These pieces of legislation and other similar ones were enacted post-commercial oil discovery to help Ghana effectively manage the anticipated revenues that its oil would generate. However, as noted by Asenso and Ackah (2022), the passage of these laws could not help solve all the challenges associated with petroleum revenue management, such as fiscal slippages. They contend that Ghana's fiscal policy has been characterized by high spending that does not lead to sustained growth or investments. This situation is exacerbated by the expenditure pressures occasioned by elections. Specifically, the 2012, 2016, and 2020 general elections caused expenditure pressures, resulting in Ghana seeking a bailout from the International Monetary Fund.

This situation and other similar challenges fly in the face of the much-vaunted robustness of Ghana's petroleum governance regime. For instance, the Petroleum Revenue Management Act 2011 (Act 815) principally seeks to achieve intergenerational equity, fiscal stability, inclusive growth, and sustainable petroleum resource management. The preamble to the law reads as follows: "an act to provide the framework for the collection, allocation, and management of petroleum revenue in a responsible, transparent, accountable, and sustainable manner for the benefit of the citizens of Ghana in accordance with Article 36 of the Constitution and for related matters." Therefore, cases of poor petroleum revenue management call into question the widely accepted robust nature of the country's petroleum governance regime. Despite the prudent arrangements, the impact of oil exploitation in Ghana remains limited. The next section focuses on one area where many observers have identified as facing challenges in the management of Ghana's petroleum industry: the management of the revenue accrued from petroleum production in the country.

CHALLENGES CONFRONTING GHANA'S PETROLEUM REVENUE MANAGEMENT

One of the challenges besetting Ghana's petroleum revenue management regime is rooted in the nature of Ghana's elite-based political coalitions (Mohan, Asante, and Abdulai 2018). The nature of the ruling coalition at the time when natural resources are discovered has important implications for how these resources are managed, whether to secure the collective interests of the citizens or the parochial interests of the ruling coalition (Poteete 2009). Ghana's politics is characterized by a winner-takes-all electoral system in which the two leading political parties—the New Patriotic Party and the National Democratic Congress—compete to advance their short-term interests of power retention. The theory of political settlements helps drive home the nature of Ghana's elite-based political coalitions. The theory focuses on how the balance of power in a polity between different coalitions shapes emerging institutions and how such institutions function in practice (Khan 2010).

Ghana's political settlement is characterized by what Khan (2010) describes as "competitive clientelism," which refers to a significant level of fragmentation in the distribution of power across political organizations and within the ruling coalition such that higher levels have more limited powers over lower levels. Within Ghana's clientelist state setting, rents from oil are centralized. Whichever of the two main political parties is in power uses them to hold on to power to pursue their parochial interests. This means that, despite the robust petroleum governance regime in place, the management of the revenue generated by the natural resource seeks to advance the interests of the few ruling elites at the expense of the citizens. Those elected to ensure that the institutions of state and the petroleum revenue management legislation enacted work effectively pursue their short-term interests. Analysts of Ghana's petroleum revenue management have raised concerns about cases of poor management of the revenue. For instance, Quartey and Abbey (2018) cited the 2015 PIAC Annual Report to drive home their concerns about some of the worrying instances of revenue mismanagement. The report mentioned cases of some extraction companies failing to pay their surface rentals, unfavorably impacting revenue generation (Quartey and Abbey 2018). The report also raised concerns about the government's abuse of petroleum revenue using many social intervention projects and the lack of transparency in the processes that led to the choice of these projects (Quartey and Abbey 2018). The report further indicated that the government spent more than the required budgetary allocation from the petroleum revenue and cautioned the government to strictly adhere to the requirement of obtaining parliamentary approval of revenue receipts to fund governmental projects (Quartey and Abbey 2018). Another area of poor governmental performance in petroleum revenue management cited by the report is the failure of the government to use part of the funds for capacity building.

Another factor responsible for the limited gains is the volatile nature of global oil prices. The volatility of oil prices remains a critical concern for resource-dependent economies like Ghana. Ghana's economy is particularly vulnerable to fluctuations in global oil prices due to its heavy reliance on petroleum revenue. Aryeetey and Ackah (2018) emphasize that sudden declines in oil prices can lead to significant fiscal deficits, reduced government revenues, and constrained economic growth. Moreover, oil price uncertainty can deter foreign investment and complicate long-term economic planning. Revenue projections in Ghana's budget are frequently based on assumptions about oil prices, making it challenging to forecast government revenues accurately. When actual oil prices deviate from these assumptions, it can disrupt budgetary allocations, hinder public expenditure plans, and result in increased government borrowing (Musa et al. 2020).

Volatile global oil prices also have dire implications for Ghana's macroeconomic stability. Fluctuations in oil prices can create inflationary pressures and exchange rate volatility. Such macroeconomic instability can affect consumer purchasing power, business planning, and overall economic performance (Amoah and Aziakpono 2017). Moreover, volatility in global oil prices has had dire social and developmental consequences for Ghana. Quartey and

Abbey (2020) contend that the unpredictability of oil prices makes it difficult for the government of Ghana to sustain social intervention programs and development projects. These uncertainties undermine poverty reduction efforts and hinder progress in achieving the Sustainable Development Goals (Quartey and Abbey 2020). They argue that the unpredictability of oil prices makes it difficult for the government to sustain social intervention programs and development projects.

The volatility of oil prices poses multifaceted challenges for Ghana's economy, fiscal planning, and developmental aspirations. Fluctuations in oil prices can lead to fiscal instability, macroeconomic challenges, and constraints on social and development spending. To address these challenges, policymakers in Ghana must focus on building resilience through flexible fiscal policies, risk management strategies, and diversification efforts. Additionally, exploring alternative revenue sources and enhancing the country's capacity to respond to oil price shocks can contribute to achieving sustainable economic growth and development in the face of volatile oil markets. We contend that one of the ways that the impact of oil exploitation on Ghana's economy can be improved is by enhancing the participation of citizens in the management of the petroleum revenue. In the following section, we demonstrate that there is little citizen participation in Ghana's petroleum revenue management and, in the succeeding section, propose an innovative way citizen participation can be enhanced.

CITIZEN PARTICIPATION IN GHANA'S PETROLEUM REVENUE MANAGEMENT

In a broader sense, citizen participation in petroleum revenue management involves engaging the public in decision-making processes regarding the utilization of the revenue. Scholars, practitioners, and policymakers of petroleum revenue management advocate for citizens' engagement in petroleum revenue management in petroleum-rich countries, as it is crucial to ensuring transparency, accountability, and sustainable development. On the whole, citizen engagement in the management of petroleum revenue is essential to ensuring that the revenue is utilized for the benefit of the entire population (Akonnor and Ohemeng 2020; Debrah and Graham 2015; Gyampo 2016; Ogbe 2022b).

We identify two kinds of citizen participation relevant to this chapter. First is the government's intentional engagement of the Ghanaian public in making decisions about the use of the petroleum revenue and, second, the genuine deliberate attempts by the oil and gas firms to engage citizens in corporate social responsibility (CSR) issues. Interviews conducted by Asare, Burton, and Dunne (2021) indicate that citizen participation in the management of the petroleum revenue has been unimpressive. Responses from these interviewees suggest that the government and the oil and gas companies take governance decisions without considering the citizens' concerns. Moreover, they aver that the government and the oil and gas companies resort to political gimmicks and rhetoric to hide the extent of this failure of citizen engagement. Asare, Burton, and Dunne's (2021) interviews reveal the harrowing realities of the lack of citizen participation in the management of Ghana's oil. There is a lack of citizen participation in policymaking. In fact, even the PIAC and other big players, like non-governmental organizations focusing on Ghana's oil governance, face challenges in their attempts to be actively involved in the petroleum revenue management. The government usually acts unilaterally. The lack of citizen participation raises grave concerns about how the government uses the petroleum revenue. Also, there is a general sense that the CSR activities of the oil companies in Ghana are superficial and just mere rhetoric. As Asare, Burton, and Dunne (2021) put it, Ghanaians are disenfranchised in respect of CSR issues. They further note that there are widespread concerns about the marginalization of the public in the country's petroleum governance amid a pronounced information asymmetry. The government and the oil and gas firms resort to using image enhancement and disclaimer techniques to maintain legitimacy.

In recognizing the integral role of citizen engagement in petroleum revenue management, the immediate question that many ask is, "How can the government engage citizens concerning petroleum revenue management?" We admit that this question is not easy to answer; however, we list three important ways that citizens can be engaged regarding petroleum revenue management. First, improved citizen participation can be achieved through the establishment of mechanisms that promote transparency and accountability in the allocation and use of petroleum revenues. This can be done by establishing independent oversight bodies, sovereign wealth funds, and/or public expenditure watchdogs. This can, inter alia, enhance citizens' monitoring capacity of the government's use of petroleum revenue. Second, citizen engagement can also take the form of the direct participation of citizens in decision-making processes regarding the allocation of petroleum revenues. This level of involvement can be achieved through public consultations, participatory budgeting processes, and civic engagement initiatives. Third, citizen engagement in petroleum revenue management can also involve raising awareness—educating the public and soliciting their views—about the implications of petroleum revenue on the economy, the environment, and society. This can promote the sustainable and equitable use of petroleum revenue, such as by implementing cash transfer schemes or direct investment in public benefits like education, healthcare, and infrastructure. Axiomatically, citizen engagement in petroleum revenue management is not only crucial for transparent and accountable revenue utilization, but it can also ensure that the revenue utilization aligns with the needs of the public (Brunnschweiler, Edjekumhene, and Lujala 2021; Lujala, Brunnschweiler, and Edjekumhene 2020; Ofori and Lujala 2015; Ogbe, Rød, and Halvorsen 2021).

The PRMA encourages Ghanaians to be active in the use and management of petroleum revenue in Ghana. Consequently, the act mandates the PIAC to inform Ghanaians and collate their views regarding petroleum revenue utilization in Ghana. In line with this, PIAC has, over the years, managed to organize town hall meetings, regional fora, and visits to the sites of some petroleum revenue–funded projects across the country. Through these mechanisms, the PIAC has engaged a cross-section of the citizens by providing them with information and responding to their questions regarding the utilization of petroleum revenue generally and the revenue-funded projects specifically.

A review of the available literature on the engagement of Ghanaian citizens in petroleum revenue management in Ghana shows that Ghanaians have not been extensively engaged. This is partly attributable to the PIAC's inability to engage more Ghanaians due to financial and staffing constraints (Graham et al. 2019; Gyampo 2016; Ogbe and Lujala 2021). As a result, most Ghanaians lack knowledge about how the revenue generated is managed. More so, some Ghanaians express negative sentiments about petroleum revenue management. For instance, Ogbe (2022b) found that Ghanaians had negative sentiments about petroleum revenue management and specific programs (like the Free Senior High School program) that petroleum revenue is used to support. However, Ogbe's (2022b) study assures that Ghanaians somewhat trust the managers of the revenue and hope for better revenue management in the future. Understandably, Ghanaians want the government to involve them in petroleum revenue management. Specifically, Ghanaians want to select the priority areas, types, and locations of petroleum revenue-funded projects (Ogbe 2022a).

Citizen participation in petroleum revenue management in Ghana has several potential benefits (Brunnschweiler, Edjekumhene, and Lujala 2021; Ogbe 2022a; 2022b; Ogbe and Lujala 2021; Ogbe, Rød, and Halvorsen 2021; Sefa-Nyarko, Okafor-Yarwood, and Boadu 2021). Primarily, it can help address the lack of knowledge among Ghanaians about petroleum revenue–funded projects in their localities (Ogbe 2022a; Ogbe and Lujala 2021; Ogbe, Rød, and Halvorsen 2021). Also, it can help the government fund projects that align with the needs and preferences of the local communities (Ogbe 2022b). Furthermore, citizen engagement can help build trust between the government and the public (Ogbe 2022b; Ogbe, Rød, and Halvorsen 2021). Citizen participation in petroleum revenue management can promote transparency, accountability, and sustainable development in Ghana.

Citizen participation in petroleum revenue management might seem like a panacea to better revenue utilization in Ghana; however, it is a complex issue, influenced by factors such as access to information and representativeness (Ogbe 2022a; Sefa-Nyarko, Okafor-Yarwood, and Boadu 2021). How can the government consult broadly with all stakeholders regarding petroleum revenue management in Ghana? We propose the use of spatial crowdsourcing, an innovative approach to enhancing citizen participation. Similarly, Ogbe and Lujala (2021) propose spatial crowdsourcing as an essential tool for informing Ghanaians and collecting their opinions regarding petroleum revenue management for effective petroleum revenue management in Ghana. The next section outlines the essential characteristics of spatial crowdsourcing and highlights the ways it can prove useful to the Ghanaian economy.

SPATIAL CROWDSOURCING: IMPROVING CITIZEN PARTICIPATION IN GHANA'S PETROLEUM REVENUE MANAGEMENT

Spatial crowdsourcing is the process wherein governments or scholars engage individuals and/or groups in collecting and disseminating spatio-temporal (e.g., socio-economic, environmental, or cultural) data (Ogbe and Lujala 2021; To, Ghinita, and Shahabi 2014). Spatial crowdsourcing leverages global positioning system–enabled devices to send and receive location-specific information (in the form of numbers, texts, pictures, or audiovisuals) to and from citizens (Miao et al. 2016; Zhao and Han 2016). As an innovative approach, spatial crowdsourcing can help the Ghanaian government inform Ghanaians and gather their opinions at their respective locations. The government can use spatial crowdsourcing to monitor and evaluate petroleum revenue–funded projects by obtaining and using feedback from project recipients (Ogbe 2022b; Ogbe and Lujala 2021). Particularly, by utilizing the power of technology (smartphones), spatial crowdsourcing can help Ghanaians actively participate in collecting and sharing data related to petroleum revenue management in Ghana. This data can include information on oil production, revenue allocation, and the impact of petroleum activities on local communities and the environment.

By engaging citizens through spatial crowdsourcing, Ghana can ensure that a wide range of perspectives and local knowledge are incorporated into decision-making processes regarding petroleum revenue management. Additionally, spatial crowdsourcing in petroleum revenue management can facilitate greater local engagement and enable citizens to contribute their unique spatial knowledge. This can lead to a more inclusive and participatory approach to petroleum revenue management in Ghana, empowering citizens to actively shape the policies and practices that govern the use of petroleum revenues in the country.

Practically, spatial crowdsourcing can help Ghanaians report and map various elements related to petroleum revenue, such as infrastructure, environmental concerns, social impact, or community needs. It can enable citizens to monitor and track petroleum revenue projects through, for instance, real-time updates and visualizations on an interactive map. This process can ensure that Ghanaians hold the authorities accountable for the allocation and execution of these petroleum revenue–funded projects. Moreover, spatial crowdsourcing can foster a feedback loop where Ghanaians can provide input, comments, and suggestions on ongoing petroleum revenue–funded projects or propose new initiatives. This interaction can encourage active participation and inclusivity in decision-making processes.

Implementing spatial crowdsourcing in Ghana's petroleum revenue management can democratize the process, empower citizens to actively engage in monitoring and decision-making, and foster a more transparent and accountable system. Additionally, it can bridge the information gap between authorities and communities, leading to more informed and inclusive policies. Through spatial crowdsourcing, Ghana can, thus, enhance transparency, accountability, and citizen engagement in the management of petroleum revenues. Admittedly, spatial crowdsourcing can face challenges such as technological disparities and guaranteeing the security of citizen-contributed information (Ogbe and Lujala 2021). However, with proper planning, infrastructure, and community engagement, spatial crowdsourcing can significantly improve citizen participation in Ghana's petroleum revenue management.

CONCLUSION

In this chapter, we have demonstrated that, though Ghana's petroleum revenue management regime is robust, it is only so in theory; in practice, it is beset with many challenges. As the chapter indicates, the discovery of oil in commercial quantities in Ghana, the inadequacy of the existing petroleum management regime at the time, and the deep national quest for ensuring that the management of the revenue generated by petroleum production benefits all Ghanaians saw the enactment of some useful pieces of legislation; however, in practice, it has not lived up to its promise largely due to factors such as the government's abuse of the management regime, lack of citizen participation, and the non-engagement of citizens in CSR decisions by the oil and gas companies. One area that faces grave challenges is petroleum revenue management. We have argued that one of the ways the challenges confronting

Ghana's petroleum revenue management can be mitigated is by enhancing citizen participation. We believe that deploying spatial crowdsourcing technology is one important approach to strengthening the petroleum management regime (especially regarding managing the accrued revenue). Despite the challenges this technology may face if used well and on a wide scale, we believe it can significantly enhance citizens' participation, thereby rendering Ghana's petroleum management regime robust in theory and practice.

REFERENCES

Abraham, K. K. A. 2019. "Petroleum Revenue Management in Ghana: The Epoch of High Expectation in Perspective." *Journal of Sustainable Development Law and Policy*, 10(1): 32–55.

Acheampong, T., and T. K. Stephens. 2022. *Petroleum Resource Management in Africa*. Cham: Palgrave Macmillan, Springer Nature.

Ackah, I., C. Bobio, E. Graham, and C. K. Oppong. 2020a. "Balancing Debt with Sustainability? Fiscal Policy and the Future of Petroleum Revenue Management in Ghana." *Energy Research & Social Science*, 67: 101516.

Ackah, I., A. Lartey, T. Acheampong, E. Kyem, and G. Ketempi. 2020b. "Between Altruism and Self-aggrandizement: Transparency, Accountability and Politics in Ghana's Oil and Gas Sector." *Energy Research & Social Science*, 68.

Acosta, A. M. 2013. "The Impact and Effectiveness of Accountability and Transparency Initiatives: The Governance of Natural Resources." *Development Policy Review*, 31: S89–S105.

Adam, A. 2017. "Ghana Petroleum Revenue Management Act: Back to Basics." Natural Resource Governance Institute. https://resourcegovernance.org/sites/default/files/documents/ghana-petroleum-revenue-management_-act.pdf, accessed January 2, 2024.

Adams, D., S. Ullah, P. Akhtar, K. Adams, and S. Saidi. 2019. "The Role of Country-Level Institutional Factors in Escaping the Natural Resource Curse: Insights from Ghana." *Resources Policy*, 61: 433–40.

Akonnor, A., and F. L. K. Ohemeng. 2020. "Towards a More Accountable Resource Governance in Developing Countries: The Case of Ghana's Oil and Gas sector." *The Extractive Industries and Society*, 7(3): 812–19.

Amoah, L., and M. Aziakpono. 2017. "Exchange Rate Behavior in Ghana: Is There Misalignment?" *The Journal of Developing Areas*, 51(4), 261–76. https://www.jstor.org/stable/26416981, accessed May 22, 2024.

Aryeetey, E., and I. Ackah, 2018. "The Boom, the Bust, and the Dynamics of Oil Resource Management in Ghana." In *Mining for Change*, 97–118. Oxford: Oxford Academic.

Asare, E., B. Burton, and T. Dunne. 2021. "Natural Resource Governance, Accountability and Legitimising Propensity: Insights from Ghana's Oil and Gas Sector." *Journal of Accounting in Emerging Economies*, 11(4): 509–32.

Asenso, J. K., and I. Ackah. 2022. "Fiscal Policy and Petroleum Revenue Management: Is Ghana on the Path to Beating the Resource Curse?" In *Petroleum Resource Management in Africa*, edited by T. Acheampong and T. Kojo Stephens, 207–53. Cham: Palgrave Macmillan, Springer Nature.

BBC News. 2007. "Ghana Will Be an African Tiger." http://news.bbc.co.uk/2/hi/africa/6766527.stm, accessed January 2, 2024.

Brunnschweiler, C., I. Edjekumhene, and P. Lujala. 2021. "Does Information Matter? Transparency and Demand for Accountability in Ghana's Natural Resource Revenue Management." *Ecological Economics*, 181: 106903.

Cameron, P. D., and M. C. Stanley. 2017. *Oil, Gas, and Mining: A Sourcebook for Understanding the Extractive Industries*. Washington, DC: The World Bank.

Chandler, J. A. P. 2020. "Developing Offshore Petroleum to meet Socio-economic objectives: Lessons from Australia, Norway and the United Kingdom." *Energy Policy*, 144: 111618.

Collier, P. 2007. *The Bottom Billion: Why the Poorest Countries are Failing and What Can Be Done About It*. Oxford: Oxford University Press

Debrah, E., and E. Graham. 2015. "Preventing the Oil Curse Situation in Ghana: The Role of Civil Society Organisations." *Insight on Africa*, 7(1): 21–41.

Doh, J., P. Budhwar, and G. Wood. 2021. "Long-Term Energy Transitions and International Business: Concepts, Theory, Methods, and a Research Agenda." *Journal of International Business Studies*, 52: 951–70.

Dominković, D. F., I. Bačeković, A. S. Pedersen, and G. Krajačić. 2018. "The Future of Transportation in Sustainable Energy Systems: Opportunities and Barriers in a clean Energy Transition." *Renewable and Sustainable Energy Reviews*, 82: 1823–38.

Edjekumhene, I., M. Voors, P. Lujala, C. Brunnschweiler, C. K. Owusu, and A. Nyamekye. 2018. "Examining Transparency and Accountability Within the Oil and Gas Sector: Impact Evaluation of Key Provisions in Ghana's Petroleum Revenue Management Act (3ie Grantee Final Report)." https://www.3ieimpact.org/sites/default/files/2019-02/GFR-TW8.1002-transparency-accountability-ghana.pdf, accessed September 30, 2023.

Ghana Petroleum Commission. 2022. "What is Local Content and Participation?" https://www.petrocom.gov.gh/local-content/#:~:text=Local%20Content%20%E2%80%93%20Petroleum%20Commission%20Ghana&text=Local%20Content%20refers%20to%20the,be%20measured%20in%20monetary%20terms, accessed September 3, 2023.

Ghose, J., S. K. Bakshi, N. Arora, R. Sharma, N. Deepa, and M. Govindan. 2018. "Natural Resource Revenue Management in Low and Middle-income Countries Experiencing Politically Fragile Conditions: A Systematic Review. Contextualisation of Review Findings for Afghanistan and Myanmar." EPPI-Centre. https://assets.publishing.service.gov.uk/media/5b101fb240f0b634b73dbe30/Contextualization_Document_final.pdf, accessed September 20, 2023.

Graham, E., R. E. V. Gyampo, I. Ackah, and N. Andrews. 2019. "An Institutional Assessment of the Public Interest and Accountability Committee (PIAC) in Ghana's Oil and Gas Sector." *Journal of Contemporary African Studies*, 37(4): 316–34.

Gyampo, R. E. V. 2016. "Transparency and Accountability in the Management of Petroleum Revenues in Ghana." *Africa Spectrum*, 51(2): 79–91.

Gyimah-Boadi, E., and H. K. Prempeh. 2012. "Oil, Politics, and Ghana's Democracy." *Journal of Democracy*, 23(3): 94–108.

Hunter, T. 2014. "The Role of Regulatory Frameworks and State Regulation in Optimising the Extraction of Petroleum Resources: A study of Australia and Norway." *The Extractive Industries and Society*, 1(1): 48–58.

Khan, M. 2010. "Political Settlements and the Governance of Growth-Enhancing Institutions." Working Paper, London School of Oriental and African Studies. https://eprints.soas.ac.uk/9968/, accessed August 20, 2023.

Kolstad, I., and T. Søreide. 2009. "Corruption in Natural Resource Management: Implications for Policy Makers." *Resources Policy*, 34(4): 214–26.

Laimon, M., T. Yusaf, T. Mai, S. Goh, and W. Alrefae. 2022. "A Systems Thinking Approach to Address Sustainability Challenges to the Energy Sector." *International Journal of Thermofluids*, 15: 100161.

Larsen, E. R. 2006. "Escaping the Resource Curse and the Dutch Disease? When and why Norway caught up with and forged ahead of its Neighbors." *American Journal of Economics and Cociology*, 65(3): 605–40.

Lujala, P., C. Brunnschweiler, and I. Edjekumhene. 2020. "Transparent for Whom? Dissemination of Information on Ghana's Petroleum and Mining Revenue Management." *The Journal of Development Studies*, 56(12), 2135–53.

Lujala, P., C. Brunnschweiler, and I. Edjekumhene. 2020. "Transparent for Whom? Dissemination of Information on Ghana's Petroleum and Mining Revenue Management." *The Journal of Development Studies*, 56(12): 2135–53.

Mähler, A. 2010. "Nigeria: A Prime Example of the Resource Curse? Revisiting the Oil-Violence Link in the Niger Delta." GIGA Working Paper, GIGA Working Paper, Hamburg.

Miao, C. Y., H. Yu, Z. Q. Shen, and C. Leung. 2016. "Balancing Quality and Budget Considerations in Mobile Crowdsourcing." *Decision Support Systems*, 90: 56–64.

Mohan, G., K. P. Asante, and A. Abdulai. 2018. "Party Politics and the Political Economy of Ghana's Oil." *New Political Economy*, 23(3): 274–89.

Musa, K. S., R. Maijama'a, and N. Muhammed 2020. "Crude Oil Price and Exchange Rate Nexus: An ARDL Bound Approach." *Open Access Library Journal*, 7(3), 1–24.

Nong, D., C. Wang, and A. Q. Al-Amin. 2020. "A Critical Review of Energy Resources, Policies and Scientific Studies towards a Cleaner and more Sustainable Economy in Vietnam." *Renewable and Sustainable Energy Reviews*, 134: 110117.

Nweze, N. P., and G. E. Edame. 2016. "An Empirical Investigation of Petroleum Revenue and Economic Growth in Nigeria." *European Scientific Journal*, 12(25).

Obi, C. I. 2010. "Oil Extraction, Dispossession, Resistance, and Conflict in Nigeria's Oil-Rich Niger Delta." *Canadian Journal of Development Studies/Revue Canadienne d'études du développement*, 30(1–2): 219–36.

Ofori, J. J. Y., and P. Lujala. 2015. "Illusionary Transparency? Petroleum revenues, Information Disclosure, and Transparency." *Society & Natural Resources*, 28(11): 1187–202.

Ogbe, M. 2022a. "Citizens' Participation in Petroleum Revenue Management in Ghana." *The Extractive Industries and Society*, 12:101175.

Ogbe, M. 2022b. "Natural Language Processing of Spatially Crowdsourced Data in Petroleum Revenue Management." *GeoJournal*, 1–21.

Ogbe, M., and P. Lujala. 2021. "Spatial Crowdsourcing in Natural Resource Revenue Management." *Resources Policy*, 72: 102082.

Ogbe, M., J. K. Rød, and T. Halvorsen. 2021. "Opinions of Ghanaians on the Management of Petroleum Revenue in Ghana." *African Geographical Review*, 1–18.

Olayungbo, D. O. 2019. "Effects of Oil Export Revenue on Economic Growth in Nigeria: A Time Varying Analysis of Resource Curse." *Resources Policy*, 64: 101469.

Oppong, N. 2020. "Between Elite Reflexes and Deliberative Impulses: Oil and the Landscape Of Contentious Politics in Ghana." *Oxford Development Studies*, 48(4), 329–44.

Osei-Kojo, A. 2023. "Analysing the Stability of Advocacy Coalitions and Policy Frames in Ghana's Oil and Gas Governance." *Policy & Politics*, 51(1): 71–90.

Ovadia, J. S. 2018. "Angola: Civil Society Actors and Petroleum Management." In *Public Brainpower: Civil Society and Natural Resource Management*, edited by I. Overland. New York, NY: Springer.

Poteete, A. 2009. "Is Development Path Dependent or Political? A Reinterpretation of Mineral-Dependent Development in Botswana." *Journal of Development Studies*, 45(4): 544–71.

Quartey, P., and E. Abbey. 2018. "Ghana's Oil Governance Regime: Challenges and Policy Solutions." CRPD Working Paper 70, Centre for Research on Peace and Development, Leuven.

Quartey, P., and E. Abbey. 2020. "Ghana's Oil Governance Regime: Challenges and Policies." In *Oil Wealth and Development in Uganda and Beyond*,edited by Arnim Langer, Ukoha Ukiwo, and Pamela Mbabazi, 331–50. Leuven, Belgium: Leuven University Press.

Quitzow, R., S. Thielges, A. Goldthau, S. Helgenberger, and G. Mbungu. 2019. "Advancing a Global Transition to Clean Energy–The Role of International Cooperation." *Economics*, 13(1): 20190048.

Rodríguez, J.-L. G., F. J. G. Rodríguez, C. C. Gutiérrez, and S. A. Major. 2014. "Oil, Poverty and Environment in Angola." *Boletín de la Asociación de Geógrafos Españoles*.

Sáez-Martínez, F. J., G. Lefebvre, J. J. Hernández, and J. H. Clark. 2016. "Drivers of Sustainable Cleaner Production and Sustainable Energy Options." *Journal of Cleaner Production*, 138: 1–7.

Sefa-Nyarko, C., I. Okafor-Yarwood, and E. S. Boadu. 2021. "Petroleum Revenue Management in Ghana: How Does the Right to Information Law Promote Transparency, Accountability and Monitoring of the Annual Budget Funding Amount?" *The Extractive Industries and Society*, 8(3): 100957.

Shobande, O. A., and J. O. Enemona. 2021. "A Multivariate VAR Model for Evaluating Sustainable Finance and Natural Resource Curse in West Africa: evidence from Nigeria and Ghana." *Sustainability*, 13(5): 2847.

Stephens, T. K. 2019. "Framework for Petroleum Revenue Management in Ghana: Current Problems and Challenges." *Journal of Energy & Natural Resources Law*, 37(1): 119–43.

Stephens, T. K., and S. Dzikunu. 2022. "Examining Ghana's Petroleum Act, 2016 (Act 919) and Other Legislative Developments." In *Petroleum Resource Management in Africa: Lessons from Ten Years of Oil and Gas Production in Ghana*, edited by Theophilus Acheampong and Thomas Kojo Stephens, 3–40. Cham, Switzerland: Springer Nature.

To, H., G. Ghinita, and C. Shahabi. 2014. "A Framework for Protecting Worker Location Privacy in Spatial Crowdsourcing." *Proceedings of the VLDB Endowment*, 7(10): 919–30.

Zhao, Y. J., and Q. Han. 2016. "Spatial Crowdsourcing: Current State and Future Directions." *IEEE Communications Magazine*, 54(7): 102–07.

Chapter 5

Gas Curse or Gas Compliment?

The Politics of Mozambique's Jackpot Natural Gas Discoveries

Angela Zivo Gapa and Antonetta Hamandishe

Mozambique stands on the verge of an eagerly anticipated extractives boom, which can potentially reshape the nation's political economy (Schubert 2020). Stalled by its protracted civil war, resource extraction in Mozambique gained traction after the 1992 peace accords and has experienced exceptional growth since 2010. The Tete and Niassa provinces are home to extensive coal reserves and a diverse array of minerals, including copper, tantalum, marble, graphite, iron ore, bauxite, gold, rubies, bentonite, and titanium, all of which have significant global demand. The country is a major player in the global aluminum, beryl, ilmenite, and zircon market. Furthermore, rich deposits of rubies were discovered in the Montepeuz area in Cabo Delgado in 2009, igniting hope for the region's impoverished communities. In 2014, the first auction of Montepeuz's rubies generated an impressive $33.5 million in revenue (Valoi 2016).

Plans are underway in Mozambique to explore extracting rare earth minerals (Yager 2021). Australian multinational Southern Cross Resources revealed that its concession in the country's Xiluvo district has 1.1 mega-tons of reserves of rare earth elements. Rare earth elements are seventeen chemical elements in the periodic table that revolutionize the clean energy space. They are crucial in manufacturing advanced technology consumer goods, including electric and hybrid automobiles, solar panels, and wind turbines. Nevertheless, despite its abundant mineral resources, Mozambique is primarily poised to emerge as a continental natural gas titan, potentially

115

becoming the world's fourth-largest exporter of natural gas (Uetela and Obeng-Odoom 2015).

One of the greatest natural gas finds in recent years is Mozambique's liquified natural gas (LNG) reserves, which are anticipated to be over one hundred trillion cubic feet (Macuane and Muianga 2020). The extraordinary natural gas discovery, made after a multiyear exploratory campaign, situates Mozambique as the new frontier in the global hydrocarbon industry. In 2006, the Mozambican government granted Italian energy multinational Eni a license to explore for gas off the state's northeastern coast, Cabo Delgado. In 2011, the company announced that it had discovered 2.4 trillion cubic meters of natural gas in the Rovuma basin off the Cabo Delgado coast, a windfall that could change the country's fortunes (Radionovich and Jossias 2021). Situated at a pivotal point in global shipping routes, Mozambique can export its LNG to various markets, including to Europe and North Africa through the Suez Canal; to West Africa, North, and South America around the Cape of Good Hope across the Atlantic Ocean; and to Asia via the Indian Ocean. Given the anticipated increase in demand for natural gas in the Asia-Pacific region from 2023 to 2035, Mozambique is well-positioned to meet this demand. The keen interest of international companies in Mozambique, such as TotalEnergies, ExxonMobil, and Oil India, further supports this (Flower 2021). Additionally, the Rovuma basin, home to most of the country's gas reserves, is located twenty-five miles offshore in Mozambique's exclusive economic zone, specifically within the Cabo Delgado province.

Similar to windfall resources in other African nations, the recent discovery of natural gas in Mozambique holds the potential to transform its economy and address issues of inequality and deprivation. With a gross domestic product of just over fifteen billion US dollars in 2019, the significant impact of this newfound resource is evident. Many have expressed optimism that revenues from the development of this resource will support the nation's social welfare, improve infrastructure, and fight poverty. Mozambique's natural gas discoveries are expected to have far-reaching economic effects and help reduce poverty. Nevertheless, the government's capacity to manage resource income, encourage equitable development, and solve current socio-economic difficulties will all affect how these resources benefit its citizens (Cust and Harding 2020).

Mozambique has outlined a strategy to establish a sovereign wealth fund, intending to ensure that the benefits of the gas discovery have a lasting, multigenerational impact. The plan involves allocating 50 percent of revenue generated over the initial twenty years of gas extraction to the fund and contributing 80 percent thereafter, with the remaining portion directed toward the country's annual budget. Furthermore, the revenue generated from natural gas is earmarked for comprehensive infrastructure development, focusing on public works projects such as railways, roads, and port construction and expansion. This initiative aims to enhance domestic mobility and connectivity to the market.

Additionally, Mozambique emphasizes investments in education and healthcare as fundamental priorities, aiming to elevate the living standards of its citizens. The two primary LNG projects in Mozambique are expected to, directly and indirectly, create thousands of jobs for Mozambicans, addressing the country's high unemployment rate of 25 percent. Additionally, natural gas revenues are aimed at rejuvenating the country's economy from the effects of the global coronavirus pandemic, which caused uncertainty and delays in regard to the country's LNG projects in light of decreased global production of natural gas during the pandemic. With uncertainty and volatility in global markets, the large international companies involved in Mozambique's LNG projects have hesitated to invest in new infrastructure. In addition to pandemic-related gas market conditions, Mozambique must be cognizant of the effects of the LNG boom to avoid the so-called Dutch disease that many other resource-rich states have experienced, as the history of resource exploitation in Africa demonstrates that natural resources frequently result in corruption, conflict, and environmental damage.

This chapter offers a comprehensive, multilevel examination of Mozambique's rapidly expanding natural gas extractive sector. It starts by outlining the political and economic landscape of Mozambique. Following this, the chapter progresses to an in-depth exploration of the government's strategies for handling the surge in hydrocarbon resources. Subsequently, it assesses the repercussions of the jihadist insurgency in the LNG-abundant region of Cabo Delgado, including the implications of international involvement. The chapter concludes by scrutinizing the populace's reaction to the discovery of natural gas and the ongoing insurgency. This is undertaken to evaluate if Mozambique can circumvent the potential pitfalls of a resource curse.

BACKGROUND TO MOZAMBIQUE'S POLITICAL ECONOMY

Mozambique is a country located in southeastern Africa bordered by the Indian Ocean to the east, Tanzania to the north, Malawi and Zambia to the northwest, Zimbabwe to the west, and Eswatini and South Africa to the southwest, making it a member of the Southern Africa Development Community (SADC). The country boasts a lengthy coastline of twenty-seven hundred kilometers along the Indian Ocean. Consequently, it benefits its four landlocked neighbors highly, providing a vital access point to global markets and crucial maritime connectivity. The country maintains strong connections with South Africa, the regional hegemon, highlighting the significance of its socio-economic progress for the advancement and stability of the SADC region (Ferim 2006).

The Frente de Libertação de Moçambique (Front for the Liberation of Mozambique) and the Resistência Nacional Moçambicana (Mozambican National Resistance) are the dominant entities in the country's political landscape. Since gaining independence from Portugal in 1975, the Frente de Libertação de Moçambique has maintained its leadership, securing decisive victories in the presidential and legislative arenas following the inception of a multiparty system in 1992. The ruling party's continuous tenure has enabled it to gain substantial influence over governmental bodies, particularly strategic institutions governing natural resources. The legitimacy of Mozambique's most recent election outcomes has been contested by the opposition, which also engaged in a minor-scale armed struggle through its militant branch against the state's military. This conflict continued until the parties reached a ceasefire agreement in 2016.

Economically, Mozambique experienced one of the highest economic growth rates in sub-Saharan Africa from 2000 to 2015. The expansion primarily stemmed from the resurgence of the service sector and the initiation of LNG production at the Coral South offshore site. In recent times, Mozambique's overall public debt has decreased, partly due to the United States' African Growth and Opportunity Act and the International Monetary Fund's Heavily Indebted Poor Countries program, deeming it to be manageable from a future-oriented perspective. According to the World Bank (2018), Mozambique's medium-term economic prognosis remains favorable, with growth forecast to rise to 6 percent between 2023 and 2025, led by the ongoing recovery in services, rising LNG production, and high commodity prices. However, the country's progress in generating employment, reducing poverty, and building human capital has been limited. The substantial wealth generated during this period has benefited only a small segment of the economy. A significant barrier to Mozambique's rapid, inclusive, and sustainable development is its extremely low human capital, indicated by a human capital index of just 0.36. The provision of fundamental education and healthcare services is inconsistent across the country, leading to regional disparities. Furthermore, the lack of robust systems to shield the most vulnerable from shocks contributes to ongoing fragility, instability, and conflict (Meek and Nene 2021).

Mozambique faces multiple vulnerabilities that could potentially undermine the benefits of its forthcoming resource boom. Political dynamics characterized by patronage and clientelism, conflicts within the ruling elite, a limited productive sector, insufficient governmental capacity, widespread poverty, and persistent budget deficits cast doubt on the prospect of the current resource boom spurring meaningful economic transformation (Macuane and Muianga 2020). A notable challenge in the oil and gas sector is the shortage of skilled human resources in top management positions (World Bank 2015). The livelihoods of a majority in Mozambique depend on natural resources, making the country highly susceptible to devastating climate-related disasters. The impending LNG projects, for instance, are projected to exacerbate climate change. Specifically, the three gas extraction initiatives in Cabo Delgado are anticipated to significantly increase greenhouse gas emissions, potentially boosting Mozambique's overall emissions by 14 percent (Mundi and Vashisht 2023).

The resource boom in Mozambique can potentially worsen existing inequities and social conflicts. Large-scale resource extraction operations may result in community dislocation, loss of livelihoods, and increased competition for limited resources such as land and water (Hinojosa-Valencia et al. 2008). Furthermore, the surge of foreign employees and investment may exacerbate social tensions and violence, especially if local groups do not believe they benefit from the resource windfall (Kotsadam and Tolonen 2016). Multiple factors are behind Mozambique's cycle of fragility, poverty, and inequality. State involvement in the economy has proven regressive, increasing the proportion of poor people. The country's governmental finances are stressed, and the ability to offer adequate public services is restricted. The enormous debt load and macroeconomic concerns endanger the economy and erode investor confidence. These factors have led to high real interest rates and impeded financial market growth. Transparency, accountability, and public involvement are also constrained, undermining confidence even more. Mozambique's governance issues would be exacerbated by the predicted flood of income from the gas industry after 2030 (World Bank 2015). Inclusive institutions will be critical to addressing fragility, conflict, and violence; creating resilience, diversifying the economy; and successfully using future natural resource earnings. Mozambique will need to address these persistent development challenges by strengthening its institutions' effectiveness and pro-poor orientation, increasing public trust, managing public finances more prudently, delivering quality public services, and promoting transparency, accountability, and citizen engagement. Inclusive governance will be critical in overcoming instability and fostering long-term development in the nation.

Since the 2016 debt crisis, the country's stability has improved, although economic prospects remain restricted. While certain industries, such as tourism and banking, have witnessed moderate growth, the extractives industry has slowed. Consumer spending must rebound to sustain growth, particularly in the services sector. The need to decrease macroeconomic uncertainty and increase investment to enable full recovery and more equitable development is thus emphasized. Mozambique faces uncertain global recovery, as the country's low levels of human capital and susceptibility to natural calamities threaten to restrict Mozambique's possibilities for broadening sources of development (World Bank 2015). Other concerns include preserving Mozambique's macroeconomic stability, considering the country's vulnerability to commodity price fluctuations, and making additional steps to restore trust via enhanced economic governance and transparency. Structural adjustments and economic diversification are pivotal to help stabilize the struggling private sector. Diversifying the economy away from capital-intensive enterprises, low-productivity subsistence agriculture, and increasingly important drivers of inclusion, such as increased education and healthcare delivery, might enhance social indices. Mozambique's economic condition remains bleak, and government debt levels approached 120 percent of gross domestic product in 2020 (BTI 2022).

Natural resource project windfalls brought a degree of relief. Mozambique's economic prospects are frequently portrayed positively since offshore gas finds might lead to economic diversification, the transformation of subsistence agriculture into agroindustry, increased revenues, and improved macroeconomic stability. However, none of the megaprojects have so far resulted in any trickle-down impact.

FRAMEWORK OF HYDROCARBON OWNERSHIP AND REGULATION IN MOZAMBIQUE

In 2016, Mozambique endured a secret debt scandal involving $2.2 billion illegally acquired from Russian and Swiss banks through state-owned and controlled enterprises, based on anticipated profits from the Rovuma Basin gas reserves. This scandal highlighted the challenge of how the Mozambique's elite could legally benefit from its impeding gas windfall. Therefore, in understanding how formal contracts facilitate rent-seeking by ruling elites, it is crucial to consider the legal framework of Mozambique's hydrocarbon sector, where contracts shape the distribution of revenues among international and national oil companies and the state (Salimo, Buur, and Macuane 2020).

Since the turn of the century, Mozambique has experienced a significant economic surge due to its extractive industries. This has prompted the enactment of various comprehensive laws concerning the country's mineral, oil, and gas sectors and their corresponding taxation frameworks. The country's legal framework strongly emphasizes state ownership of natural resources, with laws and regulations designed to govern exploration, extraction, taxation, and environmental protection. Most significant is Article 98 of the

Mozambican Constitution, which states that "the natural resources located in the soil, subsoil, inland waters, territorial sea, and continental shelf, as well as in the exclusive economic zone, are the property of the State." The Mozambican constitution affirms that ownership and administration of oil and gas resources are vested in the state. As such, the government maintains the right to participate in any project involving petroleum or natural gas operations through the state-owned company Empresa Nacional de Hidrocarbonetos, EP (ENH). The regulatory body overseeing Mozambique's oil and natural gas sector is the Council of Ministers, competent to endorse legislation related to the primary sector and awarding concessions, including approving contracts. The main law governing the sector is the Petroleum Law (Law No. 21/2014), which specifies the general framework relevant to all hydrocarbon operations and defines the rules for granting rights to perform petroleum operations. Furthermore, the Petroleum Operations Regulations (Decree No. 34/2015, amended by Decree No. 48/2018 and by Decree No. 34/2019) regulates the Petroleum Law, detailing the allocation of rights to guarantee the systematic supervision of petroleum-related processes (Rocha and Mendes 2023).

The Ministry of Mineral Resources and Energy guides and oversees the implementation of government policies related to the geological exploration and extraction of minerals and energy resources, encompassing coal and hydrocarbons (Schubert 2020). It also develops and expands natural gas, petroleum products, and electricity supply infrastructure. The Ministry of Mineral Resources and Energy is responsible for daily management, policy implementation in the oil and gas sector, and supervision by the National Institute of Petroleum (INP). The creation of the INP was officially enacted by Decree No. 25/2004 on August 20, 2004. As a national entity, the INP is the regulatory authority managing Mozambique's petroleum resources. It is entrusted with administering, promoting, and supervising hydrocarbon activities. The INP sets guidelines for involving public and private sectors in extracting hydrocarbon products and their derivatives. In addition, it oversees and monitors operations and tender procedures, ensuring the maintenance of public interest and environmental protection. Furthermore, the Petroleum Law introduced the High Authority for the Extraction Industry to regulate petroleum activities in Mozambique, which is yet to become operative (Flanders Investment and Trade 2021).

The state-owned enterprise, ENH, is responsible for prospecting, exploring, producing, and marketing petroleum products in Mozambique and exclusively represents the government in all petroleum operations, engaging in various phases and administering oil and gas allocations aimed at fostering the development of the domestic market and Mozambique's industrialization (Palmer 2023). Any investor prospecting and exploring Mozambican petroleum resources has to enter into a joint venture with ENH. In addition, the Petroleum Law mandates that the state ensure ENH's financing.

Corporate entities incorporated and registered in Mozambican territory, together with national or foreign individuals engaged in petroleum operations under concession contracts, fall under a taxation regime for petroleum operations established by the Petroleum Production Tax Law (Law No. 27/2014, amended 2017). Furthermore, the Petroleum Production Tax Regulation (Decree No. 32/2015, amended in 2022) delineates rules for the Petroleum Production Tax (IPP).

The Rules on Production, Import, Receipt, Handling, Transport, Distribution, Trade, Export, and Re-export of Petroleum Products and Decree No. 89/2019 (dated November 18, 2019) establish the legal framework governing all downstream operations (Rocha and Mendes 2023). In addition, the Strategy for Concession of Areas for Petroleum Operations (Resolution No. 39/2021) administers Mozambique's concession appraisal and production processes for both on- and offshore oil rights, supporting the advancement of the country's extractive industry. Furthermore, procedures for environmental impact assessment are codified in the Environmental Regulation for Petroleum Operations (Decree No. 56/2010), which specifies the criteria for conducting oil operations, outlining protection and control measures to prevent environmental catastrophes (Mendes 2021).

Oversight of petroleum activities in Mozambique is further regulated by the Regulation on the Licensing of Petroleum Facilities and Activities (Ministerial Diploma No. 272/2009) and Regulation of the Inspection Activity of Mineral Resources and Energy (Decree No. 34/2019). These two regulations govern all concessionaires and subcontracted parties involved in petroleum operations and set forth rules, principles, and procedures overseeing the execution of the inspection tasks concerning mineral resources and energy. In addition, the Mega-Projects Law (Law 15/2011) governs public-private partnerships, large-scale projects, and business concessions, instituting a legal framework that fosters collaboration between private partners and investors, streamlining the effective delivery of goods and services to Mozambique (Rocha and Mendes 2023).

Mozambican resource law delineates the procedures for contracting, implementing, and monitoring public-private partnerships and business concessions ventures via the Small-Scale Projects Regulation (Decree No. 69/2013), for projects that do not exceed five million Mozambican metical in investment (Mendes 2021). Private investment in the upstream sector for petroleum operations is provided through concession contracts, typically awarded via auction. Occasionally, rights are assigned through negotiations, a process that begins with the INP defining the available regions within Mozambican territory and initiating a public tender process for interested parties to submit exploration bids. These bids are evaluated on the basis of environmental safety and health standards, financial capacity, technical competence, and the Mozambican state's economic interests (Rocha and Mendes 2023).

Petroleum companies in Mozambique participating in upstream and downstream activities must obtain licenses that facilitate the setting up petroleum facilities, construction, oil pipeline exploration, production, storage, distribution, retail, and demobilization of petroleum activities (Mendes 2021). For upstream activities, fiscal terms typically involve corporate income tax and royalty-based taxation alongside bonus payments, training programs, relinquishment funds, and other financial obligations specified in the concession contract. Concessionaires are typically subject to a petroleum production tax, corporate income tax, and production-sharing mechanisms. As established by Mozambican fiscal law, a portion of revenue generated from hydrocarbon operations must be allotted to the community where the operations occur. Petroleum production tax (IPP) payment is initiated upon oil or gas extraction, with tax rates at 10 percent for petroleum and 6 percent for LNG. These rates are lowered by 50 percent for local industry production to 5 percent for oil and 3 percent for natural gas. Moreover, the tax regime provides tax stability for ten years, subject to an auxiliary 2 percent fee for IPP, effective from the eleventh year of production (Rocha and Mendes 2023).

Finally, the Rovuma Basin Decree-Law creates a distinctive legal and contractual system concerning concessionaires engaged in existing exploration and production concession contracts and special purpose vehicles in the Rovuma Basin. This is a specialized framework formulated for natural gas liquefaction projects in Areas 1 and 4 of the basin. The model exploration and production concession contract of Mozambique, endorsed through Resolution No. 25/2016, aims to align the contract model with the predominant legal framework of the oil sector as prescribed by the Petroleum Law and its ancillary regulations (Mendes 2021).

While Mozambique has made strides in establishing a robust legal and regulatory framework for its extractive industries, continued efforts are needed to address governance gaps, promote transparency, and ensure sustainable development for all stakeholders, including local communities and the environment. The past two decades have witnessed increasing calls for improved transparency in resource management in Mozambique's extractive industry. This pressure led Mozambique to join the Extractive Industries Transparency Initiative (EITI) in 2009, achieving compliant status by 2012. Since its induction in EITI, Mozambique has compiled eight reports and heightened transparency by disclosing contracts related to natural resource concessions and fortifying institutions for administration, regulation, and accountability. Complimenting these changes is the escalating engagement of civil society in discussions about the role of Mozambique's natural resources in its economic development.

THE GEOPOLITICS OF LIQUIFIED NATURAL GAS AND THE CABO DELGADO INSURGENCY

Several factors have contributed to the resource curse in Mozambique. First, the discovery of natural resources potentially worsens existing social and economic disparities since the advantages of resource exploitation are often concentrated within a small elite (Ross 2012). In Mozambique, the government's failure to distribute the proceeds of natural gas extraction equitably has stoked animosity among rural groups, creating a fertile environment for recruiting insurgents (Hanlon 2017). Second, the availability of lucrative resources draws the attention of other players, such as transnational criminal networks and foreign governments, who may want to exploit the resources for their benefit (Le Billon 2001). Furthermore, the presence of Islamic State agents and the engagement of foreign fighters demonstrates that external objectives are increasingly pushing for war in Mozambique's LNG-rich enclave. Third, the natural gas discoveries have created a motive for insurgency, further destabilizing the region and resulting in several assaults on civilians, government troops, and foreign workers engaged in natural gas installations (Mukpo 2021).

Mozambique's ongoing insurgency, mainly in the Cabo Delgado region, is most significant to its potential LNG-driven development and has prompted concerns about the future of the industry and the security of its investments. Scholars and experts attribute the insurgency to poor socio-economic conditions and organized crime, particularly heroin trafficking in the region. However, the poor management of natural resources and its role in terrorism in Cabo Delgado is often overlooked. After all, as proponents of the "grievance theory" opine, socio-economic grievances experienced by the communities in Cabo Delgado provide the impetus to insurgency. The seminal work of Collier and Hoeffler (2004) posits that violent conflicts, like rebellions and insurgencies, may be explained by atypically severe grievances such as a lack of political rights, high inequality, or ethno-religious societal divisions. They established a strong positive correlation between the onset of armed conflict and the countries' dependence on readily exploitable natural resources (Collier and LaRoche 2015). They identified the predominant factor providing the grounds for the resource curse: the local population expects that the revenues be spent on better services, whereas corrupt officials prefer to channel federally administered funds to their personal coffers, thus creating conflict. Thus, the situation in Cabo Delgado exemplifies a structural basis for insurgency based on these dynamics.

The insurgency, Ansar Al-Sanah (known locally as Al-Shabab), traces back to 2015. The insurgency's ideology is entrenched in its radical rendition of Islam introduced to the region by former expats who returned to the country, having studied in Sudan, Saudi Arabia, and the Gulf states. Ansar Al-Sanah claims that Mozambique practices a corrupt form of Islam that fails to follow the authentic teachings of Muhammad. In the lead-up to the current insurgency, the group's members infiltrated mosques in the largely Muslim communities of Cabo Delgado, threatening worshippers into adopting the group's brand of Islam, consequently alienating large segments of the population. Fundamentally, the division between the group's Salafi ideology and the local Sufi interpretation of Islam lies beneath the tensions. Over time, the group would become increasingly violent, calling for broad administration of Sharia law and a cessation of recognizing the legitimacy of the Mozambican state (Brookings 2021).

Thousands of individuals have died because of the violence, and over seven hundred thousand people have been displaced. The insurgency has caused an estimated four thousand fatalities and exiled nearly one million individuals. Approximately four million people will likely face high levels of food insecurity due to the combined effects of climate disruptions and the conflict, which also threatens the economic potential of lucrative LNG investments in the region (Caux 2024). More than 60 percent of the population has been estimated to be impoverished, and the conflict in Cabo Delgado has displaced nearly one million people. The unrest in Cabo Delgado has hindered projected returns on investments in the LNG industry, and just one offshore project worth seven billion dollars has begun production (Marshall 2021). Larger projects worth more than fifty billion dollars are anticipated to begin production between 2026 and 2028, an almost two-year delay.

A series of interrelated factors, including wide-scale poverty, lack of economic opportunity, social marginalization, and seemingly vague promises of regional development through LNG projects, have collectively contributed to fueling the insurgency in Cabo Delgado (Mukpo 2021). The large number of disenfranchised, mainly younger, males in the region means that Ansar Al-Sanah has a large base from which to recruit, and much of the group's rhetoric is centered around the rampant inequality relating to the distribution of profits from previous and ongoing natural resource extraction in the area. The issue of economic and social disenfranchisement among this group has been further aggravated by the seizure of land for natural resource extraction projects, directly intensifying their grievances. The expropriation of land in the province for use by multinational companies has created consternation and social tension among the population, resulting in some farming and fishing communities being uprooted due to expedited legal procedures. Ansar al-Sanah has reportedly raised funds through the sale of illegal timber and rubies and through poaching animals and smuggling heroin bound for South African and European markets (*Club of Mozambique* 2018).

On the August 3, 2020, insurgents captured Mocímboa da Praia, representing a tremendous blow to the government's aspirations of rolling back the insurgency. Mocímboa da Praia remains instrumental in unlocking Mozambique's gas resources, being a center for supply for gas works activities. In January 2021, the insurgents came within half a mile of TotalEnergies' onshore gas infrastructure, prompting the company to suspend its gas projects and evacuate its staff. Since the beginning of the insurgency, nearly a million Mozambicans have been displaced, with many coalescing in larger metropolitan areas within Cabo Delgado and other nearby provinces (Meldrum 2021).

The violence in northern Cabo Delgado is symptomatic of a protracted history of capitalist infiltration into peripheral regions and LNG projects, and their incentives make the tense situation worse (Gaventa 2021). To comprehend the conflict, one must consider the geopolitical divisions in the region. Cabo Delgado is geographically and socially isolated from Mozambique's urban, economic, and political capital center, Maputo. This isolation is primarily a function of the nearly two-thousand-mile distance between the region. It is further compounded by the challenging transportation links and poor road infrastructure, making access between the two areas particularly challenging and time-consuming. Cabo Delgado's population is primarily rural and agrarian, a far cry from the vibrant urban metropolis of Maputo. Furthermore, the region is linguistically isolated as the population mainly speaks Swahili and other indigenous African languages, while Portuguese, the official language of Mozambique, is more commonly spoken in Maputo. Cabo Delgado's remote location has also restricted government presence and investment, contributing to socio-economic disparities compared to the more developed south (*Review of African Political Economy* 2021). Despite its symbolic significance in the national liberation struggle, Cabo Delgado has remained economically and politically disadvantaged. Recent gas developments have exacerbated this marginalization, as the province is plagued by high levels of destitution and restricted private investment. In addition, extremists are using monetary benefits and intimidation to recruit fighters by taking advantage of local communities' aversion to foreign investors and disillusionment with the government (Meek and Nene 2021).

The Cabo Delgado insurgency seriously impacts Mozambique's natural gas political economy. The escalating conflict has hindered the progress of natural gas projects involving large multinational companies in Mozambique, leading to doubts about the sustainability and potential to draw future investments in the country's natural gas sector. As mentioned earlier, the Cabo

Delgado region has a history of extractive ventures that failed to establish meaningful connections to the domestic economy (Toews and Vézina 2018). If the insurgency persists, the enclave LNG developments in northern Cabo Delgado will unlikely yield substantial benefits for the local community or bring about significant changes in the economic landscape of Mozambique.

INFORMATION ACCESS AND CITIZEN FEEDBACK IN MOZAMBIQUE'S RESOURCE SECTOR

Recently, Mozambican citizens have expressed displeasure at how natural gas projects are operated in Mozambique. Notably, protests have been against LNG projects in Mozambique, primarily driven by concerns over these projects' social and environmental impacts on local communities. Protests against French multinational TotalEnergies' Mozambique LNG project have been centered around the displacement of local communities, environmental degradation, and the potential negative impacts on fishing and agriculture. Protesters argue that the construction of the LNG plant and associated infrastructure has led to the forced relocation of communities, loss of fertile land, and destruction of natural habitats. In addition, concerns have been raised about pollution, water contamination, and the potential for oil spills in the region, which could have severe consequences for marine life and the livelihoods of local fishermen (France 24 2023).

Another concern voiced by Mozambican citizens is the lack of transparency and consultation in the decision-making process. Mozambicans argue that local communities have not been adequately involved in discussions and negotiations regarding the LNG projects, leading to a feeling of marginalization and a disregard for their rights and interests (Rawoot 2024). These protests have been met with varying responses from the government and the companies involved. While there have been efforts to address some of the protesters' concerns, including the establishment of compensation schemes and community development programs, many argue that these measures are insufficient and do not adequately address the underlying issues. The protests against LNG projects in Mozambique highlight the complex relationship between economic development, natural resource exploitation, and the rights of local communities. They reflect a growing awareness and demand for more sustainable and inclusive approaches to resource extraction, where the interests and well-being of local communities are considered (Rawoot 2024).

Increased access to information in Mozambique has resulted in changes in political dynamics and decision-making processes. For example, civil society organizations and the media have played critical roles in distributing information on the country's natural resources, raising public awareness, and demanding transparency in resource management (Pereira 2018). The launch of the EITI in Mozambique in 2012 is one example of knowledge-access and leadership incentives. This program intends to increase transparency and accountability in natural resource management by releasing information on extractive industry earnings (EITI 2022). Mozambique's government has proved its commitment to strengthening governance and combatting corruption in the extractive industry by joining the EITI.

Despite security concerns in Cabo Delgado's northern area, the EITI Board commended Mozambique for making substantial progress in efficiently implementing the EITI and resolving critical governance problems in the extractive sector. The EITI has been critical in encouraging public conversations on the allocation of extractive resources at the sub-national level, and the Multi-Stakeholder Group has contributed to policy formation, notably on the management of future gas earnings. The government's dedication to following up on corrective measures and EITI recommendations has resulted in better transparency and data management practices. Despite the interruptions created by the COVID-19 pandemic, Mozambique's EITI implementation has maintained communication with important stakeholders outside of the Multi-Stakeholder Group, including legislators, the media, and communities impacted by extractive operations. However, data availability remains difficult because most revealed information is still in static forms rather than open ones. Mozambique's modest overall score of 82.5 points in EITI implementation was upheld by the EITI Board in 2023, contributing to enhanced transparency in the mining and oil and gas sectors (EITI 2022). According to the chair of the EITI Board, Mozambique could play a vital role in the global energy transition, and its natural resources considerably contribute to domestic resource mobilization. Despite the challenging conditions, Mozambique has maintained its implementation efforts, increasing openness in state-owned firms critical to the country's extractive sector and economy (EITI 2022).

Transparency and accessibility of information regarding natural resources are crucial for ensuring that the benefits of resource development are distributed equitably and sustainably. Mozambique must ensure that information about its natural resources is readily available to the public and that the public has access to information about the allocation of resource revenues. This can be achieved by creating a public registry of resource contracts, the publication of regular reports on resource revenues, and establishing an independent oversight body to monitor the management of resources. For example, Mozambique has made immense strides toward contract transparency in the petroleum and mining industries. The country's 2014 petroleum and mining laws mandate that any contracts executed after the laws' approval be made public. Furthermore, the government made practically all contracts before 2014 public on official websites. These disclosures have proved important to scholars and civil society organizations as they give insights into the conditions of extractive projects and allow for future income predictions. Notwithstanding these successes, attempts to promote openness about the beneficial owners of oil, gas, and mining firms have been limited. To close this gap, the Mozambican government is working with partners to develop a legislative framework to make collecting and disclosing beneficial ownership information easier (EITI 2023). In addition, by raising awareness, transferring technology, and promoting best practices, international collaboration may be essential for ensuring that resource discoveries result in sustainable development. Finally, investment and commitment to accountability and development must be balanced by legislators. By controlling natural resources directly, authorities may put sustainability ahead of high growth and income by spending money on public goods like infrastructure, governance, and human capital. Regarding social policy, the government of Mozambique has worked toward ensuring that the benefits of natural resource discoveries are shared with local people. This has been accomplished by implementing local content standards, which demand that a set amount of extractive industry employment and contracts be awarded to Mozambican residents and firms (Tanner 2010).

Knowledge access and citizen feedback are critical in influencing incentive systems, especially in resource-rich countries like Mozambique. Access to information has the potential to alter resource distribution, decision-making processes, and political dynamics inside a nation. It plays a vital role in improving resource management by enabling data-driven decision-making, fostering stakeholder engagement, promoting transparency, and facilitating collaboration and knowledge sharing. It empowers individuals and organizations to make informed choices and implement sustainable practices, leading to better conservation and utilization of resources. Increased knowledge by citizens in Mozambique results in a greater understanding of the country's natural resources, such as natural gas, coal, and minerals, attracting international investment and spurring economic progress. By accessing relevant data on resource availability, usage patterns, environmental impacts, and socio-economic factors, citizens and decision-makers can develop more effective and evidence-based strategies for resource management. In addition, participatory approaches ensure that diverse perspectives and interests are considered, leading to more equitable and sustainable resource management outcomes (De Marchi and Ravetz 2001).

CONCLUSION

Mozambique stands at a critical juncture in its developmental trajectory, poised between the promise of its jackpot LNG windfall and the potential peril of the African resource curse. In order to escape the resource curse, Mozambique requires concerted efforts to address its governance deficits, address its security challenges in the form of the jihadist insurgency in Cabo Delgado, and reconcile regional and social fragmentation to harness benefits from its resources. The pathway to Mozambique's development is fraught with myriad challenges that can only be overcome by prudent leadership, a strategic vision, a democratic mass political culture, and regional and global support. Only then can Mozambique leverage its natural gas resources to foster equitable growth and realize its developmental aspirations.

REFERENCES

Brookings. 2021. "Mozambique's Al-Shabab Insurgency, and Local and International Responses." https://www.brookings.edu/events/mozambiques-al-shabab -insurgency-and-local-and-international-responses/, accessed August 13, 2023

BTI. 2022. "Mozambique Country Report." https://bti-project.org/en/reports/country -report?isocode=MOZ&cHash=1c790e6126566391e865f6e17fd9f919, accessed June 8, 2023.

Caux, Hélène. 2024. "Displaced People in Mozambique's Cabo Delgado Plead for Peace." UN High Commissioner for Refugees. https://www.unhcr.org/africa/ news/stories/displaced-people-mozambique-s-cabo-delgado-plead-peace, accessed March 13, 2024.

Club of Mozambique. 2018. "Mozambique: Islamists Funded by Illegal Trade in Timber and Rubies." https://clubofmozambique.com/news/mozambique-islamists -funded-by-illegal-trade-in-timber-and-rubies-aim-report/, accessed September 30, 2023.

Collier, Paul, and Anke Hoeffler. 2004. "Greed and Grievance in Civil War." *Oxford Economic Papers*, 56(4): 563–95.

Collier, P., and C. Laroche. 2015. "Natural Resources Do Not Need to Be a Curse (Part 2—Avoiding the Resource Curse)." International Growth Centre. June 8. https://www.theigc.org/blogs/natural-resources-do-not-need-be-curse-part-2 -avoiding-resource-curse, accessed June 25, 2024.

Cust, James, and Torfinn Harding. 2020. "Institutions and the Location of Oil Exploration." *Journal of the European Economic Association*, 18(3): 1321–50.

De Marchi, B., and J. R. Ravetz. 2001. *Participatory Approaches to Environmental Policy*. Cambridge, UK: Cambridge Research for the Environment.

Extractive Industries Transparency Initiative (EITI). 2023 "Mozambique Achieves Moderate Score in EITI Implementation." https://eiti.org/news/mozambique -achieves-moderate-score-eiti-implementation, accessed June 13, 2023.

Extractive Industries Transparency Initiative (EITI). 2022. "Mozambique 2022 Validation Report Assessment of Progress in Implementing the 2019 EITI Standard." https://eiti.org/documents/mozambique-2022-validation -report, accessed June 24, 2025.

Ferim, V. B. 2006. "An Investigation into the Role of Hegemons in Regional Politics: a Case Study of South Africa in the SADC Region." Doctoral dissertation, North-West University, South Africa.

Flanders Investment and Trade. 2021. "Oil and Gas Industry in Mozambique, Market Report." Brussels, Belgium.

Flower, A. 2021. "LNG in the Global Context." In *Monetizing Natural Gas in the New "New Deal" Economy*. Cham: Springer International Publishing.

France 24. 2022. "Climate Groups Call for Funding Withdrawal of TotalEnergies: Mozambique Project." https://www.france24.com/en/africa /20231117-climate-groups-call-for-funding-withdrawal-of-totalenergies -mozambique-project, accessed November 1, 2023.

Gaventa, J. 2021. "The Failure of 'Gas for Development'—Mozambique Case Study." Third Generation Environmentalism Ltd., London.

Hanlon, Joseph. 2017. "Following the Donor-Designed Path to Mozambique's US$2.2 Billion Secret Debt Deal." *Third World Quarterly*, 38(3): 753–70.

Hinojosa-Valencia, Leonith, Anthony Bebbington, Leonith Hinojosa, Denise Humphreys Bebbington, Maria Luisa Burneo, and Ximena Warnaars. 2008. "Contention and Ambiguity: Mining and the Possibilities of Development." *Development and Change*, 39(6): 887–914.

Kotsadam, Andreas, and Anja Tolonen. 2016. "African Mining, Gender, and Local Employment." *World Development*, 83: 325–39.

Le Billon, P., 2001. "The Political Ecology of War: Natural Resources and Armed Conflicts." *Political Geography*, 20(5): 561–84.

Macuane, Jose Jaime, and Carlos Muianga. 2020. "Natural Resources, Institutions, and Economic Transformation in Mozambique." Working Paper 2020/136, UN University World Institute for Development Economics Research.

Marshall, Will. 2021. "The Political Economy of Mozambique's 'Faceless Insurgency.'" *Global Risk Insights*. https://globalriskinsights.com/2021/04/the -political-economy-of-mozambiques-faceless-insurgency, accessed April 19, 2024.

Meek, S., and M. Nene. 2021. "Exploring Resource and Climate Drivers of Conflict in Northern Mozambique." *Policy Briefing*, 245.

Meldrum, Andrew. 2021. "Mozambique's Jihadists Force Total to Suspend Gas Project." https://apnews.com/article/international-news-islamic-state-group -mozambique-91fd3cfdfe7f279d10ccc63deabf5193, accessed February 22, 2022.

Mendes, T. A. 2021. "Mozambique Petroleum Legal Framework: Comparative Assessment of Mozambique Stabilization Clauses." Doctoral dissertation, Universidade Católica Portuguesa.

Mukpo, Ashoka. 2021. "Gas Fields and Jihad: Mozambique's Cabo Delgado Becomes a Resource-Rich War Zone." *Mongabay*. https://news.mongabay.com/2021/04/gas -fields-and-jihad-mozambiques-cabo-delgado-becomes-a-resource-rich-war-zone/, accessed September 13, 2023.

Mundi, Hardeep Singh, and Shailja Vashisht. 2023. "Cognitive Abilities and Financial Resilience: Evidence from an Emerging Market." *International Journal of Bank Marketing*, 41(5).

Palmer, Bob. 2023. "Oil Regulation: Mozambique" Lexicology Law Business Research, Mayer Brown. https://www.vda.pt/xms/files/05_Publicacoes/2023/ Livros/2023_Oil_Regulation_-_Mozambique.pdf, accessed June 25, 2024.

Pereira, R., 2018. "Assessing the implementation of the National Archives and Records Service Act at Eduardo Mondlane University in Mozambique." *ESARBICA Journal: Journal of the Eastern and Southern Africa Regional Branch of the International Council on Archives*, (37): 221–44.

Radionovich, R. G., and V. J. Jossias. 2021. "The Oil Industry in Mozambique: Brief Historical Overview of Oil Exploration in Mozambique." *Московский экономический журнал*, 12: 338–43.

Rawoot, Ilham. 2024. "Inside the Campaign to Stop the Largest Gas Projects in Africa." https://wagingnonviolence.org/2024/02/inside-campaign-to-stop -mozambique-lng/, accessed February 20, 2024.

Rocha, Paula Duarte, and Tiago Arouca Mendes. 2023. "Energy: Oil & Gas 2023." https://practiceguides.chambers.com/practice-guides/comparison/731/11346 /18421-18426-18437-18452-18455-18462, accessed February 22, 2023.

Ross, M. L. 2012. *The Oil Curse: How Petroleum Wealth Shapes the Development of Nations*. Princeton, NJ: Princeton University Press.

Salimo, P., L. Buur, and J. J. Macuane. 2020. "The Politics of Domestic Gas: The Sasol Natural Gas Deals in Mozambique." *The Extractive Industries and Society*, 7(4): 1219–29.

Schubert, J. 2020. "Willful Entanglements: Extractive Industries and the Co-Production of Sovereignty in Mozambique." *Ethnography*, 21(4): 537–58.

Tanner, C. 2010. "Land Rights and Enclosures: Implementing the Mozambican Land Law in Practice." In *Struggles over Land in Africa: Conflicts, Politics and Change*, edited by Ward Anseeeuw and Chris Alden, 105–30. Cape Town: Human Sciences Research Council.

Toews, Gerhard, and Pierre-Louis Vézina. 2018. "Why Natural Resource Finds Are More than Just a Curse: The Case of Mozambique." *The Conversation*. http: //theconversation.com/why-natural-resource-finds-are-more-than-just-a-curse-the -case-of-mozambique-93963, accessed April 10, 2023.

Uetela, P., and F. Obeng-Odoom. 2015. "Natural Gas and Socio-Economic Transformation in Mozambique." *The Journal of Energy and Development*, 41(1/2): 47–66.

Valoi, Estacio. 2016. "The Blood Rubies of Montepuez." *Foreign Policy*. https: //foreignpolicy.com/2016/05/03/the-blood-rubies-of-montepuez-mozambique -gemfields-illegal-mining/, accessed February 22, 2024.

World Bank. 2018. "Mozambique Economic Update: Less Poverty, but More Inequality." https://www.worldbank.org/en/country/mozambique/publication/ mozambique-economic-update-less-poverty-but-more-inequality, accessed June 11, 2023.

World Bank, 2015. Mozambique Energy Sector Policy Note. https://documents .worldbank.org/en/publication/documents-reports/documentdetail /135711468180536987/mozambique-energy-sector-policy-note, accessed June 11, 2023.

Yager, T. 2021. *The Mineral Industry of Mozambique*. Minerals Yearbook, 32–1 https: //www.usgs.gov/media/files/mineral-industry-mozambique-2016-pdf, accessed May 22, 2024.

Chapter 6

The Political Economy of Oil Discovery in Turkana, Kenya

Prospects and Challenges

Babere Kerata Chacha, Kenneth O. Nyangena, and Charles Okongo Imbiakha

Natural resources play a pivotal role in the economic development of developing nations, and Kenya is no exception. The discovery and exploitation of natural resources, especially in Africa, often become focal points for political maneuvering, with significant implications for the country's economic trajectory. The historical context of resource discovery in Kenya is deeply rooted in colonial legacies and post-independence struggles for resource control. During the colonial era, external powers exploited Kenya's resource wealth, setting the stage for subsequent political tensions (Okoth 2001). Consequently, Kenya's political landscape substantially influences the regulatory frameworks governing oil and mineral exploration and extraction.

The evolution of extractive laws and policies in Kenya reflects the government's response to changing political dynamics (Kibua 2015). Establishing regulatory bodies and formulating extractive policies have become arenas for political negotiation and influence. Key political figures, including government officials, politicians, and local leaders, play a crucial role in shaping the course of resource discoveries. Their involvement in licensing, allocation of extractive rights, and decision-making processes can either facilitate or hinder responsible resource exploration (Kagwanja 2018). The influence of political actors in the oil and mineral sectors also raises concerns about transparency, accountability, and the fair distribution of benefits.

The economic implications of resource discovery are, therefore, central to political discourse in Kenya. Political discussions and policy debates often

center around the themes of revenue generation, job creation, and infrastructure development that are intricately tied to extractive activities (Kaburu
2019). The distribution of economic benefits often becomes contentious,
highlighting the need for inclusive and sustainable practices. Local communities residing in areas with oil and mineral deposits are critical stakeholders
in the politics of resource discovery. However, their voices, which are often
marginalized in decision-making processes, are integral to understanding the
broader social impact of oil and mining activities (Ong'wen 2016).

With this background in mind, the recent discovery of oil reserves in
Turkana, Kenya, has sparked a complex political landscape characterized by
competing interests, power dynamics, and socio-economic implications. This
chapter delves into the intricate politics surrounding Kenya's oil discovery,
exploring the role of various stakeholders, the challenges posed, and the
potential ramifications for both local and national levels of governance. By
examining the social and political dynamics within Turkana's burgeoning oil
enclave, the chapter uncovers the transformative impact of foreign multinational corporations (MNCs) engaged in extensive extractive development and
activities that continually shape stakeholder interactions in the region.

Our argument posits that the expansion of enclave oil operations in
Turkana influences how citizenship is experienced and performed in the
region. It explores the many perspectives, challenges, and interactions of
rural African groups with enclave development within or adjacent to their
territories. In the context of rural communities residing near extractive sites, it
is worth examining the impact of enclave oil development on the emergence
of rearticulated forms of citizenship. These communities often rely on oil
firms to meet their economic and social requirements, leading to the complex
interplay between them.

This chapter is structured as follows. First, the chapter unpacks the dilemma
of "Turkana Tragedy" to illustrate how the Turkana people anticipated and
hoped that the nation's plentiful resources would raise living standards and
help the region's local population. The chapter then shows the dynamics of
political accountability and transparency, positioning the role of civil society
organizations and citizens in decision-making processes and the use of oil
revenues. We then delve into the social history of the Turkana people and how
this marginalized group emerged through colonial and post-colonial experiences. Furthermore, we explore how the debates and major arguments in the
literature on both national and international political economy have centered
on the role of MNCs in the developing world under the conceptual presuppo-
sitions of legitimacy theory and environmental justice theory. All this is done
to describe corporations' responsiveness to local external stimuli by questioning the concept of "social contract." Finally, we survey the background of
oil exploration in Turkana, showing how the multinational Tullow company

signed agreements with the Kenyan government and how its exclusion politics intersected with the ideals of the 2010 constitution and devolution praxis.

THE TURKANA TRAGEDY

"Now is the time to eat; God has heard us at last." This was the reaction of a marginalized pastoralist community in Turkana upon learning in 2012 that commercial oil reserves had been found in their county (Mkutu and Mdee 2020). It was anticipated and hoped that the nation's plentiful resources would help the local population in the region where they were extracted and provide tangible benefits. This windfall was accompanied by governance issues that impacted the application of laws and policies in sectors like the environment, culture, economy, security, and society. Implementing the 2010 constitution in Kenya ushered in a decentralized form of government, necessitating significant restructuring.

The discovery of oil deposits in the Turkana region of Kenya set off a chain of events that complicated the political environment, resulting in opposing interests, shifting power dynamics, and socio-economic repercussions. It raised concerns about the potential for the resource curse. This happens when resource-rich countries experience economic and political challenges, including corruption and mismanagement of revenues. In addition, Kenya has a diverse ethnic and regional landscape, which complicates the matter, as the distribution of oil wealth added a layer of complexity to existing tensions.

In contrast, local communities were worried about the potential negative impact on their livelihoods and balancing economic development with environmental sustainability. More importantly, there have been negotiations with oil companies on exploration and extraction rights. These negotiations often involved complex contracts and agreements, leading to debates about the terms and conditions, including the share of revenues allocated to the government and local communities. In addition, the issue of political accountability and transparency led civil society organizations and citizens to call for openness in decision-making processes and the use of oil revenues.

The history of the Turkana people has been tumultuous. Having been established as one of Kenya's most influential pre-colonial ethnic groups, they were soon to be seen by the Western anthropologists s as "a pool upon which the British drew migrant laborers and soldiers" and by colonialists as "backward pastoralists or noble savages" (Chacha 2009). At other times, they were virtually cut off from the market. Ochieng (1998) claims that the Turkana experienced crises of the worst kind in practically every decade of the twentieth century, changing from a wealthy, proud, and self-reliant pastoralist group into petty commodity peasants, cattle rustlers, and famine relief clients. Nevertheless, despite all of the capriciousness and disruptions, there has been one outstanding continuity: their unique history, intricate relationships with one another, and intriguing ways in which they have responded to the forces of change.

Both African and Africanist scholars have contributed significantly to the rapidly expanding field of Turkana history and anthropology by revealing intricate linguistic, ritual, agricultural, and social organization. They have also tended to work toward a theoretical and practical understanding of the process of politico-economic transformation. With a stronger hostility to land consolidation and registration, anthropologists have long viewed Turkana land as a "problem area" concerning "development," citing the low levels of production and poor-quality stocks on which they focus (Grim 1994). For instance, Ochieng (2005) states that the slow pace of economic development was due to Turkana's adherence to the ceremonial value system and the fact that most of their desires were for brides and cattle. The Turkana peasants are often stereotyped as staunch conservatives. However, this chapter dispels that notion and shows that the late nineteenth century saw the highest rate of economic change of any later era.

By carefully reading colonial literature, one can discern many viewpoints, particularly those that contrast the administrative approach with that of white settlers and missionaries, not to mention Africans. However, a superficial characterization of people based on their occupation, economic priorities, class, race, or even religion can be used to distort their contributions to knowledge or to determine the course of evolution. While each was unmistakably a product of its time and space, being sons of Anglican clerics, Huntingford and Louis Leakey, for example, were both of British ancestry and engaged in anthropological and ethnographic research during the 1920s and 1930s. It is striking that neither perfectly fit into any neat category of European society in colonial Kenya. They both occasionally took on tasks for the Kenyan government. They were always willing to share their knowledge of "local customs" whenever native authorities, uncaring settlers, or enthusiastic missionaries encountered mistrust or overt opposition. Massam (1968) admitted that the Turkana were pagans when he claimed that their religion was too nebulous to provide them with any defense against magic.

Like many other pastoralists in Kenya, the Turkana have long endured a torrent of negative and false perceptions and narratives that have harmed their well-being. These are determined by their means of subsistence, their surroundings, and their cultural customs. The marginalization, exclusion, and discrimination of this population are reflected in and contribute to significant stereotypes and myths.

According to Ochieng (1990), the Sessional Paper Number 10 of 1965, which was the foundation for later policy and the marginalization of dry regions, left compelling narratives about the arid and semi-arid lands. This encompasses the narrative of security, insecurity, and conflict that has been prolonged by the state of emergency. Specifically, the prevailing condition of insecurity has shaped perceptions of the region and its people, framing interactions with state institutions in similar terms, as noted by the author. The allocation of government funding predominantly favored security, law, and order in these sectors, often overlooking the importance of adhering to the rule of law (Ochieng 1990: 122). The overarching narrative that painted mobile pastoralism as irrational, unproductive, and environmentally harmful was comprehensive, touching on economic, socio-cultural, and environmental aspects.

ANALYTIC FRAMEWORK: MULTINATIONAL CORPORATIONS AND RESOURCE EXPLORATION IN AFRICA

This section provides an overview of local and global literature on the role of MNCs in oil exploration. During the past few decades, one of the major arguments in the literature on international political economy has centered on the role of MNC in the developing world. While critics of MNCs see them as key agents of the international economy, their advocates tend to see these enterprises as fighting the dragon of underdevelopment (Asogwa 2000). Additionally, legitimacy and environmental justice theories are applied in analyzing the region's socio-economic and environmental dimensions of oil exploration and extraction. Environmental justice theory focuses on the fair distribution of environmental benefits and burdens across different social groups. They particularly address the concerns of marginalized communities such as the Turkana.

Those who view MNCs as engines of development maintain that they contribute scarce resources, namely capital, technology, managerial, and marketing skills. Moreover, they create jobs and alleviate the balance of payment deficits of their host states. On the other hand, critics of MNC operations in developing nations claim that they harm the local economies of their host states (Chukwuemeka and Obingene 2002). They contend that when compared with domestic firms, MNCs destroy jobs because they employ capital-intensive technologies inaccessible in host developing countries.

Wright and McMahan (1992) noted that MNCs' technology transfer to less-developed countries seldom increases their exports as they have a tradition of placing business values above the host country's. In addition,

Robert (2001) reveals that MNCs alter social, economic, and political cleavages. MNCs control the main activities in exploring and exploiting natural resources in Africa. This is due to their substantial financial muscle and technical expertise in resource-related activities. Developing countries hope to reap benefits from engaging these corporations, and sometimes they do. However, this relationship has a downside in that their activities negatively affect the social and political stability of the people. Muigua (2018), while acknowledging that the place of MNCs in the global economy cannot be wished away, attempts to show how the engagement between developing countries and MNCs can be made more fruitful and mutually beneficial. Tirimba and Macharia (2014) argue that the benefits of MNCs in African countries are typically lost through transfer pricing to the main branches of the MNCs in the home countries.

Mena et al. (2010) contend that the stakeholder framework, which emphasizes striking a balance between the interests of MNCs' suppliers, shareholders, and management and those of their external stakeholders, such as governments and host communities, offers strong support for a broad approach to MNC governance mechanisms and accountability. Cadbury (2003) in addition, underlined the necessity of "aligning the interests of individuals, corporations, and society as nearly as possible." "The way ahead" for modern corporations "lies in ensuring that the fruits of good governance, its ability to add value, are widely and wisely shared, thus playing a positive part in the goal of the developed and developing world to alleviate poverty" (Cadbury 2003: 5).

Legitimacy theory is adopted in the literature to describe the responsiveness of corporations to local external stimuli by "implementing and developing voluntary social and environmental disclosure of information in order to fulfill their social contract," a contemporary necessity for their "survival in a jumpy and turbulent environment" (Burlea and Popa 2013: 1579). As a result, society's impression and perception of the organization (concerning the social, moral, and economic interests of the local stakeholders) are taken with utmost seriousness when it reports its activities for fear of being opposed or sanctioned by the local environment through boycott, social pressure, or legislative and judicial mechanisms. In political philosophy and legal theory, legitimacy is primarily discussed in two ways: normatively or legally, and descriptively or sociologically. According to Meyer and Sanklecha (2009), descriptive legitimacy looks at whether the people who are the focus of the relevant norm, policy, institution, or entity—such as the state or an organization—consider it to be legitimate. In the normative sense, legitimacy examines whether the notion satisfies specific requirements or prescriptions to determine whether the underlying assumption underpinning its descriptive sense is correct (Meyer and Sanklecha 2009: 2). Hurd (1999: 381) states that legitimacy is "the normative belief by an actor that a rule or institution ought to be obeyed." The definition of legitimacy provided by Suchman (1995: 574)—"a generalized perception or assumption that the actions of an entity are desirable, proper, or appropriate within some socially constructed system of norms, values, beliefs, and definitions"—is comparable to this definition in the descriptive or sociological sense. In the discussion that follows, this is the form of legitimacy that is at question.

In addition to legitimacy theory, stakeholder theory is useful for combining and considering the interests of many sites regarding the impact of business activity, which helps explain why MNCs in Africa lack environmental responsibility. The notion of stakeholders offers a basis for discerning the diverse cohorts and persons that are directly impacted by the environmental degradation of their host communities. This is especially important when considering the operations of extractive companies that exploit natural resources like gas and oil, which are known to have a detrimental effect on the environments in which they operate, particularly in places with weak governance and lax regulatory frameworks. In such circumstances, people and organizations in host communities will undoubtedly be very interested in halting the degradation of their surroundings and pursuing the appropriate remedies. These people and organizations make up the group of local stakeholders.

The current circumstances provide justification for adopting a human rights–centered approach to governing the operations of MNCs. However, the establishment of such a regulatory framework has encountered significant opposition and remains underdeveloped due to the fact that MNCs are non-state actors. Critics of MNCs pushing for increased public accountability highlight their substantial economic control. The aforementioned advocacy arises due to the perception that corporations, possessing significant economic influence, are able to elude public oversight and engage in activities that negatively impact employees, consumers, vulnerable communities, or the environment (Koenig-Archibugi 2019: 235). There is, therefore, a growing demand for enhanced transparency and responsibility inside MNCs (Eweje 2006).

BACKGROUND OF OIL EXPLOITATION IN TURKANA

Turkana is one of the forty-seven counties formed by the County Government's Act of 2012 of the Constitution of Kenya 2010. The county is located in the Rift Valley Province of Kenya. At seventy-seven-thousand square kilometers, Turkana is the second largest county, estimated to cover about 13 percent of Kenya's surface. This vast land has an economic advantage, for beneath its surface lie huge oil deposits that are currently being explored and will see extraction on an industrial scale in the years to come—which will raise hopes for a county with a population of slightly over one million. Turkana County stretches across nearly twenty-eight thousand miles of northwestern Kenya—a hot, arid region rife with conflict and short on infrastructure and social services. Among its largely pastoral population (over eight hundred thousand), 94 percent live in poverty and 87 percent are illiterate (with literacy rates for women a dismal 4 percent). In 2012, an exploratory group from British-based Tullow Oil tapped into gas and oil reserves on Turkana land, leaving the long-isolated region primed for change. Kenya's president hailed the discovery as "a major breakthrough," and the minister of energy proclaimed, "The resources will be used to transform Turkana County and lift the community from poverty" (Ackah-Baidoo 2012).

Lake Turkana, previously known as Lake Rudolf, is the preeminent characteristic and most significant natural resource within the basin and surrounding area. Lodwar, the most populous urban center in Turkana County, is estimated to have a population of around thirty-six thousand individuals (Horn Institute 2018). The climate of the Turkana region is characterized by a blend of arid conditions resembling a desert environment, together with sparse grasses. The region's inhospitable environment has consistently presented a significant obstacle to the progress of this locality, primarily favoring pastoralism as the principal economic activity involving cattle rearing, along with some involvement in camel, sheep, and goat husbandry. This is further supplemented by limited agricultural practices and reliance on fishing (Johannes, Zulu, and Kalipeni 2015).

The arid climate has precipitated a challenging existence for the indigenous communities residing within this geographical area. Scarce resources often give rise to conflicts, which commonly manifest as violent cross-border cattle raids originating from Uganda, Sudan, and Ethiopia. These conflicts mainly occur among pastoralist communities that compete for limited pasture, water, and livestock (Johannes, Zulu, and Kalipeni 2015). The national perceptions of Turkana County have undergone a transformation, shifting from being viewed as a place that was backward, neglected, and geographically isolated to now being recognized as a developing influential entity and a source of optimism for Kenya's overall progress and advancement.

Obonyo (2013) asserts that Kenya's oil and gas exploration dates back to 1903 in the era of the British colonial administration through to the 1960s when the first drilling was done on the Lamu Oil Basins. The biggest milestone in Kenya's oil and gas industry was achieved when massive crude oil deposits—estimated to be in millions of barrels—were discovered in the Eastern and Southern Lokichar Basin of Turkana County, North-Western Kenya (Obonyo 2013).

The discovery of crude oil deposits quickly attracted the attention of investors, among them being the British-affiliated Tullow Oil. On March 26, 2012, President Mwai Kibaki announced the discovery of oil in Turkana County by the Anglo-Irish firm (BBC 2012). The president described this as a new beginning on the journey to make Kenya an oil producer and major economic player internationally. Since this announcement, Turkana County has had feverish interest (Johannes, Zulu, and Kalipeni 2015).

Tullow was first visible in Kenya in 2010, after signing agreements with Africa Oil and Centric Energy to gain a 50 percent operating interest in five onshore licenses: 10BA, 10BB, 10A, 12A, and 13T. In 2012, Tullow Oil first discovered crude oil in the South Lokichar Basin at the Ngamia-1 well (Cordaid 2015). The Ngamia-1 exploration well in Kenya marked the start of a significant program of drilling activities across the area. The Ngamia-1 well successfully got over two hundred meters of oil pay, the second largest East Africa onshore tertiary rift basin opened by Tullow. Since then, exploration has been recorded in the South Lokichar Basin at the Amosing, Twiga, Etuko, Ekales-1, Agete, Ewoi, Ekunyuk, Etom, Erut, and Emekuya oil fields.

GOVERNMENT LEGISLATION ON MANAGEMENT OF NATURAL RESOURCES IN KENYA

Mineral legislation establishes the foundational framework for legal regulations concerning all extractive resources within Kenya. Hence, it is crucial to comprehensively examine the legislative framework governing the mineral sector prior to engaging with the legislation pertaining to Kenya's oil sector. According to Mining Act No. 12 of 2016, mineral rights holders must prioritize, to the greatest extent feasible, the utilization of resources, products, services, and manpower originating from Kenya. Additionally, mineral rights holders must present thorough programs on recruiting and training of Kenyans. The granting of mineral rights is contingent on the approval of this scheme. According to Ackah-Baidoo (2012), the legislation allows individuals with mineral rights to establish a comprehensive community development agreement. This agreement aims to ensure socially responsible investment and prioritize employment opportunities for residents living in close proximity to mining operations. In general, the regulation of mineral activities encompasses a range of legislative acts that govern several stages, including exploration and mining. These acts typically involve the issuance of permits or licenses for exploration, as well as leases, licenses, or concessions for production or mining during the full lifespan of a mine.

Conversely, mineral rights typically confer to the possessor the authority to explore and exploit a certain region for a specified duration. The move from exploration to mining is contingent upon identifying natural resources in economically viable amounts. According to the findings of Dale (2012), individuals can obtain mineral rights, transfer them, and potentially have them revoked, but only in strict adherence to legal regulations. The author additionally asserts that the expropriation of their property in accordance with this legislation can only take place for reasons that benefit the public and must involve the fair and reasonable compensation of the affected parties. This idea and its perspective provide evidence by referencing the civil law systems of certain Latin American nations, which have embraced the concept of treating mineral rights as tangible assets, attracting interest from international investors (MacEachern et al. 2010).

Kenya greatly benefits from ratifying regional and global pacts that underpin its commitment to its national policy framework. The current legal and policy framework for oil and gas in Kenya includes both existing and proposed laws and policies, divided between what existed before the discovery of oil in 2012 and that which has been drafted after the discovery (Cordaid 2015). The 2010 Constitution of Kenya is the primary and the most important legal and policy document that enshrines national legislation on managing natural resources in the country. Article 62 of the constitution states that all extractive resources, as defined by law, are public land, which shall vest in and be held by the central government in trust for the Kenyan people and shall be administered on their behalf by the National Land Commission. It follows that oil and gas resources are vested in the national government in trust for the people of Kenya.

Further, the obligation to share benefits derived from natural resources is anchored on Article 102 of the constitution, which implores the state to ensure sustainable exploitation, utilization, management, and conservation of the environment and natural resources and ensure equal sharing of the benefits. These obligations are further stipulated in the Petroleum Bill, which specifies the exact percentage of petroleum revenue that shall be shared between the national government, the county government, and the local community. The Petroleum Bill also establishes a sovereign wealth fund, which obliges the Kenyan government to pay at least 5 percent of its revenue share into it. A 2015 report by the Cordaid Group titled the "Assessment of Community Perceptions of Oil Exploration in Turkana County, Kenya," gives an elaborate formula on the percentage of revenue that shall be shared between the national and county governments and the local community as follows:

- 75 percent of the revenue goes to the national government;
- 20 percent of the revenue to go to the county government—this amount should not be more than double the amount allocated to that county by the Commission on Revenue Allocation;

- 5 percent to the local community—provided this amount does not exceed a quarter of the amount allocated to that county by the Commission on Revenue Allocation.

Aside from the constitution, there exist several other pieces of legislation relevant to oil exploration that include:

(i) The Petroleum Exploration and Production Act 1986
(ii) Subsidiary Legislation under the Petroleum Act
(iii) Petroleum Exploration and Production Regulations 1984
(iv) Petroleum Exploration and Production (Training Fund) Regulations 2006
(v) the Environment Management and Coordination Act 1999 (Cordaid 2015)

Proposed legislations include the Petroleum (Exploration, Development, and Production) Bill 2015; Petroleum Exploration, Development, and Production Local Content Regulations; The National Sovereign Wealth Fund Bill 2014; and the National Energy and Petroleum Policy 2015. Another critical piece of legislation is the Community Land Bill 2014, which addresses the question of compensation for land that is used by oil and gas companies (Cordaid 2015). It is important to note that although the "footprint" of specific oil exploration and production facilities (including good pads and campsites) is generally small, there are all the associated facilities (residential, educational, market, and recreational), as well as access roads for those working on the oil exploration/production sites, which take up much larger areas of land (Horn Institute 2018).

Moreover, the land needed for pipelines (even if buried for safety purposes and kept to a minimum width) will be permanently taken over, through a way-leave that gives the company a "right of way" over community land. According to international standards, compensation is compulsory for this type of land takeover (Cordaid 2015). At the county level, the Turkana County Government also has legislation on managing oil discovery in the county. Based on the 2010 constitution, the devolution process offers significant governance and revenue-sharing opportunities (as well as challenges) related to natural resources management, including oil (Institute of Development Studies 2017).

County government institutions in Turkana are relevant to oil exploration, and include the county Ministries of Environment, Energy and Natural Resources; Land, Physical Planning and Urban Areas; and Finance and Economic Planning that deal with revenue collection and distribution. The work of these institutions complements the work of the national government to ensure oil discovery in Turkana brings social and economic benefits to the grassroots. In addition, the county assembly has a specialized committee on energy and natural resources to oversee the operations of Tullow and other oil actors in Turkana County.

THE KENYAN CONTEXT: TURKANA OIL "CURSE"

A historical examination reveals resource exploitation and mismanagement patterns, shaping Kenya's current state. The colonial legacy of resource extraction and post-independence struggles for control have left lasting imprints on the nation's mineral sector (Nyamóngo 2005). The resource curse is intricately linked to governance challenges in Kenya. Corruption, lack of transparency, and inadequate regulatory frameworks have contributed to the mismanagement of natural resources (UN Economic Commission for Africa 2015).

Weak institutions and political interference further exacerbate the problem, hindering effective resource governance. While resource wealth holds the promise of economic development, the resource curse often results in economic instability. Over reliance on volatile commodity prices, the "Dutch disease" phenomenon, and unequal distribution of wealth create economic imbalances (World Bank 2019). The failure to diversify the economy and invest in other sectors leaves the country vulnerable to the fluctuations of the global commodities market.

The resource curse in Kenya has profound socio-economic consequences, affecting local communities and exacerbating existing inequalities. Displacement, environmental degradation, and social tensions arise from the uneven distribution of benefits and the neglect of community interests (Sifuna 2017). The failure to integrate local communities into decision-making processes further compounds these challenges.

To integrate effectively with the local Turkana community, Tullow Oil has implemented various strategies to actively include and interact with the communities residing in the regions where it operates. In 2010, Tullow assumed operational control from Africa Oil. Subsequently, an association known as the Lokichar Basin Development Committee was established, consisting of eleven representatives from local communities, the national government, and Tullow. This committee oversaw the social investment relationship with all communities in Block 10BB (Cordaid 2015). Tullow employed a team of approximately thirty community liaison officers (CLOs) to engage with local people in Turkana. These CLOs were responsible for overseeing operations in the three oil exploration blocks, namely 10BA, 10BB, and 13T, encompassing the regions of Turkana North, East, and South (Kisero 2012). The approach to community engagement might be likened to a reactive strategy, where CLOs constantly address one issue after another, leaving little room for comprehensive community awareness and meaningful interaction.

In recent times, Tullow has indicated a shift in its community engagement methodology, wherein it is presently formulating a novel and more structured "field stakeholder engagement strategy." This entails implementing modifications to the structure and enhancing the education of CLOs, who have been rebranded as field stakeholder engagement officers, as well as community communications officers, government and public affairs officers, village socialization officers, and other individuals comprising the "social performance" team (Cordaid 2015). Moreover, the revised approach encompasses an enhanced grievance mechanism featuring a proactive cohort of data collectors and a pledge to address complaints within a thirty-day time frame. Additionally, it incorporates a comprehensive outreach initiative targeting both rural and urban areas, which emphasizes the collection and dissemination of information and prioritizes active listening and comprehension.

The oil business has a unique prospect for mitigating unemployment and poverty. The proclivity of parties, such as the government, to make exaggerated commitments and subsequently fail to fulfill them poses significant dangers that may result in heightened disillusionment with the oil business inside the Turkana region (Johannes, Zulu, and Kalipeni 2015). The individuals residing in the Turkana region, who were previously assured of securing prominent roles within Tullow Oil operations, were ultimately assigned to low-skilled employment, such as traffic marshals, which provided remuneration below five hundred Kenyan shillings (equivalent to six US dollars) per day. The discovery of oil in Turkana County has resulted in heightened polarization among various ethnic groups, exacerbating existing competition and violent conflicts over the control of water sources and grazing grounds. It has also strained the relationship between customary and contemporary land-tenure systems, leading to increasing tension. Instances of such warfare have been documented in the oil-abundant regions of Turkana, specifically in the vicinity of Ngamia 1 (Survey 2012).

According to Johannes, Zulu, and Kalipeni (2015), the oil discovery in Turkana County has generated interest among individuals who are not inhabitants of the area. The historically disenfranchised native community in Turkana has expressed apprehension about the potential consequences of the oil discovery, fearing that it may exacerbate their social and economic marginalization. Recent research indicates that there is a growing body of data suggesting that local populations have been marginalized and disenfranchised from participating in decision-making processes related to the oil industry. Residents of Turkana are dealing with a variety of issues, some of which include land grabs by those who are seen as being from "outside," widespread corruption, and competition between different ethnic groups.

All of these problems, along with others, might lead to full-blown violent conflicts, including those between different ethnic groups, between Turkana County and the government, and between Turkana County and investors or Tullow Oil.

According to Kisero (2012), the Turkana community perceives a sense of exploitation by government officials at the national level who are poised to gain advantages from Kenya's oil finds while disregarding the marginalized Turkana population. Numerous indigenous herders residing in Turkana express concerns regarding the potential emergence of external and internal conflicts resulting from oil findings. They believe the Kenyan government has neglected its involvement in crucial decision-making procedures about land transactions, local job opportunities, oil-related licensing, and contractual agreements. The local populace was not adequately notified about the discovery of oil; their awareness of it was primarily derived from news and media coverage (Johannes, Zulu, and Kalipeni 2015).

Most revenue is directed toward Nairobi, resulting in disproportionate benefits for other regions of the country, while the Turkana region is left with limited economic opportunities. There is widespread concern regarding the potential mobilization of individuals who seek to assert their perceived entitlements, which could lead to confrontations with government authorities due to long-standing distrust and perceived grievances against the government. Additionally, if oil revenue management is inadequate, there is a risk of conflicts arising between ethnic groups (Ndanyi 2012). Moreover, there is a burgeoning apprehension regarding the potential loss of land, particularly in light of the ongoing privatization of land to external entities, which runs counter to the customary system that governs pastoral areas and exclusively acknowledges communal ownership and utilization. The current process of land privatization fails to acknowledge the adverse consequences on pastoralists and their entitlements, exacerbating the potential for further conflict within an unstable region (Johannes, Zulu, and Kalipeni 2015).

A legal center in Kenya known as Kituo cha Sheria, which offers guidance on problems relating to human rights to empower the poor and disadvantaged, discovered that the exploration efforts in Turkana County resulted in some observable advancements (Johannes, Zulu, and Kalipeni 2015). These improvements are seen as blessings to the wider community and the county (Horn Institute 2018). They include infrastructure such as transportation and communication, social amenities such as schools and hospitals, and economic advantages such as small-scale trade.

On the other hand, Turkana residents firmly believe in oil development potential. Still, they are less convinced whether exploration and appraisal activities have yielded dividends (Institute of Development Studies 2017). Crude oil drilling requires a lot of water. It is even problematic in places where water is scarce (Zabbey and Olsson 2017). Tullow has been using hydraulic fracturing in Turkana County that produces large quantities of wastewater that sometimes may contain harmful dissolved chemicals and other hazardous products.

INCLUSION AND EXCLUSION POLITICS: THE 2010 CONSTITUTION AND DEVOLUTION

Turkana County has been the nation's major hub for oil exploration efforts. The discovery of oil in Turkana sparked optimism for the region's economy and prosperity, but it also created problems with inclusion, resource distribution, and equitable benefit-sharing. The question of land rights and community participation in decision-making processes is one important component. Like many other indigenous communities across the world, the Turkana people have had difficulty getting their opinions heard when it comes to issues involving the exploitation of resources on their territories. Concerns have been raised over the possible environmental effects of oil exploration on the nearby ecosystems and the Turkana people's way of life. Politics of inclusion and exclusion are frequently at the core of these problems. Fair representation, involvement, and benefit-sharing between the government, oil firms, and local people are frequently contested issues. Kenya's constitution, especially the 2010 version, strongly emphasizes local governance and devolution to guarantee that people have a voice in distributing and managing resources in their areas. But putting these constitutional ideals into practice can be difficult, and there may be times when some communities feel left out or underrepresented when making decisions about resource extraction.

Kenya has been under a highly centralized government system for over half a century that resulted in the political and economic exclusion of many ethnic communities while bringing about inequitable political and economic benefits to a few individuals hailing from specific ethnic communities. The 2010 constitution, as a result, introduced a devolved system, among others, to do away with such a political system and culture of exclusion. Relations among some ethnic communities in Kenya have been characterized by deep animosity and suspicion, which heighten during election periods. This is so mainly because individuals hailing from a few ethnic communities dominated the country's political structures and economic resources, to the exclusion of other communities, both before and after Kenya became an independent country. The people in authority used the state apparatus to benefit themselves, their kin, their friends, and their regions economically. The exclusion was exacerbated as the country increasingly became centralized, contributing to intermittent conflicts, which often occur following general elections, the worst being the 2007 post-election violence. Kenya adopted a new constitution in 2010 with a view, among other things, to curbing this decades-long interethnic animosity.

We argue that by creating forty-seven counties and sub-national territorial and political units, the 2010 Kenyan constitution enhanced the opportunities for the political inclusion of hitherto excluded communities. Moreover, the 2013 election results show that several previously excluded communities have become represented at the county level and have gained control of one or more of the counties where they form the majority. The system of devolution that Kenya adopted has not, however, entirely done away with the possibility of some ethnic communities being excluded. Several ethnic communities now form a new minority at the intracounty level since the devolved system has not provided a county for each territorially structured ethnic community. Moreover, many who have migrated from what traditionally would have been viewed as their "home county" to other counties now form intracounty minorities. Practice shows a trend in which the communities forming the majority in some counties are excluding those who are in the minority in those counties. Furthermore, the national executive still retains significant political and economic clout and hitherto excluded communities are not guaranteed representation.

The political exclusion of and economic discrimination against the various ethnic communities and the urgency to curb these problems triggered persistent demands for constitutional reform in the 1980s. At the center of the call for constitutional reform was the demand to remove and replace the centralized government system with a decentralized one. There was an even stronger demand for equitable representation of all regions and communities in the national government, which had been the domain of a few communities and individuals. These demands could not be ignored after the 2007 post-election violence. Thus, serious moves were begun toward constitutional reform, resulting in the adopting of the 2010 constitution. The constitution, among other things, introduced a devolved system of government composed of forty-seven counties and a national government.

However, at the beginning, most Turkana residents feared that an influx of investors and prospectors would disrupt their livelihoods and exacerbate corruption, environmental degradation, and tribal conflict. Tullow failed to engage the community before it began production and was met with resistance and hostility. The Kenya Land Alliance and Friends of Lake Turkana, both Ford partners, stepped in to educate residents about land rights and protections granted by the constitution, and they helped establish the Community Parliament as a forum for airing grievances, sharing information, and organizing (Côte and Korf 2018). Tensions came to a head in late 2013, when locals staged demonstrations arguing that they were being overlooked for employment and contracts (Hall et al. 2017). Tullow suspended operations to review its policies and ultimately agreed to double its social investment in the region and offer more advanced training to locals so they might qualify for higher cadre jobs (Lind 2018).

With such support from Ford partners, local leaders have made numerous inroads over time. Tullow has now instituted systems to address community concerns, build relationships, and understand local needs and challenges, and it has established community centers where local people can engage with the company and register grievances. In addition, Tullow is now involved in social investment projects throughout Turkana related to health, environment, education, and water (Tyce 2020).

Within such discourses, community members residing in or near extractive sites are referred to as stakeholders or beneficiaries (Eweje 2007). Such language is impartial and apolitical, overlooking complicated and shifting relationships between social groups in and around sites of extraction. Our analysis takes the power-laden relationships between corporate actors and rural communities seriously, starting with the fact that private companies have emerged as competitors with the state for providing protection to citizens (Isin and Nyers 2014).

CONCLUSION

Through an examination of the dynamic social and political dynamics within Turkana's burgeoning oil enclave, we have been able to demonstrate an analysis that uncovers the transformative impact of foreign corporations engaged in extensive extractive development as well as activities that continually reshape the interactions among important stakeholders in the region. More concretely, our argument posits that the expansion of enclave oil operations in Turkana is exerting an influence on how citizenship is both experienced and performed in the region. The literature (Ackah-Baidoo 2012; Ferguson 2005; 2006; Le Billon 2004; 2005; MacEachern et al. 2010) explores the many perspectives, challenges, and interactions of rural African groups with enclave development within or adjacent to their territories. In rural communities residing near extractive sites, it is worth examining the impact of enclave oil development on the emergence of rearticulated forms of citizenship. These communities often rely on oil firms to meet their economic and social requirements, leading to a complex interplay between them.

Therefore, this study contributes novel viewpoints to the ongoing discussions regarding the tactics employed by significant external capital to delineate and subsequently establish control over resources for extraction in regions where the influence of a central governing body is relatively minimal (Côte and Korf 2018; Peluso and Lund 2011; Rasmussen and Lund 2018; Sikor and Lund 2009). Significantly, there is a current trend of making substantial expenditures in resources and the accompanying infrastructure in regions where governance has traditionally been managed through hybrid structures that prominently engage locally trusted institutions (Boege, Brown, and Clements 2009; Hönke 2012). It is postulated that the investment in oil activities will be accompanied by an augmented governmental presence, potentially fostering a reconfiguration of local governance relations and institutions. According to Watts (2001: 207), the author argues that the "strategic and economic influence of oil serves to intensify and magnify the prominence, or more precisely, the perceptibility, of the state in public affairs, as well as that of transnational capital in society."

In sum, the proliferation of oil operations in isolated rural regions, propelled by political and economic motivations and the subsequent introduction of new resource valuations, have significant implications for the political landscape and conflicts near these newly established installations and infrastructure. These effects persist regardless of the effectiveness of an enclave model. The oil finding in Turkana is characterized by a multitude of intricate and interrelated political factors, which embrace various dimensions, including economic, social, environmental, and geopolitical aspects. Through the utilization of openness, inclusion, and a steadfast dedication to the well-being of all parties involved, Kenya can effectively leverage the potential advantages associated with oil while simultaneously mitigating the risks and conflicts that may arise. The prioritization of reconciling the interests of various stakeholders is crucial to guarantee that the oil discovery effectively contributes to the holistic advancement and stability of the nation.

REFERENCES

Ackah-Baidoo, Abigail. 2012. "Enclave Development and 'Offshore Corporate Social Responsibility': Implications for Oil-Rich Sub-Saharan Africa." *Resources Policy*, 37(2): 152–59.

Ake, C. 1981. *African Political Economy*. Essex: Longman Group.

Asogwa, J. 2000. *African Traditional Economies and Their Transformation*. Farnham, UKL Ashgate Publishing.

BBC. 2012. "Kenya Oil Discovery after Tullow Oil Drilling." https://www.bbc.com/news/world-africa-17513488, accessed August 30, 2023.

Boege, Volker, M. Anne Brown, and Kevin P. Clements. 2009. "Hybrid Political Orders, not Fragile States." *Peace Review*, 21(1): 13–21.

Burlea, S., and L. Popa. 2013. "The Transition to Democracy in Africa: Challenges and Opportunities." *Journal of African Development*, 1579.

Cadbury, W. 2003. *The Humanitarian Impulse: NGOs and the Refugee Crisis in Africa*. Westport, CT: Praeger Publishers.

Chacha, B. K. 2009. "Agricultural History of the Abakuria of Kenya from the End of the Nineteenth Century to the Mid-1970s." Masters thesis, Egerton University.

Chukwuemeka, E., and A. Obingene. 2002. *International Politics, A Contemporary Perspective*. Enugu: JTC Publishers.

Cordaid. 2015. *Oil Exploration in Kenya: Success Requires Consultation: Assessment of Community Perceptions of Oil Exploration in Turkana County, Kenya*. Annual Report, August.

Côte, Muriel, and Benedikt Korf. 2018. "Making Concessions: Extractive Enclaves, Entangled Capitalism and Regulative Pluralism at the Gold Mining Frontier in Burkina Faso." *World Development*, 101: 466–76.

Dale, R. 2012. *Development in Africa: Governance and Policy Reform in the Global Era*. Boulder, CO: Lynne Rienner Publishers.

Eweje, G. 2006. *Sustainable Development in Africa: Challenges and Opportunities*. Cheltenham, UK: Edward Elgar Publishing.

Eweje, G. 2007. *African Development: Economic, Social and Political Dimensions*. London: Palgrave Macmillan.

Ferguson, J. 2005. *Global Shadows: Africa in the Neoliberal World Order*. Durham, NC: Duke University Press.

Ferguson, J. 2006. *Expectations of Modernity: Myths and Meanings of Urban Life on the Zambian Copperbelt*. Berkeley: University of California Press.

Grim, B. J. 1994. *Economics of Agricultural Development in Kenya*. Lanham, MD: University Press of America.

Hall, Damon M., Gerardo R. Camilo, Rebecca K. Tonietto, Jeff Ollerton, Karin Ahrné, Mike Arduser, John S. Ascher, et al. 2017. "The City as a Refuge for Insect Pollinators." *Conservation Biology*, 31(1): 24–29.

Hönke, Jana. 2012. "Multinationals and Security Governance in the Community: Participation, Discipline and Indirect Rule." *Journal of Intervention and State-building*, (6): 57–73.

Horn Institute. 2018. "The Negative Impacts of Oil Exploration and Discovery on the Turkana Community." Horn Policy Brief 10, Nairobi. https://horninstitute.org /wp-content/uploads/2019/02/No.-10-The-Negative-Impacts-of-Oil-Exploration -and-Discovery-on-the-Turkana-Community-Spreads.pdf, accessed September 30, 2023.

Hurd, T. 1999. "Legitimacy and Authority in International Politics." *International Organization*, 53(2): 379–408.

Institute of Development Studies. 2017. "Governing Black Gold: Lessons from Oil finds in Turkana, Kenya." Research Briefing, Brighton, UK.

Isin, E. F., and P. Nyers. 2014. *Routledge Handbook of Global Citizenship Studies*. London: Routledge.

Johannes, Eliza M., Leo C. Zulu, and Ezekiel Kalipeni. 2015. "Oil Discovery in Turkana County, Kenya: A Source of Conflict or Development?" *African Geographical Review*, 34(2): 142–64.

Kaburu, W. 2019. *Police Reforms in Kenya: The Politics of the Implementation Process*. Durban, South Africa: African Centre for the Constructive Resolution of Disputes (ACCORD).

Kagwanja, P. 2018. *Kenya's Uncertain Democracy: The Electoral Crisis of 2007*. London: Routledge.

Kibua, T. N. 2015. *Economic Policy and Administration in Kenya*. Nairobi: University of Nairobi Press.

Kisero, J. 2012. "Minister's Firm Sold Turkana Oil Block for Sh800m." *Daily Nation*.https://nation.africa/kenya/news/minister-s-firm-sold-turkana-oil-block-for -sh800m--805954, accessed March 1, 2024.

Koenig-Archibugi, M. 2019. "Global Governance." In *The Handbook of Globalisation*, 3rd ed., edited by Jonathan Michie, 334–46. Cheltenham, UK: Edward Elgar Publishing.

Le Billon, Philippe. 2004. *The Geopolitical Economy of Resource Wars*. New York: Routledge.

Le Billon, P. 2005. *Geopolitics of Resource Wars: Resource Dependence, Governance and Violence*. London: Routledge.

Lind, J. 2018. *Governance and Livelihoods in East Africa: Transformations in Agrarian Systems*. London: Routledge.

MacEachern, J., George Pemberton, Murray Gingras, and Kerrie Bann. 2010. "Ichnology and Facies Models." *Facies Models*, 4: 19–58.

Massam, B. H. 1968. *Colonial Rule and African Political Development in Kenya*. Oxford: Oxford University Press.

Mena, M., W. R.Ochieng, and D. M. Anderson. 2010. *Kenya: The Struggle for Democracy*. London: Zed Books.

Meyer, J. W., and M. Sanklecha. 2009. *Globalization and Governance in Africa: Transformations in Political Authority*. London: Palgrave Macmillan.

Mkutu, Kennedy, and Anna Mdee. 2020. "Conservancies, Conflict and Dispossession: The Winners and Losers of Oil Exploration in Turkana, Kenya." *African Studies Review* 4: 831–57.

Muigua, Kariuki. 2018. "Securing the Realization of Environmental and Social Rights for Persons with Disabilities in Kenya." *Journal of CMSD*, 2(1).

Ndanyi, J. 2012. *Land Reforms and Agricultural Development in Kenya: A Historical Perspective*. Nairobi: East African Publishers.

Nyamongo, I. 2005. *Health, Disease and Healthcare in Africa: Ethnographic Approaches*. Farnham, UK: Ashgate Publishing.

Obonyo, J. 2013. "Influence of Oil Exploration on the Livelihoods of the Turkana Community: A Study of Tullow Oil Company in Lokichar Location of South Turkana Sub-County." University of Nairobi, Nairobi.

Ochieng, W. R. 1990. *Themes in Kenyan History*. Nairobi: East African Educational Publishers.

Ochieng, W. R. 1998. *Historical Studies and Social Change in Western Kenya*. Nairobi: East African Educational Publishers.

Ochieng, W.R. 2005. *Decolonization and Independence in Kenya, 1940–93*. Melton, UK: James Currey Publishers.

Okoth, A. 2001. *A History of Africa: African Nationalism and the De-colonisation Process*. Nairobi: East African Publishers.

Ong'wen, O. 2016. *The State and the Kenyan Economy: An Institutional Perspective*. Berlin: Heinrich Böll Foundation.

Peluso, Nancy Lee, and Christian Lund. 2011. "New Frontiers of Land Control: Introduction." *Journal of Peasant Studies*, 38(4): 667–81.

Rasmussen, Mattias Borg, and Christian Lund. 2018. "Reconfiguring Frontier Spaces: The Territorialization of Resource Control." *World Development*, 101: 388–99.

Robert, S. 2001. *The Politics of Transition in Africa: State, Society and Economic Transformation in Kenya*. London: Routledge.

Sifuna, D. 2017. *Education and Development in Kenya: Historical Perspectives and Contemporary Challenges*. Nairobi: University of Nairobi Press.

Sikor, Thomas, and Christian Lund. 2009. "Special Issue: Access and Property: A Question of Power and Authority." *Development and Change*, 40.

Suchman, M.C. 1995. "Managing Legitimacy: Strategic and Institutional Approaches." *Academy of Management Review* 20(3): 571–610.

Survey, K. 2012. "Kenya Population and Housing Census 2012." Kenya National Bureau of Statistics.

Tirimba, Ondabu Ibrahim, and George Munene Macharia. 2014. "Economic Impact of MNCs on Development of Developing Nations." *International Journal of Scientific and Research Publications*, 4(9): 1–6.

Tyce, M. 2020. "The Kenyan National Treasury: A 'Pocket of Effectiveness' Curtailed." ESID Working Paper 150, University of Manchester. https://papers.ssrn.com/sol3/papers.cfm?abstract_id=3661612, accessed July 16, 2024.

UN Economic Commission for Africa. 2015. "Economic Report on Africa 2015: Industrializing through Trade." United Nations. https://repository.uneca.org/handle/10855/22767, accessed July 16, 2024.

Watts, Michael. 2001. "Petro-Violence: Community, Extraction, and Political Ecology of a Mythic Commodity." *Violent Environments*, 189–212.

World Bank. 2019. "Kenya Economic Update: Transforming Agricultural Productivity to Achieve Food Security for All." https://www.worldbank.org/en/country/kenya/publication/kenya-economic-update-transforming-agricultural-productivity-to-achieve-food-security-for-all, accessed June 25, 2024.

Wright, Patrick M., and Gary C. McMahan. 1992. "Theoretical Perspectives for Strategic Human Resource Management." *Journal of Management*, 18(2): 295–320.

Zabbey, Nenibarini, and Gustaf Olsson. 2017. "Conflicts–Oil Exploration and Water." *Global Challenges*, 1(5).

Chapter 7

Cameroon's Extractive Revival

The New Policy on Mineral Exploitation

Fernand Guevara Mekongo-Mballa, Parfait Oumba, and Angela Zivo Gapa

December 22, 2023, marked the date of the official preparatory works related to the exploitation of the transboundary Mbalam-Nabeba iron ore deposit between Cameroon and Congo under the aegis of the Hong Kong–based firm Bestway. This project is the flagship of Cameroon's new mining policy. It is expected to generate twenty-five billion US dollars in royalties and various taxes to the state and decentralized local administrative units over a fifty-year period. Correspondingly, ten thousand direct and indirect jobs and subcontracts for local companies are expected. Earlier in the year, two other projects related to mineral resources exploitation were also launched: one related to the iron ore deposit in the locality of Kribi-Lobé under the aegis of the Chinese company Sinosteel SA, and another related to iron in the locality of Grand-Zambi, under the aegis of the Cameroonian company G-Stone (Ndouyou 2023; *Business in Cameroon* 2023). These projects are the realization of the ambition expressed by the Cameroonian government to make the mining sector an important pillar of its development with a view of achieving the status of an emerging country by the year 2035, as mentioned in the Growth and Employment Strategy Paper and the National Development Strategy (2020–2030) for Structural Transformation and Inclusive Development (Republic of Cameroon 2021; Ministry of Economy, Planning and Regional Development 2020).

This ambition aims to remedy a paradox: Cameroon has significant mining potential, but according to the 2020 Extractive Industries Transparency

Initiative (EITI) report on Cameroon, it only contributed 0.12 percent of the state budget in 2020 (EITI 2022: 15). From a broader perspective, this ambition aims to disprove Sachs and Warner's (1995) argument that countries endowed with natural resources experience a slower growth rate than countries that have less, hence experiencing a resource curse.

Since achieving independence in 1960, Cameroon's development has primarily revolved around its agricultural sector. However, in the 1980s, the petroleum industry emerged as the country's primary source of foreign exchange. Since then, oil revenues have dwindled, and attention has shifted toward extracting other minerals, including gold, diamond, bauxite, cobalt, uranium, nickel, and rare earth elements, to boost its economic development (Fonjong 2004).

Structurally, Cameroon's economy and politics bear a strong resemblance to those of African countries afflicted by the resource curse (e.g., Nigeria, Angola, the Democratic Republic of Congo, Sierra Leone, Congo Brazzaville, Equatorial Guinea, and Sudan). The resource curse (also known as the paradox of plenty) highlights the struggle faced by numerous resource-rich countries to capitalize on their natural wealth fully and for their governments to address public welfare demands adequately. Despite the anticipation of improved development following the discovery of natural resources, these nations often experience heightened levels of conflict and authoritarian governance, along with diminished economic stability and growth rates compared to their resource-scarce counterparts (Gapa 2020). Scholars of the curse contend that the wealth derived from oil, minerals, and gas possesses unique characteristics, setting it apart from other forms of wealth. These distinctive features include substantial initial investments, extended production periods, location-specific extraction requirements, significant scale often characterized as substantial rents, volatility in pricing and production, these resources' finite nature, and the industry's inherent secrecy (Natural Resource Governance Institute 2015).

Politically, Cameroon functions as an autocracy, with considerable power concentrated in the executive branch, notably under President Paul Biya, who has held office for over four decades and is presently Africa's oldest head of state. According to Nting (2019), this situation implies that revenues from mining may be diverted to fund mechanisms of repression aimed at safeguarding the government's short-term political elite interests, thereby hindering Cameroon's long-term economic development. To mitigate such risks, the government aims to establish a system where revenues derived from mineral exploitation are directly invested in the provision of social services to local communities. Thus, the current optimism regarding the prospective economic benefits of the new mining code should be approached with caution.

This chapter aims to highlight Cameroon's new mining policy and the challenges it faces to produce the expected results, specifically improving the living conditions of Cameroonians. The chapter is structured as follows: a discussion on the state of scientific research on the study will precede an analysis of Cameroon's old mining policy before considering the reasons that pushed the legislators to adopt a new one. Finally, the chapter will identify and analyze the prospects and challenges of the new mining policy.

OVERVIEW OF THE LITERATURE ON CAMEROON'S MINING SECTOR

The literature concerning the mining industry in Cameroon is predominantly structured around themes using quantitative, qualitative, and juridical prisms. Quantitatively, Goueth (2001) highlights Cameroon's impressive mining potential, which comprises at least fifty-two mining resources, some of which are world class. Iron, bauxite, rutile, diamond, nickel, cobalt, gold, limestone, and rare earth deposits are found in Cameroon. Qualitatively, research focused on the implementation of Cameroon's old mining policy. Lickert (2013) analyzed the latter under the prism of power relations and the misappropriation of resources it generated. She highlighted the option taken by the state to privatize the exploitation of mining resources while retaining its regulatory prerogatives, the legal limits of the code, the involvement in the mining field of actors close to power, and the lack of transparency in the relationships between mining companies and the Cameroonian government, which excluded local authorities and populations. Other studies have addressed the issue of natural resource exploitation in Cameroon in a sectoral approach. Examples include studies on small-scale artisanal mining (Weng et al. 2014; Eboumbou and Logo 2023), extractive mining practices in eastern Cameroon (Voundi 2021), the repercussions of natural resource exploitation in the Bakassi region (Kimengsi and Lambi 2015), and the influence of corruption on natural resources and export diversification in Cameroon (Ngameni et al. 2023).

From a juridical perspective, Guessele (2020) addresses the protection of human rights in state contracts related to the exploitation of natural resources in Cameroon. She argues that natural resources are one of the pillars on which developing countries like Cameroon build their economic growth. Due to limited resources, the state relies on foreign transnational companies to finance and implement extractive projects. Cameroon intends to boost its economy through state contracts by exploiting natural resources, including minerals. The experience of many African countries demonstrates that the exploitation of natural resources has negatively affected the environment and human livelihoods. Hence, there is the question of the preeminence of profits made by companies at the expense of human rights and nature, prompting the integration of a human rights and environmental security approach to mining, given the stronger concern for balancing financial, societal, and environmental imperatives in Cameroon. Guessele (2020) finds that despite the legal and institutional system, there is still a long way to go to effectively protect human rights under current investment contracts related to natural resource exploitation in Cameroon.

Himbé (2018) studied the 2016 mining code, concluding it contained seeds of innovations that improved mining governance in Cameroon. Among these innovations were provisions related to transparency in extractive industries, the creation of three different funds related to mining activity, and the integration of environmental safeguards before, during, and after the completion of mining activities. Mve (2015) highlights the principles governing mining activity in Cameroon, considering the various issues related to the sector. The work provides different juridical responses to Cameroon's mining issues, including the management of revenues generated by mining activities, the safeguarding of the socio-economic rights of affected populations, oversight of the relationship between the state and mining multinationals in Cameroon, and evaluating policies implemented in relation with the exploitation of mining resources.

Various studies highlight the growing importance of mining in Cameroon, both in the business and development sectors and in science and academia. However, these studies do not consider the recent mining code promulgated by the republic's president in December 2023 and its innovations because of its recency. Coupled with the effective launch of the aforementioned mining projects and the creation of the new national mining company Société Nationale des Mines (SONAMINES), Cameroon's new mining policy emerged. Given these new parameters, it is pertinent to begin by examining Cameroon's previous mining policy to assess the coherence of the new one.

CAMEROON'S OLD MINING POLICY: FROM RELATIVE DISINTEREST TO GRADUAL AWARENESS OF THE MINING POTENTIAL

Mining operations in Cameroon trace their origins to the colonial era, with documented activities spanning from 1924 to 1928. During this time, French colonial authorities initiated a mining inventory program within their jurisdiction of the Cameroonian territory (Mpomzok and Iliassou 2021). Those activities culminated during World War II before declining until the early 2000s (Ouedraogo 2009). Indeed, the Cameroonian government's interest in mining is very recent. Initially, Cameroon did not establish a mining policy but instead adopted various legal instruments to regulate the sector. Only two laws relating to mining activity were adopted from accession to independence until the beginning of the 2000s. These laws governed the various technical and administrative aspects of mining activity in Cameroon, with the underlying concern for the state to exercise permanent control over its natural resources. Hence, the 1964 law-bearing regime of mineral substances in Cameroon forged a principle that has remained constant in Cameroon's mining policy: that of the sovereignty of the state over its sub-soil.

By determining which mineral resources were strategic and to whom to sell them, the competition of Cold War powers was implicit, as it required that allies in the periphery (mostly the newly independent Third World states) should not sell their strategic resources to their potential adversaries, the Communist bloc. From this period until the beginning of the 2000s, apart from exploratory studies to assess its mining potential, Cameroon's mining policy materialized solely through the creation of ALUCAM, a factory intended to produce aluminum from alumina extracted in Guinea. This lack of genuine interest of the government in the mining sector resulted in a meager contribution of the mining sector to the gross domestic product of Cameroon. The disinterest can be explained by the fact that in addition to the important role already played by cash crops such as cocoa and wood, the oil production that started by the end of the 1970s already constituted an additional resource to the national budget. Furthermore, the volatility of international market conditions was not encouraging for the exploitation of mineral resources.

The economic crisis in the 1980s, with the fall in the price of raw materials and commodities and the drop in oil production due to the maturation of some of Cameroon's oil deposits, were determining factors in orienting governmental perception toward the mining sector. It prompted the financial institutions (International Monetary Fund and World Bank) to encourage developing countries to revise their mining codes to make them more attractive to international investors and, subsequently, diversify their economies. Indeed, the countries most impacted by the economic crisis were those with abundant natural resources, particularly oil and mining. Still, until then, these had not contributed to an effective improvement in the living conditions of their populations.

Law No. 001 of April 16, 2001, bearing the mining code in Cameroon, initiated a change of course in the national mining policy. Anchored in the principle of state ownership of its sub-soil, it endorsed the privatization of mining activity with recognition of the ownership of the products resulting from their exploitation to the holders of mining titles. The state retained a central and regulatory role. For example, mining companies benefited from more rights by conducting mining prospection and informing the mines directorate at the

Ministry of Mines of their results. In addition, given its lack of technical and logistical resources, the state depended on mining companies to carry out its tasks. This was the case for the cartographer from the Ministry of Mines, who found himself asking mining companies to provide him with a means of transport to carry out his field control missions as stipulated in the old mining code (Lickert 2013: 115). In addition, this resulted in an exclusive system involving only the central state and mining companies, granting research or exploitation permits at the discretion of the president of the republic or the Ministry of Mines. Apart from weakening the state itself, this undermined the authority of local stakeholders. This policy also excluded local populations from the revenues generated by mining activities that almost always took place on their ancestral lands, from which they obtained no benefits.

On the other hand, this law maintained ambiguity between the artisanal mining normally reserved for nationals and the semi-mechanized mining accessible to foreigners, the latter investing in the gray zones created by the mining code to engage in activities reserved for nationals. Likewise, it did not mention the international commitments made by Cameroon concerning transparency in the extractive industries, the environmental considerations about mining activities, or the poor organization of quarry activities. Furthermore, it weakened the collaboration among the various administrations responsible for executing the mining policy (Himbé 2018). The various amendments enacted through Law No. 2010/011 on July 29, 2010, aimed at infusing the mining policy with greater social and local emphasis, proved insufficient in addressing all existing deficiencies.

At the institutional level, Cameroon's mining policy experienced major changes and innovations, beginning with the creation of the Ministry of Mines, Industry and Technological Development (MINMIDT), which led the charge in implementing the mining policy. The merging of mines, industry, and technological development departments within this ministerial institution was explained by the aim of transforming the mining sector beyond mere extraction into a catalyst for the country's border-based industrialization through the local processing of various extracted ores. Resultantly, a capacity-building program for the mining sector, Projet de Renforcement des Capacités du Secteur Minier, was implemented between 2012 and 2017 to put into practice various reforms so that the mining sector would effectively contribute to the country's development. It was, therefore, necessary to improve the knowledge of mining potential and make related information access on the mining industry more transparent, make administration more efficient, ensure positive impacts at the local level, and ensure that mining development was done in harmony with other imperatives such as environmental preservation and other land use activities.

In addition to the Projet de Renforcement des Capacités du Secteur Minier, the Artisan Mining Support and Promotion Framework (CAPAM) was created in 2003 to better structure the artisanal mining sector and redirect its production into the formal economy. Its mission, conferred following Decree No. 2014/2349/PM of August 1, 2014, was to collect the state share in every mining activity. Furthermore, it controlled and monitored the production of companies engaged in semi-mechanized mining activities and collected their corporate tax. The 2016 mining code attempted to remediate the shortcomings of the 2001 code and included in its scope of action mining activities other than solids, which had until now been neglected by sectoral legislation. It also incorporated the extraction of geothermal deposits, spring waters, mineral waters, and thermo-mineral waters. The code also innovated by integrating environmental requirements such as the Environmental and Social Impact Study before any mining activity except artisanal mining and the restoration of sites after extraction. It introduced the concept of "local content," defined as "the set of activities focused on the development of local capacities, the use of local human and material resources, the transfer of technologies, the subcontracting of local companies, services and products and the creation of measurable additional values for the local economy," which must be included in any mining project save for those relating to artisanal mining (Oyewole 2018).

Remarkably, Cameroon's old mining policy established three specific funds to implement a new policy. First, the mining sector development fund was intended to finance mining prospecting, funded by annual contributions based on gross production from owners of small and industrial mines, operators of semi-mechanized artisanal mines, and operators of semi-mechanized industrial or artisanal quarry substances. Secondly, the fund for the rehabilitation, restoration, and closure of mining and quarry sites was established for environmental restoration at the end of their operation. This fund was supplemented by the same actors as those of the mining sector development fund, based on the estimated costs of implementing the environmental preservation and rehabilitation program as defined in the environmental and social impact study. The sums dedicated to this fund were free of income tax, subject to their effective use for the intended purpose, and held in an escrow account with the central bank. Finally, the special account for the development of local capacities was created to finance the economic, social, cultural, industrial, and technological development of Cameroon through the development of human resources, businesses, and local industry. The amount of contributions was pegged between 0.5 and 1 percent of the total amount of turnover, excluding taxes of the mining or quarry company. The terms of collection and management of contributions were also established by agreement between the state, the duly mandated public body, the representatives of the populations, and the contributing mining or quarrying companies.

In terms of transparency, the 2016 mining code included in its corpus the commitments that all mining title holders declare all payments made to the state, their compliance with the obligations of the Kimberley process, and the EITI. Furthermore, measures were implemented to mitigate conflicts of interest alongside the requirement for traceability, notably within the diamond and gold sectors, and identifying all stakeholders involved in mining rights. These measures prohibited public administration officials or organizations supervised by the MINMIDT from engaging in mining activities. Additionally, there were prohibitions against holding direct or indirect financial stakes in mining companies or their subcontractors. Lastly, the legislation outlined taxes, customs duties, and economic incentives pertinent to mining title holders.

Overall, Cameroon's old mining policy was marked by a gradual evolution in awareness of Cameroon's mining potential and the impact it could have on the development of the country and the improvement of the population's living conditions. It led to a proliferation of norms and institutions aimed at regulating the mining sector intensively. However, the creation of SONAMINES and the adoption of a new mining code in 2023 suggest that the national mining policy is under permanent construction. This is why addressing the factors that motivated a new mining policy in Cameroon is appropriate.

FACTORS CONTRIBUTING TO DEVELOPMENT OF CAMEROON'S NEW MINING POLICY

Despite the progress observed in normative and institutional provisions, recent developments in the national mining policy suggest that pitfalls must be addressed for the mining sector to fulfill its potential. These include issues such as transparency deficits, adverse environmental effects of mining operations, and the absence of tangible benefits for local populations.

The Lack of Transparency in the Mining Sector

The issue of transparency in the mining sector is recurrent in Cameroon. Despite transparency provisions incorporated into the 2016 mining code, many disparities exist between official mining production figures and their estimates. For example, a joint study by the International Criminal Police Organization (INTERPOL) and Enhancing Africa's Response to Transnational Organized Crime mentions large disparities between local estimates of officially exported gold and declarations of gold imports from

Cameroon to the United Arab Emirates (UAE). For 2017, official statistics from Cameroon report only four kilograms of gold exported to the UAE, while the country announced 10.9 tons imported from Cameroon (INTERPOL 2021). A cross-section data analysis from the "General Report on the Second Mining Governance Forum" (Eboumbou and Logo 2023) facilitated estimating the discrepancy gap on the Cameroonian side. Referring to the average price of an ounce of gold in 2017 (i.e., 1,275.60 US dollars for the month of November that year), the official value of Cameroonian exports to the UAE was recorded as 184,593 US dollars, while official UAE gold imports from Cameroon were estimated at 448,306,451 US dollars (BDOR 2017). The discrepancy on the Cameroonian side is, therefore, significant. Even more concerning is that over the 2008 to 2018 period, gold imports from Cameroon to the UAE increased from 0.30 tons to 11.7 tons, according to the aforementioned study (INTERPOL 2021). In addition, according to the EITI, gold collected in Cameroon under the legal supply chain in 2017 amounted to 701 kilograms, while the US Geological Service estimated artisanal gold production at two thousand kilograms for this same year. A significant part of gold production and its income thus goes unaccounted for in the official national statistics.

Moreover, there appeared to be a duplication of responsibilities between the CAPAM and the MINMIDT. Specifically, the CAPAM had the authority to enter into production contracts with foreign investors for semi-mechanized mining, while the MINMIDT issued mining authorizations for the same region. Moreover, myopic decisions, such as hastily issuing research or exploitation permits for extracting gold presumed to be submerged due to the construction of the Lom Pangar dam in the country's eastern region, had unanticipated consequences. It resulted in an influx of foreign mining operators into the semi-mechanized mine, who operated on the ground with artisanal mining permits after establishing informal arrangements with legitimate permit holders. Their growth shifted the focus of CAPAM from artisanal mining to semi-mechanized mining, hence marginalizing artisanal mining. As a result, it was insufficiently integrated into the official commercialization circuit, perpetuating a substantial loss of revenue for the state.

Most importantly, because the quality of institutions depends on those who run them, the line was not always clear between public and private interests. For example, between the functions of the director of CAPAM and his personal activities, Lickert (2013: 117) states: "We sometimes find him during negotiations as a representative of private interests (sometimes his own as an independent shareholder) and at the same time as a representative of financial interests of the state as a state shareholder through CAPAM," but also, "he admits to signing personal checks in the name of CAPAM, and himself ensures the sale of Cameroonian gold and diamonds in Dubai and Bangkok while waiting for precise regulations in this area to be defined." Hence, representatives of the administrative authority could sign legal documents in their personal capacity (Lickert 2013: 114). Ultimately, regarding procedural matters, despite regulations specifying that granting operating authorizations should commence with local-level verifications conducted by MINMIDT representatives, it is not uncommon to encounter operators in the field who possess authorizations directly issued from the capital. Thus, the administration circumvents its own regulations.

Finally, the emergence of semi-mechanized mining appears to embolden its operators. The frequent encroachment of semi-mechanized mining operators on artisanal mining land led to conflicts and exposed shortcomings in land management. Additionally, regarding the marketing of their products, artisanal miners found themselves vulnerable to unscrupulous collectors who lacked permits and traceability documents and who dictated prices to the miners, leaving them with no choice but to comply.

The Negative Environmental Consequences of Mining Activities

Many mining companies began their activities without having previously conducted an Environmental and Social Impact Study. Carried out without appropriate oversight, mining activities generate negative environmental consequences that may be irreversible. Although the decree from MINMIDT prohibited the use of mercury, cyanide, and other toxic products in mining activities in Cameroon, a joint report from the Publish What You Pay and MISEREOR coalition revealed a mercury content of greater than 0.15 Mg/L on the Nguengue River near the China Mining company in the Eastern Cameroon region. The same report also showed a content of 0.22 Mg/L in the washing tank of the Wolf Mining company in the village of Colomine district of Ngoura (MISEREOR and Publish What You Pay 2019). These practices contaminate water, soil, and groundwater, and, through the food chain, destroy animal biodiversity, arable land, and agro-pastoral areas, all of which ultimately harm human health. In addition to the use of prohibited products, the report, as mentioned earlier, revealed that several companies violated the 1996 environmental law which prohibits them from carrying out the river diversion of rivers (the Zhang company in Bétaré-Oya) or drying up streams (Lu and Hang in Batouri), or conducting mining activities in within watercourses (Métalicom and Optimum mining in Batouri). Finally, it should be noted that mining activities primarily involve excavation. The various wells dug by mining operators were never filled after exploitation, thus exposing animals and individuals to mortal dangers by falling and/ or drowning. The adverse impacts of mining activities on the environment and populations generated conflicts between miners and farmers, breeders, fishermen, and foresters, indicating a lack of socio-economic benefits for the affected populations.

Limited Socio-Economic Benefits to Local Populations

One of the embodiments of the "natural resource curse theory" is the absence of the "trickle-down effect" on poverty reduction, especially at the local level. This "trickle-down effect" can manifest through socio-professional, educational, health, or other opportunities offered directly by mining operators at the local level or by the redistribution of taxes levied on mining activities to local communities. Concerning employment, it is evident that as projects relating to industrial mining are still new, the mining sector is essentially driven by semi-mechanized mining, which, as its name indicates, utilizes machinery that necessitates fewer personnel than artisanal mining practices. Furthermore, employers in the semi-mechanized sector tend to recruit those who share their languages and culture. Such is generally the case with Chinese mining operators.

On the other hand, the redistribution method of the revenues generated by mining has not yet contributed to producing positive benefits for local populations. A plausible explanation is that the method of collecting and redistributing income, as provided for in the 2016 mining code, was still incomplete. Indeed, the state entity responsible for monitoring and controlling the production, marketing, and promotion of the transformation of substances resulting from artisanal and semi-mechanized artisanal mining activities was not yet effective.

Likewise, the redistribution of taxes from semi-mechanized mining was incomplete. As demonstrated by the general report of the second Forum on Mining Governance, the latest legislative provision to date, Law No. 2016/017 of December 14, 2016, bearing the mining code, provided in Article 28 that the state levies a final synthetic mining tax of 25 percent of the gross production of each site of the semi-mechanized exploitation of mineral substances. Pending the decree implementing this provision, CAPAM was responsible for collection. This included:

- 2.2 percent of the monthly corporate tax advance payment;
- 5 percent of the ad valorem tax; and
- 17.8 percent to be distributed between the fund for the development of the mining sector, the structure in charge of supervising and promoting artisanal mining activities, the local municipality, and the local community.

In practice, two principles determined the share owed to the state: the fixed monthly share principle and the production-sharing principle. Under the fixed monthly share, a predetermined amount was assigned for each component of the overall tax. On the other hand, the production-sharing principle involved distribution of shares based on production.

CAMERON'S NEW MINING POLICY

Cameroon's new mining policy of December 2023 was enacted to support the effective extraction of Cameroon's mining potential. It plans to achieve this, on the one hand, by channeling artisanal production into the official mining circuit and, on the other hand, by effectively regulating mining production on an industrial scale. The policy aims to provide socio-economic benefits to the population and contribute to making Cameroon an emerging country by 2035.

The policy has three major components: enhanced involvement of local authorities, establishing a state entity responsible for extraction oversight, and implementing a new mining code.

An Increased Role for Local Authorities

The new mining policy in Cameroon aims to be administratively more inclusive. Hence, decentralized local authorities are entrusted with the administration of artisanal mining. Due consideration is also provided for them in the redistribution taxes levied on mining activities. Consequently, the general tax code has been updated. It specifies in Article 239(5) the methods of distribution of the ad valorem tax resulting from mining activities:

- 25 percent for the compensation of the populations impacted by mining activities, provided to the territorially relevant municipality;
- 10 percent for collection costs, recovery, and support for technical monitoring and control of the activities concerned, distributed at the rate of 50 percent for the tax administration and 50 percent for the administration in charge of the mines; and
- 65 percent for the public treasury.

Furthermore, the new mining code officially endorses production sharing as the method for economic valorization by the state of its sovereign rights over its mineral resources. Henceforth, the state levies a synthetic tax of 25 percent on each production in the semi-industrialized mining sector. Overall, the production-sharing system provides more revenues for the state and local communities, and the principle of fixed monthly shares generates income monthly for Cameroonian stakeholders.

The Creation of SONAMINES

The lack of control over the revenues generated by artisanal mining activities and the limits observed in the CAPAM action prompted the state to take more decisive measures. Hence, a presidential decree created the national mining company SONAMINES on December 14, 2020. It is primarily responsible for the inventory of mining indices; the exploration, extraction, transformation, and packaging of mineral substances; the acquisition of participation in mining companies; participation in negotiations and monitoring in the execution of state contracts; the collection and conservation of documentation on mineral matters in collaboration with the MINMIDT; the contribution to transparency in the mining sector; the promotion of information on mining issues; and various other actions contributing to its development. In light of the latest mining code, SONAMINES is authorized to collect the synthetic mining tax within the framework of the finance law.

The major innovation of Cameroon's new mining policy, SONAMINES, is that it is exclusively responsible for purchasing and marketing gold and diamonds throughout the national territory. This prerogative addresses the numerous abuses and shortcomings identified in marketing minerals under the previous mining policy.

The Adoption of a New Mining Code

Cameroon's 2023 mining code encourages investments in the mining sector and supports the country's socio-economic development. To this end, it stands out from previous codes with certain innovations. At the conceptual level, it clarifies the notion of artisanal mining by defining it as "an operation that uses traditional methods and processes to extract and concentrate top- or sub-soil mineral substances at a maximum depth of ten meters and obtain marketable products" Law No 2023/014 of December 2023 relating to the Mining Code, Chapter 2, Section 3).

One of its main innovations is the recognition and reinforcement of the prerogatives of SONAMINES, the public entity duly mandated by the state to oversee mining activities. It lies at the core of driving forward mining endeavors within Cameroon, ensuring the state maintains a minimum 10 percent ownership stake in the capital of companies engaged in semi-industrial or industrial mining sectors. In addition, to increase transparency and traceability in the possession, transportation, transformation, and commercialization of mineral substances, SONAMINES is responsible for requesting a certificate of authenticity from the mining administration before exporting precious and semi-precious substances. Furthermore, it guarantees the supply of precious and semi-precious minerals to the local market. It ensures the control and monitoring of production, marketing, and transformation or valorization operations of precious and semi-precious rocks from artisanal and semi-mechanized mining. In terms of procedures and quality assurance, it introduces operations such as hallmarking, but above all, refining and stamping by SONAMINES before the exportation of gold from Cameroon to strengthen transparency and control. Hence, the increase in taxation linked to research and extraction permits, especially in the field of small mines and industrial mines, and the appearance of new tax items did not appear in the 2016 mining code. These include the mineral waste license, the refining plant license, or the license to open a manufacturing workshop for articles made from precious and semi-precious stones.

Cameroon's new mining code has tax and customs incentives during the research and extraction phase. It prescribes compliance of the accounting system of mining companies with that of the Organisation pour l'harmonisation du droit des affaires en Afrique (Organization for the Harmonization of Corporate Law in Africa). Regarding control and surveillance, it establishes a synergy between agents of the Ministry of Mines and those of other administrations involved in mining policy. It includes the extraction of mining waste as an activity. Finally, drawing on the experiences of land tensions between artisanal mining operators and those in semi-industrial mining, it facilitates access to land by initiating the related procedure upon validation of the pre-feasibility study. However innovative and voluntary it may be, the success of Cameroon's new mining policy will depend on its ability to address crucial challenges.

CHALLENGES RELATING TO THE IMPLEMENTATION OF THE NEW MINING POLICY

Cameroon's new mining policy will not be enacted in a vacuum. Decades of neglect, followed by two decades of attempts to make up for lost ground, characterized by a proliferation of institutional and regulatory frameworks and the adoption of three mining codes in approximately twenty years—this clearly demonstrates the magnitude of the task at hand. The first but not least is undoubtedly the resistance it will encounter in its implementation. Indeed, the prerogatives vested in SONAMINES in collecting and marketing gold and diamonds throughout the national territory will likely clash with existing practices.

Internally, corruption punctuates the mining sector, particularly in mining regions such as eastern Cameroon, where strong suspicions of collusion between mining operators and the central and local administration—to the detriment of the population and the natural environment—exist and call into question the country's resource governance model (Voundi 2021). In addition to corruption, economic entrepreneurs, sometimes with the support of political entrepreneurs, circumvent the law. Faced with the legal provision that reserves artisanal mining only for nationals, companies owned by local authorities subcontract mining activities to Chinese entities in violation of the provisions of the mining code on conflicts of interest. The code prohibits public officials within the public administration and employees of a public body affiliated or supervised by the ministry responsible for mines from engaging in mining activities or holding direct or indirect financial stakes in mining companies or their subcontractors (Voundi 2021).

At the international level, the porosity of the borders, the absence of resources, and local compliance make Cameroon a preferred transit point for the illegal export of precious and/or semi-precious stones, particularly gold, from the Central African Republic. Companies such as the British Oriole Resources, specializing in gold extraction, challenged the mining code, expressing concerns that it granted excessive privileges to SONAMINES and increased fees for mining companies (Mbadi 2023).

Overseeing the implementation of local content poses a great challenge to the administration of the mining policy. Protest movements, such as those of Campo inhabitants of Campo versus Sinosteel (Lickert 2013) and of the inhabitants of the seven Mobilong neighboring villages concerning the activities of C&K Mining, abound over issues of lack of employment, compensation, and other benefits (Voundi 2021). In addition, local communities face numerous frustrations due to the threat of land grabs by mining operators. These conflicts demonstrate the need for positive socio-economic benefits for local populations in mining enclaves. However, in many cases, the administration responsible for ensuring the effective implementation of mining contracts' "local content" clauses elude these obligations when conflicts arise between local populations and mining companies.

Another recurring question is the length of time between the founding texts of a new mining policy and the texts related to their implementation (Guessele 2020). In 2018, at least ninety provisions of the 2016 mining law were still awaiting implementation decrees and other specific texts (Himbé 2018). Five years later, the application texts for the funds mentioned in the 2016 mining code and included in the 2023 law are still pending. In addition, the law bearing the 2023 mining code contains no less than sixty-five provisions that require decrees to be issued for their implementation. These provisions include organizing the management of the artisanal mine by the decentralized territorial authorities and organizing the regime for strategic mineral substances. In addition, the code lays out the modalities of distribution of the state's share between the public treasury, the duly mandated body, and the decentralized territorial authorities. It also sets aside a mining sector development fund and a restoration and rehabilitation fund for mining and quarry sites.

Finally, considering its assigned missions, the question remains whether SONAMINES will truly have the necessary means to fulfill them. Indeed, artisanal mining, which largely escapes state control, requires significant material and human resources to be channeled into the official circuit. Artisanal miners are scattered all over the East and Adamaoua regions of the country, some hardly accessible by road to be effectively monitored. Hence, it is important to strengthen this institution's logistical and human resources with other administrations involved in mining policy. The swearing-in of 194 mining inspectors in 2023 can be interpreted as a positive signal. In this regard, the stakes are significant concerning the autonomy and integrity of regulatory bodies and ensuring they are adequately equipped to carry out their duties. If these prerequisites are satisfactorily fulfilled, they will undoubtedly contribute to transforming the new mining policy in Cameroon into a blessing rather than a curse.

CONCLUSION

Cameroon's mineral resources remain largely untapped as the country stands at a critical juncture toward the revival of mineral extraction. Despite its challenges, the country's mineral industry represents a vital sector of its economy with significant promise and future potential for growth and development. It stands to be established whether Cameroon will go the route of countries like Tanzania, which have pursued extractive codes with a heavy emphasis on resource nationalism, or the way of states like Ghana and Botswana, which have embraced economic diversification. Either way, in order to escape the resource curse, the institutional framework of Cameroon needs to become more democratic, focusing less on executive power and more on the devolution of authority to local mining communities.

The new mining policy and governmental efforts to improve transparency to attract foreign investment will be essential to Cameroon's mining revival. It seeks to remedy the shortcomings of prior extractive law in Cameroon, incorporating the attractiveness, competitiveness, and financial profitability concerns by integrating SONAMINES to help fast-track the implementation of transformational mining projects and increase the solid minerals sector's contribution to the gross domestic product in the short or medium term. There is great optimism that by implementing the new mining code, Cameroon would considerably improve the mineral sector's profitability. Adopting sustainable practices and responsible resource management will drive the extractive industry's competitiveness and sustainability. Beyond improving the regulatory and legal framework, Cameroon requires more investment in infrastructure development, technical innovation, and human capital to unlock its full potential.

The new mining code has not gone unchallenged, however. According to Mbadi (2023), four British and Canadian mining firms have united in trying to halt the new law, which they believe confers exorbitant powers on SONAMINES and flouts international transparency agreements like EITI (Mbadi 2023). It can also be argued that Cameroon's ongoing push for mineral exploitation poses the likely risk of triggering political instability and conflicts. Without effective economic planning, corruptible politicians will likely prioritize political patronage further, resulting in local mining communities' economies lacking direct benefits.

To address this governance dilemma in resource-rich Cameroon, there is a need to enhance transparency, responsibility, and accountability mechanisms through the process of democratization. Democratic principles undermine despotic tendencies and facilitate the involvement of civil societies and local communities in resource management, ultimately leading to beneficial outcomes for both the local and national economies of Cameroon.

REFERENCES

BDOR. 2017. "Cours de l'Or du 02/11/17: Retrouvez l'evolution des cours de l'Or du Jeudi 02 Novembre 2017." https://www.bdor.fr/actualites-or/cours-de-l-or-du -021117, accessed September 15, 2023.

Business in Cameroon. 2023. "Grand Zambi Iron Ore: G-Stones Reportedly Ready to Start Exploitation in the Next Few Months." August 30, 2023. https: //www.businessincameroon.com/mining/3008-13380-grand-zambi-iron-ore-g -stones-reportedly-ready-to-start-exploitation-in-the-next-few-months, accessed December 15, 2013.

Eboumbou, S., and P. B. Logo. 2023. "General Report on the Second Mining Governance Forum– (MG F), Theme: Artisanal and Small-Scale Mining Exploitation: Opportunities and Challenges for Local Development." Yaoundé, January 18–20, 2023.

Extractive Industries Transparency Initiative (EITI). 2022. "Cameroon 2020 EITI Report: Report on Cameroon's Extractive Sector." https://eiti.org/documents/ cameroon-2020-eiti-report, accessed January 10, 2024.

Fonjong, L. N. 2004. "Changing Fortunes of Government Policies and its Implications on the Application of Agricultural Innovations in Cameroon." *Nordic Journal of African Studies*, 13(1): 13–29.

Gapa, A. Z. 2020. "Natural Resources and African Economies: Turning Liability to Asset." In *The Palgrave Handbook of African Political Economy*, edited by O. S. Oloruntoba and T. Falola, 679–97. London: Palgrave Macmillan.

Goueth, N. 2001. "Ressources minières au Cameroun." SOPECAM, Yaoundé, Cameroon.

Guessele, I. O. 2020. "La protection des droits de l'Homme dans le cadre de contrats d'Etat relatifs à l'exploitation des ressources naturelles au Cameroun." Doctoral thesis, Année Académique.

Himbé, L. D. 2018. "Le nouveau Code minier camerounais, au cœur des standards de la gouvernance extractive contemporaine." HAL Open Science 01664344.

International Criminal Police Organization (INTERPOL). 2021. "L'exploitation aurifère illégale en Afrique Centrale." https://www.interpol.int/content/download /16493/file/2021%2007%2027%20FRENCH%20PUBLIC%20VERSION _FINAL_L%27exploitation%20aurif%C3%A8re%20ill%C3%A9gale%20en %20Afrique%20Centrale.pdf?inLanguage=fre-FR, accessed November 15, 2023.

Kimengsi, J. N., and C. M. Lambi. 2015. "Reflections on the Natural-Resource Development Paradox in the Bakassi Area (Ndian Division) of Cameroon." *Journal of African Studies and Development*, 7(9): 239–49.

Lickert, V. 2013. "La Privatisation de la Politique minière au Cameroun: Enclaves Minières, rapports de pouvoir trans-locaux et captation de la rente." *Politique Africaine*, (3): 101–19.

Mbadi, O. 2023. "Cameroon's New Mining Code 'Excessive,' Say British and Canadian Miners." *The Africa Report*, December 22. https://www.theafricareport .com/331286/cameroons-new-mining-code-excessive-say-british-and-canadian -miners/, accessed February 28, 2024.

Ministry of Economy, Planning and Regional Development. 2020. "ND30: National Development Strategy 2020–2030: For Structural Transformation and Inclusive Development." http://bibliotheque.pssfp.net/livres/NATIONAL_DEVELOPMENT _STRATEGY_2020_2030.pdf, accessed on January 10, 2024.

MISEREOR and Publish What You Pay. 2019. "Transparence et fraude envi-ronnementale dans le secteur minier au Cameroun: Cas de l'exploitation artisanale semi mécanisée à l'Est et dans l'Adamaoua." https://www.dmjcm.org/etude-fraude -environnementale/.

Mpomzok, A, and Ndam I. 2021. "Voies de communication et développement des activités minières au Cameroun." *Editions Francophones Universitaires d'Afrique*. https://fr.scribd.com/document/576653346/Alfred-Mpomzok, accessed December 12, 2023.

Mve, U.D. E. 2015. *L'encadrement juridique de l'exploitation minière au Cameroun.* Paris: L'Harmattan.

Natural Resource Governance Institute. 2015. "The Resource Curse: The Political and Economic Challenges of Natural Resource Wealth." NRGI Reader, New York.

Ndouyou, J. 2023 "Kribi-Lobe: les travaux preparatoires lances." *Cameroon Tribune*. https://www.cameroon-tribune.cm/article.html/61036/fr.html/kribi-lobe -les-travaux-preparatoires-lances, accessed December 15, 2023.

Ngameni, J. P., S. B. Ngassam, G. N. Tiwang, and A. Tchounga. 2023. "Natural Resources and Exports Diversification in Cameroon: Does Corruption Matter?" *Research in Globalization* 6: 100134.

Nting, R. T. 2019. "The Political Economy of Mineral Exploitation in Cameroon." *African Research Review*, 13(1): 1–13.

Oyewole, B. 2018. "Overview of Local Content Regulatory Frameworks in Selected ECCAS Countries." UN Conference on Trade and Development, Geneva, Switzerland.

Ouedraogo, F. 2009. "Diagnostic du secteur minier du Cameroun." Rapport Final, ADE, Commission Européenne.

Republic of Cameroon. 2021. "Cameroon: Growth and Employment Strategy Paper 2010/2020: A Reference Framework for Government Action Over the Period 2010–2020." Republic of Cameroon, Yaoundé. https://www.cameroonembassyusa .org/main23/images/documents_folder/quick_links/Cameroon_DSCE_English _Version_Growth_and_Employment_Strategy_Paper_MONITORING.pdf, accessed on December 15, 2023.

Sachs, J. D., and A. Warner. 1995. "Natural Resource Abundance and Economic Growth." NBER Working Paper 5398, National Bureau of Economic Research, Cambridge, MA.

Voundi, E. 2021. "Extractivisme minier dans l'Est-Cameroun et controverses socio-environnementales: quelles perspectives pour un développement paisible des communautés locales?" *Belgeo. Revue belge de géographie*, (2).

Weng, Lingfei, et al. 2014. "Asian Investment at Artisanal and Small-Scale Mines in Rural Cameroon." *The Extractive Industries and Society*, 2(1): 64–72.

PART III

Old Money

New Resource Discoveries in Traditional Resource States

Chapter 8

A Political Settlement Analysis of Extractive Governance Practices in Zimbabwe

Tinashe Sithole

Zimbabwe is rich in natural resources, including valuable minerals such as gold, diamonds, and platinum (Mtapuri 2017; Malinga 2018; Samanga 2019). More recently, Zimbabwe is poised to play a critical strategic role in advancing the global energy transition toward cleaner energy through its recent windfall discovery of lithium. The discovery makes Zimbabwe the world's sixth-largest reserve of lithium deposits (Glass 2022). Despite this wealth, a lack of widely shared benefits from extractive resource governance leads to persistent inequalities and poverty among the population. In recent years, scholars and policymakers have increasingly focused on comprehending the political and economic factors that influence extractive resource governance in Zimbabwe and their implications for development. Previous studies on extractive resource governance in Zimbabwe have focused on issues such as corruption, mismanagement, and the influence of multinational corporations (Bond and Sharife 2012; Munier 2016; Spiegel 2015; Simpson 2018). However, there needs to be more analysis of the political settlements that underlie these dynamics and shape the distribution of benefits from extractive resource governance.

This chapter applies a political settlement analysis to study extractive resource governance in Zimbabwe. This approach provides a framework for examining the underlying power dynamics and interests that influence the distribution of benefits from extractive resources and the consequences for development (Khan 2010). The political settlement framework is a vital lens through which we can comprehensively grasp the African resource curse and its connection to authoritarianism. The broader resource curse literature underscores the transformative process in resource-rich nations as they evolve into "rentier states," predominantly relying on revenue from oil, gas, and minerals and consequently contributing to authoritarian rule. Rulers inheriting weak states grapple with immediate fiscal needs and prioritize high-rate resource extraction for short-term political survival. However, it is crucial to recognize that not all resource-rich nations inevitably succumb to authoritarianism. Research by Haber and Menaldo (2011: 23) challenges this conventional wisdom, highlighting that, over the long run, oil and mineral reliance may not be a guaranteed path to dictatorship. The intricate dynamics of political and institutional history, alongside regional and cultural contexts, play a substantial role in shaping the political landscape, adding complexity to our understanding of authoritarian regimes in resource-rich nations. Using a political settlement lens, this chapter critically analyzes the complex and often opaque dynamics of extractive resource governance in Zimbabwe to inform more effective strategies for promoting equitable and sustainable development. How do political settlements affect the governance of newly discovered extractive resources in Zimbabwe? This chapter underscores the critical role of elections in shaping political settlements. The interests of the Zimbabwe African National Union-Patriotic Front (ZANU-PF) in extractive resources make them central in shaping Zimbabwe's political landscape.

Since the extractive sector is a politically sensitive topic in Zimbabwe, this research utilized a gatekeeper who assisted in gaining access to stakeholders in the extractive industry as part of its data collection.[1] Within social science research, gatekeepers are critical mediators for gaining access to participants and study locations (Andoh-Arthur 2019). The research was guided by several questions, including the following: What role do political actors play in shaping the direction of extractive (extractive sector, diamonds, and gold) resource governance? How have sanctions on the ZANU-PF government shaped resource governance in Zimbabwe? How have the relationships between dominant elites, mineral extraction, and the state affected patterns of inclusive development over time? How does political culture shape extractive resource governance practices in post-liberation Zimbabwe? How do electoral processes impact Zimbabwe's governance and management of extractive resources? Secondary data included a systematic review of relevant academic literature, anecdotal evidence from the media, grey literature, and reports published by the governments and local and international non-governmental organizations.

The first section of this chapter provides the conceptual framework informing the analysis and discusses the evolution of political settlements in independent Zimbabwe. The concepts of political settlements and extractive resource governance practices in Zimbabwe's resource governance discourse are discussed next, followed by the liberation movement's political culture and values that emerged from the liberation war. A brief overview of Zimbabwe's extractive resource governance practices comes next, and after that is a discussion of the critical institution the Zimbabwe Mining Development Corporation (ZMDC). The last part discusses resource redistribution in Zimbabwe, the logic behind the actions driving the reforms or lack thereof, and the substance of the equitable redistribution of resources in the country. Given new resource discoveries, particularly lithium, the impact of sanctions on the ZANU-PF government in shaping Zimbabwe's extractive resource governance becomes crucial.

CONCEPTUAL FRAMEWORK: THE POLITICAL SETTLEMENT APPROACH

The political settlement framework refers to the relationships, norms, institutions, and power dynamics that shape power distribution and influence in society (Khan 2010). Debates around this framework often center around questions of power-sharing, inclusion, representation, and legitimacy (Bebbington et al. 2018; Frederiksen 2018; Botlhale 2022). These debates may involve various stakeholders, including the state, civil society, political parties, and ethnic or religious groups. The ultimate goal is to achieve a stable and inclusive political settlement that allows for effective governance and addresses the needs and interests of all citizens.

Power-sharing entails distributing power and influence among different actors, such as the state, civil society, political parties, and ethnic or religious groups (Kyed and Gravers 2015: 3). This is important for representation, which is the mechanism through which different groups can participate in decision-making processes and have their voices heard. This representation matters as it determines the inclusiveness of the process. Inclusiveness is the extent to which different groups are included in the political settlement and have access to resources and opportunities (Di John and Putzel 2009: 5). As society is formed of contending groups and classes with different interests, the ultimate test of inclusiveness needs to be anchored in the distribution of rights and entitlements, which are the outcomes of the settlement. In this case, the governance of extractive resources is often viewed as an outcome of a political settlement as those in power make decisions about resource extraction, allocation of revenues, and regulatory framework (Sithole 2022: 45–46). Thus, when the process is inclusive, it often impacts legitimacy.

Legitimacy is the perceived validity and acceptability of political institutions and actors based on their performance and the extent to which they are seen to represent the interests of the people (Khan 2010). Deliberative democracy, in theory, suggests that the legitimacy of a decision-making process and, in this case, a political settlement is derived from public participation in the process, reflecting on the process's inclusivity (Habermas 1998). On the other hand, determining how inclusive or exclusionary a political settlement is should not be understood simply by looking at the extent of participation in the bargaining process (Di John and Putzel 2009). Further analysis of the distribution of rights across groups and classes in the society on which the settlement is based is a better indicator of the inclusivity of a political settlement. The outcome of this process is the establishment of institutions, which are the formal and informal rules, norms, and structures that govern the distribution of power and influence in a society (North 1993). Equally, this chapter analyzes the institution, the ZMDC, that governs extractive resources in Zimbabwe.

In addition, the political settlement framework emphasizes the importance of political culture, defined as the norms, values, and beliefs that shape the relationships and behaviors of political actors in society (Formisano 2001). Swedlow (2013: 264) argues that political culture determines who gets what, when, why, and how. Within the context of the political settlement in Zimbabwe, ZANU-PF has played a central role in shaping the process and outcomes. This political culture is shaped by the historical context (i.e. the events, processes, and legacies) that have shaped the political settlement in Zimbabwe. Southall (2014: 83) notes that the post-liberation agenda of liberation movements was in all cases, to effect "Africanization" or "transformation," justified by the need to correct colonial racial imbalances. Consequently, the liberation movement's political culture is framed in the language of the pursuit of justice. Thus, key institutions of governance have become intertwined with the liberation movement's ideals, values, and ideologies (Sithole 2022: 124). These components are interrelated and interact in complex ways to form the political settlement in Zimbabwe. The political settlement framework seeks to understand these relationships and their implications for stability, governance, and social development in post-1980 Zimbabwe. In addition, it illuminates how new resources are being governed against the backdrop of the resource curse's multifaceted challenges.

An analysis of Zimbabwe's historical context of the liberation struggle and the demands for the restoration of justice and dignity for the African majority underscores the interests and incentives driving the political settlement. It is important to emphasize that the interests and incentives of the political actors drive political settlements, which may be motivated by factors such as power, resources, ideology, or public opinion. The ZANU-PF government has held power for over forty years, relying on the newfound extractive resource revenue to prop up its waning influence. Therefore, the liberation movement's interests are emphasized in this regard. These interests and incentives have shaped the content and dynamics of the political settlement. Lastly, political settlements involve negotiation, compromise, and conflict resolution processes, which can have different outcomes for different actors. These outcomes may include changes in the distribution of power, resources, or rights, and they may have long-term consequences for the stability and effectiveness of the political settlement. This is important in emphasizing how, after the regime gained power post-1980, ZANU-PF used extractive resource governance to further their interests and accumulate power in every subsequent election. Equally, the removal of Robert Mugabe in 2017 reflects the changes in the distribution of power and resources, which contributed to the stability of the political settlement and his removal from power.

TOWARD AN ANALYTIC FRAMEWORK

Political actors play a central role in shaping the direction of political settlements, as their interests guide negotiation and interaction. The interests and incentives of the political actors to control access and revenues from extractive resources are a key driving force in a political settlement, as they shape the actors' goals and behavior. These interests and incentives can be influenced by the settlement's institutions, norms, values, and external factors such as the economy, society, and international relations (in this case, sanctions against Zimbabwe). Sanctions against the ZANU-PF government have contributed to the lack of transparency in extractive resource governance, enabling revenue generation for power retention, election funding, and rewarding the military, a key power broker. Moreover, one cannot understate these extractive resources' political and economic significance because they are expected to play a crucial role in building the economy, especially in job creation, which is critical for sustaining the regime (Bond and Sharife 2012; Centre for Natural Resource Governance [CNRG] 2021). In Zimbabwe, the election processes are fiercely contested and resemble a high-stakes, zero-sum game where ZANU-PF goes to great lengths to secure its power. The party heavily relies on revenue from extractive resources to finance its campaign activities and sustain its waning influence, making its hold on power inextricably linked to these resources. The outcomes of the election have long-term consequences for the stability and effectiveness of the settlement and the distribution of power, resources, and rights among the political actors.

Figure 8.1 illustrates the interactions and influences among the different components of Zimbabwe's political settlement. The control over extractive resources and access to them has underpinned the social stratification and class formation process in Zimbabwe (Murombedzi 2016: 59). Thus, they have become a source of power for the government of Zimbabwe. ZANU-PF

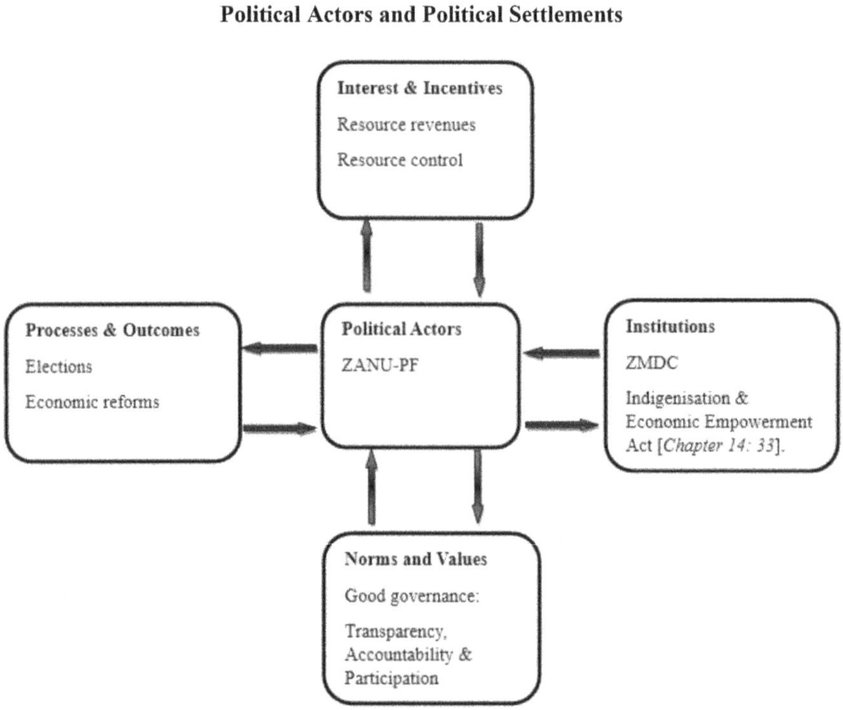

Political Actors and Political Settlements

Figure 8.1. Political Actors and Political Settlements. *Source*: Author.

has historically pursued economic policies prioritizing state control and indigenizing key industries such as mining and agriculture (Malinga 2018). Thus, the new resource discoveries have meant that ZANU-PF's economic control over newly discovered resources in Zimbabwe provides the party with substantial political leverage and raises concerns about transparency and equitable distribution (Bond and Sharife 2012). This control has enabled ZANU-PF to wield influence in negotiations with foreign investors and secure alliances with China and Russia, bolstering its political hold (Maguwu and Hamauswa 2019). However, it has also amplified the risk of corruption and a lack of accountability in resource management, which has impeded the equitable distribution of wealth and benefits to local communities.

ZANU-PF has leveraged institutions such as ZMDC and appropriated the Indigenisation & Economic Empowerment Act Chapter 14: 33 to skew resource redistribution to favor its clientele. Allegations of corruption surrounded ZMDC, resulting in the European Union imposing an asset freeze due to its affiliation with the ZANU-PF faction of the government (Croft 2013). Unfortunately, the ZANU-PF government, through the ZMDC, has exploited mineral resources for the benefit of political elites, especially funding ZANU-PF activities.[2]

In addition, the ZANU-PF liberation movement's political culture has undermined "good governance" principles such as transparency, accountability, and participation. The norms and values of the liberation movement's values ideology are often evoked to justify redistribution policies that skew resource redistribution in favor of its political elites. Content analysis of policies such as the Indigenisation and Empowerment Act illustrates key themes framed in a language of transformation and the pursuit of justice often invoked to justify governance policies (Andreasson 2010). Unfortunately, resource redistribution has disproportionately favored ZANU-PF-aligned individuals, and any deviation from this risks destabilizing the political settlement. In the context of the sanctions on Zimbabwe by the United States, the ZANU-PF has relentlessly pursued self-serving policies. These policies have led to politically exposed individuals' egregious abuse of state resources, all under the guise of pursuing transformation and justice against Western imperialism.

For ZANU-PF, extractive resource control is the ultimate source of power for governments in post-independence Africa and Zimbabwe (Murombedzi 2016: 59). Indeed, the political and economic salience of these extractive resources cannot be understated due to the role they play in building the economy in instances such as job creation, which is critical for regime sustenance (Transparency International 2020: 2). In this case, they have been instrumental in funding ZANU-PF campaigns.

The election outcome in Zimbabwe has had long-term consequences for the stability and effectiveness of the settlement and for the distribution of power, resources, and rights among citizens. The governance of extractive resources in Zimbabwe will demonstrate how the ZANU-PF regime is central in shaping the political settlement and inclusive development over time.

DEFINING ZIMBABWE'S POST-INDEPENDENCE POLITICAL SETTLEMENT

Political settlement in Zimbabwe refers to the set of arrangements and institutions, formal and informal, that determine how power is exercised and how conflicts are managed within the country. In the context of Zimbabwe, the term often refers to the political, economic, and social arrangements put in place following the country's independence from colonial rule in 1980. The political settlement in Zimbabwe has exhibited several key features, including authoritarianism (and neopatrimonialism) (Masunungure 2011; Raftopoulos 2019). The ruling party, ZANU-PF, has maintained a tight grip on power since independence, with political opposition suppressed and civil liberties restricted (Bratton 2014). Suppression of opposition voices led to a concentration of power in the hands of a small political elite. As a result, the ruling party has used clientelistic practices, such as the distribution of state resources and jobs, to maintain political support and control (Van de Walle 2007). The clientelistic practices have created a dependent political culture where citizens look to the state to provide them with goods and services.

Elite capture has occurred, with the ruling elite asserting control over key sectors of the economy, including the extractive sector and land (Barnes and Child 2014), further reinforcing the dominance of the ruling party and the current political settlement. To maintain its dominance in the political settlement, the ZANU-PF government has suppressed opposition political parties and limited freedom of speech and assembly (Mazango 2017). In the post-Mugabe era, Zimbabwe has witnessed a sequence of political reforms designed to consolidate authoritarian rule. For instance, legislation such as the Criminal Law (Codification and Reform) Amendment Act 2023 was passed, negatively impacting the political participation and role of civil society in holding the government accountable (Sithole 2023). Consequently, the government has faced accusations of suppressing political opposition, civil society, and the media, leading to constraints on freedom of speech and the press. This combination of factors, such as violent intimidation to silence opposition and manipulate the electoral process, has meant that ZANU-PF has maintained its grip on power. Thus, the distribution of power in the political settlement has favored ZANU-PF.

On the other hand, the formation of the national unity government in Zimbabwe in 2008 marked a significant change in the country's political settlement. The national unity government was formed due to negotiations between the ruling ZANU-PF party and the opposition Movement for Democratic Change after the disputed presidential elections of 2008 (Mapuva 2010: 255). The national unity government was established as a power-sharing agreement between ZANU-PF and the Movement for Democratic Change. This marked a significant change from the previous arrangement in which ZANU-PF monopolized power. One can infer that there was a significant change in the political settlement in Zimbabwe, which allowed for increased political space, improved human rights, and improved international relations (Magocha and Mutekwe 2021).

The issues mentioned here of political repression and human rights abuses contributed to the international isolation of Zimbabwe. Zimbabwe faced widespread international condemnation, including sanctions and travel bans imposed by the United States. This further isolated the country and made it difficult for foreign investment to take place, which impacted the extractive sector governance and the political settlement in the country (Masunungure and Badza 2010). Overall, the political settlement in Zimbabwe is marked by authoritarianism, clientelism, elite capture, political repression, and international isolation, all negatively impacting the country's political, economic, and social development. The dynamics and characteristics of Zimbabwe's political settlement significantly influence governance, particularly in managing newly discovered extractive resources. Unfortunately, these characteristics contribute to the lack of inclusivity, enabling corruption and exacerbating existing social inequalities, leading to a further decline in the well-being of marginalized communities.

NEGLECT OF "GOOD GOVERNANCE" PRINCIPLES IN ZIMBABWE

From 1980 to 2020, Zimbabwe consistently neglected good governance principles. Good governance is based on six core principles: "participation, fairness, decency, accountability, transparency, and efficiency" (Du Preez 2015: 31). While these principles claim universality, their interpretation remains specific and inherently shaped by underlying value systems, which in turn manifest in institutions. Building good governance systems in Africa raises questions on ensuring equitable redistribution of resource benefits for sustainable development in reducing inequality. How can transparency and accountability be enhanced within the governance systems of extractive resources to ensure that newly discovered resource revenues are managed and benefit the whole country? The assumption is that good governance principles provide an inclusive framework for embedding common values in extractive resource governance.

In the governance of extractive resources, good governance principles primarily focus on the state, ensuring responsible, accountable, and equitable resource management. Good governance in managing extractive resources can often be heavily contested, as various stakeholders may have conflicting interests and views on how these resources should be governed and distributed. Despite this, the broad interpretation of good governance in extractive resources converges on many points, primarily emphasizing transparency, accountability, and equitable benefit-sharing for sustainable development. The resource nationalism view perceives good governance as a strong role of state ownership of resources and using revenue funds to improve the well-being of the citizens (Andreasson 2015: 316). On the other hand, the human rights view broadens the conception of good governance to include protecting the rights of affected communities, workers, and indigenous groups to ensure that resource projects do not marginalize them. The democratic inclination of "good governance" principles is crucial for African countries facing the dual challenges of democratization and development.

EVOLUTION OF POST-COLONIAL ZIMBABWE'S EXTRACTIVE RESOURCE SECTOR

The evolution of post-colonial extractive resource sector governance practices in Zimbabwe from 1980 to 2020 has witnessed several key trends. First, the government has played a central role in the extractive resource sector in Zimbabwe, with the nationalization of several key industries, including mining, in the early years of Mugabe's rule. As such, there have been allegations of political interference in the extractive resource sector, with the government and its connected individuals alleged to have benefited disproportionately from the sector and repressing any form of opposition or criticism related to the extractive sector. From 1980 to 1985, mining in Zimbabwe remained regulated by the colonial government policies and legislation, especially the Mines and Minerals Act Chapter 27 21:05 of 1965 (Kaseke, Chaminuka, and Musingafi 2015: 90). Reforms in the early 1990s enhanced the state's role in regulating the mining sector. The government of Zimbabwe enacted the Zimbabwe Mining Development Corporation Act (Chapter 21: 08), which established the ZMDC (Kaseke, Chaminuka, and Musingafi 2015: 91). ZMDC has served as the government's investment vehicle in the mining sector. The recent Al Jazeera Gold Mafia story highlights the challenges and trends that have impacted the governance of extractive resources in Zimbabwe, where ZANU-PF-affiliated public officials can smuggle extractive resources with impunity (Al Jazeera English 2023).

Moreover, there have been persistent allegations of corruption and a need for more transparency in the extractive sector, with little information about the allocation of license contracts and revenues generated by the sector. One interviewee noted: "To be able to get a license to operate a mine with ease, you need to speak to someone in ZANU-PF as this will guarantee you protection in case there are issues." According to the *Mining Technology* report (2022), "It is being estimated that the smuggling to South Africa and the UAE is costing Zimbabwe nearly $1.8bn in lost mining earnings." As a result, the Zimbabwe government's regulatory framework for the extractive resource sector has faced criticism for its weaknesses, limited oversight, and enforcement of laws and regulations. For instance, in 2022, Zimbabwe banned the export of raw lithium as it sought at least first-stage processing within the country for the critically important metal. However, this did not stop the smuggling of raw lithium. Mailey (2015: 7) notes that: "The equation typically boils down to three components:

1. corruptible senior figures in a government responsible for managing the natural resource sector coupled with weak oversight institutions,
2. unscrupulous multinational investors who partner with senior government officials to exploit resource-rich states while evading scrutiny, and
3. loopholes in the international economic legal system that allow external investors and corrupt officials alike to transfer revenues out of resource-rich states and into the international financial system with limited reporting requirements."

Another key trend that has characterized resource governance in Zimbabwe includes limited public participation. The public, especially local communities and civil society, has had limited opportunities to participate in the decision-making and governance of extractive resource sector activities, particularly in awarding licenses, contracts, and the management of revenues. For instance, there have been clashes between mining communities and Chinese mining companies in Zimbabwe, evicting locals from their ancestral lands (Kawadza 2022). Other reports note that locals fear intimidation and victimization if they report abuses in mining communities because the foreign mining companies enjoy protection from the local chief, councilors, and politicians (International Crisis Group 2020).

In addition, Zimbabwe has faced widespread international condemnation, including sanctions and travel bans imposed by other countries. Arguably, this further isolated the country and made it difficult for foreign investment to take place, which impacted the extractive sector governance. This has inadvertently contributed to illicit trade and smuggling of extractive resources such as Gold, as noted in the Al Jazeera Gold Mafia documentary (Al Jazeera English 2023). From 1980 onwards, one can argue that Zimbabwe's extractive resource sector governance was marked by government control, political interference, lack of transparency, weak regulatory framework, limited public participation, and international isolation.

THE MUGABE ERA AND THE GOVERNANCE OF ZIMBABWE'S MINERAL RESOURCES

Robert Mugabe, who ruled Zimbabwe from 1980 to 2017, significantly impacted the governance of extractive resources in the country. Mugabe's regime was criticized for its lack of transparency and accountability in the mining sector and for failing to address environmental and social issues. One study found that Mugabe's government granted mining concessions to a small group of elites, who could capture the benefits of the extractive sector, while the broader population saw little benefit (Bond and Sharife 2012; Saunders

2014). This contributed to widespread discontent and social conflict in the mining areas.

The Mugabe regime was also accused of using the extractive sector as a source of illicit financing and personal enrichment (Saunders 2014). For example, the Marange diamond fields, which were discovered in 2006, were marred by allegations of human rights abuses, illicit diamond trading, and lack of transparency (Kanyumba and Mugova 2019). After years of political turmoil, including the 2008 election crisis, Mugabe's regime was eventually replaced by a unity government in 2009, which brought together members of his party and the opposition. The unity government attempted to address some of the challenges of extractive sector governance in Zimbabwe. Still, there were ongoing concerns about the influence of Mugabe-era elites and the lack of meaningful reform.

LIBERATION MOVEMENT POLITICAL CULTURE IN ZIMBABWE

Liberation movement political culture is a form of governance that legitimizes who gets what, when, and how based on liberation war credentials. It skews resource redistribution in favor of its elites while transcending ethnic lines. Its values include ideological orientations such as resource nationalism, which sought the power of the state to control natural resources (Sithole 2022). While its values include economic empowerment and social and political transformation of the African majority, the same values have seen it placing the political party above the state. Consequently, this has allowed them to use the extractive industry to advance class interests. Such loyalist values generated during the struggle could only endure by infusing them into extractive resource governance institutions. New resource discoveries still need to deliver economic promises for poverty alleviation, as the political culture deliberately favors its clientele over fair resource redistribution.

The liberation movement political culture in Zimbabwe promotes partisan behavior and selectively rewards individuals who align with the ruling party's ideology. It is rooted in the experiences of the liberation movement and framed in a language of pursuing justice and dignity for African citizens. Chikwanha (2022: 127) notes, "The permanent mantra of ZANU-PF has become a quest for the seemingly elusive liberation for most citizens. Freedom remains clothed in unquestioned demonstrations of loyalty and constant kowtowing to whatever current political discourse in the rulingparty is."

The liberation movement's political culture values were introduced into the state through the ruling party's operations, determining the who, when, and how of access to mining rights. Ultimately, the culture prioritizes loyalty and discourages dissent.

The ZANU-PF government in Zimbabwe prioritizes political affiliation in the distribution of resources, which goes against democratic principles like accountability and transparency. Despite this, the political culture of the liberation movement continues to impact the governance of extractive resources in the country. It creates a skewed distribution of extractive resources in favor of the ruling party through controlling party networks and pursuing national unity across ethnic lines. This is evident in the allocation of mines to ZANU-PF youths during elections (Kabonga 2016; Mkodzongi and Spiegel 2020), highlighting the embeddedness of this political culture and its impact on citizenship and resource distribution (figure 8.2).

RESOURCE REDISTRIBUTION IN A NEOPATRIMONIAL STATE

The justification for resource redistribution stems partly from the complex drivers of inequality in Zimbabwe (Kriger 2006). The neopatrimonial model of governance employed by ZANU-PF deeply infiltrates all aspects of society, including socio-economic and political spheres. This system allows citizens to access government services and benefits through the party's structure.

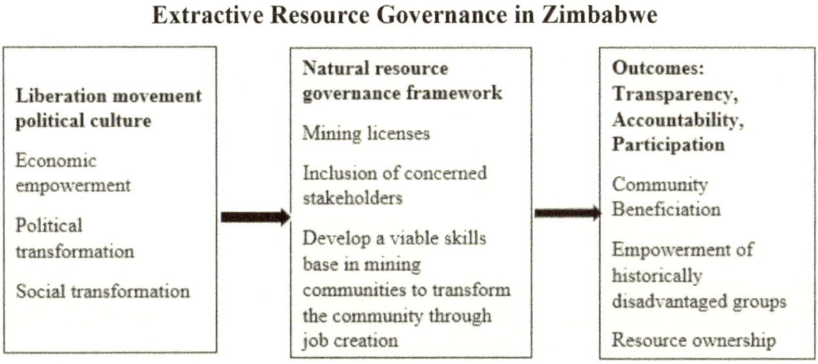

Extractive Resource Governance in Zimbabwe

Liberation movement political culture Economic empowerment Political transformation Social transformation	Natural resource governance framework Mining licenses Inclusion of concerned stakeholders Develop a viable skills base in mining communities to transform the community through job creation	Outcomes: Transparency, Accountability, Participation Community Beneficiation Empowerment of historically disadvantaged groups Resource ownership

Note: The figure illustrates that while mining laws and regulatory frameworks establish the terms of what a country might gain from extraction and determine the revenues and responsibilities for actors involved in the industry, the process of establishing the legal and institutional framework for sector activities has not always been transparent, with many opportunities for vested interests to influence the regulatory process. This ultimately undermines transparency, accountability, and participation.

Figure 8.2. Extractive Resource Governance in Zimbabwe. *Source:* Author.

Many citizens seeking to gain from the system have chosen self-inclusion. This is evident in cases where individuals have portrayed themselves as liberation fighters and loyalists, such as those who participated in land seizures. Neopatrimonialism binds participants to the party's dictates to pursue rewards, whether coerced or voluntary. For example, many high-ranking army officers benefited from farm invasions, now owning fertile land in the country (Chikwanha 2022: 130).

In Zimbabwe, resource redistribution typically occurs in a way that benefits a small group of political elites rather than being distributed fairly and equitably. Resource redistribution has often taken the form of distributing state-controlled resources, such as licenses, contracts, and land, to individuals or groups with close ties to the political elite. These resources are distributed in ways that serve to strengthen the political power of the elite rather than to promote the economic development or well-being of the general population.

KEY STRUCTURE: ZIMBABWE MINING DEVELOPMENT CORPORATION

The ZMDC is a government-owned entity in Zimbabwe primarily responsible for developing, managing, and promoting the country's mining industry. It is a vehicle for the government to participate in various mining ventures and activities. The corporation engages in joint ventures, partnerships, and investments in domestic and international mining projects. Over the years, ZMDC has engaged in various mining projects and partnerships, including those related to gold and diamond mining. The corporation has faced its share of challenges and controversies, particularly concerning transparency and governance issues in the mining sector.

ZANU-PF has taken advantage of its position as the incumbent party and has received support from various government-owned entities, contributing to projects that were ostensibly presented as government initiatives. This conflation of party, government, and state functions is employed to avoid scrutiny concerning the funding of ZANU-PF by public entities and to obscure allegations of ministers diverting public funds from state-owned enterprises for personal gain, often under the pretext of party financing. Consequently, the ZMDC has financed ZANU-PF activities, masquerading as government programs (CNRG 2021: 7).

In the 2008 and 2018 elections, ZANU-PF funded its election campaigns using mineral resources and external donors. Before the 2008 presidential run-off election, leading up to the violent run-off on June 27, 2008, reports suggest that the ZANU-PF received a significant one-hundred-million-dollar injection of funds through a questionable arrangement orchestrated by a businessman with interests in farming, fuel, and mining (CNRG 2021: 7). This businessman channeled the funds to ZANU-PF, disguising it as a "loan" from Lefever Finance Limited (BVi). Lefever Finance Limited had a joint venture with ZMDC, Todal Mining (Pvt) Limited, which owned the Bokai mine. Lefever Finance Limited held a 60 percent stake in Todal Mining (Pvt) Limited, with ZMDC owning the remaining 40 percent (CNRG 2021: 7). Allegedly, these funds were used to support the army's efforts to manipulate the outcome of the March 29, 2008, election in favor of ZANU-PF, ultimately leading to the June 27, 2008, presidential election run-off. MDC's Morgan Tsvangirai withdrew from the race during this run-off, citing the army's alleged killing of over two hundred of his supporters.

Furthermore, with each election, ZANU-PF, facilitated by ZMDC, illicitly sold mineral resources and mines to finance its campaigns. For instance, in 2009, Reclam, a non-mining company, notably partnered with ZMDC's Marange Resources to establish Mbada Diamonds, which mined Marange gems in Manicaland. Reclam injected one hundred million US dollars into the joint venture company (Mbada Diamonds) as part of the agreement (CNRG 2021: 10). Reportedly, a portion of this one hundred million US dollars was made available to ZANU-PF in 2010 in preparation for the 2013 elections. Mbada Diamonds funded a significant portion of the party's activities leading up to the 2013 elections, with a substantial portion of the funds derived from the one hundred million US dollars secured for the party through the illegal sale of diamonds to Hong Kong (CNRG 2021: 12). This reliance on extractive resources has become crucial for sustaining the regime, as ZANU-PF's governance of extractive resources now shapes the stability of its political settlement. Consequently, the discovery of new resources has led to ZMDC being used by ZANU-PF to finance its political activities.

Therefore, ZANU-PF has leveraged its incumbency, and institutions like the ZMDC have systematically undermined the natural resource governance framework. Concurrently, sanctions on Zimbabwe have compelled the government to adopt alternative strategies for concealing illegal activities and forming partnerships with China in the mining sector. Unfortunately, the primary beneficiaries of these extractive resources have predominantly been ZANU-PF and its affiliates, leaving communities and sector activities bereft of transparency and rife with opportunities for vested interests. This complex web of political and economic dynamics underscores the urgent need for transparency, accountability, and equitable resource distribution in Zimbabwe's extractive industries to benefit all its citizens and promote sustainable development.

THE TRAGEDY OF MINING-AFFECTED
COMMUNITIES IN ZIMBABWE

Several key themes characterize the tragedy of mining-affected communities in Zimbabwe. To begin with, numerous communities have endured forced displacement from their ancestral lands to accommodate mining activities, resulting in the heartbreaking loss of homes, livelihoods, and cultural heritage. Additionally, mining operations have wrought severe environmental devastation, including deforestation, water contamination, and soil erosion, adversely affecting community well-being and the sustainable management of their lands. Furthermore, these communities often need to be included in the economic benefits that the mining sector could bring, such as employment and business opportunities. In some cases, mining activities have diminished existing economic prospects (Kawadza 2022).

Moreover, the inadequate compensation for losses and harm has deepened the suffering experienced by these communities. To compound matters, the limited involvement of mining communities in the decision-making and governance of the extractive sector exacerbates their marginalization, perpetuating the cycle of negative impacts. Even in the face of new resource discoveries, there is little hope for change due to the current non-inclusive nature of the political settlement. Genuine prospects for transformation can only emerge when the political settlement derives its legitimacy from Zimbabwe's citizens' active participation and consent. Comprehensive reforms are imperative to address the multifaceted tragedy mining-affected communities face in Zimbabwe.

First, the government's control over extractive resources has often been used for political gain, with key decisions about the allocation of licenses and contracts being influenced by political considerations rather than economic or technical factors. The allocation of extractive resources has often been done in a lack of transparency, with little information about the process being made available to the public. This has made it difficult for mining communities, civil society, and the media to hold stakeholders accountable, and it has also led to allegations of corruption and abuse of power. In Zimbabwe, public participation in decision-making and governance of extractive resources has remained limited. This has made it difficult for communities and other stakeholders to have a say in managing resources, leading to negative impacts on local communities without their consent.

The impact of the Chinese in the mining industry has resulted in some environmental and social impacts. Reports in Zimbabwe suggest how Chinese mining companies have violated labor practices and environmental laws without repercussions (Kawadza 2022). In 2020, the Minister of

Environment, Climate, Tourism, and Hospitality warned Chinese-owned mines against violating environmental laws and regulations (Mupesa 2020). One interviewee noted: "China operates on the premise that it does not interfere in the internal affairs of other countries. . . . In fact, they have an enormous influence on the internal affairs of Zimbabwe by allowing repression as a bargain for going in and extracting Zimbabwe extractive resources." The extractive resource sector in Zimbabwe is associated with various negative environmental and social impacts, such as deforestation, pollution, and displacement of local communities. The government has faced criticism for its failure to mitigate these impacts or compensate affected communities.

The current political settlement has resulted in elite capture. For instance, extractive resources are controlled and distributed in ways that serve to strengthen the political power of the elite, rather than promoting the economic development or well-being of the general population. This elite capture has reinforced the dominance of the ruling party ZANU-PF and maintained the current non-inclusive political settlement. As a result, ZANU-PF uses the resource revenue to prop up its waning influence. Despite ZMDC's intended role of using extractive resources for the betterment of Zimbabwe's citizens, ZANU-PF has undermined equitable resource distribution, giving the liberation movement's political culture the upper hand in shaping resource governance in Zimbabwe.

ZIMBABWE'S LITHIUM DISCOVERIES: THE ROLE OF POLITICAL SETTLEMENT, PROSPECTS, AND CHALLENGES

In Zimbabwe, the discovery of lithium, a coveted resource in the global transition to a net-zero economy, has raised questions about its governance, potential benefits, and the influence of the entrenched political culture. In the following, the author explores how the country's political settlement intertwines with new lithium discoveries and its implications for the nation's future. Zimbabwe's political settlement significantly influences the governance of its emerging resources, particularly lithium. The government's immediate fiscal needs often drive high-rate resource extraction to secure essential rents for short-term political survival, a phenomenon seen especially during election periods (CNRG 2021). The ZANU-PF government relies on these revenues to fund its campaigns, with many having vested interests in the resource industry. However, the uneven distribution of resource benefits characterizes the political culture of the ruling ZANU-PF party. Without a shift toward a more inclusive political settlement, the newfound lithium discoveries may inadvertently exacerbate authoritarianism. External players, particularly China, leverage their influence in order to access Zimbabwe's mineral wealth. For instance, a class alliance between external players, particularly China, and ruling ZANU-PF party officials has facilitated the illicit smuggling of lithium at Bikita Minerals following the Chinese takeover (NewsHawks 2023; Pavlovic and Chivanga 2023).

Zimbabwe's lithium reserves are remarkable, claiming the largest lithium reserve in Africa and ranking sixth globally (Pavlovic and Chivanga 2023). It hosts numerous ongoing lithium exploration projects. Since 2021, several high-profile developments have showcased the nation's potential to become a significant player in the global lithium market. Notable lithium projects in Zimbabwe feature a $422 million acquisition of the Arcadia mine by Zhejiang Huayou (world's biggest cobalt producer) (Pavlovic and Chivanga 2023). Premier African Minerals partnered with Li3 Resources Inc. to secure a 50 percent stake in Mutare-based lithium assets. Additionally, Hong Kong's Sinomine acquired a complete 100 percent interest in African Metals Management Services and Southern African Metals and Minerals for $180 million, concentrating on the Bikita Lithium Mine (Pavlovic and Chivanga 2023). Experts estimate that Zimbabwe could meet up to 20 percent of the world's lithium demand if it fully exploits its vast lithium reserves. Chinese investors have played a pivotal role in these developments, contributing significantly to the investment momentum.

Despite Zimbabwe's lithium wealth, a disturbing issue continues to plague the industry: smuggling. Numerous reports highlight individuals, often with close ties to powerful ZANU-PF politicians and mine employees, who are involved in the daily illegal export of substantial quantities of lithium, effectively depriving the nation of vital revenue (NewsHawks 2023). Notably, the government took steps to address this problem by banning the export of unprocessed lithium, aiming to encourage local value addition. However, the illicit trade persists, with some ruling party officials allegedly contributing to the problem, and the involvement of Chinese nationals further complicates the situation (NewsHawks 2023).

Zimbabwe must confront its deeply entrenched political culture to harness the benefits of new lithium discoveries. Establishing a rule-based mining sector characterized by transparency and accountability is essential for success. Political will becomes paramount, with government leaders prioritizing the nation's interests over personal gain. Upholding the rule of law, enforcing regulations, and promoting a patriotic judiciary can significantly curb mineral smuggling and other illicit activities that impede the nation's progress.

In all, Zimbabwe is at a crossroads with its abundant lithium resources. The governance of these resources holds the key to the nation's economic development, political stability, and the well-being of its citizens. By addressing its prevailing political culture and embracing a more inclusive and transparent resource governance framework, Zimbabwe can ensure that new resource discoveries genuinely benefit the nation and its people rather than contribute to authoritarianism and illicit activities.

CONCLUSION

Zimbabwe's extractive resource governance remains influenced by ZANU-PF, with its liberation movement political culture undermining equitable redistribution. Key institutions like ZMDC benefit the political party. This chapter shows that elite capture of the extractive sector has allowed the ruling elite to capture key sectors of the economy, including the extractive sector, which has further reinforced the dominance of the ruling party and the current political settlement. Another key issue is the lack of transparency and accountability. The allocation of extractive resources in Zimbabwe has often been done with a lack of transparency, with little information being made available to the public about the process. This has made it difficult for communities, civil society, and the media to hold stakeholders accountable, and it has also led to allegations of corruption and abuse of power.

Due to international isolation, Zimbabwe has had to make new allies to ensure the country's economic stability. Consequently, there have been negative environmental and social impacts associated with the Chinese allies in the mining sector, with issues including deforestation, pollution, and displacement of local communities. Affected communities have criticized the government for neither mitigating these impacts nor compensating them.

Overall, the political settlement in Zimbabwe is characterized by authoritarianism, clientelism, elite capture, lack of transparency and accountability, political repression, and negative environmental and social impacts, which all harm the governance of the extractive resources sector in the country. In conclusion, it is evident that the political settlement in Zimbabwe has exerted significant influence over the governance of its extractive resources, leading the ruling party to leverage the assets to bolster its diminishing influence. Consequently, discovering new resources alone may not alter the country's fortunes as political stability remains intricately tied to these resources. What Zimbabwe truly requires is an inclusive political settlement that encompasses the interests of all its citizens, paving the way for a more sustainable and equitable future.

NOTES

1. The chapter analysis gathered data through a literature review and Zoom interviews with fifteen researchers, civic organizations, and academics, all intentionally selected. These interviews took place from May 2021 to September 2021. The primary data collection categorized respondents into three groups: researchers, academics, and civic organizations. This categorization aimed to capture various perspectives on natural resource governance practices and political settlements while minimizing researcher biases. The interviews were part of the author's fieldwork for their doctoral study, which received ethical clearance from the Faculty of Humanities at the University of Johannesburg. The doctoral study specifically examined how political settlements influence the governance of extractive resources in post-independence Zimbabwe and South Africa. This chapter, however, exclusively concentrates on Zimbabwe.

2. See CNRG (2021), which details how ZANU-PF through the ZMDC has facilitated shadowy deals that have helped to fund ZANU-PF election campaigns.

REFERENCES

Al Jazeera English. 2023. "Gold Mafia - Episode 1 - The Laundry Service I Al Jazeera Investigations." March 23. Video, 48:00:00. https://www.youtube.com/watch?v=evWEuVR1XIs&t=2734s, accessed April 23, 2023.

Andoh-Arthur, Johnny. 2019. *Gatekeepers in Qualitative Research*. Thousand Oaks, CA: SAGE Publications Ltd.

Andreasson, Stefan. 2015. "Varieties of Resource Nationalism in Sub-Saharan Africa's Energy and Minerals Markets." *The Extractive Industries and Society*, 2(2): 310–19.

Andreasson, Stefan. 2010. "Confronting the Settler Legacy: Indigenisation and Transformation in South Africa and Zimbabwe." *Political Geography*, 29(8): 424–33.

Barnes, Grenville, and Brian Child, eds. 2014. *Adaptive Cross-Scalar Governance of Natural Resources*. New York: Routledge.

Bebbington, Anthony, Abdul-Gafaru Abdulai, Denise Humphreys Bebbington, Marja Hinfelaar, and Cynthia Sanborn. 2018. *Governing Extractive Industries: Politics, Histories, Ideas*. London, UK: Oxford University Press.

Bond, Patrick, and Khadija Sharife. 2012. "Zimbabwe's Clogged Political Drain and Open Diamond Pipe." *Review of African Political Economy*, 39(132): 351–65.

Botlhale, Emmanuel. 2022. "Political Settlements Analysis of Natural Resource Governance in Botswana." *Politikon*, 49(3): 274–90.

Bratton, Michael. 2014. *Power Politics in Zimbabwe*. Boulder, CO: Lynne Rienner Publishers.

Centre for Natural Resource Governance (CNRG). 2021. "Mortgaging the Future in Return for Power: Zimbabwe's Natural Resources and the 2018 Election." Penhalonga, Zimbabwe.

Chikwanha, Barbara A. 2022. "The Liberation Culture and Missed Opportunities for Security Sector Reform in Zimbabwe: 1980–2018." *African Security Review*, 31(2): 123–38.

Croft, Adrian. 2013. "EU to Lift Sanctions on Zimbabwe Diamond Mining Firm." *Reuters*. https://www.reuters.com/article/zimbabwe-elections-eu-idINDEE98G0D020130917, accessed September 15, 2023.

Di John, Jonathan, and James Putzel. 2009. "Political Settlements: Issues Paper." Discussion Paper, University of Birmingham, Birmingham, UK.

Du Preez, Mari-Lise. 2015. "Interrogating the 'Good' in 'Good Governance': Rethinking Natural Resource Governance Theory and Practice in Africa." *New Approaches to the Governance of Natural Resources: Insights from Africa*, 25–42.

Formisano, Ronald P. 2001. "The Concept of Political Culture." *Journal of Interdisciplinary History*, 31(3): 393–426.

Glass, Fausto Carbajal. 2022. "Preventing Environmental Crime and Human Vulnerability through the MGPOC Framework: The Case of Zimbabwe's Lithium Industry." *Journal of Illicit Economies and Development*, 4(1).

Frederiksen, Tomas. 2018. "Corporate Social Responsibility, Risk and Development in the Mining Industry." *Resources Policy*, 59: 495–505.

Haber, Stephen, and Victor Menaldo. 2011. "Do Natural Resources Fuel Authoritarianism? A Reappraisal of the Resource Curse." *American Political Science Review*, 105(1): 1–26.

Habermas, Jürgen. 1998. *Between Facts and Norms: Contributions to a Discourse Theory of Law and Democracy*. Translated by William Rehg. Cambridge, MA: MIT Press.

International Crisis Group. 2020. "All That Glitters is Not Gold: Turmoil in Zimbabwe's Mining Sector." Crisis Group Africa Report 294. https://www.crisisgroup.org/africa/southern-africa/zimbabwe/294-all-glitters-not-gold-turmoil-zimbabwes-mining-sector, accessed November 24, 2023.

Kabonga, Itai. 2016. "Youth and Development in Ward Three of Chegutu District, Zimbabwe." *International Journal of Research in Social Sciences*, 6(2): 344–55.

Kanyumba, Blessing, and Shame Mugova. 2019. "Labour Management Issues in Marange Diamond Mines." In *Opportunities and Pitfalls of Corporate Social Responsibility: The Marange Diamond Mines Case Study*, 115–22. Cham: Springer International Publishing.

Kaseke, Kwaedza E., Lilian Chaminuka, and Maxwell C. C. Musingafi. 2015. "Mining and Minerals Revenue Distribution in Zimbabwe: Learning from our Surroundings and Past Mistakes." *Journal of Economics and Sustainable Development*, 6(6).

Kawadza, Sydney. 2022. "Laws, Regulation and Culture Clashes within China-Zimbabwe Mining Communities." Wits Centre for Journalism Africa-China Reporting Project, September 27. https://africachinareporting.com/laws-regulations-and-culture-clashes-within-china-zimbabwe-mining-communities/, accessed March 2, 2023.

Khan, Mushtaq. 2010. "Political Settlements and the Governance of Growth-Enhancing Institutions." School of Oriental and African Studies, University of London, London.

Kriger, Norma. 2006. "From Patriotic Memories to 'Patriotic History' in Zimbabwe, 1990–2005." *Third World Quarterly*, 27(6): 1151–69.

Kyed, Helene Maria, and Mikael Gravers. 2015. "Integration and Power-Sharing: What are the Future Options for Armed Non-State Actors in the Myanmar Peace Process?" *Stability: International Journal of Security and Development*, 4(1).

Magocha, Blessing, and Edmore Mutekwe. 2021. "Narratives and Interpretations of the Political Economy of Zimbabwe's Development Aid Trajectory, 1980–2013." *TD: The Journal for Transdisciplinary Research in Southern Africa*, 17(1): 1–12.

Mailey, John R. 2015. *The Anatomy of the Resource Curse: Predatory Investment in Africa's Extractive Industries*. Washington, DC: Africa Center for Strategic Studies.

Malinga, Wayne. 2018. "'From an Agro-Based to a Mineral Resources-Dependent Economy': A Critical Review of the Contribution of Mineral Resources to the Economic Development of Zimbabwe." *Forum for Development Studies*, 45(1): 71–95.

Mapuva, Jephias. 2010. "Government of National Unity (GNU) as a conflict prevention strategy: Case of Zimbabwe and Kenya." *Journal of Sustainable Development in Africa*, 12(6): 247–63.

Masunungure, Eldred V. 2011. "Zimbabwe's Militarized, Electoral Authoritarianism." *Journal of International Affairs*, 47–64.

Masunungure, Eldred V., and Simon Badza. 2010. "The Internationalization of the Zimbabwe Crisis: Multiple Actors, Competing Interests." *Journal of Developing Societies*, 26(2): 207–31.

Maguwu, Farai, and Shakespear Hamauswa. 2019. "BRICS and the New Scramble for Zimbabwe in the Aftermath of the Military Coup." *BRICS and Resistance in Africa: Contention, Assimilation and Co-optation*, 119.

Mazango, Eric. 2017. "Media Games and Shifting of Spaces for Political Communication in Zimbabwe." *Westminster Papers in Communication and Culture*, 2: 33–35.

Mkodzongi, Grasian, and Samuel J. Spiegel. 2020. "Mobility, Temporary Migration and Changing Livelihoods in Zimbabwe's Artisanal Mining Sector." *The Extractive Industries and Society*, 7(3): 994–1001.

Mining Technology. 2022. "Zimbabwe Bars Raw Lithium Export to Capitalise on Price Surge in Global Market." https://www.mining-technology.com/news/zimbabwe-raw-lithium-export/?cf-view, accessed July 29, 2023.

Mtapuri, Oliver. 2017. "Re-thinking Mining in Embattled Africa: A Calculative Sociological Logic." *Mining Africa. Law, Environment, Society and Politics in Historical and Multidisciplinary Perspectives*, 215.

Munier, Nathan. 2016. "The One Who Controls the Diamond Wears the Crown! The Politicization of the Kimberley Process in Zimbabwe." *Resources Policy*, 47: 171–77.

Mupesa, Conrad. 2020. "Mines, Firms Warned Against Environmental Violations." *The Herald*, July 9. https://www.herald.co.zw/mines-firms-warned-against-environmental-violations/, accessed March 2, 2023.

Murombedzi, James C. 2016. "Inequality and Natural Resources in Africa." *World Social Science Report*, 59–62.

NewsHawks. 2023. "Bikita Lithium Smuggling Rife." September 27. https://thenew-shawks.com/bikita-lithium-smuggling-rife/#google_vignette, accessed September 29, 2023.

North, Douglass. 1993. "Institutions and Economic Performance." In *Rationality, Institutions and Economic Methodology*, edited by Bo Gustafsson, Christian Knudsen, and Uskali M, 242–61. Milton Park, UK: Taylor & Francis Group.

Pavlovic, Clinton, and Tapiwa Chivanga. 2023. "Zimbabwe: A New Focus for Lithium Mining." *Mining Weekly*. https://www.miningweekly.com/article/zimba-bwe-a-new-focus-for-lithium-mining-2023-04-18, accessed April 18, 2023.

Raftopoulos, Brian. 2019. "Zimbabwe: Regional Politics and Dynamics." In *Oxford Research Encyclopedia of Politics*. London, UK: Oxford University Press.

Samanga, Ruvimbo. 2019. "The Impact of the Zimbabwean Space Agency's Programme for the Mapping of Mineral Reserves on Foreign Direct Investment in Zimbabwe." Doctoral dissertation, University of Pretoria.

Saunders, Richard. 2014. "Geologies of Power: Blood Diamonds, Security Politics and Zimbabwe's Troubled Transition." *Journal of Contemporary African Studies*, 32(3): 378–94.

Simpson, James G. R. 2018. "Monitoring Marange: Human Rights Surveillance, the Kimberley Process, and Zimbabwe's Blood Diamonds." Doctoral dissertation, University of Oxford.

Sithole, Tinashe. 2023. "Zimbabwe's 'Patriotic Act' Erodes Freedoms and May Be a Tool for Repression." *The Conversation*. https://theconversation.com/zim-babwes-patriotic-act-erodes-freedoms-and-may-be-a-tool-for-repression-209984, accessed July 31, 2023.

Sithole, Tinashe. 2022. "A Comparative Study of Natural Resource Governance Practices in the Post-Liberation War States: The Case of Zimbabwe and South Africa." Doctoral dissertation, University of Johannesburg, South Africa.

Southall, Roger. 2014. "Threats to Constitutionalism by Liberation Movements in Southern Africa." *Africa Spectrum*, 49(1): 79–99.

Spiegel, Samuel J. 2015. "Contested Diamond Certification: Reconfiguring Global and National Interests in Zimbabwe's Marange Fields." *Geoforum*, 59: 258–67.

Swedlow, Brendon. 2013. "Political Culture." In *Encyclopedia of Modern Political Thought*. Thousand Oaks, CA: SAGE Publications Ltd. https://doi.org/10.4135/9781452234168, accessed June 25, 2024.

Transparency International. 2020. "US$12 Billion Mining Economy by 2023: What Are the Key Enablers?" https://kubatana.net/wp-content/uploads/2020/08/Weekend-Digest-31-July.pdf, accessed December 12, 2020.

Van de Walle, Nicolas. 2007. "Meet the New Boss, Same as the Old Boss? The Evolution of Political Clientelism in Africa." In *Patrons, Clients and Policies: Patterns of Democratic Accountability and Political Competition*, 50–67. Cambridge: Cambridge University Press.

Chapter 9

"Why Should We Pay Tax?"

Fiscal Policy and Tax Morale in Sudan (1999–2019)

Jacopo Resti and Hassan Bashir Mohamed Nour

Since the 1970s, the literature on the "resource curse" has explored the mechanisms that link natural resource wealth to less democratic governance and accountability (Ross 2018). Numerous studies provide evidence of the so-called rentier effect, a scenario where a substantial flow of oil revenues in governments' coffers leads to reduced tax reliance and the development of patronage networks (Mahdavy 1970; Ross 2001). The underlying assumption is that taxation and democracy are closely related: when governments try to raise tax revenues, they are met with public demands for state responsiveness and accountability (Bräutigam, Fjeldstad, and Moore 2008).[1] Conversely, when external rents substantially fund governments, they are freed from the need to raise taxes and are thus less accountable to their citizens (Beblawi and Luciani 1987). In the long run, the availability of these rents, notably oil revenues, inhibits the state's capacity to extract taxes from its citizens, leaving it vulnerable to rent-seeking and unable to promote socio-economic development (Chaudhry 1989; Knack 2009; Ross 2018).[2]

Notwithstanding the role played in the country's national history and in topical developments since the waning of the oil boom and secession of South Sudan, the study of taxation in Sudan has been neglected. Outstanding issues drawing international scholarly attention have primarily revolved around Sudanese politics, conflict, and international intervention. In-depth treatment of taxation appears occasionally as an appendix of the broader political economy of the Sudanese state, seldom analyzed in the context of the oil economy and state-society relations (Benson 2019). The new wave of research studies and policy reports on fiscal policy and taxation in Sudan underscores this topical interest and calls for a synchronous and thorough scholarly attention (Fjeldstad 2016; El-Battahani and Gadkarim 2017; Logan et al. 2021).

Against this backdrop, this chapter analyzes key trends and patterns of contemporary fiscal policy and taxation in Sudan during and after the oil economy from 1999 until 2019. This time frame enables a cohesive historical perspective as it overlaps with the rule of President Omar-al-Bashir as the chief leader of the Al-Ingaz (Salvation) regime, starting in 1999 with the demise of the military-Islamist duopoly that had ruled the country since the 1989 coup, and ending twenty years later with the ousting of Omar-al-Bashir in 2019. It encompasses two distinctive sub-periods, namely during (1999–2010) and after (2011–2019) the oil boom, allowing for comparison of trends and patterns across decades.

This period witnessed significant political fluctuations that left long-lasting effects on macroeconomic stability and society at large, marked by the decline in gross domestic product (GDP) growth and the dramatic drop in the exchange rate of the Sudanese pound that placed a serious economic burden on Sudanese citizens. These socio-economic pressures have been mounting since the secession of South Sudan, eventually leading to the fall of al-Bashir in the wake of a popular revolution that broke out in December 2018 and ended his rule on April 11, 2019. Taxation increasingly became topical during this period, as seen in the number of key milestones in Sudanese tax reform, including the establishment of taxpayer's offices in the mid-2000s, the digitalization of the tax system, and the application of electronic bills since 2015.

As elaborated in the first section of this chapter, from 1999 to 2010 the Sudanese economy relied heavily on revenues from oil production, estimated at five hundred thousand barrels per day. These revenues financed the federal budget (around 50 percent of total revenues) and constituted about 95 percent of foreign exchange sources. This helped recover economic stability, effectively supporting GDP growth and reducing the tax burden and pressure on the consumer price index. Oil revenues relegated taxation to near oblivion, the only notable exception being the value-added tax (VAT) and tax hikes in 2009, when a plunge in oil revenue was forecast. However, revenues from oil, primarily extracted from southern Sudan, were not invested to promote the country's wealth and development due to widespread corruption and the ideological nature inherent to the military regime. After 2005, the country witnessed the division of financial resources between North and South Sudan, with the allocation of quotas for the oil-producing areas affected by the war, especially the regions of Abyei, South Kordofan, and South Blue Nile. This division was enshrined in the Comprehensive Peace Agreement (CPA), signed in Naivasha, Republic of Kenya, between the National Congress Party, the ruling party in Sudan, and the Sudan People's Liberation Movement led by John Garang.

The second period, addressed in the second section, stretches from 2011 to 2019. With the secession of South Sudan in 2011, Sudan lost its most important source of public budget and foreign exchange. Since then, the Sudanese economy has been in a chronic state of stagflation. Under fiscal austerity, the government tried to make up for oil losses by imposing new tax measures and local fees, while relying heavily on VAT, which accounted for about 70 percent of tax revenues. Yet, even when budgets witnessed a resurgence of taxes to fill widening deficits, tax revenue remained extremely low compared to Sudan's peers. In addition, tax reforms faced die-hard tax exemptions, a narrow tax base in a large informal economy, and cosmetic fiscal decentralization. The post-secession period also witnessed the phenomenon of gold mining, which supported the Sudanese economy by providing a source of income for millions of Sudanese, directly or indirectly. Nevertheless, revenues from gold have hardly fed the federal budget, and a large part of the production is smuggled abroad (Elbadawi and Suliman 2018).

Absent a genuine commitment to national economic and social development by the Al-Ingaz regime, widespread corruption and tax evasion, favoritism toward regime supporters, as well as US economic sanctions and Sudan's designation on the list of countries sponsoring terrorism, all led to weak fiscal governance and significantly harmed distributive justice. Sudanese citizens could hardly perceive any benefits from natural resource management and public expenditure, thus plunging tax morale and fiscal policy in its weakest state. These challenges are mirrored in the chapter's third section, which sheds more light on Sudanese attitudes toward taxation and motivations behind tax payment by reviewing findings on tax morale from field data collection in Khartoum in 2022.

THE OIL BONANZA (1999–2010)

Sustained Uneven Growth

In 1999, when Sudan's first oil was pumped, the military-Islamist duopoly forged during the Ingaz revolution by President Omar al-Bashir and Sheikh Hassan al-Turabi ended. Internal rivalries emerged as the Islamists took a belligerent stance in foreign and domestic politics, calling for an Islamist revolution that excluded the army. Prospective oil revenues fueled quarrelling in the financial arena around rent distribution among the elites. Eventually, President Al-Bashir split the Islamists, bringing key figures such as Ali Osman Taha into the military camp and expelling al-Turabi (Roessler 2016).

While the power struggle was moderated in Khartoum by the ruling elites, in the state's peripheries, the fissure within the Islamists translated into war in Darfur (de Waal 2015).

The benefits of the oil boom concentrated in the "near periphery" in central and northern Sudan by absorbing hundreds of thousands into the civil service and military payrolls ("payroll peace"). Increased public spending enabled the government to centralize power and secure political loyalties in the army, the security apparatus, and Islamists from the ruling party (Alsir 2014). In 2005, the CPA ended nearly a half-century of war between Sudan and what is now South Sudan. The CPA enshrined a political settlement based on a new collusive duopoly between the National Congress Party, the successor to the National Islamic Front, and the Sudan People's Liberation Movement,[3] marking the shift from religious and ideological radicalism to economic centrism. With the words of de Waal, "Sudan was a rentier political marketplace funded by oil" (de Waal 2015: 82).

After decades of poor economic growth (Ali and Elbadawi 2003), during the "oil decade" Sudan experienced the highest levels of growth in its history, averaging 6.1 percent of GDP annually between 1999 and 2010, and 7.9 percent between 2004 and 2008 (International Monetary Fund [IMF] 2008). Although smaller in shares to GDP compared to the agricultural and service sector, the oil economy became crucial to Sudan's external and fiscal balances at the start of the twenty-first century. Oil exports made up, on average, 85 percent of total exports between 2001 and 2010, with a peak of about 95 percent in 2009 (Abbas 2010). Oil revenues also became the primary source of public finances and rose to more than 50 percent of total government revenues in the same period, outsizing tax revenues.[4] The oil bonanza translated into historic high figures for real GDP and expenditure per capita. Both indicators peaked in 2008, boosted by high oil export volumes and world prices. In 2008, real GDP per capita stood at 142,500 Sudanese pounds, while expenditure per capita rose to 20 percent of GDP, almost doubling expenditures from the 1989 to 1999 period (IMF 2012; Logan et al. 2021).

The economic boom was driven primarily by increases in physical capital from domestic as well as foreign direct investment, notably from Asian national oil companies led by China, India, and Malaysia[5] that displaced previous American corporations such as Chevron (Patey 2014). Contrary to the 1990s, the contribution of total factor productivity to economic growth has been negligible during the oil decade, and even reported negative rates in 1999, 2004, 2008, and 2009 (World Bank 2015). In other words, the boom reflected increased attractiveness for capital investments in the oil economy and not gains in productivity from other economic sectors.

The rise of the petroleum sub-sector led to levels of investment above 25 percent of GDP after 2000 (World Bank 2009a), which nonetheless overwhelmingly concentrated on infrastructural projects in the Hamdi triangle, excluding the vast peripheries from the massive patronage system of the "payroll peace" and fueling resentment (de Waal 2019). The latter was met by increased spending on defense, national security, and public order, which accounted for roughly 40 percent of the budget, sacrificing health, education, and water services (World Bank 2007). This oil-induced growth came at the expense of agriculture, which continued to feature Sudan's historically low productivity and crop yields. The agricultural share of GDP fell from more than 40 percent to less than 30 percent during the oil decade, while agricultural productivity fell to 1 percent from a 6 percent high at the start of the 1990s (World Bank 2015).

The manufacturing sector also remained in its infancy without undergoing any structural transformation: most of the Sudanese labor force was absorbed by the agricultural and service sectors, where wages and productivity were lower. Rather than experiencing a transition to an increasingly diversified industrial economy, the country transitioned to a highly concentrated export basket dominated by crude oil (World Bank 2015). The lack of product diversification is also striking when compared to regional peers for the period 2000 to 2012.

Public management of oil revenues carried the usual symptoms of the so-called Dutch disease (Suliman 2016), including rampant inflation exceeding 10 percent annually on average. Sudan's economic diversification remained modest, lost competitiveness, and non-oil products (e.g., sesame and livestock) lost substantial shares in the export basket (IMF 2008). Overreliance on oil added to uncertain political developments in relations with South Sudan (Patey 2010). While calls for economic diversification and private-sector-led growth remained on paper (World Bank 2009a), estimates of a short-term exhaustion of oil reserves fell on deaf ears (Zachrisen 2010).

The Fall of Tax and the Rise of Value-Added Tax

At the national level, the share of non-tax revenues from oil exceeded shares of tax revenue in total revenue until 2009, relegating other tax sources to minor budget shares. In 2004, tax revenue in Sudan was below 40 percent of total federal government revenue, a substantial decrease compared to pre-oil tax shares that averaged two-thirds of total revenues. Within this smaller tax share, indirect taxes rose significantly, reaching 80 percent of tax revenue, a historic high in Sudan (Ahmed, Babiker, and Bell 2004). The rise in indirect taxation appears difficult to explain given the general decrease in trade taxes from the 1990s, marked by the market-oriented liberal policies of the National Comprehensive Strategy (1992–2002).

The answer lies in what was soon to become the main tax source in Sudan: the VAT. VAT was adopted in Sudan with the VAT Law in 2000. The tax measure was portrayed as particularly efficient for raising revenue in a largely informal economy at a time when the government was still struggling to shrink deficits and the oil boom was yet to burst. VAT carried more benefits than existing sale taxes, such as the possibility to refund producers for the VAT they paid for input goods and mitigate the complete loss of revenue in case of tax evasion by retailers. Nonetheless, being a regressive tax, VAT was to have a strong incidence on Sudanese households by targeting a wide range of basic goods and services, further deteriorating consumption levels of the poor.[6] The VAT burden was thus shouldered by Sudanese consumers and added to that of excises duties, which had almost doubled in the 1990s (Ahmed, Babiker, and Bell 2004). The adoption of VAT, along with new legislation on import duties in the early 2000s, was also a flywheel for the structural development of the tax administration. Between 2004 and 2007, the large, middle, and small taxpayers' offices were established by the Taxation Chamber to streamline collection and relations with Sudanese taxpayers.

The fall in tax shares was also precipitated by sharp cuts in tax rates between 2000 and 2008. In 2000, business profit tax applied to all economic sectors in Sudan at a rate of 35 percent (5 percent for agricultural corporations). By 2008, business profit tax rates were more than halved at 15 percent for most sectors and 10 percent for industrial corporations, while the agricultural sector had been exempted since 2001 (figure 9.1). That oil and tax

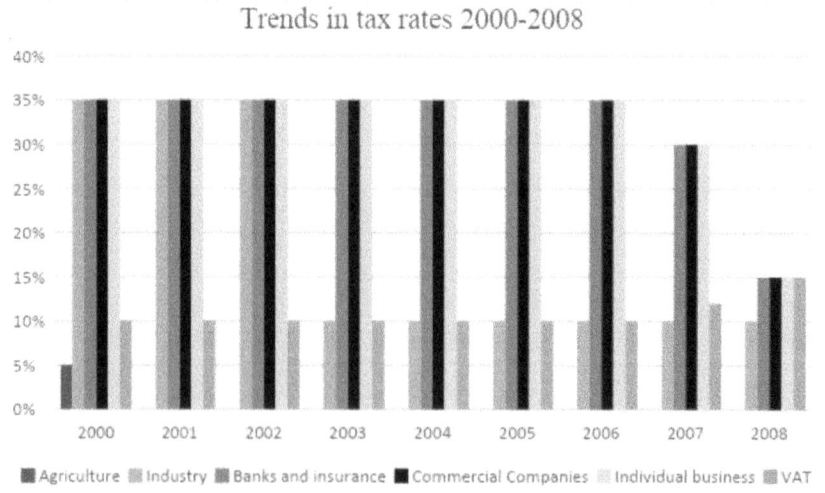

Figure 9.1. The Fall in Tax Rates during the Oil Boom (2000–2008). *Source:* Author created based on information from Sudan Taxation Chamber Tax Amendments records.

revenue played as connected vessels would be evident again in 2009 when the government doubled taxes on communications and introduced a new import tax to cover a forecast plunge in oil revenue and a widening budget deficit (*Sudan Tribune* 2008).

TIMES OF CRISIS (2011–2019)

Crude Days

The heyday of the oil economy ended abruptly in 2011 with the secession of South Sudan. With the separation of the South, the country's main regional hub of oil fields, Sudan lost 75 percent of its oil revenues. Oil production fell from 460,000 barrels per day to around 100,000 (IMF 2013), and exports from 8 billion US dollars in 2011 to 0.4 billion in 2013 (World Bank 2015). In the months that followed secession, Sudan swiftly transitioned from being a net exporter of crude oil to a net oil importer. Most importantly, the share of oil to total government revenues fell from more than 50 percent to around 15 percent in 2012, with public revenues declining overall by 33.5 percent between 2011 and 2012 (IMF 2012; World Bank 2015). Looking at trends in shares to GDP, the decline in oil contribution to the national economy dates back to 2009 when domestic production decreased, and international prices collapsed in the context of the Great Recession. In three years (2010–2013), oil revenues to GDP fell from 7 percent to less than 1 percent. This loss was partly offset by increases in non-tax revenues (e.g., sale of public assets, import tariffs, stamp duties), which averaged around 10 percent of GDP in 2010 to 2012. As far as tax revenues are concerned, no significant variations were observed over the period 2008 to 2013, with average shares around 3 percent of GDP (figure 9.2).

The gap in public revenues opened a significant deficit of roughly 4 percent in 2012, after two years of a sustained balanced budget. Widening budget deficits pushed the government to resort to the vicious practice of deficit monetizing through direct borrowing from the Central Bank of Sudan. This monetary expansion through the central bank, already experienced in the 1990s, led to a significant increase in inflation rates since 2011. The latter tripled on average from 10 percent to 30 percent in the years after secession, with peaks close to 50 percent (World Bank 2009b). Sudan's enduring international isolation and related economic and financial sanctions, in force since 1997, had cut the country off international financial institutions' reach, thereby limiting options for foreign financing.[7]

Besides its remarkable impact on the economy and ensuing recession, the effects of the oil shutdown revealed the deep-seated inequalities and

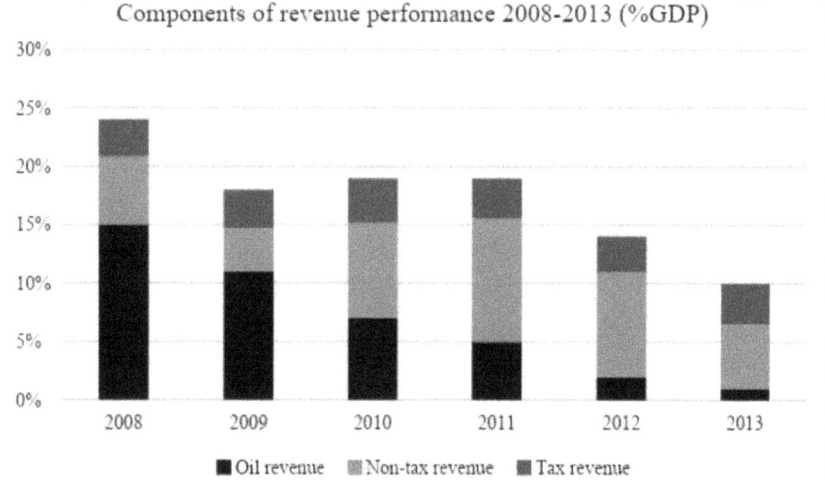

Components of revenue performance 2008-2013 (%GDP)

Figure 9.2. Components of Revenue to GDP in Sudan (2008–2013). *Source:* **Author created based on information from Ministry of Finance & National Economy Annual Budgets.**

economic inefficiencies of the Al-Ingaz regime's "salvation" model. Its "black gold" was not used to help the flourishing growth of "green gold," and the capital-intensive hydro-agricultural mission failed as an alternative engine of growth to fund industrial expansion and social services in a rentier political marketplace dominated by oil (Verhoeven 2015).

In June 2012, the government proposed a response plan and announced austerity measures. The austerity package targeted both the revenue and expenditure sides of the national budget, including tax hikes as well as cuts in public expenditures (World Bank 2012). The VAT rate increased from 15 to 17 percent, the import tax from 10 to 13 percent, and the business profit tax on the banking sector doubled from 15 to 30 percent (figure 9.3). Non-tax measures included widespread privatization and the sale of public assets. Stamp duties were applied on financial transactions and international flights, and new import tariffs completed the package.

The plan also cut government expenditures by 8.6 percent, especially on development spending plans, which were reduced by over 50 percent. Fuel subsidies that characterized the oil decade were cut by more than 20 percent and development transfers to states almost by 10 percent. Salaries and wages were the only budget item that increased. This included compensations to federal employees who suffered from soaring inflation rates above 35 percent in 2012. Federal transfers to states were also cut to a third of pre-secession levels (IMF 2012). Government expenditures declined to 13.6 percent of GDP in 2012, down from over 20 percent during the oil boom. Austerity

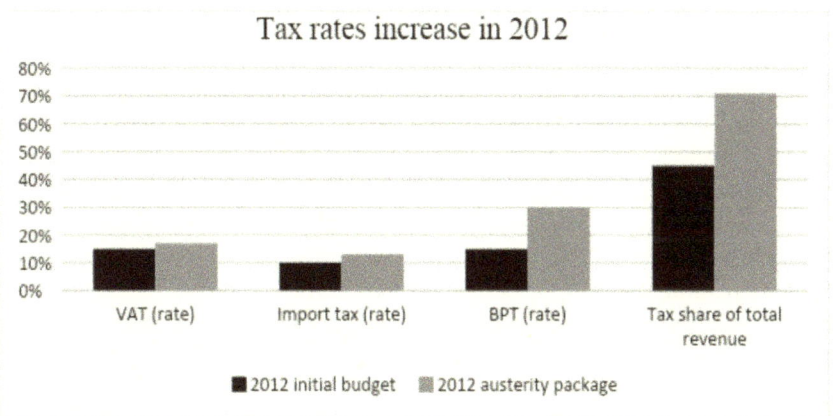

Figure 9.3. The 2012 Austerity Package. *Source:* Author created based on information from Ministry of Finance & National Economy and World Bank (2012).

measures notwithstanding, adjustments were insufficient to offset increasing deficits (World Bank 2012).

Following a year of fiscal austerity, the tax system accounted for 64 percent of total revenues in 2013, compared to 71 percent in 2012 and 45 percent in 2011. Sudan's tax system remained reliant on indirect taxation, which made most of the tax revenue collected in 2013, outsizing direct income tax to less than 10 percent. Overall, indirect taxes accounted for 60 percent of total revenues in 2013, of which more than two-thirds were raised through VAT (41 percent) and a third from customs and excises taxes.

The Gold Mirage

In the wake of secession, Sudan emerged as one of the top gold exporters in the world. The government regarded the gold sector as a prospective substitute for oil revenues, supported gold mining at the federal and state policy levels, and encouraged its production and export.[8] While gold accounted for only 13 percent of exports in 2011, this share rose to 42 percent in 2012 and 36 percent in 2013 (IMF 2014). In 2014, gold production was announced to have reached seventy-one tons by the minister of mining, with export revenues exceeding one billion US dollars, placing Sudan fourth in Africa behind South Africa, Ghana, and Tanzania (*Sudan Tribune* 2015). In the same year, export revenues from gold exceeded oil exports for the first time (Central Bank of Sudan 2014).

The Central Bank of Sudan has enacted a gold-buying policy to bring the mining sector under government control and establish itself as the dominant buyer in the domestic gold market and exclusive exporter of gold while combating smuggling by offering competitive prices to local producers and traders (World Bank 2015). For the first time, a gold refinery was constructed in Khartoum in 2012, which all companies must use to obtain the bank's authorization to export refined gold (Chevrillon-Guibert 2016).[9] This policy has nevertheless contributed to expanding the money supply by the central bank, as state agents paid gold traders in local currency, another major factor in driving domestic inflation. Coupled with deficit financing, the gold-buying policy has undermined macroeconomic stability, export competitiveness, and the sustainability of external debt (Elbadawi and Suliman 2018).

The gold sector has adopted the same governance features of "black gold": an "enclave economy" with production centers in the peripheries and revenues controlled by the central government via dedicated state agencies and the gold market located in Khartoum (Patey 2014). Government reach over the mining sector has extended beyond export to tax revenues. Whereas tax operations used to be run by local authorities that taxed artisanal production for own revenue, since 2015 the government mandated the Sudanese Mineral Resources Company with tax collection on the ground, fueling revolts among mining communities (Chevrillon-Guibert 2016).

Since 2012, the ability of the government to generate fiscal revenues from the gold sector has been greatly constrained. Gold mining remains artisanal (almost 90 percent of the country's production), with mining activities scattered over eight hundred small mines, and lacks a modern industrial mining environment (Marwan 2015). Meanwhile, the richest sites discovered in Darfur have remained under the control of the Arab militia, with the result that large shares of gold production and export do not appear in official figures (MacGregor 2017). To counter smuggling and attract foreign currency, in 2020 the central bank allowed private traders to export gold up to 70 percent of their production, provided they deposited proceeds in local banks and that they sold the other 30 percent to the central bank (Reuters 2020).

Enduring Challenges: Tax Exemptions, Informality and Fiscal (De)Centralization

Since 2011, tax reforms in Sudan have encountered multiple challenges that have slowed or hindered progress in improving tax collection and revenue. Most of these challenges are common to other low-income countries. They relate to the country's economic structure, such as high levels of poverty, low productivity, and a weak tax administration. Obstacles in raising revenue can also result from deliberate decisions in tax policy (Moore 2013). Studies on the politics of taxation have demystified its revenue function, providing evidence of its use as an "instrument of rule" (Moore 2018; Benson 2019). Among these challenges, some are particularly daunting in Sudan. These include tax exemptions, a large informal sector, and tax evasion (Awad 2020). Overall, it can be argued that tax policy has been *unable and unwilling* to raise more revenue.

Tax exemptions can be claimed according to a wide range of legislative acts, agreements, and resolutions in Sudan. Economic activities benefiting the most from these exemptions are concentrated in the agricultural sector. Since 2001, the sector is fully exempted from both corporate income tax and VAT. The industrial sector also enjoys a special corporate income tax rate of 10 percent, instead of the 15 percent that applies to other corporate businesses. Interestingly, public servants aged fifty or older are exempted from personal income tax. The latter applies a flat rate of 15 percent for personal incomes above a minimum threshold (144,000 Sudanese pounds in 2018).

VAT exemptions have become increasingly critical for government revenues, especially since South Sudan's secession. The VAT rate in Sudan is 17 percent for goods and services and 30 percent for the communication sector. According to the Tax and Custom Reforms Committee (Ministry of Finance and Economic Planning 2014), in 2013, VAT accounted for over 75 percent of total tax revenues. Contrary to its legislative provisions, VAT exemptions have been granted beyond basic goods and services. These extensions have been eased by the fact that the minister of finance has long been the only exempting authority.[10]

Furthermore, bilateral agreements between ministries and government agencies have contributed to mass VAT exemption, especially on imports, beyond basic goods and service categories disciplined by the VAT law. As shown in figure 9.4, VAT-exempted imports were around 60 percent of total imports between 2011 and 2014, generating a revenue loss of over eleven billion Sudanese pounds, around two billion US dollars (2014 prices). Large tax exemptions are reflected in VAT collection efficiency. Although Sudan's tax rate is similar to its regional peers (17 percent), collection efficiency is very low in comparison[11] (IMF 2016).

Taxing informality is a challenge many low-income countries share (Joshi, Prichard, and Heady 2014). The informal sector is characterized by small profits and numerous economic agents, who are hard to reach because they lack accurate tax records and are geographically scattered across the country in small entrepreneurial units. In these settings, the administrative costs of taxation can rise significantly and outsize revenue potential. Unified forms of taxation may also fail to raise revenue by discouraging taxpayers from graduating from single or presumptive taxes to the conventional system in the longer term (Bonjean and Chambas 2003).

A conservative estimate shows that more than 60 percent of the Sudanese economy belongs to the informal sector, mostly based on agriculture, where the economy is at subsistence levels (IMF 2020).[12] The large informal sector

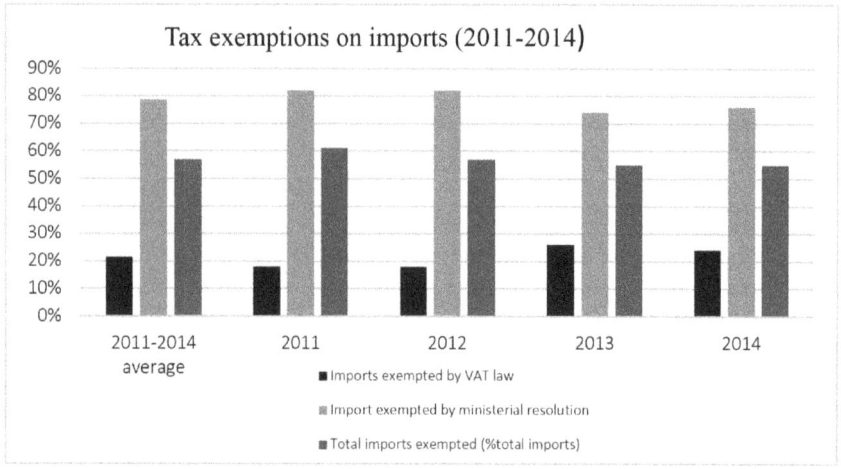

Figure 9.4. VAT Exempted Imports 2011–2014 (Percent of Total Imports). *Source:* Author created based on information from MFEP Tax and Custom Reforms Committee (2014).

in Sudan reflects a narrow tax base due to low registration rates of taxpayers in the tax administration system. The number of registered taxpayers in Sudan (i.e., holding a tax identification number) is 250,000.[13] Considering a working age population (fifteen to sixty-four years of age) of twenty-two million, one of every hundred Sudanese potential taxpayers is registered in the tax system. It is, hence, not surprising that Sudan's tax revenue heavily relies on indirect taxes and increasingly on VAT since its adoption in 2000. Direct taxes can be applied only to a limited tax base (tax identification number holders) that is largely unaware of tax procedures and uncooperative toward the Sudanese tax administration that is perceived incompetent, inefficient, and corrupt.[14] This partly explains the unsatisfactory performance of the self-assessment scheme introduced in 2008, a modern taxation system relying on voluntary compliance by taxpayers. The scheme has registered fluctuating revenues in the years following its implementation (Ministry of Finance and Economic Planning 2014). Low levels and flat rates of direct taxes limit the potential for redistribution among the different population groups, especially the poor. Comparison with peer countries shows that Sudan has the highest threshold for paying personal income tax and, at the same time, the smallest spreads between the highest and lowest personal income rates, signaling a very regressive tax system (Abbas 2010).

Notwithstanding reforms, tax revenue in Sudan remains very low on average and was 6 percent of GDP in 2018 (IMF 2020). As mentioned, this is partly explained by the legacy of "unearned" sources of non-tax revenue, notably oil, the large informal economy, and the narrow, evasion-prone tax base, including widespread tax exemptions provided by the Law on Investment and other legislative acts, ministerial resolutions and agreements. In the period 2011 to 2018, government revenue was relatively low, around 10 percent of GDP, compared to the oil decade (15 percent). Indirect taxes (i.e., VAT, customs, and excise taxes) have been the main source of revenue and policy response to the fall in non-tax revenues since 2011, albeit insufficient to offset the latter. Shares of direct taxes (corporate and personal income) remained negligible, averaging less than 1 percent of GDP since 2011 (IMF 2020; Logan et al. 2021). Between 2013 and 2018, the largest single source of tax revenue was VAT, reaching almost 70 percent of total revenues, while direct taxes averaged just over 20 percent.[15] These trends have reinforced the regressive features of Sudanese taxation and skewed the tax burden on consumption of basic goods and services, hindering the redistributive potential of the tax system. Revenues from income tax (both personal and corporate) in Sudan over the past twenty years have been the lowest among other non-resource-rich countries in sub-Saharan Africa, Middle East, and Central Asia, and well below peer averages close to 3 percent of GDP (IMF 2020).

Acknowledging the importance of revenue mobilization at the local level, in 2019 the new constitutional declaration maintained the same three levels of government (federal, state, and locality) and, together with the Juba Peace Agreement, signed in 2020 between the government and the Sudan Revolutionary Front, reaffirmed the commitment to implement fiscal decentralization in Sudan and included provisions for local revenue raising (The Juba Peace Agreement 2020). Despite this de jure arrangement, fiscal decentralization remains largely unachieved in practice, and related policies did not lead to a meaningful transfer of power to ordinary citizens at the local level (Logan et al. 2021). The centralization and lack of tax revenue responsibilities at the local level has led to a proliferation of non-tax fees, stamp and user charges applied by local tax authorities in their efforts to mobilize local revenue. The urgency to raise revenues since 2011 and the lack of supervision by the federal government have encouraged arbitrariness in the assessment of liabilities and collection by tax officers and intermediaries on the ground (Fjeldstad 2016).

Although fiscal reliance on federal transfers by the sub-national government was reduced (at the expense of local fees and charges), a fiscal equalization system and gap-filling mechanism are still missing: transfers to states and localities lack transparency in allocation, predictability in disbursement, and are allegedly politicized (El-Battahani and Gadkarim 2017). As a result, "the geographical inequality" (de Waal 2014) of Sudan today is roughly the same as in the early 1980s: the bulk of federal transfers is concentrated in central regions within a one-day drive from Khartoum, the Hamdi triangle, with over one-quarter of all transfers flowing to the state of Khartoum and Gezira between 2012 and 2018 (Logan et al. 2021). The states where the gap between own revenue and expenditure needs is wider, notably in the South, West, and Red Sea, are largely neglected.

TAX MORALE IN POST-REVOLUTIONARY SUDAN

"Tax is a national duty . . . and a social responsibility."

—Sudan Taxation Chamber

"Only 6% of Sudanese pay their income tax, I have my salary deducted at source and the tax revenue goes to the military, it's not fair."

—Sudanese public servant

A relatively recent and growing body of literature focuses on the connections between taxation and state-building through the eyes of taxpayers, studying people's views and attitudes toward taxation. The concept of tax morale received growing attention as the "intrinsic motivation to pay taxes" (see Feld and Frey 2007; Frey and Torgler 2007; Torgler 2007), influenced by both pecuniary and non-pecuniary factors. More practically, the question of why ordinary citizens pay tax and, even more recently, of why few citizens pay tax, with special regard to the African continent, has gained topical interest and is often at the core of empirical studies on tax morale (McCulloch, Moerenhout, and Yang 2021; Resnick 2021).

The quotations at the top of this section illustrate the contradictions emanating from perceptions of a national, collective morale or social duty to pay tax, on the one hand, and individual views on whether the tax system is "fair" and whether the government "deserves" a share of taxpayers' income, on the other. This paradox may not be unique to Sudan, but its magnitude and puzzle are. Very few Sudanese pay tax, while their political, economic, social, and cultural motivations toward tax payment are not well known.

Findings from field data collected in Sudan in 2022 show that perceptions of poor service delivery, lack of tax information, and weak sanctions are associated with low tax morale and compliance.[16] Not a single respondent is satisfied with public service delivery in Khartoum (e.g., access to education, health, roads, waste management) and the majority of them perceive public service to have worsened in the last three years (2019–2022). When asked about their willingness to pay taxes if the money was spent on improving public service delivery, almost 90 percent of respondents from the formal economy states it would. This overwhelming majority is split into two halves: those who would always pay more taxes for better services (40 percent), regardless of income, and those who would pay if their income was higher (40 percent). Results from the informal economy are even more clear-cut. Over 70 percent of the sample would always pay taxes for better services, and only 15 percent would pay if their income was higher. Only 10 percent would never pay taxes in exchange for public services.

The recurring link between tax payments and expectations of public service delivery is exemplified by the following quote from a Sudanese office keeper of an international organization in central Khartoum:

> Look! We are in the wealthiest residential area of Khartoum, the capital of Sudan—the rich of the rich—and this is the state of the roads, no electricity, offices get flooded with heavy rain, no drainage system, no public services! Why should we pay tax?[17]

As far as perceptions of tax enforcement are concerned, close to 80 percent of the respondents from the formal economy perceive the severity of sanctions for non-compliance in Khartoum to be mostly "low" (44 percent) or "moderate" (33 percent). Furthermore, over 50 percent of respondents perceive tax avoidance to be "easy, with recourse to certified accountants." When asked about individual perceptions of business compliance, around 65 percent of them perceive that more than 50 percent of businesses in Khartoum are non-compliant (through evasion or avoidance).

Similarly, 85 percent of respondents from the informal economy perceive sanctions mostly as "moderate" (50 percent) or "low" (35 percent). When caught in a tax dispute for not paying taxes, over 50 percent of the sample perceives its resolution as "easy to solve informally or amicably." Concerning the likelihood of other taxpayers being non-compliant, over 60 percent of the sample from the informal economy perceives that people meet their tax obligations "sometimes," while only 15 percent of respondents declare that taxpayers are "always" compliant.

Weak tax enforcement in the form of sanctions and audits is reflected in the following quote on tax evasion by the owner of a large business in Khartoum:

> I had not paid corporate tax of my big business for more than a decade! . . . when tax authorities eventually found out, the consequence was the payment of an apparently severe fine. In reality, it was less than a tenth of the total tax liability that we managed to evade. We had to close the business on the same day but reopened shortly afterwards with a brand-new company name, same management, same people.[18]

Tax avoidance as a widespread practice is also witnessed by certified accountants in Khartoum. When commenting on their job, one of these stated:

> A certified accountant is a highly requested profile in Sudan, our job is to exploit the loopholes in the tax law and make rich financial disclosures of large businesses look as meagre as possible.[19]

Finally, on the lack of tax literacy and information, around 70 percent of the sample from the formal economy perceives that information on tax payment is either absent (40 percent) or not accessible (30 percent). Moreover, more than 80 percent declare they never participated nor heard of tax campaigns or education programs in Khartoum. Similarly, 75 percent of the sample from the informal economy perceives information on tax payment as absent or scarce, while 65 percent has never heard nor participated in tax programs.

The low level of tax literacy is well illustrated by the following quote from an international business developer in Khartoum, discussing the qualification and availability of tax consultants:

> When we had to develop a curriculum for vocational training, we included a module on tax education for the private sector, given its relevance in our needs assessment. When we realized we could not find a qualified tax advisor, we had to drop the module.[20]

Although non-representative of the broader population of taxpayers, preliminary findings suggest that perceptions of poor service delivery, lack of tax information, and weak tax enforcement are associated by Sudanese respondents with weak tax morale. Overall, respondents regard these three determinants as reasonable justifications for non-compliance. With minor variations, this applies to both groups of respondents from the formal and informal economy. Quite intuitively, in low-income countries with very low levels of tax takes and compliance like Sudan, multiple determinants seem to play a role in influencing people's motivations toward tax payment. More interestingly, the fact that the majority of respondents are willing to pay taxes for tangible returns in public service delivery is less obvious in a country where the oil economy and other state rents have historically mist up the fiscal contract with taxpayers (de Waal 2007; 2015; Fjeldstad 2016). Nevertheless, targeted respondents may have greater expectations from tax payment in the form of public service delivery due to their urban location and proximity to service providers, and relatively high socio-economic status. Rural taxpayers have generally lower expectations of public service, especially in poor agrarian societies where land taxes are merely seen as "tributes" to rulers (Prichard 2015). Further research will have to look at tax morale in less urbanized and more peripheral settings, especially in the agricultural sector that is driving the Sudanese economy.

CONCLUSION

The historical period covered by this chapter (1999–2019) provides a broad framework to analyze fiscal policies, oil revenues, and tax morale in Sudan, while allowing for a comparison of key trends and patterns across decades (during and post-oil). Ultimately, the following considerations highlight some of the most insightful empirical findings and theoretical contributions.

First, sustained oil rents between 2000 and 2008 overshadowed taxation, with tax rates significantly reduced over the same period. Interestingly, these cuts targeted direct taxes, a burden taxpayers could "feel." As shown, business profit tax was more than halved for most economic sectors between 2000 and 2008. The industrial sector also benefited from special rates while the agricultural sector was fully exempted since 2001. Evidence suggests that oil and tax revenue played as connected vessels also the other way round, when declining oil revenues in 2009 prompted tax hikes on communications and imports and increased VAT rates (i.e., indirect taxes). These findings hold interesting theoretical contributions as they appear consistent with rentier effects, particularly with the "taxation effect," simply put that oil-rich states tax at low rates to prevent or avoid taxpayers' demands for state responsiveness and accountability (Beblawi and Luciani 1987; Ross 2001). More importantly, the "taxation effect" received less attention than other oil wealth effects on Sudanese authoritarianism. The "spending effect," where oil wealth is spent on patronage and the military apparatus, and the "group formation effect," where state largesse inhibits civil society's mobilization for liberalization, have been comparatively more debated in Sudanist scholarship (Elnur 2009; de Waal 2015; Verhoeven 2015; Gallab 2016).

Second, government revenue has relied overwhelmingly on indirect taxes. Shares of indirect taxes have averaged around half of government revenue and three-quarters of tax takes over the last few decades. When tax revenues were at their lowest during the oil boom, shares from indirect taxes were at their highest. In this regard, VAT deserves special consideration. VAT was introduced in 2000 and soon became (and still is) the main source of tax revenue, outsizing, by far, all other taxes. While direct tax rates fell during the oil boom, VAT was increased twice between 2005 and 2008, from 10 to 15 percent (to 17 percent in 2013). VAT was a needed substitute for trade taxes that were sacrificed in the name of market liberalization in the 1990s, and a better expedient in refunding producers and mitigating tax evasion by retailers than existing sale taxes. VAT was also fit for taxing the huge informal sector and was more cost-effective than direct taxes.

Interestingly, the amount of VAT raised is only a small fraction of potential VAT revenues. As shown, many businesses have been exempted from paying VAT on imports. Collection inefficiencies and selective exemptions beyond basic goods and services prescribed by the VAT law raises questions on whether and to what extent tax exemptions in Sudan are discretional and serve as an "instrument of rule" that sacrifice revenue to maximize political support (Piracha and Moore 2016; El-Battahani and Gadkarim 2017; Moore 2018). Tax reforms transferring the exempting authority from the minister of finance to the council of ministers in 2014 have not curbed exemptions.

The sheer reliance on indirect tax revenues also highlights the limited external validity of historical evidence from the West which theorized taxation as a means of institutional development and accountability (i.e., state-building). Fiscal sociology assumes that primarily direct taxation makes taxpayers "feel" the fiscal burden, favoring tax bargaining between the state and society (Bracco, Porcelli, and Redoano 2013). The shift to more indirect taxation may alter citizen's demands for accountability based on a "fiscal contract" with the state (Bird & Gendron 2007; Bird 2008). These features inevitably impact the relationship between taxation and state-building in countries like Sudan, pointing to distinctiveness rather than similarity with historical accounts of state formation in the West (Tilly 1990).

Third, preliminary findings from fieldwork on tax morale in Sudan show that perceptions of poor service delivery, lack of tax information, and weak tax enforcement (audit, sanctions) are associated with low tax morale and compliance in Khartoum. Findings that respondents from the formal and informal economy alike have expectations of service delivery from tax payment, albeit from an urban, unrepresentative sample, is already an interesting insight worth deepening in a country lacking historical evidence about the connection between taxation and state-building (Fjeldstad 2016). Further research should focus on taxpayers' intrinsic motivations that are more context-dependent (personal values, cultural, religious, and social norms, etc.). In order to complement analyses of taxpayers' expectations from their fiscal exchange with the state, research should also address taxpayers' actual behaviors and engagement with tax authorities, with special regard to the dynamics of tax bargaining (Prichard 2015).

As noted by other authors (Benson, Alneel, and Makawi 2023), ongoing academic and public debate in Sudan around the crisis of the state has shifted from adopting predominantly peace-based narratives of the CPA-era emphasizing ethnic, religious, and cultural fault lines, to developing a new narrative placing the political economy at its core. In particular, socio-economic rights and demands, advocating for a fair redistribution of the state economic resources with the peripheries and safety nets for the poor, have been fueling the revolution since 2018. After all, calls for "peace, justice and freedom" by protest movements were incubated during the endless queues in front of bakeries and gas stations all over Sudan.

Today, "Sudan's unfinished democracy" (Berridge, de Waal, and Lynch 2022) and ongoing conflict underscore the importance of a fiscal contract on economic governance as a constitutive, inescapable element in negotiating a political settlement between state and societal actors. This contribution feeds into this new brand of scholarship and civic activism, brought to the surface by the "the promise and betrayal of a people's revolution" that places socio-economic issues related to public wealth, revenue distribution, and taxation at the heart of the country's crisis and, hopefully, rebirth.

NOTES

1. The chapter "Why Should We Pay Tax?" is part of Jacopo Resti's forthcoming doctoral dissertation.

2. The authors would like to thank Dr. Awad Babeker Eisa and Akram Abdel Gayoum Abbas for their precious guidance and support during the study. Our research endeavors are dedicated to all Sudanese people facing hardship and suffering from war and displacement.

3. The political movement founded in 1983 by Dr. John Garang de Mabior, who envisaged a "New Sudan" where religious and cultural hegemony of traditional ruling tribes at the center would be broken while the South and other peripheries would drive change.

4. According to the Ministry of Finance and Economic Planning annual budgets, oil revenues were even more vital for the Government of South Sudan, accounting for 98 percent of total revenues since the mid-2000s.

5. These include China's National Petroleum Corporation, Petronas from Malaysia, and ONGC Videsh from India.

6. Interviews with Sudanese taxpayers in Khartoum, August 2022. Bird (1992) estimated that indirect taxes accounted for almost all taxes paid in low-income countries. The tax burden ranged between 10 and 20 percent of low-income families' income that is almost entirely spent on consumption good and services rather than savings.

7. On November 4, 1997, the Clinton administration issued Executive Order 13067, blocking US relations with the Government of Sudan on the grounds of its association with terrorist groups. The Executive Order expired on October 12, 2017, ending the twenty-year sanction regime.

8. Notable policies and regulations adopted in this regard are the following: The Regulation of Traditional Gold Mining of 2012, The Mines and Minerals Development Act of 2015, and The Mineral Wealth and Mining Resources Development Act of 2015.

9. Companies must also repatriate the foreign currency from gold exports and justify its use when withdrawn from the central bank which ensures that sale proceeds are not diverted to offshore accounts. The immediate policy goal was to replenish the central bank of sorely needed foreign currency reserves by establishing a monopolistic system in the artisanal gold trade.

10. Until 2014, the minister of finance and economic planning used to be the only government body endowed with exempting authority. As part of the efforts to reform the tax system and limit exemptions, this authority was assigned to the council of ministers in 2014.

11. The IMF estimated VAT efficiency in Sudan—revenue collected in percent of GDP divided by the standard tax rate—at 0.19 in 2016, in contrast to a median of 0.37 from twenty-one peer countries.

12. This is well above the average of African low-income countries, estimated around 40 percent.

13. Personal interviews with tax officers in Khartoum, August 2022.

14. Interviews with taxpayers in Khartoum, August 2022.

15. From the archives of the Sudan Taxation Chamber, Collection Department. The rate of VAT was raised in 2013 from 15 to 17 percent (first rate was 10 percent in 2005).

16. Field data collection on tax morale with Sudanese respondents was carried out in Khartoum through face-to-face questionnaires, interviews, and field observation in July and August 2022, enabling a first data sample on Sudanese attitudes and perceptions of taxation from the formal and informal economy. Data collection relied on a (non-probability) sample of local taxpayers and key informants from tax offices, firms, businesses, local markets, and international organizations. The questionnaires were pre-tested with researchers from the Economic and Social Research Bureau in Khartoum, and revised to improve formulation, readability in Arabic, and ease the data collection from a non-technical public audience.

17. Personal interviews with individual taxpayers in Khartoum, August 2022.

18. Personal interviews with business representatives in Khartoum, August 2022.

19. Personal interviews with tax accounting offices in Khartoum, August 2022.

20. Personal interviews with vocational training experts in Khartoum, August 2022.

REFERENCES

Abbas, S. M. 2010. "Fiscal Adjustment in Sudan: Size, Speed, and Composition." IMF Working Paper 10/79, International Monetary Fund, Washington, DC.

Ahmed, M. M., R. A. Babiker, and M. E. Bell. 2004. "An Analysis of Fiscal Policies in The Sudan: A Pro-Poor Perspective." George Washington Institute of Public Policy, George Washington University.

Ali, A. A. G., and I. A. Elbadawi. 2003. "Explaining Sudan's Economic Growth Performance." Cambridge General Economic Surveys of Africa: Eastern and Southern Africa.

Alsir, S. 2014. *The Oil Years in Sudan: The Quest for Political Power and Economic Breakthrough*. Toronto, Canada: The Key Publishing House Inc.

Awad, B. E. 2020. "The Impact of Tax Evasion and Tax Avoidance in Developing Countries (Case Study Sudan)." Doctoral thesis, Al Nealain University.

Beblawi, H., and G. Luciani. 1987. *The Rentier State in the Arab World*. London: Croom Helm.

Benson, M. S. 2019. "Taxation, Local Government and Social Control in Sudan and South Sudan, 1899–1956." Doctoral thesis, Durham University.

Benson, M. S., M. Alneel, and R. Makawi. 2023. "The Everyday Politics of Sudan's Tax System: Identifying Prospects for Reform." The London School of Economics and Political Science.

Berridge, W., A. de Waal, and J. Lynch. 2022. *Sudan's Unfinished Democracy: The Promise and Betrayal of a People's Revolution*. London, UK: Hurst Publishers.

Bird, R. M. 2008. "Tax Challenges facing Developing Countries." International Studies Program Working Paper 08–02, Andrew Young School of Policy Studies, Atlanta, GA.

Bird, R. M., and P. Gendron. 2007. *The VAT in Developing and Transitional Countries*. New York: Cambridge University Press.

Bonjean, C. A., and G. Chambas. 2003. "Taxing the Urban Unrecorded Economy in SubSaharan Africa." CERDI Working Papers 200316, Centre for eResearch and Digital Innovation, Clermont-Ferrand, France.

Bracco, E., F. Porcelli, and M. Redoano. 2013. "Political Competition, Tax Salience and Accountability: Theory and some Evidence from Italy." SSRN Scholarly Paper ID 2244783, Social Science Research Network, Rochester, NY.

Bräutigam, D., O.-H. Fjeldstad, and M. Moore. 2008. *Taxation and State-Building in Developing Countries—Capacity and CSonsent*. Cambridge: Cambridge University Press.

Central Bank of Sudan. 2014. *Foreign Trade Statistical Digest October-December 2014*. Khartoum: Central Bank of Sudan.

Chaudhry, K. A. 1989. "The Price of Wealth: Business and State in Labor Remittance and Oil Economies." *International Organization*, 43(1): 101–45.

Chevrillon-Guibert, R. 2016. "The Gold Boom in Sudan." *International Development Policy | Revue Internationale de Politique de Développement*, 7(1).

de Waal, A. 2019. "Sudan: A Political Marketplace Framework Analysis." Occasional Paper 19, World Peace Foundation at Tufts University and the Conflict Research Programme.

de Waal, A. 2015. *The Real Politics of the Horn of Africa: Money, War and the Business of Power*. Cambridge: Polity Press.

de Waal, A. 2014. "Visualizing Sudan: Geographical Inequality." Tufts University World Peace Foundation Reinventing Peace blog, May 7. https://sites.tufts.edu/reinventingpeace/2014/05/07/3-visualizing-sudan-geographical-inequality/.

de Waal, A. 2007. "Sudan: International Dimensions to the State and its Crisis." Occasional Paper 2, Crisis States Research Centre.

Elbadawi, Ibrahim Ahmed, and Kabbashi Madani Suliman. 2018. "The Macroeconomics of the Gold Economy in Sudan." Working Paper 1203, Economic Research Forum, Khartoum, Sudan.

El-Battahani, A., and H. A. Gadkarim. 2017 "Governance and Fiscal Federalism in Sudan, 1989–2015: Exploring Political and Intergovernmental Fiscal Relations in an Unstable Polity." University of Bergen, Bergen.

Elnur, I. 2009. *Contested Sudan: The Political Economy of War and Reconstruction*. London: Routledge.

Feld, L. P., and B. S. Frey. 2007. "Tax Compliance as the Result of a Psychological Tax Contract: The Role of Incentives and Responsive Regulation." *Law & Policy*, 29(1): 102–20.

Fjeldstad, O. 2016. "Revenue Mobilization at Sub-National Levels in Sudan." Sudan Report, CMI.

Frey, B., and B. Torgler. 2007. "Tax Morale and Conditional Cooperation." *Journal of Comparative Economics*, 35(1): 136–59.

Gallab, A. A. 2016. *Their Second Republic Islamism in the Sudan from Disintegration to Oblivion*. New York: Routledge.

International Monetary Fund (IMF). 2020. "Sudan: Selected Issues Paper." Country Report 20/73, International Monetary Fund, Washington, DC.

International Monetary Fund (IMF). 2016. "Sudan: Article VI Consultation—Staff Report; Press Releases; and Statement by The Executive Director for Sudan." Country Report 16/324, International Monetary Fund, Washington, DC.

International Monetary Fund (IMF). 2014. "Sudan: Article IV Consultation and Second Review Under Staff-Monitored Program—Staff Report; Press Releases; and Statement by The Executive Director for Sudan." Country Report 14/364, International Monetary Fund, Washington, DC.

International Monetary Fund (IMF). 2013. "Sudan: Article IV Consultation." Country Report 13/317, International Monetary Fund, Washington, DC.

International Monetary Fund (IMF). 2012. "Sudan: Selected Issues Paper." International Monetary Fund, Washington, DC.

International Monetary Fund (IMF). 2008. "Sudan: Article IV Consultation." Country Report 08/174, International Monetary Fund, Washington, DC.

Joshi, A., W. Prichard, and C. Heady. 2014. "Taxing the Informal Economy: The Current State of Knowledge and Agendas for Future Research." *The Journal of Development Studies*, 50(10): 1325–47.

Knack, S. 2009. "Sovereign Rents and Quality of Tax Policy and Administration." *Journal of Comparative Economics*, 37: 359–71.

Logan, S., A. Nyembo, B. Owen, M. Saab, and C. Sacchetto. 2021. "Fiscal Federalism in Sudan." Working Paper, International Growth Centre State Fragility Initiative.

MacGregor, A. 2017. "Musa Hilal: Darfur's Most Wanted Man Loses Game of Dare with Khartoum . . . For Now." Aberfoyle Security Special Report, December 12. https://www.aberfoylesecurity.com/?p=4096, accessed August 30, 2023.

Mahdavy, H. 1970. "The Pattern and Problems of Economic Development in Rentier States: The Case of Iran." In *Studies in the Economic History of the*

Middle East: from the Rise of Islam to the Present Day, edited by M. A. Cook, 428–67. London: Oxford University Press.

Marwan, A. 2015. "Sudan's Gold Boom." *Gulf News*, November 28. https://gulfnews.com/uae/environment/sudans-gold-boom-1.1626644, accessed August 30, 2023.

McCulloch, Neil, Tom Moerenhout, and Joonseok Yang. 2021. "Building a Social Contract? Understanding Tax Morale in Nigeria." *The Journal of Development Studies*, 57(2): 226–43.

Ministry of Finance and Economic Planning. 2014. "Tax and Custom Reform Committee." Final Report.

Moore, M. 2018. "Taxation and Development." In *The Oxford Handbook of the Politics of Development*, edited by C. Lancaster and N. van de Walle, 224–55. London, UK: Oxford University Press.

Moore, M. 2013. "Obstacles to Increasing Tax Revenues in Low-Income Countries." Working Paper 15, International Centre for Tax and Development, Brighton.

Patey, L. 2014. *The New Kings of Crude: China, India, and the Global Struggle for Oil in Sudan and South Sudan*. London: Hurst.

Patey, L. 2010. "Crude Days Ahead? Oil And the Resource Curse in Sudan." *African Affairs*, 109(437): 617–36.

Piracha, M., and M. Moore. 2016. "Revenue-Maximising or Revenue-Sacrificing Government? Property Tax in Pakistan." *The Journal of Development Studies*, 52(12): 1776–90.

Prichard, W. 2015. *Taxation, Responsiveness and Accountability in Sub-Saharan Africa: The Dynamics of Tax Bargaining*. Cambridge, UK: Cambridge University Press.

Resnick, D. 2021. "Taxing Informality: Compliance and Policy Preferences in Urban Zambia." *The Journal of Development Studies*, 57(7): 1063–85.

Reuters. 2020. "Sudan Opens Up Gold Market in Bid to Raise Revenue." https://www.reuters.com/article/idUSKBN1Z81M2/#:~:text=KHARTOUM%20(Reuters)%20%2D%20Sudan%20has,the%20country's%20cash%2Dstrapped%20treasury, accessed January 9, 2024.

Roessler, P. 2016. *Ethnic Politics and State Power in Africa: The Logic of the Coup-Civil War Trap*. Cambridge, UK: Cambridge University Press.

Ross, M. L. 2018. "The Politics of the Resource Curse: A Review," In *The Oxford Handbook of the Politics of Development*, edited by C. Lancaster and N. van de Walle, 200–23. London, UK: Oxford University Press.

Ross, M. L. 2001. "Does Oil Hinder Democracy?" *World Politics*, 53(3): 325–61.

Suliman, K. 2016. "Understanding and Avoiding the Oil Curse in Sudan." In *Understanding and Avoiding the Oil Curse in Resource-rich Arab Economies*, edited by I. Elbadawi and H. Selim, 421–60. Cambridge: Cambridge University Press.

Sudan Tribune. 2015. "Sudan Produces 43 Tons of Gold during the First Half of 2015." https://sudantribune.com/article54145/, accessed July 1, 2023.

Sudan Tribune. 2008. "Sudan Hikes Taxes as Oil Revenues Set to Dive." https://sudantribune.com/article29351/, accessed January 1, 2024.

The Juba Peace Agreement. 2020. "The Comprehensive Peace Agreement between The Government of The Republic of The Sudan and The Sudan People's Liberation Movement/Sudan People's Liberation Army." Sudan Open Archive.

Tilly, C. 1990. *Coercion, Capital, and European States, AD 990–1990*. Oxford: Blackwell.

Torgler, B. 2007. *Tax Compliance and Tax Morale: A Theoretical and Empirical Analysis*. Cheltenham, UK: Edward Elgar.

Verhoeven, H. 2015. *Water, Civilisation and Power in Sudan: The Political Economy of Military-Islamist State Building*. Cambridge: Cambridge University Press.

World Bank. 2015. "Realizing the Potential for Diversified Development. Sudan Country Economic Memorandum." World Bank, Washington, DC.

World Bank. 2012. "Sudan Country Economic Brief." Issue 2012-02, World Bank, Washington, DC.

World Bank. 2009a. "Sudan Investment Climate Assessment." World Bank, Washington, DC.

World Bank. 2009b. "World Bank Open Data, Inflation, Consumer Prices (Annual %)—Sudan (2009–2013)." World Bank, Washington, DC.

World Bank. 2007. "Sudan Public Expenditure Review Synthesis Report." Report 41840-SD, World Bank, Washington, DC.

Zachrisen, Gunnar. 2010. "Sudan vil bli olje-importør." https://www.panoramanyheter .no/afrika-miljo-og-energi/sudan-vil-bli-olje-importor/272735, accessed March 11, 2024.

Chapter 10

Political Power versus Economic Power?

The Case of Zambia's Mining Sector

Edward Lange

Zambia is a mining country with vast mineral resources potential due to its geographic location. Since the 1930s, the mining industry has been its economic backbone. It has a large known resource base of copper, cobalt, gold, nickel, platinum, zinc, lead, iron, manganese, gemstones (including emeralds), uranium, and coal. The country also has a potential for hydrocarbon production, specifically petroleum. Zambia boasts a wide range of industrial minerals capable of underpinning the anticipated growth in the mining, manufacturing, and agricultural sectors, such as feldspars, talc, phosphates, kaolin, gypsum, silica sand, fluorite, graphite, and barite (Phiri, Wang, and Nyambe 2016). However, due to the seemingly weak governance system, the mining sector is currently grappling with significant issues related to crime and lawlessness, causing considerable damage and hindering its potential for growth and national benefit.

Copper extraction has dominated Zambia's economic and political development since the Roan Select Trust European exploration of the region in the late 1880s under the British South Africa Company. Despite copper accounting for over 75 percent of its current exports, the country has high poverty rates and inequality. In addition, Zambia's rural and peri-urban areas have remained marginal to its development regardless of the recurrent rallying demands and cries for economic diversification in support of the stagnant agricultural sector.

This chapter, therefore, discusses Zambia's economic overdependence on mining, which has contributed to its growth failure. This failure is directly linked to the relationship between political decisions and the social economic development and has perpetuated and ignited mixed reactions from the general citizenry, including complaints from indigenous people on how they have not benefited from the extraction of mineral resources. The motivation of this chapter is the clear link that exists between democratic governance and natural resource governance. For Zambia, it is evident that the mining sector is a major contributor to foreign direct investment, while mining tax revenues contribute a significant portion of total government revenue. The sector is also a significant source of formal employment—both directly and indirectly—resulting from it being a more mature sector of the economy. Therefore, it is worth exploring the reasons why Zambia's mineral wealth has not translated into sustained and inclusive development despite this being considered the post–resource curse era.

The mining sector has witnessed several challenges, including policy inconsistency, political interference, lack of a consistent legislative and policy framework, and the stagnation of the artisanal and small-scale mining (ASM) sub-sector. This chapter analyzes issues like (a) the state of ASM in the rural parts of Zambia; (b) the new mineral resource development policy and the current government election manifesto; (c) political statements, mining sector policy reforms, and the local economic situation on the ground; (d) the emerging scavenging of minerals, illegal mining, and the role of political system; and (e) how to streamline political power away from national economic sectors.

All of these elements are linked to a lack of a clear vision of the sector. Although Zambia is a proponent of the Africa Mining Vision, the country has not yet developed a stand-alone Country Mining Vision. Issues such as limited consultations and lack of participation of key stakeholders have created a disconnect between mineral endowment and poverty eradication efforts. Although the mining sector remains a key strategic sector, the country has not managed to convert its mineral wealth fully for the benefit of the Zambian people. The ruling United Party for National Development (UPND) manifesto attests to this when it argues that the mining sector remains a significant part of the Zambian economy but is faced with key challenges, which include the lack of local participation in this industry, a lack of transparency and accountability regarding revenue management, and uncertainties about energy supply and property rights (UPND 2021). According to the World Bank (2016), other challenges include the lack of consistency surrounding fiscal policy and the lack of support for diversifying the economy and leveraging infrastructure for the general population. Hence, one cannot separate the national political economy from the mining sector, as it encompasses the entire spectrum of social and economic structures within a Zambian community.

OVERVIEW OF MINING SECTOR'S
CONTRIBUTION TO THE ECONOMY

Zambia is a unitary republican state with the executive, legislature, and judiciary operating as autonomous organs of government. The executive is headed by the president of the country, the legislature by the speaker of the National Assembly, and the chief justice heads the judiciary. Elections in Zambia take place within the framework of a multiparty democracy and a presidential system. The president and National Assembly are simultaneously elected for five-year terms. Zambia has been a regional model of peaceful and multiparty political transitions, yet corruption and persistent democratic weaknesses threaten this stability.

After Zambia's independence in 1964, the country's development was inspired by rapid growth in the copper sector in the late 1960s and early 1970s due to favorable world copper prices (Roan Consolidated Mines Public Relations Department 1978). Despite the increase in copper prices, workers were unsatisfied as most worked on short-term contracts. This situation left them vulnerable as unions did not represent short-term workers (Ferguson 1999). As a result, the government stated its plan to purchase shares in mining enterprises during the Mulungushi economic reforms of 1968 which were part of the "Zambian Economic Revolution" (Burdette 1977). The Matero reforms were introduced by the government in 1969 and resulted in the government owning 51 percent of the mining corporations (Parpart and Shaw 1983). In 1970, the Zambia Industrial Mining Corporation took over the two mining businesses, renaming them Roan Select Trust and Nchanga Consolidated Copper Mines (Fraser 2017). It was in 1973 that the Zambian government ended the purchase of shares in mining companies (Sardanis 2011). In 1982, there was the merger of Roan Select Trust and Nchanga Consolidated Copper Mines, resulting in the creation of Zambia Consolidated Copper Mines Limited (ZCCM), with 60.3 percent of the shares being owned by the Zambian government and the remainder belonging to the Anglo American Corporation (Simutanyi 2008). Apart from the drop in copper prices, the sector has faced a slew of issues, including a lack of investment, overstaffing, and obsolete equipment; with production costs soaring, the underground mine progressed to deeper levels, and in 1994, the Republic of Zambia was among the thirty poorest countries in the world (World Bank 2016). The government privatized the mines in 2000 and kept only a minority shareholding through ZCCM (Larmer 2016).

The August 2021 elections ushered in Zambia's third transition of power, offering opportunities for democratic governance and fiscal reforms while setting high public expectations for the government to deliver on democracy's dividend. The UPND, referred to as the "New Dawn" under the leadership of Hakainde Hichilema, was voted into office until the year 2026. The UPND promised to increase the mining sector's contribution to the national economy. After two years in power, it was ripe for the electorate to ask pertinent questions about the management of the mining sector by the New Dawn government.

From the preceding discussion, it is clear that power dynamics are in effect, illustrating relationships where one entity holds social-formative authority over another, compelling obedience to their desires. Politicians want to rule, control resources, appease the electorates by giving them jobs, and generate more revenue on the personal level so that they can remain in control and strong. Companies, on the other hand, have access to resources and financing, and offer jobs and other services needed to ensure a sustainable and organized economy. The government has the authority to make laws and policies, and manage national resources by providing an enabling environment for both its people and the business community. Therefore, balancing power relations is one of the key elements of a resource-rich jurisdiction that ensures a well-represented citizenry.

According to the Zambian Central Statistics Office, the contribution of the sector to the national economy in Zambia increased to 3,682.50 million ZMW in the fourth quarter of 2021 from 3,561.70 million ZMW in the third quarter of 2021 (Zambian Central Statistics Office 2023). According to the 2022 Extractive Industries Transparency Initiative (EITI) report, the contribution of the extractive sector to the country's gross domestic product reduced by 3 percent and its contribution to exports reduced by 5 percent. The domestic revenue increased by 5 percent in 2022 (Zambia EITI 2023). A recent review of Zambia's mining sector governance and investment attractiveness by the World Bank shows the country remains an appealing place for investment due to its favorable geology, long history of mining, political stability, low risk of expropriation, high levels of security, and a relatively favorable economic environment (World Bank 2016). However, the same review also identified some bottlenecks constraining the growth potential of Zambia's mining sector.

President Hichilema's inaugural speech re-invigorated the relevance and importance of the sector to economic sustainability and the realization of the 2030 Sustainable Development Goals (National Assembly of Zambia 2021). The president informed the nation that the mining sector would continue to play a key role in accelerating economic growth. The president bemoaned the fact that despite the long mining history and large mineral resource endowment, Zambia still faces several challenges in the sector; these changes include low levels of local participation and ownership, lack of transparency and accountability as well as inconsistent fiscal policy. The president assured the nation that his "New Dawn" administration was determined to ensure increased local participation and ownership in the sector, more jobs being created, as well as increased investments in the mining sector. Harnessing the opportunities available in the mining sector will be crucial to the country's economic revival. Increased copper and other mineral production must be ensured, as well as maximizing the benefits from various minerals such as gold, cobalt, and manganese, among others. There must be promotion of further exploration and value addition by offering appropriate incentives in the sector. He emphasized the need to position the country to be a leading manufacturer of mineral value-added products such as electrical cables and copper-based accessories to meet the growing demand of such products, which will translate into more employment opportunities for the Zambian people, especially the youth.

President Hichilema used his speech at the annual African Mining Indaba held in Cape Town in May 2022 to sell to the international investment community his vision for the nation's vital mining sector (Vandome 2023). He informed the gathering that the country is well-positioned to capitalize on the global drive for the minerals critical to green transitions and the ambition is to more than treble the country's copper production to three million tons per year. The speech was well-received by industry players who have long waited for the country's political and regulatory regimes to match the nation's resource potential. Promises of a transparent, predictable, and fair regulatory environment created a hopeful buzz among investors. Furthermore, the centrality of the sector has been expressed by the government's target to grow production of copper to two million tons by 2026 and to three million tons by 2031 (Lim 2022).

THE LEGISLATIVE AND POLICY FRAMEWORK OF ZAMBIA'S RESOURCE SECTOR

Each political party in government reviews and realigns legislation and policies to their respective manifesto. It is, therefore, important to critically assess the adaptability and suitability of the existing legal framework. Currently, the primary law governing the mining sector is the Mines and Minerals Development Act (No. 11 of 2015) of the Laws of Zambia, as read together with the Mines and Minerals Development (Amendment) Act (No. 14 of 2016). The Mines and Minerals Development Act became effective on July 1, 2015, although the date of assent is August 14, 2015. It repealed and replaced the Mines and Minerals Development Act No. 7 of 2008. Administration is regulated under the Mines and Minerals Development (General) Regulations, SI 7 of 2016. The government's policy is not to participate in exploration or other mining activities, or in any shareholding activity other than in a regulatory and promotional role. The right to explore or produce minerals is authorized by a license granted under the Mines and Minerals Development Act No. 11 of 2015. The Mines and Minerals Development Act deals with mining rights, licenses, large-scale mining in Zambia, gemstones mining, health and safety, environmental protection, and geologic services on analyses, royalties, and charges. The sector is administered by the Geological Survey Department, the Mines Development Department, the Mining Cadastre Department, and the Mines Safety Department of the Ministry of Mines and Minerals Development.

There is notable ambiguity within the Mines and Minerals Development Act 2015 Act on the extent it interfaces with other legislations, namely Lands and Forestry Acts. The licensing committee is appointed by the minister of mines and mineral development; at the same time, the minister has authority to overrule the committee's decisions. The current act allows the government to withhold compensation and re-settlement agreements from the public, which creates room for mistrust, reduces accountability, breeds mistrust, and threatens justice. There is a gap regarding non-mining rights, with respect to gold mining and lack of definition of "strategic mineral" which needs to be included in the act. This has been because of the process of enacting the same law, as there were no adequate consultations and most stakeholders' submissions were not considered by the government. The Mineral Royalty Sharing Mechanism, as was provided for under Article 136 of the Mines and Minerals Development Act of 2008, was omitted and is absent in the current law.

The Ministry of Mines and Mineral Development lacks the requisite capacity to superintend over the mineral resources for the country effectively. In its current form, the ministry has several operational and administrative challenges ranging from human resources to infrastructure and technology. Zambia has mineral deposits in almost all ten provinces, but the ministry has offices only in about six provinces. These offices are also not fully operational due to inadequate staff. The government has no staff stationed at the point of production permanently but relies on production figures supplied by the mining companies. The Mines Safety Department is highly centralized and fails to respond to eventualities such as mine accidents.

The government replaced the Mineral Resources Development Policy of 2013 with the Mineral Resources Development Policy of 2022, which responds to the identified inadequacies in dealing with the many new issues taking place both locally and internationally in the mining industry. These issues include new challenges that have emerged in the industry such as low investment in mineral exploration and mining, low participation of Zambians in the mineral value chain, inadequate growth coupled with the informality of the ASM sub-sector, and the plan to operationalize the new government ambitions to ramp up copper production to three million metric tons per annum by 2031.

In their manifesto, the UPND government promised to undertake a major mining sector policy reform including tax policy and administration reform that will bring various stakeholders on board to design a sound policy and administration system, with broad policy considerations that will stand the test of time. This, therefore, means that the revision of the policy provided the UPND government an opportunity to make the correct decisions on the identified inadequacies of the listed policies, strategies, and legislations. On October 14, the cabinet approved the revised Mineral Resources Development Policy and its Implementation Plan 2022–2026.

The implication is the government detected some challenges that character-ized the policy and legislative framework; both the 2013 Mineral Resources Development Policy and the Mines and Minerals Development Act of 2015 were inadequate to position the sector as an engine for growth and development; and they could not respond to the reforms of the ASM, local content, value addition, and the energy transition drive. It was also clear that the sector was not set to respond to the triple challenges—poverty, unemploy-ment, and inequality—facing Zambia.

The aspirations of the "New Dawn" government to drive the economy through prudent natural resource management can be achieved through a supportive legislative and policy framework. During his end-of-year message for the year 2023, the minister of mines informed the nation that the UPND government in its manifesto is anchored on the vision of having a united and prosperous Zambia with equal opportunities across ethnic, religious, and gender considerations, living in harmony in a free democratic society, and thus carrying forward Zambia's vision 2030. The minister highlighted the following as being key focus areas:

a. undertake a major mining sector policy reform including tax and admin-istration policies reforms
b. enhance monitoring and oversight mechanisms and technologies to reliably ascertain the volume and content of mining output for taxation purposes to ensure Zambians receive their fair share
c. promote small-scale mining as it has potential to generate more local jobs and supports the retention of earning within the country
d. put in place a policy and plan to facilitate local ownership and increased participation of Zambian players in the industry

The government has so far put in place the following: Minerals Regulation Commission Bill, Geological and Minerals Development legal framework, local content regulation, Mining Appeals Tribunal, introduction of 4 percent presumptive tax for the ASM sub-sector, strategies for three million tons of copper, Critical Minerals Strategy, issues of Konkola Copper Mines (KCM) and Mopani Copper Mines Plc (MCM), energy transition, mining licensing, and formalization of ASM.

ARE THE NEW DAWN GOVERNMENT POLICY REFORMS RESPONSIVE?

Zambia's New Dawn policy reform has been lauded as progressive. However, the limited participation and technical approach exclude relevant stakeholder views. In its current form, it remains a threat to indigenous people's rights because it is biased toward civil servants. Coincidentally, the previous government in 2020 developed a draft Statutory Instrument—"The Mines and Minerals Development (Local Content) Regulations 2020" (GRZ 2020)—to regulate the development of mining local content in Zambia. Large-scale mining license holders are required to submit annual returns to the director of mining cadastre showing compliance with conditions and obligations attached to the license, including local business development. The ministry does not publish reports consolidating this information for effective monitoring and evaluation purposes. In the draft Mining Local Content Regulations (GRZ 2020), the term "local content" covers the employment and training of Zambians ("Zambianization"), the procurement of local content products, technology transfer programs, social development initiatives, and the localization of professional services. The policy framework for mining local content in Zambia is underpinned by Vision 2030, the Seventh National Development Plan, and the respective mining, industrial, employment and science and technology policies.

The UPND government has continued with the process of putting in place a policy and a plan to facilitate local ownership and increased participation of Zambian players in the industry. The findings of a study conducted by the African Development Bank in 2019 revealed that the mining sector procures between four billion to five billion US dollars annually in goods and services. However, only about 10 percent of this originates from Zambians. Therefore, localizing a significant portion of mining procurement would promote the participation of Zambians across the mining value chain.

In addition to copper, Zambia boasts other mineral resources including base metals, precious, industrial, gemstones, and energy minerals. It is important to mention that the country's overdependence on copper has impacted negatively on the exploitation of these minerals, making it susceptible to fiscal risks emanating from production and price volatility.

According to the Center for Trade Policy and Development's Monday opinion edition of April 25, 2022, entitled "Economic Diversification in Mining Sector Part One" (Center for Trade Policy and Development 2022), several pieces of policy and legal documents speak to the economic diversification within Zambia's mining sector. The Ministry of Mines and Minerals Development and the Ministry of Commerce Trade and Industry created Zambia's export diversification strategy for gold and gemstones in 2020. The strategy aims to achieve diversification through the lens of ASM. This strategy is robust because it explicates the strategic objectives and the proposed interventions on a sector-by-sector basis.

Further to what was articulated in the UPND inaugural speech, true to his party's manifesto, President Hichilema informed the world that in mining, his administration would strive to increase copper and other mineral production to three million tons per annum so that Zambia can reclaim its place as one of Africa's leading mining countries. He further noted that his government envisages to promote the expansion of the mining value chain as well as the promotion of mineral diversification. Further, it will encourage the production and processing of gemstones, gold, nickel, manganese, iron, and industrial and other minerals. This effort is confused by the seeming reliance and dependence on copper as evidenced by the three million tons copper strategy.

There has been a lot of mistrust between the government and the people on how the issue of license issuance and allocation has been handled in the past. This problem has been a breeding area for corruption and abuse by officers and politically connected individuals. The government suspended operations at the cadastre and instituted investigations, and it approved some recommendations from the 2022 findings of the Mining Cadastre Audit Report. The approved recommendations include re-opening the Mining Cadastre Department following the completion of the audit exercise; floating of the bids for the blocked mining rights to companies which are wholly or partly owned by Zambians; restricting the number of mining rights an entity or company or related companies should have to only five; ensuring that foreign entities, wishing to acquire mining rights, partner with Zambians or companies owned by Zambians; and utilization of information and communication technology in the conduct of business to avoid human interaction. The cabinet further agreed to address the issues which have compromised the issuance and management of mining rights; implement decisive measures to unlock investment in the mining industry; and enhance efficiency, transparency, and accountability in the administration of mining rights. Finally, the government announced the migration from manual application to online mining as of December 15, 2023.

POLITICAL DECISIONS FOR THE
DECLINING COPPERBELT ECONOMY

The two biggest copper mining companies in the copperbelt are MCM and KCM. These mines serve as a gauge for the mining industries and, by implication, the Zambian economy's health. The Copperbelt is the country's major contributor to gross domestic product, with mining accounting for 90 percent of the total (Callaghan 2013). Smaller Copperbelt mines such as Lubambe Copper Mine, Chibuluma Mines, NFC Africa Mining, CNMC Luanshya, Chambishi Copper Smelting Company, Sino-Metals, and Chambishi Metals also add to Zambia's copper output.

Based on the previous deals that the government undertook, it was clear that there was low capacity to negotiate, as evidenced by the Glencore deal in which the company, through its subsidiary Carlisa Investments Corp., in which Glencore holds 81.2 percent of the shares, in March 2021 completed the sale to ZCCM Investments Holdings PLC of its 90 percent interest in MCM. Glencore continues to retain offtake rights in respect of MCM's production. The retaining of offtake rights is a complete rip off, and it is not clear if the government through ZCCM-Investment Holding understood the concept. This undertaking has impacted the community negatively as the government has failed to manage or run the asset (Banda 2016). Uncertainty surrounding the government's controversial ownership of MCM and KCM has not helped the prospect of capital injection in the mining firms that have operations in Kitwe, Mufulira, Chingola, and Chililabombwe. The two firms have been struggling to pay suppliers and contractors who are equally failing to pay their respective workers.

The KCM and MCM situation has been a gigantic issue that required people to face it with sober minds and calm spirit to avoid hastily handling the matter. The miners, their mine workers' unions, the suppliers, the contractors, creditors, and indeed other key stakeholders should exercise patience with a good attitude because the government is on top of things. There is a need to give the current government sufficient room in which to operate and negotiate with the potential investors in the best interest of the nation. This is more so in that the issue of both KCM and MCM was inherited by the current government administration, which has shown a lot of political will to address once for all. Indeed, in 2019, the government decided to institute a liquidation process of KCM contrary to advice from various stakeholders to use a different route if they indeed wanted to address the matter. The liquidation route from the start seemed to have been a challenging one and time wasting; hence, where the country is today.

Similarly, the MCM issue started when Glencore, the majority share-holder, decided to place the mine on care and maintenance, which did not go well with the ruling Patriotic Front administration. One year before the 2021 general elections, the Patriotic Front administration was desperate to get re-elected and decided to get into a share buyout that complicated matters. A bad deal was cut through a transaction resulting in 1.5 billion US dollars while the Zambian government retained 100 percent shareholding through ZCCM-Investment Holding. We are aware that the administration then deliberately agreed to some terms and conditions which were at best counter to national interest and that could have contributed to the current scenario. The "New Dawn" government administration has had to contend with many complicated matters to try and unlock the opportunities in these mining units.

Zambia's ASM sub-sector has been struggling to enhance and estimate the real contribution to the national economy. This is mainly because most activities are not formalized and are often associated with illegal mineral supply chains. In many parts of the country, ASM activities are increasingly being as important as large-scale mining activities, especially the numbers of people employed. There has not been readily available information of the exact number of laborers in the sector. It has therefore been challenging for the government together with concerned parties to take care of worker rights and representation. There is no clear and outstanding model of ownership, neither is there a framework for profit-sharing mechanisms in Zambia. Zambians in most cases own only papers, while foreigners own the minerals and the extraction in the name of partnerships.

The ASM sub-sector has grown considerably in the recent past and is not only a source of livelihood of people but also contributes significantly to the country's socio-economic development. The sub-sector has been identified to have high potential to increase its contribution to the mainstream national economy as well as revenue and wealth generation. A significant proportion of people engaged in the sector are women, youths, and children. Women work as miners and are also involved in other aspects of the ASM value chain, including ore processing, panning, and transporting goods while also additionally playing a critical role in supporting the industry through their activities as shopkeepers and cooks. However, women are usually marginalized in ASM communities and have limited decision-making power because they are rarely recognized as miners.

Zambia is an EITI implementing country, joined EITI as a candidate on May 15, 2009, and became fully compliant with the EITI 2011 Standard on September 19, 2012. Zambia EITI has been using the EITI process and data disclosures to inform discussions on the mining fiscal regime and benefit sharing. Zambia EITI has also been working to inform regulatory reform and improve the underlying procedures for monitoring production and export data from extractive industries. Transparency and accountability are always a hot topic as there is continuous mistrust between the people, the government, and the mining companies, operators,or developers who in most cases are the multinational corporations. While the membership and implementation of EITI has added value and credibility to the country's transparency profile, the initiative is not enough to seal all the loopholes of ensuring that all production is captured and accounted for.

THE SCRAMBLE FOR NEWLY DISCOVERED OF MINERALS IN ZAMBIA

Zambia's Ministry of Mines is taking proactive measures to harness the potential of the newly discovered minerals such as sugilite gemstone and other unexploited mineral deposits. By developing a comprehensive strategy for responsible and sustainable management, the government aims to ensure that the exploitation of these minerals benefits Zambian citizens.

As indicated in the preceding section, there is a thin line between ASM and illegal mining. This sub-sector is usually associated with criminal activities. Because of the number of people involved in the extraction of minerals at small-scale level, it has become a fertile avenue for political party mobilization activities. The current government's greatest challenge is on how to balance between political appeasement and genuine youth employment creation. The proceeds from such activities have not been adequately accounted for as it trades informally and there is no documentation. The government has therefore taken a step and included this as part of the three million strategies by recognizing the potential of slag dumps and tailing dumps in most brown mine sites dotted around the country. It is therefore based on this assumption and projection of the potentiality that strategic objective three is to facilitate the exploitation from all the decommissioned mineralized tailings and slag dumps.

To allow citizens benefit from these mineral resources, political party cadres have been afforded an opportunity to participate in the mining value chain through the formation of mine cooperatives for purposes of acquiring mining licenses. While these interventions are underway, the illegal and criminal activities have continued in the name of youth empowerment. Unwarranted disasters have repeatedly occurred where lives have been lost, when if the correct action was taken life could have been saved. The following is a description of two accidents that happened due to the involvement of political party cadres in mining activities.

The Black Mountain, located between Wusakile and Nkana West in Kitwe, is owned by Nkana Alloy, who are the major shareholders with the government having a minor stake through ZCM-IH. The ruling party, then Patriotic Front, mobilized its youths, popularly known as "Jerabos," and started extracting materials without prior consent from the owners. In trying to harmonize the situation, the government negotiated that the minority shares for ZCCM-Investment Holdings were going to be transferred to the community, which legally was not done. The activities by the youths continued. In May 2018, community members and motorists complained about blasting at the mountain which destroyed 130 houses in Wusakile Township. The government assured the nation that the situation was under control and that the Mines Safety Department was monitoring the operations at the site. On June 20, 2018, the Black Mountain collapsed and more than ten people died.

The unfortunate occurrence could have been avoided, but it was not easy for the government politically; measures were supposed to be put in place as the operations were not in line with mine regulations, but again the issue was on what and how to handle the youths who were illegally mining at the mountain. In their quest to regulate the operations, the government registered a cooperative for youths called Chapamo, meaning working together. The illegality continued even after the change of government. The activities have continued for fear of losing popularity by the current government. This whole episode is because of having a docile civil society that allows lawlessness; there is a need to have a cadre of competent fearless lawyers who will begin to hold politicians accountable. It was clear that some corrupt politicians sanctioned this unsafe mining. The leaders chose being populist at the expense of laid down rules and regulations.

During campaigns prior to the 2021 elections, Hichilema promised to give the same mountain to the Jerabos once voted into power. Now what is surprising is that no one cared to follow the rules after the final deal was struck to give 10 percent to the Jerabos. It is all about economic power to propel political power, while the general citizenry keeps complaining of not benefiting from their God given mineral endowments.

Due to lack of economic activities, many youths in the town of Chingola of the Copperbelt province have resorted to turning the former and disused Nchanga Open pit sites into a lucrative source of bread and butter. While the rest of the world celebrated the World AIDS Day on December 1, 2023, this mine community was engulfed in grief, as an unprecedented catastrophe struck the mining town of Chingola, where an estimated thirty-six illegal miners were feared to have been buried alive at the Sensele mine, highlighting the perils lurking in the shadows of unauthorized mining operations. The grim incident has prompted the government to immediately cease mining operations at the ill-fated site. So far out of the suspected number of victims only twelve have been retrieved out of which only one survived, while eleven were dead and have been put to rest at an official burial site with the support of the government.

Following this horrific accident, Mines Minister Paul Kabuswe announced the closure of operations at the Sensele mine. The decision came post his visit to the harrowing accident site in Chingola. This decision by the government was in support of the rescue and recovery operations which were aimed at retrieving the bodies of the victims. The collective collaborative efforts of the rescue teams, including the local authorities, mining officials, and emergency services, were aimed at locating and recovering the trapped miners.

Surprisingly, in the name of poverty and empowerment, while on the other side of the same mine site the searching was ongoing, the illegality was also continuing on the side of Sensele Copper mine where another fatal accident was recorded in which a forty-nine-year-old illegal miner of Chiwempala area died after the earth fell on him while doing illegal mining at the open pit mine near Debra's site on December 24, 2023.

Yes, there have been widespread complaints about benefiting from these assets by the citizens, but the persistence of these illegal mining activities in various communities, which are allegedly driven by factors such as economic hardships and lack of alternative employment opportunities,needs not to be allowed. Such unauthorized operations often lack proper safety measures and oversight, due to political appeasement, which ultimately culminate in tragic accidents and subsequent fatalities. The government has periodically conducted crackdowns on illegal mining, emphasizing the importance of adhering to safety regulations to prevent such tragedies. The question that will continue to beg an honest answer is: who benefits from these illegal activities, the government or politically connected individuals?

In the recent past, Luapula province has been the center of illegal activities in the mining sector. The various incidents have just brought to light the unreported historical cases of mining-related crimes in Zambia. One notable occurrence involves Luapula Province Minister Derrick Chilundika, who has been implicated in the illegal mining of sugilite. On July 5, 2023, President Hakainde Hichilema took immediate action by dismissing him from his position as minister for Luapula province. Subsequently, he and eighteen others, including senior and junior police officers, businessmen, and ruling UPND party officials, were arrested by the Zambia Police Service.

It is therefore important to critically analyze the availability of sugilite and preparedness of the government to derive maximum benefit from the mineral especially the host community, whose major economic activity is fishing. Further, there is a need to assess the level of political party patronage and influence on matters of national interest, especially in the mining sector. Finally, we will attempt to share some information regarding the little known sugilite and the potential economic benefits. Luapula is one of Zambia's ten provinces and is in the northern part of the country. The province was named after the Luapula River which acts as a boundary with the Democratic Republic of Congo. Luapula province extends along the northern and eastern banks of the Luapula river from Lake Bangweulu to Lake Mweru, including waters and islands of those lakes, and is inhabited by Bemba-speaking peoples (including the Lunda, Kabende, Aushi, Chishinga, and Bemba). Traditionally, Luapula is not a mining region compared to the Copperbelt and Northwestern provinces. The province has been predominantly a fishing area and subsistence farming is another source of livelihood for the many households in most of the districts. Sugilite is a rare mineral and a gemstone best known for its vibrant pink to purple color. High-quality specimens are sought after by mineral collectors and lapidarists (people who cut and polish gems). Sugilite is a sodium potassium lithium silicate mineral. Small amounts of manganese produce the pink to purple color displayed by some specimens of sugilite. The composition of sugilite varies because iron, manganese, and aluminum can substitute for one another. The acknowledgment and acceptance by government that the mineral in question has not been in its database of mineral occurrence in Zambia and at the same time acknowledging the illegal extraction of the mineral under discussion is a clear demonstration of lack of capacity by the government. This requires urgent practical attention and more than just policies and regulatory reforms. After noticing increased activities of illegal mining of the mineral, the government through the Geological Survey Department conducted a verification inspection from February 10 to 15, 2022, to ascertain the occurrence of sugilite. The findings revealed that during the exploration by Bayan Construction Limited, there were illegal mining activities of manganese by the surrounding communities which exposed sugilite mineralization.

The fact the government did not know about the presence of this mineral and the collusion between civil servants and political party leadership especially from the ruling is a clear manifestation of a weak governance system, a system that feeds on the fertility of poverty and disorganization and low technical capacity by the technocrats. If minerals are to be extracted prudently, there is a need for the government to invest in the geographical survey mapping of minerals across the country. It is also important to grow the sense of patriotism among public workers and put in place effective measures to prevent corruption by detaching party officials from the mainstream governance system.

Perhaps greater opportunities will be garnered from developing critical minerals in Zambia. Critical minerals are used to in mobile phones, computers, fiber optic cables, semiconductors, banknotes, defense aerospace, and medical applications. Many critical minerals are also used in low-emission technologies, such as electric vehicles, wind turbines, solar panels, and rechargeable batteries. Critical minerals are cardinal in clean energy transition, especially in battery performance.

The government has recognized the fact that, despite the abundant natural resources like gold, cobalt, coltan, lithium, copper, etc., Zambia has not been able to fully exploit these resources to help in the economic development of the country for the benefit of the Zambian people. It is against this background that it has become necessary to pay attention to all the stages of the value chain of non-renewable mineral resources, starting from awarding of contracts and licenses for exploration and production to integrating mining with sustainable development plans. As the global demand for critical minerals, many countries have looked to Africa's abundant reserves of cobalt, lithium, copper, and other minerals vital to the manufacturing of modern technologies. Zambia, therefore, has realized the urgent need to develop a strategy to get the best opportunities from its critical mineral resources. The strategy, therefore, calls for structural transformation of the mining sector in Zambia through effective management of exploration, exploitation, value addition, and its trade.

Securing access to these strategic, high-value commodities is a key focus for continental bodies and governments around the world, and many Western nations and multinational corporations and African countries including Zambia are working to achieve this goal as ethically and sustainably as possible.

ORGANIZED LABOR AND HUMAN RIGHTS IN ZAMBIA'S MINING INDUSTRY

In line with the international conventions and instruments, Zambia has developed various policies and enacted specific laws protecting human rights and governing business activities. Zambia, like all states, has an obligation to respect human rights and fundamental freedoms as enshrined in the international conventions and instruments that the country has signed and ratified such as the Universal Declaration of Human Rights. In addition, the mining companies adhere to various international conventions and practices under the auspices of international organizations such as International Labor Organization and United Nations.

According to the labor force survey of 2019, it is stated that in Zambia, youth unemployment rate was estimated at 17.9 percent. The youth unemployment rate was higher in urban areas at 18.1 percent than in rural areas at 17.6 percent. The youth unemployment rate among females was higher in urban areas at 20.9 percent than in rural areas at 14.4 percent. There is unemployment and underemployment, poor quality and unproductive jobs, unsafe work and insecure income, rights that are denied, and gender inequality in the study areas.

Zambia is a part of the UN Global Compact Initiative, the International Labor Organization Declaration on Fundamental Principles and Rights at Work, and the International Labor Organization Tripartite Declaration of Principles concerning Multinational Enterprises and Social Policy. The right to form a collective labor organization is a fundamental aspect of the employee/employer relationship within the liberal democracy. As individuals, workers previously possessed only inefficient leverage in negotiating the conditions of labor. Selling your labor force in a capitalist society has, since industrialization, been accompanied by collective struggles against employers.

According to Beatrice B. Liatto, during the first ten years of independence, the edge within this struggle was gained by politically oriented leaders who regarded trade union interests as subordinate to the party and government's need to accumulate (Liatto 1989). She asserts that from the early 1970s, economistic ally-oriented trade unionists have ascended to the leadership of the labor movement. Ideally, in Zambia and the mining sector these leaders claim to place emphasis on the economic interests of workers and the need of the trade union movement to maintain its organizational autonomy, perceiving this to be a necessary part of the country's development. The emerging and development of unionism has heightened tension between labor and the state, inducing further incorporative efforts. The state's activities in this regard have been reinforced by continuing industrial action, often initiated by the rank and file, which itself serves as a measure of the inadequacy of any previous strategy aimed at worker quiescence.

Despite the sector being heavily unionized, unions have been unable to protect workers. Most Zambian miners are disappointed with their unions. There is too much mob psychology, working culture, and blind loyalty. The disappointment is made worse by the tendency of unions to portray themselves as strong when in fact the situation has provided room for corruption and cowardice.

The mining sector today in Zambia has seven unions representing workers. These unions include the following: Mine Workers Union of Zambia; National Union of Miners and Allied Workers; United Mine Workers Union of Zambia; Consolidated Miners and Allied Workers Union of Zambia; Miners and Allied Workers Union of Zambia; Miners, Technicians and Artisans Union of Zambia; and the Zambia National Union of Nurses. It sounds correct to conclude that trade unions in Zambia support democracy, because of corruption and their close association with political institutions and management. It is evident, therefore, that in the mining sector union actions are related to actual political regime changes. The context of political activities and mine unions are more concerned about organizational survival than ideological commitments. In Zambia's mining industry, wages and working conditions have consistently declined for forty years. This is attributed mainly to changes of labor laws. For now, it's difficult to organize strikes due to multiple unions in one sector, the increase in the practice of subcontracting of workers which has become easier and common, and wages negotiated at each workplace rather than for the industry because workers belong to different unions.

Historically, Zambia's mining unions were too powerful and militant. Workers were motivated by the principle of "The People United Will Never Be Defeated." Union leaders argued that they negotiated the highest salaries by understanding economic data and by threatening strikes. But instead, they worked closely with employers' union for purposes of institutional survival and sustainability and started engaging in some businesses with mining companies, which eventually made them believe that their union as a financially influential entrepreneurial entity, because of the businesses it ran. They understood these debt-centric businesses as a sign of unions' strength, rather than workers' poverty.

Most union leaders belong to mainstream political parties; it is an undeniable fact that these union leaders used to be typically popular miners who held leadership positions in their church and community. They assisted their co-workers daily by resolving disputes with management and providing material support to struggling peers. They were also nominally in charge of negotiating wages.

Zambia is party to several regional and international protocols on gender equality and women's empowerment such as the Southern African Development Community Protocol on Gender and Development, the African Charter on Human and Peoples' Rights, the Maputo Protocol on the Rights of Women in Africa, the Convention on the Elimination of All Forms of Discrimination Against Women, the Convention on the Rights of Children, and the Beijing Declaration and Platform for Action. Zambia has historically been associated with patriarchal tendencies that have significantly affected the country's human and economic development. The norms, behaviors, and roles associated with being a woman, man, girl, or boy, as well as relationships with each other, are some of the characteristics that define gender in a Zambian society. As a social construct, gender varies from society to society and can change over time (World Health Organization 2021). Gender concerns related to the mining sector—including both large- and small-scale mining operations—have highlighted that the sector is overwhelmingly male dominated, and scholars have suggested that high levels of gender-based inequality remain, including sex segregation of jobs, women occupying lower-status roles,or linked effects of idealized notions of nuclear families and male breadwinner roles, and other cultural and legislative factors (Lahiri-Dutt 2015).

For Zambia, women's growing participation in mining should be understood considering the mining sector's importance for the country's economy. As Zambia is party to several regional and international protocols on gender equality and women's empowerment, it is important to understand the gendered impacts of mining as a human rights issue. Women have the same "right to development" as men.

Generally, it is agreed that business must contribute positively to the society at large (Hamann and Kapelus 2004). As indicated in the introduction, the notion of corporate social responsibility (CSR) is especially contentious in terms of the impact, implementation, and measurement of the concept. The three pillars of sustainable development, namely, economic, social, and environment, also play a major role in the construction of the concept of CSR and largely contribute to the controversies associated with the concept. The concept of CSR has been studied so many times. However, the practice of CSR continues to be problematic, and the interpretation differs from one corporation to the other, from one society to the other. One area of contestation is whether CSR should be regulated. Many governments in Africa have started regulating CSR for purposes of standardizing the quality of investment. Zambia has not, although there has been an ongoing debate around the subject between civil society organizations and the Chamber of Mines, through the Canadian High Commission. The Zambian government has been reluctant to regulate it by way of developing a national CSR strategy. As the situation stands today, Zambia has no legal enforcement mechanism of CSR and as such most mining houses are disconnected from communities and reality. Lack of regulation of CSR in Zambia means companies have no legal obligation to give an account of how they are implementing their programs and who they are doing it for. It also means the companies are not accountable to explain their investments and impact to the Zambian government (Elorza 2019). CSR within the extractive industry is a relevant and contentious issue globally. Issues pertaining to equality, human rights, and sustainable development are pervasive throughout the extractive industry's economic, social, and environmental arenas.

There is still no consensus on the definition of CSR regarding the measurement of performance or impact or how to determine which of the various "developmental" components of the concept—namely, economic, social, or environmental—takes precedence over the other where there are competing interests.

CONCLUSION

According to both available literature and situation on the ground, Zambia's country's economic overdependence on copper mining has contributed to its growth failure; this failure is directly linked to the disjointed relationship between political decisions and the social economic development. Ideally, there is supposed to be a clear link between national political economy and the mining sector, and this involves the whole range of social economic structure of a Zambian community.

In Zambia, it has become fashionable for every political party in government to change or review and realign legislations and policies to their respective manifesto. According to the "New Dawn" government, the sector was not able to respond to the triple challenges—poverty, unemployment, and inequality—facing the country. The inconsistency in policy and legislative framework has contributed to the investment instability. Further, political party patronage in ASM has created a struggle for supremacy, and there is a constant political tug of war between government machinery and political party emissaries. For newly discovered minerals and the need for citizens to benefit from these mineral resources, political party cadres have been accorded an opportunity to participate in the mining value chain through, the formation of mine cooperatives for purposes of acquiring mining licenses. These efforts have been politically driven and have led to loss of lives. The widespread complaints about benefiting from these assets by the citizens have been genuinely responded to, but the persistence of these illegal mining activities in various communities, which are allegedly driven by factors such as economic hardships and lack of alternative employment opportunities, needs not to be allowed.

The fact the government did not know about the presence of sugilite in Luapula province and the collusion between civil servants and political party leadership is a clear manifestation of a weak governance system—a system that feeds on the fertility of poverty and disorganization and low technical capacity by the technocrats. Most union leaders belong to mainstream political parties; it is an undeniable fact that these union leaders used to be typically popular miners who held leadership positions in their church and community. They assisted their co-workers daily by resolving disputes with management and providing material support to struggling peers. They were also nominally in charge of negotiating wages.

It is evident from the foregoing that power relations are at play here—it is a clear example of relationships in which one part has social-formative power over another and can get the other part to do what they wish by compelling obedience. Politicians want to rule, they want to control resources, they want to appease the electorate by giving them jobs, and they want to generate more revenue at the personal level so that they can remain in power. Companies have access to resources, they have access to financing, they have jobs and other services needed to ensure a sustainable and organized economy. The government has the authority to make laws, policies and manage national resources by providing an enabling environment for both its people and the business community. Therefore, balancing power relations is one of the key elements of a resource-rich nation that ensures a well-represented citizenry.

REFERENCES

Banda, T. 2016. "Knowledge Asymmetry and Agency Costs: Zambia's Copper Mining Regulatory Framework." Doctoral dissertation, Cornell University.

Burdette, M. M. 1977. "Nationalization in Zambia: A Critique of Bargaining Theory." *Canadian Journal of African Studies/La Revue Canadienne des études Africaines*, 11(3): 471–96.

Callaghan, C. 2013. "Mineral Resource Based Growth Pole Industrialisation— Base Metals Report." Regional Integration Research Network Open Dialogues for Regional Innovation. https://www.academia.edu/10227072/Mineral_Resource _Based_Growth_Pole_Industrialisation_Growth_Poles_and_Value_Chains, accessed June 25, 2024.

Center for Trade Policy and Development. 2022. "Economic Diversification in Mining Sector Part One." Lusaka, Zambia.

Elorza, L. 2019. "Corporate Social Responsibility in Zambian Copper Mines." Southern African Institute for Policy and Research. http://saipar.org/wp-content/ uploads/2020/03/Verma.Elorza.ActionAid-1.pdf, accessed May 22, 2024.

Extractive Industries Transparency Initiative (EITI). 2022. "EITI Progress Report 2022." https://eiti.org/documents/eiti-progress-report-2022, accessed May 22, 2024.

Ferguson, James. 1999. *Expectations of Modernity: Myths and Meanings of Urban Life on the Zambian Copperbelt*. Oakland: University of California Press.

Fraser, A., 2017. "Post-Populism in Zambia: Michael Sata's Rise, Demise and Legacy." *International Political Science Review*, 38(4): 56–472.

Government of the Republic of Zambia (GRZ). 2020. "The Mines and Minerals Development (Local Content) Regulations 2020." http://www.businesslicenses.gov .zm/consultation/regulations/the-mines-and-minerals-development-local-content -regulations-2020/comments, accessed June 25, 2024.

Hamann, R., and P. Kapelus. 2004. "Corporate Social Responsibility in Mining in Southern Africa: Fair Accountability or Just Greenwash?" *Development*, 47(3): 85–92.

Lahiri-Dutt, K. 2015. "The Feminisation of Mining." *Geography Compass*, 9(9): 523–41.

Larmer, Miles. 2016. *Rethinking African Politics: A History of Opposition in Zambia*. London, UK: Routledge.

Liatto, B. B. 1989. "*Organised Labour and the State in Zambia.*" Doctoral dissertation, University of Leeds.

Lim, H. 2022. "Transparency, Institution, and Investment: The Case of the Extractive Industries Transparency Initiative (EITI)." *Social Science Research Network*, working paper. https://papers.ssrn.com/sol3/papers.cfm?abstract_id=4245586, accessed June 25, 2024.

National Assembly of Zambia. 2021. "Statement by Mr. Hakainde Hichilema, President of the Republic of Zambia During the General Debate at the Fifth United Nations Conference on the Least Developed Countries (LDCS): Doha, Qatar." https://estatements.unmeetings.org/estatements/14.0485/20230305140000000 /582jnvwNMpIH/stkqtBAAqGrd_en.pdf. (Site discontinued.)

Phiri, C., P. Wang, and I. A. Nyambe. 2016. "Geology and Potential Hydrocarbon Play System of Lower Karoo Group in the Maamba Coalfield Basin, Southern Zambia." *Journal of African Earth Sciences*, 118: 45–262.

Parpart, Jane L., and Timothy M. Shaw. 1983. "Contradiction and Coalition: Class Fractions in Zambia, 1964–1984." *Africa Today*, 30(3): 23–50.

Roan Consolidated Mines, Public Relations Department. 1978. *Zambia's Mining Industry: The First 50 Years*. Produced for the Mining Industry by the Public Relations Department, Roan Consolidated Mines Limited.

Sardanis, Andrew. 2011. *Africa: Another Side of the Coin*. London: I. B. Tauris.

Simutanyi, Neo. 2008. "Copper Mining in Zambia: The Developmental Legacy of Privatisation." Paper 165, Institute for Security Studies.

United Party for National Development (UPND). 2021. "United Party for National Development (UPND) Manifesto." https://www.sh.gov.zm/wp-content/uploads /2021/12/UPND-MANIFESTO-Updated-00.pdf, accessed May 23, 2024

Vandome, Christopher. 2023. *Zambia's Developing International Relations*. Washington, DC: Chatham House.

World Bank. 2016. "How Can Zambia Benefit More from Mining (Arabic)." https: //documents.worldbank.org/en/publication/documents-reports/documentdetail /710031638421772490/how-can-zambia-benefit-more-from-mining, accessed May 22, 2024.

World Health Organization. 2021. "Gender and Health." https://www.who.int/health -topics/gender#tab=tab_1, accessed May 22, 2024

Zambia Extractive Industries Transparency Initiative (EITI). 2023. "Report on Zambia's Extractive Sector." https://eiti.org/countries/zambia#:~:text=Overview %20and%20role%20of%20the%20EITI&text=There%20has%20been%20public %20debate,monitoring%20production%20and%20export%20data, accessed May 22, 2023.

Zambian Central Statistics Office. 2023. "Zambia Census Statistics." https://www .zamstats.gov.zm/, accessed May 23, 2023.

Chapter 11

New Resource Discoveries, Old Patterns of Accumulation, Politics, and Development in Nigeria

Dung Pam Sha

Nigeria is one of Africa's largest resource-endowed countries. The resource economy began in the 1890s, when the colonial state and capital explored, extracted, and exploited resources such as tin, columbite, coal, and bauxite in Jos, Enugu, and other parts of the country, harvesting millions in pounds. In the 1960s, oil was discovered in the Niger Delta region of the now post-colonial state and has since fetched millions of dollars for the government over the decades. Recently, Nigeria discovered new sites for fossil fuels and many for solid minerals, including gold, lead, blue, and sapphire in the northern part of the country, particularly in the Kolmani community of Gombe state and Nasarawa state. These recent discoveries have raised many concerns among citizens about whether the Nigerian story of the resource curse will be different.

This chapter aims to show that despite new resource discoveries that generate income for the state, old patterns of capital accumulation in the interest of a few elites, violent politics to control the state, and unequal and disjointed development prevail within Nigeria's resource economy. The chapter argues that while resources are natural endowments to nations meant to be a blessing to citizens, they usually become a curse when class greed and state capture obstruct their utilization and management. Resource discoveries have instead inflicted pain on many countries. In Nigeria, resource extraction has initiated conflicts between the state and indigenous peoples. In addition to oil, minerals in their raw form are mined illegally under the protection of state elites and exported by transnational elites and companies, leaving no record

249

of proceeds in the state treasury. Violent competition for political power in these resource-endowed communities has intensified because the state guarantees control over the distribution of oil and mineral resource rents. Indeed, this control facilitates the pilfering of rents through obscure government expenditures.

Consequently, social provisioning by the state has diminished in Nigeria as social protection programs are weakly resourced, resulting in widespread poverty. The chapter recognizes the utility of the Dutch disease, rent-seeking, institutional, state, and dependency models in explaining the resource curse in Nigeria but argues that, separately, they do not provide a holistic understanding of the phenomenon. The author, therefore, proposes in this chapter that an integrated political economy approach would provide a more comprehensive understanding of the paradox in the country. This proposed approach draws its strength from these extant methods and interprets their strong points from a political economy perspective.

The term "resource curse" is used in this chapter to refer to a situation where fuel and mineral resource–rich developing countries tend to generate negative developmental outcomes, including poor economic performance, collapsing growth rates, high levels of corruption, ineffective governance, and increased political violence (Di John 2010). Capital accumulation is also used to describe how the state receives rents and how it is re-invested into economic development and welfare purposes (Radley and Lehmann-Grube 2022). This is state accumulation. It is also used here to refer to the profits received by private sector operators who re-invest in production. The source and the endpoint of the rents of accumulation are important to consider here. The rent, meant for the state, is diverted by state officials for private accumulation (Iyayi 1986). Similarly, the refusal by actors in the extractive sector to declare and disclose the quantities of resources extracted also blocks state accumulation.

Development is used in the chapter to refer to positive changes in citizens' material living conditions due to oil and solid mineral rents. Development becomes unequal when disparities exist between the social classes of the rich and the poor, between genders, and between geographical regions of the country (Amin 1976).

The chapter is written in five sections. The second section discusses the extant theoretical perspectives on resource curse and suggests the need to develop an integrated theoretical framework for understanding the phenomenon. The third section takes an overview of resource discoveries in Nigeria from the colonial to the present period and proposes that the manner of the discoveries and resource extraction created the basis for the resource curse. The fourth section examines the major drivers of resource curse in Nigeria, while the fifth section discusses the manifestation of a country that has experienced the curse. The fifth section concludes the chapter by drawing attention to the lessons learned from the Nigerian experience and proffers suggestions on how resources can become a blessing to the people.

RESOURCE CURSE: STATE OF THE DISCOURSE

The literature on resource curse has received substantial attention by scholars and activists and, as a result, many theoretical perspectives have been shared by its proponents. Recently, Gapa (2020) explained why African economies need to develop despite many resources. These reasons include sustainable development and development challenges including environmental problems, desertification, resource conservation, decline in biodiversity, poor border controls, lack of human security, and the displacement of communities from their traditional lands (Gapa 2020: 684). While this set of factors constitutes a major challenge to Africa, this chapter will also review other prominent theoretical models in explaining the African problem such as the Dutch disease and the rent-seeking, institutional, state, and dependency perspectives.

The assumption of the Dutch disease model is that a booming natural resources sector can lead to a decline in the development of tradable sectors such as the manufacturing and sometimes the agricultural sector. This situation occurs when labor is pulled into the natural resource sector and shifts production away from the manufacturing sector. The shrinkage of the manufacturing sector is dubbed the "disease" because it is the source of chronic slow growth and can lead to a socially inefficient decline in growth (Sachs and Warner 1995). The symptoms of Dutch disease include a) real exchange rate appreciation, b) slower manufacturing growth, c) faster service sector growth, d) higher overall wages, and e) overreliance on a single sector which is vulnerable to a fluctuating global market. The Dutch disease model has been used to explain the resource curse phenomenon. Here, the decline in manufacturing undermines economic growth because as the sector fails to develop, the non-tradable sectors continue to expand (Sachs and Warner 1995: 23). Finally, natural resources–abundant countries often fail to pursue export growth because of high price levels and lack of exports promotion (Sachs and Warner 1995).

The Dutch disease model has been able to provide an understanding of the cause of resource curse in some nations. However, the model has failed to explain why nations such as Norway, Botswana, Australia, and others have developed using their resource endowments. The answer to these could be found in other causes such as the quality of institutions, the structure of economy, the nature of the state, and the political regime type.

A second model, the rent-seeking model, argues that abundant natural resources have the tendency of increasing the number of entrepreneurs engaged in rent-seeking and this in turn reduces the number of entrepreneurs running productive firms. A reduction in the number of productive firms reduces income which in turn lowers welfare (Torvik 2002). The model emphasizes the role of power groups and institutional frameworks and suggests that economies experience lower economic growth because of the distortionary redistributive activities by governments (Akylbekova 2015). Power groups try to appropriate the rents generated by natural resources. In the process, the natural resources sector is the one that is squeezed because of harmful rent-seeking activities, thus producing no wealth to be used for welfare. In the model, the economy consists of the formal and informal sectors. The taxes generated from the formal sector constitute the source of fiscal transfers to power groups in society. The power groups work hard to protect their profits from taxation and, therefore, undertake to hide their profit in the informal/shadow sector, which has a lower rate of return. The official sector has high returns, and countries with powerful groups respond to increased revenues by high fiscal spending and slower economic growth. This is possible because public capital expenditures are not used efficiently and appropriated revenues are consumed and invested in the informal sector or abroad (Akylbekova 2015). The utility of the rent-seeking model lies in the fact that it shows how those cheap rents, instead of promoting development and welfare, end up being wasted by the elites. The problem with the model is that it does not consider other causes of resource curse such as the quality of institutions, rules, regulations, and norms in society.

Yet another explanatory model, the institutions model, sees weak formal and informal institutions as causal factors of resource curse. The formal institutions consist of written rules and constraints that contribute to political stability, prevent corruption, enhance public sector efficiency, and protect private property rights from misappropriation by private parties or government. The informal institutions consist of moral codes and norms about right and wrong and are not part of a written legal framework (Gapa 2013). A breakdown of these institutions will certainly weaken the way society is governed. Using this understanding, scholars have linked the resource curse phenomenon in many countries to the presence of weak institutions. A study conducted by Mehlum, Moene, and Torvik (2002) showed that countries rich in natural resources constitute both growth losers and growth winners. The major rationale for these diverging experiences is the differences in the quality of institutions. They found out that more natural resources tend to push aggregate income down, in situations where institutions are "grabber friendly." More resources raise income when institutions are "producer friendly." Their study showed that the quality of institutions determines whether countries avoid the resource curse. Countries that observe rule of law are those with high institutional quality; therefore, they escape the resource curse. Using the institutional model, Gapa's studies (2013) revealed that Botswana escaped the resource curse because of its unique institutional quality rooted in the political culture compatible with the institutions of development and democracy. This in turn facilitated its economic and political development. The legitimacy and historical continuity which the regime enjoyed facilitated the robustness of both formal and informal institutions. The country's ability to manage its identities through assimilation facilitated the harmony among the ruling elites and citizens. Indeed, the institutional perspective opened up the discussion on why countries fail despite their endowment.

It is argued that the existing conceptualization of the resource curse suffers from "methodological nationalism" (Siakwah 2017) because it pays no attention to the position of these resource-rich countries in the global capitalist system. The system is characterized by exploitative relations where the actors in the centers or metropoles of the world system exploit its peripheries/satellites. Economic surpluses are extracted from the peripherals to metropoles. In the process, the resource-rich countries are underdeveloped (with low growth, poverty, unemployment, etc.) while the metropoles experience a high level of development. The peripheries are forced to be producers of raw materials which they export, thus giving no room for manufacturing and for independent development utilizing these resources (Amin 1974). This is the position of the underdevelopment and dependency school scholars. Using what he calls network approach, Siakwah (2017) argues that the resource curse is a tendency conditioned and molded by a "globalized assemblage" which is the interactions between and among states, national and local politics, transnational interests, technologies, and globalized structures and actors. The merit of the dependency perspectives is its ability to factor in the external conditions that produce and sustains the resource curse. The weakness of the perspective is found in the way the internal factors and actors are downplayed in explaining the resource curse such as the quality of institutions, state weakness, state capture and the nature of the ruling class.

The state-and-class theoretical perspective draws its strength from the Marxist theories of the capitalist state (Frankel 1979). The state is seen as the central organizing agency for the society, and it plays the role of providing cohesion for the entire socio-economic and political system. In a situation where the state does not play this role, it will be impossible for such a society to use its natural endowments to achieve development. Resource-rich countries experience the curse essentially because a self-interested ruling class controls the state. Such a state in extreme cases is captured and deliberately made to serve the interest of the class that controls it. In such a situation, the state cannot control resource extraction in a transparent and accountable manner because state officials compromise or lack the actual ability to play its constitutional roles.

This perspective has been employed by Iyayi (2007) in his study of the Niger Delta region in Nigeria when he argues that the major source of the resource curse in Nigeria is the nature of the state, ruling class, and accumulation, which is primitive as it allows for corruption and pilfering of state resources for private consumption. Resource extraction leads to the underdevelopment of the oil-bearing communities and in Nigeria because surpluses are transferred to developed areas and sectors outside the oil-bearing communities and the country. In addition, the extraction has triggered injustice to the citizens in the oil-bearing communities because they are estranged from benefiting from the surpluses generated from resource extraction. The merit of this perspective is its focus on the state and the ruling class that control rents and violate national rules, regulations, and norms of society to deny the development of the countries endowed with resources. The weakness of this perspective is its major attentions on the state to the exclusion of other drivers of the resource curse such as rent-seeking and weak institutions.

From the review of the theoretical models, none of them have sufficiently explained the resource curse phenomenon. The author suggests a model that combines similar views expressed by the models and ties them together to provide an explanatory view of the resource curse. This integrated political economy model holds the view that there is utility in the various perspectives attempting to explain the resource curse. These perspectives believe countries experiencing the curse have witnessed worse economic performance, affecting politics, citizens' welfare, and development. The drivers of the resource curse include the presence of a weak state, weak adherence to rules and regulations, a ruling class with a high appetite for rent-seeking and consumption, primitive accumulation of state resources, and a lack of commitment to investing in growth-yielding sectors such as manufacturing and agriculture. In addition, resource extraction is supported by an international system interested in sustaining a raw material export orientation from resource-rich countries. Escaping the curse will thus depend on subverting the dominant control of the state by the present character of the elite. This is possible when coalitions of people's groups are determined to challenge the status quo. When this condition is met, the focus of managing the economy should be on preventing the Dutch disease and curtailing rent-seeking behavior while strengthening societal norms, rules, and regulations.

THE STATE, CAPITAL, AND RESOURCE
DISCOVERIES IN NIGERIA

Colonialism was an essential factor in the extraction of resources in Nigeria. The colonial state provided the policy, legal, and institutional environment for resource extraction fueling economic growth in the British metropole—the British capital mined tin, columbite, gold, coal, manganese, etc. During the post-colonial period, Nigeria discovered and began extracting oil and gas in commercial quantities in 1967. Since then, foreign capital has dominated the oil sector in Nigeria. A major player in the industry is Shell PLC, which the British government owns. The company is a joint venture composed of Nigerian National Petroleum Corporation (NNPC; 55 percent), Shell (30 percent), TotalEnergies (10 percent), and Agip (5 percent). The company has more than one hundred producing oil fields and a network of more than six thousand kilometers of pipelines flowing through eighty-seven flow stations. The Shell Petroleum Development Company operates two coastal oil export terminals. Shell accounted for 50 percent of Nigeria's total oil production (899,000 barrels/142,900 m^3 per day in 1997) from more than eighty oil fields. Other foreign companies that dominate Nigeria's oil industry include Chevron Nigeria Limited, an American company operating as a joint venture with NNPC (60 percent stake) and Chevron (40 percent stake). In addition, ExxonMobil operates as a joint venture between the NNPC (60 percent stake) and ExxonMobil (40 percent stake). ExxonMobil also holds a 50 percent interest in a production-sharing contract for a deep-water block offshore (Frynas, 1999).

Other companies consist of Nigerian Agip Oil Company Limited, which is an Italian company operating as a joint venture between the NNPC (with 60 percent state), AGIP (with 20 percent), and ConocoPhillips (with 20 percent). Total Petroleum Nigeria Limited is a French joint venture between NNPC (60 percent) and Elf (now Total) with 40 percent. Texaco, which has merged with Chevron, is an NNPC-Texaco-Chevron joint venture with NNPC possessing 60 percent of holdings, Texaco (20 percent), and Chevron (20 percent). The other players in the industry are independent and indigenous oil and gas companies, including Addax Petroleum Nigeria Limited, Aiteo Group, AMNI International Petroleum Development Company Ltd, Consolidated Oil Limited, Dubri Oil Company Ltd, Emerald Energy Resources Ltd, and Yinka Folawiyo Petroleum Company Ltd. (Frynas, 1999).

Nigeria is now the second-largest oil and gas producer in Africa. Since gaining independence, its economy and budgets have primarily depended on the petroleum industry's surpluses. As of February 2021, the oil sector contributed about 9 percent of the country's gross domestic product (GDP).

In addition, Nigeria is a major exporter of crude oil and petroleum products to the United States. With the reactivation of the solid mineral industry in the country in the 1990s through rhetoric and few actions, the state has attracted foreign and local capital by providing an environment for the exploration and exploitation of mineral resources found in many in all states of the federation. Between 2016 and 2020, the Nigerian state issued more exploration licenses to foreign and local capital for mineral resources and a few mining leases (Nigerian Extractive Industries Transparency Initiative [NEITI] 2022). In a period of five years spanning from 2016 to 2020, the Nigerian government issued a total number of 7,664 licenses for mineral extraction, a trend pointing to a gradual return to solid mineral mining, which experienced a significant decline due to the discovery of oil and gas in the late 1960s (NEITI 2022).

The institutions created to regulate resource extraction in the country include the NNPC, the solid mineral regulatory compliance institutions such as the Ministry of Mines and Steel Development with departments like the Mines Inspectorate Department, Mines Environmental Compliance Department, and Artisanal and Small-scale Mining. The other institutions that have not played adequate roles in stemming the tide of corruption in the mineral extraction business and which require strengthening include the Mines Environmental Compliance Department, Mining Cadastre Office, Nigerian Geological Survey Agency, Nigerian Steel Raw Materials Exploration Agency, Federal Inland Revenue Service, Nigerian Customs Service, and Corporate Affairs Commission (NEITI 2022).

THE RESOURCE CURSE IN NIGERIA

It has been established that the oil boom witnessed in Nigeria in the 1970s did not translate to economic growth, development, or the welfare of citizens. Sala-i-Martin and Subramanian (2003: 14–19) demonstrated how oil expenditures led to wasteful investments in Nigeria. Since the 1970s, there has been a notable decrease in capacity utilization in predominantly state-owned manufacturing, highlighting inefficiencies in government investments. This decline serves as evidence of wasteful expenditure. In addition, Sala-i-Martin and Subramanian (2003) pointed out that waste was seen in the use of oil revenues to finance the construction of the Ajaokuta steel complex in the 1970s without producing any product in commercial quantity. Furthermore, the oil boom led to an increase in the size of the government. This stimulated rural labor migration into the urban centers for job opportunities. In the process, agricultural production declined while the prices of food increased.

It is also crucial to note that in Nigeria, private accumulation and the resource curse are driven by class interests, creating a structural foundation for the curse. Both national and foreign interests own oil wells, and state support is provided through the Ministry of Petroleum Resources. Private capital has established dominant control of the oil sector partly because of their financial muscle and technical expertise in the industry, which the state officials cannot match. However, private interests in Nigeria tend to manifest through manipulation of contract deals, production-sharing agreements, declaration of production outputs and disclosure of profits, and non-payment of royalties and taxes to the state. This is included in accounts of the failure to transfer petroleum and solid mineral revenues to the government's treasury and their redirection (Gapa 2013).

Nigeria has lost large quantities of resources to theft and other criminal activities. Criminal enterprise within Nigeria's oil industry ranges from petty crimes in oil communities to capture by government officials in conjunction with multinational companies with guaranteed protection from the military. It is reported that an average of 437,000 barrels of oil is stolen on a daily basis by criminals in Nigeria (Oduor 2022). It is also reported by NEITI that Nigeria lost 619.7 million barrels of crude oil valued at 16.25 trillion Nigerian naira (46.16 billion US dollars) to crude oil theft between 2009 and 2020 (Faminu 2023). An Ernst & Young audit estimated that around 133 billion US dollars' worth of crude oil and refined products are stolen or adulterated every year (Khartukov 2021). Misappropriation and misaccounting of funds is also prevalent, particularly the underdeclaration of oil produced by oil companies.

State capture is another strong driver of the resource curse. The state has been controlled so that its capacity to stop the resource curse phenomena is severely weakened. The reasons for the suboptimal performance of Nigerian institutions in addressing the resource curse include the fact that most of the officials have witnessed deficits in resource transfers and poor personnel. With these in mind, they are indirectly prevented from monitoring the implementation of resource extractions. Top-level administrative personnel are drawn into questionable relationships with the political class, thus compromising their integrity. Mkandawire (2015) describes this kind of relationship as neopatrimonial and clientelist. For instance, top bureaucrats take up positions as board members of transnational oil and mineral resource conglomerates. The Corruption Perceptions Index shows that Nigeria has persistently been rated and ranked as a corrupt nation. These compromises and many other instances attests to that fact. What has become clear with resource institutions is the lack of transparency in the process of resource extraction—minerals are mined by artisanal, small-scale companies and sold to exporters without declaration and disclosure to the state. For instance, NEITI (2022) reported that financial flows from 96 extractive companies were reconciled but at the conclusion of the exercise, the initial difference of N2.45 billion was reduced to N54.25 million. The unreconciled difference of N54.25 million is traceable to the six non-responsive extractive companies due to: a) failure/refusal to complete and submit the approved data gathering templates b) failure to allow the auditors access to their premises; and c) failure to turn up for the tripartite reconciliation meeting.

At another level, both artisanal, small-scale operators and big buyers escape from paying taxes and royalties. As a result, the Transparency International Index shows that Nigeria is highly corrupt. The magnitude of corruption affects the gamut of resources available for meeting the needs of the citizens of the country. Governance is weakened as the state cannot garner resources to fulfill its responsibility to citizens and even maintain state institutions. The legitimacy is therefore called into question.

Another driver of the Nigerian resource curse is the state constitutional framework which supports the concentration of resource extraction at the federal government level. The constitution of the Federal Republic of Nigeria and the Mineral Act 2004 grant the federal government the responsibility of allocating licenses, collecting rents from companies in the oil and solid mineral mining sector, and monitoring and evaluating the operations in the oil and gas sector. The overconcentration of powers to the central government, coupled with the absence of capacity by the federal government to control the mining operations, has left the full exploitation of the natural endowment lacking. The data released by the Federal Ministry of Solid Minerals in Nigeria shows that the resources, especially the solid minerals, are underutilized (Federal Republic of Nigeria 2016: 20). Nigeria has 2,750 metric tons of coal but only 0.04 metric tons is being mined; of 10.0 metric tons of lead/zinc, only 0.6 metric tons are mined; of ten thousand metric tons of iron ore, only 0.07 metrics are mined; of two hundred metric tons of gold, only 0.14 metric tons are mined; and of 2,300,000 metric tons of limestone, only eleven metric tons are mined (NEITI 2022).

The government at the sub-national levels is forced to depend on the federal government for the scant monthly allocations of the rents. The oil- and mineral-bearing communities have formed strong perceptions that resource extraction from their lands is being used in developing the entire country while their areas are left desolate in terms of development. Another driver of resource curse is the deployment of rents to sustain class hegemonic politics instead of development. Politics in Nigeria is an expensive game. For instance, in a contest for a political office, picking up a nomination form at the party level (Majeed 2022), running the campaign for the primary elections, and organizing the campaign for the national elections consume huge amounts. The elections are highly monetized. The import of this is that the resources often used for politicking are state resources that the political elite in the various ruling parties use to fund political party activities and elections. The state is, therefore, denied resources to meet the needs of citizens and the curse.

The global political economy has been another factor that has driven the resource curse. The colonial extraction of solid mineral resources like tin, columbite, manganese, gold, coal, etc., meant that the resources were not processed domestically. Therefore, the country lost the initial opportunity to develop. Surplus extraction and the appropriation by the centers of global capitalism meant the development was hampered internally. This is the classic case of underdevelopment. The global economy made Nigeria a source of raw materials and prevented it from self-autonomous development. Because oil is a strategic resource and globally scarce, it is in high demand worldwide, making it valuable. Thus, global competition creates an incentive for state capture and corruption. The phenomenon continued to constrain domestic resource processing in support of raw material exports during independence from the colonial state. This makes one believe that global mining companies supporting the home states have helped drive Nigeria's resource curse. The current demand for Nigeria's oil and gas and solid minerals comes from Europe, the United States, Canada, and China.

In 2020, there were about thirty mineral types exported from Nigeria. Mineral ores and concentrates such as zinc, lead, and manganese were the major contributors to the total export volume, with 21,590 tons, representing 65 percent. A total of 80 percent and 85 percent of the total export volume and value was exported to China in 2020 (NEITI 2022). There is a significant difference between the governance of oil and mineral resources. On the one hand, the oil sector governance structure has sufficient regulations and some weak levels of supervision by the Nigerian state and the relevant institutions. The Ministry of Petroleum is under the Office of the President and with a minister to assist the president in the act of monitoring and supervision. On the other hand, the governance structures of the mineral resources during the colonial period were designed, organized, and regulated by the colonial state. There was sufficient regulation and supervision by the state, and the revenue generated was appropriated by the colonial state. The governance structure of the mineral sector in the country today is different from that of the colonial period and of oil today. There is a low level of supervision of the mineral sector in the country. Supervision of mineral exploration and extraction is currently under an inefficient Ministry of Mineral Resources. The ministry lacks the capacity and ability to establish presence and dominance in the operation within the sector. The revenue gained by the NNPC, the state corporation in charge of controlling the operations of the oil fields in the country, accounts for 76 percent of federal government revenue and 40 percent of the entire country's GDP. As of 2000, oil and gas exports account for 98 percent of Nigerian export earnings (World Bank. 2004). The oil sector's contribution to the country's GDP since 1970 has fluctuated. From a contribution of 37 percent in 1978, the GDP contribution experienced a sharp decline in 1981 due to the pilfering of the resources at the source, theft at the treasury level, and at the point of distribution and redistribution. The volatility of the international market has also compounded the situation. This implies that the ruling class does not prioritize citizens' needs, the basic foundation for inclusive development, and those in governance circles. The revenues that were recorded show that the peak periods for revenue were 1974, where it contributed to about 27 percent, 1979 (41 percent), 1993 (28.7 percent), and 2000 (22 percent). In all the other periods from 1970 to 2020, the revenue remained below 20 percent, the lowest being 1.6 percent in 1982 and 2.8 percent in 2015 (World Bank 2024). In addition, the revenues that flow into the collective treasury controlled by the federal government of Nigeria showed some slight increase from the year 2022 with a revenue of S1,296.240 (CEICDATA 2022). The NEITI also reports that between January 1, 2007, and December 31, 2019, the solid mineral sector contributed 496.28 billion Nigerian naira (2,347.12 million US dollars) to the government's receipts during this period (NEITI 2022), but with the same results of no performance economically, as will be shown in the next section of the chapter.

THE IMPACT OF NEW OIL AND MINERAL EXTRACTION

There is a negative correlation between resource extraction and Nigeria's development level and quality. The resource extraction process captured by local and foreign capital independently or under the supervision of a captured state has failed to deliver coordinated and inclusive development. Despite the huge resource availability, the state has demonstrated an inability to provide a sound and stable framework for its development. Its growth rates have been fluctuating downward over the years.

During the 1970s, Nigeria went through a significant "oil boom," which accounted for approximately 25 percent of its GDP. By 2002, the contribution of oil to the GDP had lessened to 15 percent, yet it still resulted in a substantial inflow of funds into the nation's treasury. Retired Nigerian military official Yakubu Gowon succinctly described the situation by stating, "Money is not Nigeria's problem, but how to spend it." (Olayinka, 2014). Indeed, the Nigerian oil boom heralded massive elite spending on would-be "white elephant projects." (Mehlum et al. 2002). Millions of dollars were stolen from state coffers during this period, thus contributing to the resource curse. The oil boom was thus preceded by recessions and depressions in late 1970s and 1980s, and in 1993 and 1995, with growth rates reaching negative levels. Negative growth was experienced in 1967 with −15.74 percent and in 1981 with −13.13 percent (Macrotrends 2021b).

How resources are extracted shapes the way politics functions in a country. Politics in resource-cursed countries is very competitive because state control guarantees access to the resources the state distributes. For instance, state actors have control over the allocation of oil wells, licenses for the exploration of mineral resources, and the monthly allocation of revenues to central and sub-national governments. The state also awards contracts for infrastructural development from annual budgets and allocates licenses for imports and exports. This role incentivizes the political elites to want to capture and establish control of the state. As a strategy for ascending to power, the ruling political elite often appeals to ethnic, religious, and regional sentiments (Gapa 2013). Though they periodically agree to rotate power at the sub-national and central levels, such consensus breaks down, creating space for political violence. In this case, elections become contentious and volatile, often leading to violence. In Nigeria, the pre-election period is often marred by killings and ransom kidnappings of political opponents. On election day, the opportunistic political parties and the financially buoyant politicians buy voters to capture the electoral management body and security forces in order for the election results to be announced in their favor. This creates violent post-election situations in the country.

New resource discoveries have established new political dynamics at the local and national levels in Nigeria. One observable phenomenon is the contestations about the territorial ownership of the location of the new resources. State elites and their communities make claims and counterclaims regarding the original owners of the location as has happened between Bauchi and Gombe states with the discovery of one billion barrels of crude oil reserves and five hundred billion standard cubic feet of gas oil in commercial quality in the Kolmani oil and gas field. Kolmani was issued the Oil Prospecting Licenses 809 and 810, cutting across Kolmani One, Two, Three, Four, and Five, and had as of 2023 attracted over three billion dollars in investments. It is revealed that Kolmani One is in Bauchi state in Alkaleri, while the other four oil wells are in Gombe (Adepegba et al. 2022). In Nigeria, ownership entitles the elites and the community some limited access to the gains of extractions. The failure to resolve these disagreements have led to violent conflicts that have disrupted economic activities including investments in the extractive sector. The case of disagreements among communities in the Niger Delta is a case in point.

The politics of location is related to the politics of land ownership. The inhabitants of the land where mineral deposits are found have triggered a discussion around two issues: artisanal mining outside state control and how this leads to the curse and the conflicts that are witnessed leading to exacerbation of the curse. First, there is large-scale artisanal mining that is taking place outside the purview of the state and its agencies. Here resource extraction is done in communities without taxation while the proceeds are sold in informal markets to big buyers who are either domestic companies or foreign businessmen who in turn transport these products outside Nigeria. In this way, the inland revenue agencies at the sub-national and national levels remain spectators of these informal transactions. Large revenues are unaccounted for and lost in the process.

Second is the issue of conflicts inspired by illegal mining by artisanal and small-scale miners. Illegal mineral extraction in Nigeria has often led to violent local conflicts, especially in the northern region. It is reported (*ENACT Observer* 2020) that sponsors of illegal mining compete over control of the mining fields and employ violence to secure this control. The tactics employed include creating divisions among communities and declaring artisanal mining as illegal in favor of bigger illegal miners. They also secure the protection of the state officials at national and sub-national levels.

Furthermore, the funders of illegal mining also sponsor rural banditry and cattle rustling in mining communities. When this happens, local violent conflicts among local cattle breeders and rearers occur, leading to the displacement of local populations and creating opportunities for illegal miners to operate.

At another level, the artisanal miners, who are typically from poor and marginalized communities, often contest the right of the state to deny them active extraction of mineral deposits. Typically, when community actors are denied access and when their demands for access are not met appropriately and promptly, the situation degenerates into political violence (Bassey 2009: 179–84). Related to this is the politics of appropriation: who gets what, when, and how of the resource extraction proceeds? Therefore, the politics of extraction is about access, accumulation, and control of the state apparatus.

Another classic example of a resource curse in Nigeria is its negative impact on employment. The Dutch disease theory explains this situation clearly as it draws attention to the lack of diversification in the economy when such an economy is dependent on natural resource exports. The theory holds that the country's currency appreciates due to the export of oil, while other industries in the economy become less competitive leaving the economy dependent on a capital-intensive sector instead of a labor-intensive sector like manufacturing or agriculture. This in turn negatively affects employment rates and leads to a lack of diversification in the economy (Sala-i-Martin and Subramanian

2003). Resource curse can therefore be gleaned from the quality of employment opportunities available in the country, its poverty levels, and the types of jobs supported by the economy. It is therefore paradoxical that a country with vast resources is unable to provide jobs for its people.

From 1991 to 2021, unemployment rates have steadily risen from 4.12 to 9.79 percent. This implies that despite the resources available in the country, the state has failed to address the rising levels of unemployment in Nigeria (Macrotrends 2021a). Additionally, poverty alleviation efforts continue to elude Nigeria. In Nigeria, 40.1 percent of people were deemed poor according to the 2018/2019 National Monetary Poverty Line, and 63 percent are multidimensionally poor according to the National Multidimensional Poverty Index 2022 (UN Development Programme 2022). Multidimensional poverty was higher in rural areas, where 72 percent of people were deemed poor, compared to 42 percent of people in urban areas (Eluemunor 2018).

Of all the regions in the country, the Niger Delta, which provides 99 percent of the oil and gas, witnessed one the highest levels of poverty in the land (Bird 2004). Most of the states within the Niger Delta experienced poverty rates ranging from 19.2 to 33.1 percent. In addition to poverty, gas flaring has compounded environmental conditions in the Niger Delta region. Oil extraction by oil companies emits significant amounts of hazardous waste products into the environment, which will often cost vast amounts of money to dispose of. As a result, the gas is burnt into the air, a phenomenon called "gas flaring." Despite continuous warnings and deadlines from the Nigerian government, foreign companies involved in oil extraction continue the practice of gas flaring.

The impact of gas flaring is monumental, and it harms not only the environment but human beings and livestock as well. In addition, it contributes to global warming with its many implications. The phenomenon in the Niger Delta is described:

> Flames as tall as 10-story buildings burn day and night in the village of Ebedei, in Nigeria's Niger Delta. But the heat from these fires is neither soft nor warm, it's fierce and prickly. The constant noise sends wild animals fleeing, and people must shout to be heard over the roaring flames. Fields of crops, once green, have turned yellow or stopped growing entirely. The village no longer enjoys the respite of cool or darkness of night. In the oil-rich Niger Delta of southern Nigeria, 2 million people live within 4 kilometers (2.5 miles) of a gas flare. Below the flames, oil is being extracted. (Schick, Myles, and Okelum 2018)

Oil spillage has also exacerbated poverty in the region. It is estimated that thirteen million barrels (1.5 million tons) of crude oil have been spilled since 1958 from over seven thousand oil spill incidents, a yearly average of about

240,000 barrels (Ordinioha and Brisibe 2013). A study on the Niger Delta found that oil spillage has adverse effects on the livelihoods of communities and the ecosystem. It showed that:

> An average of 240,000 barrels of crude oil are spilled in the Niger Delta every year, mainly due to unknown causes (31.85%), third-party activity (20.74%), and mechanical failure (17.04%). The spills contaminated the surface water, groundwater, ambient air, and crops with hydrocarbons, including known carcinogens like polycyclic aromatic hydrocarbon and benzo (a) pyrene, naturally occurring radioactive materials, and trace metals that were further bio-accumulated in some food crops. The oil spills could lead to a 60% reduction in household food security and were capable of reducing the ascorbic acid content of vegetables by as much as 36% and the crude protein content of cassava by 40%. These could result in a 24% increase in the prevalence of childhood malnutrition. Animal studies indicate that contact with Nigerian crude oil could be hemotoxic and hepatotoxic, and could cause infertility and cancer. (Ordinioha and Brisibe 2013)

Resource abundance in Nigeria continues to be negatively correlated with the health of the citizens because resource revenues are appropriated away from social sectors such as health. This explains why a naturally endowed country has its healthcare sector in severe stress, confronting challenges like low government budget allocation, deteriorating medical infrastructure, poor compensation, outbound medical tourism, and the subsequent emigration of skilled healthcare workers. The federal government allocated 5 percent of its budget to health in 2021, compared to the 15 percent it pledged as part of the 2001 Abuja Declaration (Gatome-Munyua and Olalere 2020).

Nigeria has one of the fastest-growing populations globally with 5.5 live births per woman and a population growth rate of 3.2 percent annually (International Trade Administration n.d.). It is estimated to reach four hundred million people by 2050. Medical professionals are scarce, with only about thirty-five thousand doctors nationwide despite a demand exceeding 237,000. This is partially due to the massive migration of healthcare workers overseas. Nigeria loses at least two billion dollars every year to medical tourism, according to the Nigerian Medical Association (International Trade Administration, 2023). The resources allocated to the sector have been dwindling, and it is not a good story to tell of a country endowed with resources. In the year 2000, 3.2 percent of the GDP was allocated to health, 5.05 percent in 2003, 3.30 percent in 2010, 3.35 percent in 2015, and 3.09 percent in 2018 (World Bank 2020).

CITIZENS' DEMAND FOR ACCOUNTABILITY
AND THE STATE'S RESPONSE

Citizens' knowledge of the resource curse has grown over time due to several factors, including the growth of civil society committed to addressing the devastation of the environment in the oil-bearing communities, and the supportive role of international civil society focusing on the rights of the people in resource-based societies. There has been massive knowledge production through the documentation of the harm that oil and gas exploitation has had in the communities by civil society, academics, and international development partners ((Defence of Human Rights 2000, Civil Liberties Organization 2001, Committee for the, Bassey, Nnimmo 2003). These developments have been more pronounced in the oil-producing states in the Niger Delta region of Nigeria. This level of activism has not been seen in the solid mineral–bearing states of the country for two reasons: first, the mineral resource extraction in many locations is still in its infancy, and, second, it is not as coordinated as in the oil sector. Informalization of work is prevalent and, therefore, the growth of a working class with trade union organization is absent. There is weak state regulation of mining operations in the resource-bearing fields, which poor artisanal miners currently dominate.

It is crucial to note the role of social media in raising people's consciousness about the resource curse in resource-based communities and other citizens. The media has allowed people to tell their stories and the stories of their living conditions in the midst of plenty. It is also crucial to interrogate the extent to which knowledge production and people's consciousness about the resource curse can influence a change in the problem in Nigeria. From the account of developments in the country's oil- and gas-producing regions, knowledge of the resource curse resides in all community members (Civil Liberties Organization 2001).

Indeed, a derivable lesson from the Niger Delta story is that knowledge has been used as a weapon to increase consciousness, and consciousness drives collective action. Collective action has produced some concrete results for the people of the Niger Delta region, although class interests are reversing the gains made by the people. This is because resources allocated to the region to drive development are being pilfered by the elite in charge of state institutions. Despite this limitation, knowledge can be a weapon to fight the resource curse.

The Nigerian state provides no incentive structure to stop the resource curse. The illegal extraction of oil and solid minerals by the elites in connivance with foreign companies and the primitive appropriation of the oil revenues have not been met with any frontal decision to deal with these illegalities. The state has taken limited steps to respond to daily pressure from citizens to halt the menace of oil bunkering or theft of solid mineral resources. They often engage the armed forces to patrol oil installations and areas of oil pipeline vandalism. There have yet to be concerted efforts to monitor oil companies' production and distribution operations effectively. The companies are known to underdeclare and underdisclose the exact quantities of oil and gas produced. As noted earlier, there is a transparency deficit in the declaration of exact revenues, royalties, and taxes paid to the state, as disclosed by NEITI. The lesson from the Nigerian story is that captured and weak states cannot stop the resource curse since their officials are devoted participants in the crime.

RECOMMENDATIONS

The ruling class in control of the weak state apparatus is perpetually rent-seeking, and their behavior makes politics less developmental, unequal, and less inclusive. For resource endowments to be a blessing in Nigeria, this chapter argues that a number of reforms are required in the area of resource extraction, the model of accumulation, and the pattern of politics and development. The following suggestions may not radically halt the resource curse but have the potential to reverse the curse incrementally.

The first recommendation is to implement reforms that deal with state capture. Broadly speaking, the Nigerian state has to be freed from a corrupt political leadership that converts state property to personal property and in agreeance with political and economic cabals that maintain and sustain control over the state. This will require constructing a developmental state. The specific reforms should be built on mechanisms to strengthen transparency, accountability, service delivery capabilities, and a culture of constitutionalism and rule of law.

A second recommendation is to strengthen institutional governance. State regulatory compliance institutions such as the NNPC and Ministry of Mines and Steel Development require strengthening to enable them to monitor resource extraction. These institutions should be cleared to block corrupt influences and strengthen transparency in resource extraction.

Third, Nigeria should implement reforms to deal with class interests. To reduce class capture in the extractive industry, reforms must end the unchecked pilfering of rent meant for the state and the natural resources at the extraction point. Attempts should be made to address the illegal operations of state officials and multinational oil and mineral resource companies. The reforms should include deploying extensive sanctions on class actors that violate mining extraction laws, particularly those relating to declaration and disclosure.

A fourth recommendation is that state constitutional reform support the devolution of resource extraction to sub-national governments. The present situation where the federal government controls the mining sector should be revised to allow full exploitation of the natural endowment for the common good. Therefore, the Nigerian Constitution and the Mineral Act 2004 should be revised.

Reforms to block resource rents from being recycled to sustain ruling class hegemonic politics must be put in place. This measure should include the enforcement of the country's Constitution, the Electoral Act, and the Anti-money Laundering Act on campaign financing. Strict monitoring and sanctions should be imposed on violators.

Finally, Nigeria needs a leadership committed to ending the resource curse. A set of leaders must emerge and be committed to building an inclusive and welfare state. Such leaders should be able to reduce the adverse influence of the global political economy on the mining sector through policy design and deploy resource revenues to meet citizens' basic needs—food, health, education, housing, and other Sustainable Development Goals; have policies that will balance efforts at domestic resource processing and exports of raw minerals; and ensure that resource extraction has a positive multiplier effect on the other sectors of the economy.

For these reforms to be achieved, collective action in politics is required. This can be done by building a broad coalition against the resource curse. Such a coalition should include major civil society coalitions in the extractive sector, labor unions, professionals, the business community, development partners with international mandates, and anti-corruption institutions in partnership with the presidency, the National Assembly, the regulatory bodies in charge of the mineral sector, and sub-national governments.

CONCLUSION

The chapter has demonstrated that despite the discoveries of new mineral resources in Nigeria, there has not been a fundamental change in the behavior of the state, the elite that controls the state, and the robustness of the political economy. This situation results from the resource curse that has plagued the country for many years. The chapter makes the point that resources are natural endowments to countries meant to be a blessing to citizens. However, they have become a curse because of class greed complicated by state capture, which prevents using these endowments for socio-economic benefit. Resource discoveries have instead inflicted pain on the citizens of resource-rich countries, and economic growth has been severely weakened. Resource competition in Nigeria has become divisive along ethnic, religious, and regional fault lines. Here, the competition has turned violent, particularly during election cycles. The ruling classes also failed to reach a consensus on everything ranging from revenue distribution and allocation to jurisdictional issues. Despite this, elites from both sides of the political divide benefit from state capture of resource endowments.

Optimistically, citizens' knowledge of the oil curse has increased over time, eliciting demands from the oil-bearing communities for better provision of resources and redistribution from the state to mitigate the consequences. The conversion of citizens' knowledge into collective action led by a developmental-democratic leadership will have the high potential of pulling the country out of the curse.

REFERENCES

Adepegba, Adelani, Okechukwu Nnodim, Armstrong Bakam, and Chima Azubuike. 2022. "Bauchi, Gombe Fight Over New Oil Wells." *Punch Newspapers*. https://punchng.com/bauchi-gombe-fight-over-new-oil-wells/, accessed June 1, 2023.

Akylbekova, Dina. 2015. "Analyzing the Resource Curse Theory: A Comparative Study of Kazakhstan and Norway." Department of Economic History, Lund University. https://lup.lub.lu.se/student-papers/search/publication/7760298, accessed July 1, 2024.

Amin, Samir. 1976. *Unequal Development: An Essay on the Social Formations of Peripheral Capitalism*. London: Monthly Review Press.

Amin, Samir. 1974. *Accumulation on a World Scale: A Critique of the Theory of Underdevelopment*. London: Monthly Review Press.

Bassey, Nnimmo. 2003. "Oil and Gas Exploration and Exploitation in the Niger Delta: The Social and Demographic Challenges." In *Empowerment in Action: ERA's Community Intervention in the Niger Delta*, edited by G. U. Ojo, 47–64. Ibadan: Kraft Books.

Bassey, Nnimmo. 2009. "Knee Deep in Crude." Environmental Field Report volume 1, Environmental Rights Action/Friends of the Earth, Lagos.

Bird, Frederick. 2004. "Wealth and Poverty in the Niger Delta: A Study of the Experiences of Shell in Nigeria." In *International Businesses and the Challenges of Poverty in the Developing World*, 34–63. Berlin: Springer Link.

CEICDATA. 2022. "Nigeria Gross Federation Account Revenue: Oil." https://www.ceicdata.com/en/nigeria/government-revenueand-expenditure/gross-federation-account-revenue-oil, accessed October 10, 2023.

Civil Liberties Organization, 2001. *Blood Trail: Repression and Resistance in Niger Delta*. Lagos: CLO.

Committee for the Defense of Human Rights. 2000. *Boiling Point: The Crisis in the Oil Producing Communities in Nigeria.* Lagos: Committee for the Defense of Human Rights.

Di John, Jonathan. 2010. "The 'Resource Curse': Theory and Evidence." https://www.realinstitutoelcano.org/en/analyses/the-resource-curse-theory-and-evidence-ari/, accessed May 1, 2023.

Eluemunor, Emeka. 2018. "Poverty Assessment of the Niger Delta." https://beamexchange.org/resources/1332/, accessed February 1, 2024.

ENACT Observer. 2020. "Mining and Extractives/Illegal Mining Drives Nigeria's Rural Banditry and Local Conflicts." https://enactafrica.org/enact-observer/illegal-mining-drives-nigerias-rural-banditry-and-local-conflicts, accessed April 1, 2024.

Faminu, Gbemi. 2023. "Nigeria Loses N16.25 trn to Crude Oil Theft in 12 years." https://businessday.ng/business-economy/article/nigeria-loses-n16-25trn-to-crude-oil-theft-in-12-yrs-neiti/, accessed October 12, 2023.

Federal Republic of Nigeria. 2016. *Road Map for the Growth and Development of the Nigerian Mining Industry.* Abuja: Federal Ministry of Solid Minerals.

Frankel, Boris. 1979. "On the State of the State: Marxist Theories of the State after Leninism." *Theory and Society,* 7(1/2): 199–242.

Frynas, Jedrzej Georg. 1999. *Oil in Nigeria: Conflict and Litigation between Oil Companies and Village Communities.* Münster: Lit Verlag.

Gapa, Angela. 2020. "Natural Resources and African Economies: Turning Liabilities to Assets." In *The Palgrave Handbook of African Political Economy,* edited by Samuel Ojo Oloruntoba and Toyin Falola. London, UK: Palgrave Macmillan.

Gapa, Angela. 2013. "Escaping the Resource Curse: The Sources of Institutional Quality in Botswana." Doctoral dissertation, Florida International University.

Gatome-Munyua, Agnes, and Nkechi Olalere. 2020. "Public Financing for Health in Africa: 15% of an Elephant Is Not 15% of a Chicken" Africa Renewal. https://www.un.org/africarenewal/magazine/october-2020/public-financing-health-africa-when-15-elephant-not-15-chicken, accessed December 12, 2023.

Iyayi, Festus. 1986. "The Primitive Accumulation of Capital in a Neo-Colony: Nigeria." *Review of African Political Economy,* 13(35): 27–39.

Iyayi, Festus. 2007. *The Niger Delta: Issues of Justice and Development Agenda.* Abuja: Centre for Democracy and Development.

International Trade Administration, Nigeria, n.d. "Total Market Size for Healthcare." https://www.trade.gov/countrycommercial-guides/nigeria-healthcare, accessed December 12, 2023.

Khartukov, Eugene M. 2021. "Oil Theft: A Frightening International Perspective." *Oilman Magazine,* March 7. https://oilmanmagazine.com/article/oil-theft-a-frightening-international-perspective, accessed October 10, 2023.

Macrotrends. 2021a. "Nigeria Unemployment Rate 1991–2021." https://www.macrotrends.net/countries/NGA/nigeria/unemployment-rate, accessed June 7, 2023.

Macrotrends. 2021b. "Nigeria Gross Domestic Product 1960–2021." https://www.macrotrends.net/countries/NGA/nigeria/domestic-product, accessed June 7, 2023.

Majeed, Bakare. 2022. "Update 2023: APC Fixes Presidential Forms for N100 Million, Adopts Indirect Primaries." *Premium Times Nigeria*, April 20. https://www.premiumtimesng.com/news/headlines/524823-updated-2023-apc -fixes-presidential-forms-for-n100-million-adopts-indirect-primaries.html?tztc=1, accessed August 3, 2023.

Mehlum, Halvor, Karl Moene, and Ragnar Torvik. 2002. "Institutions and the Resource Curse." Memorandum 29, Department of Economics, University of Oslo.

Mkandawire, Thandika. 2015. "Neopatrimonialism and the Political Economy of Economic Performance in Africa: Critical Reflections." *World Politics*, 67(3): 1–50.

Nigerian Extractive Industries Transparency Initiative (NEITI). 2022. "Solid Minerals Industry Report 2020." https://neiti.gov.ng/cms/wp-content/uploads/2022/08/Final -2020-SMA-Report.pdf, accessed July 7, 2023.

Oduor, Michael. 2022. "437,000 Barrels of Oil Stolen on Daily Basis by Criminals in Nigeria." https://www.africanews.com/2022/09/08/437000-barrels-of-oil-stolen -on-daily-basis-by-criminals-in-nigeria/, accessed October 12, 2023.

Olayinka, Collins. 2014. "Nigeria: At 80 Gowon Explains—'Nigeria's Problem Is Not Money, but How to Spend It.'" https://allafrica.com/stories/201410202349 .html, accessed June 7, 2023.

Ordinioha, Best, and Seiyefa Brisibe 2013. "The Human Health Implications of Crude Oil Spills in the Niger Delta, Nigeria: An Interpretation of Published Studies." *Nigerian Medical Journal*, 54(1): 10–16.

Radley, Ben, and Patrick Lehmann-Grube. 2022. "Off-Grid Solar Expansion and Economic Development in the Global South: A Critical Review and Research Agenda." *Energy Research and Social Science*, 89: 102673.

Sachs, Jeffrey D., and Andrew M. Warner. 1995. "Natural Resource Abundance and Economic Growth." NBER Working Paper 5398, National Bureau of Economic Research, Cambridge, MA.

Sala-i-Martin, Xavier, and Arvind Subramanian. 2003. "Addressing the Natural Resource Curse: An Illustration from Nigeria." IMF Working Paper 03/139, International Monetary Fund, Washington, DC.

Schick, Leonore, Paul Myles, and Okonta Emeka Okelum. 2018. "Gas Flaring Scorches Niger Delta." https://www.dw.com/en/gasflaring-continues-scorching -niger-delta/a-46088235, accessed October 10, 2023.

Siakwah, Pius. 2017. "The Political Economy of the Resource Curse in Africa Revisited: The Curse as a Product and Function of Globalized Hydrocarbon Assemblage." *Development and Society*, 46(1): 83–112.

Torvik, Ragnar. 2002. "Natural Resources, Rent Seeking and Welfare." *Journal of Development Economics*, 67(2): 455–70.

UN Development Programme. 2022. "National Multidimensional Poverty Index 2022." New York.

World Bank. 2020. "Current Health Expenditure (% of GDP)—Nigeria." https: //data.worldbank.org/indicator/SH.XPD.CHEX.GD.ZS?locations=NG, accessed October 10, 2023.

World Bank. 2004. *Taxation and State Participation in Nigeria's Oil and Gas Sector.* Technical paper; no. ESM 057, Energy Sector Management Assistance

Programme (ESMAP), Washington, DC. http://hdl.handle.net/10986/18078, accessed May 17, 2024.

World Bank 2024. "Oil Rents (% of GDP)—Nigeria." https://data.worldbank.org/indicator/NY.GDP.PETR.RT.ZS?locations=NG, accessed October 10, 2023.

PART IV

The Way Forward

Conclusion

Resource Futures: African Strategies for a New Era in Resource Politics

Angela Zivo Gapa

Africa, ostensibly rich in oil, natural gas, precious stones, and minerals, stands at a critical junction in its twenty-first-century development trajectory. The continent is positioned as a key participant in the global commodities market due to its wealth in minerals and hydrocarbon resources. It is fast gaining recognition as the new frontier for resource exploration in light of the green technology revolution. A sizable amount of the world's oil, gas, and mineral reserves are found on the continent, including vital industrial minerals like cobalt and lithium and precious metals like gold and platinum, which are essential to developing the electric vehicle and renewable energy industries. Furthermore, Africa has immense potential in the rare earth mineral space (Okoh and Onuoha 2024).

Despite Africa's wealth in natural resources, this has yet to benefit African countries. Domestically, most African countries have suffered the scourge of the resource curse either through the Dutch disease (Enders and Herberg 1983), revenue volatility (Poelhekke and van der Ploeg 2007), corruption (Pendergast, Clarke, and Van Kooten 2011), clientelism (Lemarchand 1972), and sometimes resource conflict (Le Billon 2005; Alao 2007). The effects of the African resource curse have been pervasive, spanning from diamond mines in Central and West Africa to the oil enclaves of the Gulf of Guinea. Countless lives have been affected by conflict resources, which motivate and sustain resource conflicts (Le Billon 2008). In addition, the mishandling of immense revenues derived from non-renewable natural resources has negatively affected infrastructure development that supports health, education, and transportation systems across the continent. Empirical evidence demonstrates a clear link between resource-rich nations and diminished investment in human capital, heightened corruption, and declines in economic diversification. These factors frequently lead to stagnation in economic growth for countries that would otherwise be considered privileged due to their resource endowments (Araji and Mohtadi 2018).

The curse of African resources extends globally, manifesting in a prevailing geopolitical bias within resource markets worldwide (i.e., the filtering of the global political economy of natural resources through the prism of the grand strategy of influential nations [Narizny 2007]). This bias often overrides more nuanced events that consider the involvement of political and social actors within Africa, covered in the resource curse literature. As a result, research on new resource discoveries tends to be geopolitically influenced by the supply-security concerns of the European Union, the United States, China, and Russia. While historically influenced by the interplay of internal and external factors, African countries can only better negotiate lucrative agreements in the natural resource space by enhancing their agency in developing strategies to balance the interests of more powerful global actors (Lala 2020).

For much of Africa's history, African countries have experienced constrained autonomy in the global political economy of natural resources. With their rich endowment of strategic commodities, African countries are now more critical than ever to leverage their resources to finance core socio-economic objectives, reduce poverty, utilize the resources, and strengthen global trade partnerships. African nations grapple with complex challenges as they strive to optimize the benefits of their natural resources to improve their populations while simultaneously ensuring incentives for corporations to make substantial and lasting investment choices (Collier 2007). The decision-making processes of both governments and companies occur amid significant uncertainty, knowledge imbalances, and strong motivations for specific interest groups to exploit resulting advantages. Consequently, African policymakers must formulate strategies that address economic transformation dynamics while adhering to ideals of sustainable development (Cust and Zeufack 2023).

This chapter delves into the prospects of non-renewable natural resource management in Africa in light of the post–resource curse era. It focuses on four predominant paradigms—resource nationalism, resource liberalism, resource diplomacy, and resource decentralization—all to enhance African agency in the global natural resource realm in the hopes of mitigating the resource curse.

RESOURCE NATIONALISM: REASSERTING STATE SOVEREIGNTY IN AFRICAN RESOURCE MANAGEMENT

In natural resource governance parlance, African agency is often synonymous with state intervention, resource nationalism, and risk amid unquestionable opportunity. Resource nationalism is an ideology advocating for asserting state control and ownership over the natural resources within a country's territorial boundaries (Emel, Huber, and Makene 2011). This approach prioritizes national interests, funneling revenue into national development projects to ensure that resource exploitation's benefits contribute significantly to national development. This typically includes actions such as nationalizing resource industries, wherein the state assumes direct ownership or substantially controls resource extraction and production processes (Singh and Massi 2016). The objective of resource nationalism is to optimize state authority over resource wealth, ensuring that the advantages derived from resource exploitation primarily benefit the nation and its inhabitants. From this standpoint, much erstwhile understanding rests upon a territorial conceptualization of how political power is exercised in controlling the economic distribution of rents derived from natural resource sectors (Emel, Huber, and Makene 2011).

In the post-colonial era, African countries have attempted to assert their sovereignty and pursue greater control over their natural resources, many establishing regulatory frameworks, legal systems, and institutions aimed at resource nationalism (Andreasson 2015). They have also sought to negotiate better terms for resource extraction with international companies to ensure that the benefits are shared more equitably. African countries will attain agency in natural resource management when they can autonomously and proficiently oversee their natural resources in accordance with their distinct priorities, values, and sustainable development objectives. Therefore, African nations must assume a leading role in the decision-making processes concerning the exploitation, conservation, and utilization of their natural resources.

The commodity supercycle facilitated the push toward the developmental state, spurred by global financial crises and the emergence of the BRIC nations, allowing African client states to reconsider their development paths and forge new relationships with non-traditional partners. China has become an active lender offering "infrastructure for oil" in Angola, South Sudan, and Ghana (Alves 2013). In Nigeria, oil multinationals de-invest in the country due to a lack of security in the Niger Delta and a desire to increase their focus on offshore projects, which were supposed to be protected from sabotage. According to Ostrowski (2023), the key driver behind contract renegotiations in Africa was the resurgence of the notion of state-led development, as the concept had been sidelined at the height of the neoliberal debates of the late 1980s. An increasing number of contemporary African examples abound where the politics of natural resources is articulated in a shifting language of control, national identity, reshoring offshore resources, and autonomous choice of development pathways. In Tanzania, liberal reforms to produce equitable socio-economic benefits combined to produce popular discontent over multinational corporations. The Tanzanian government implemented extensive reforms in its mining sector, passing several pieces of legislation empowering the government to renegotiate contracts, increase its sharehold-ing rights, and elevate royalties on minerals and metals. The Tanzanian presi-dent oversees the mining sector and has preferred supporting artisanal miners, revoking licenses from multinational companies Barrick and Glencore, and opening up the land for numerous small-scale miners, all in the interest of resource nationalism (Emel, Huber, and Makene 2011). Another example is Senegal, which is currently trending toward resource nationalism, pro-pelled by political instability ahead of the presidential election in February 2024. The main opposition candidate, Ousmane Sonko, has anchored his campaign on a strongly nationalistic outlook, vowing to renegotiate con-tracts and enhance government control over the country's nascent oil and gas industry. The incumbent president, Macky Sall, thus faces pressure to enact stricter local content laws than their oil multinational partners deem appropri-ate for an emerging producer. This effort aims to achieve a 50 percent local participation target across the hydrocarbon industry by 2030 under legislation supported by parliament (Roberts 2023).

Among the newest African countries to embrace resource nationalism to safeguard its mineral wealth from foreign exploitation is Zimbabwe. In December 2022, the Mnangagwa government initiated a ban on raw lithium ore exports to curb the economic impact of artisanal mining while at the same time encouraging investments in state-approved production facilities. Henceforth, in January 2023, a broader ban was legislated, encompassing all base mineral ores, a move aimed to spur the establishment of domestic lithium-processing facilities, thereby boosting national revenue and job opportunities, deemed essential for maximizing the value of the country's lithium reserves. Zimbabwe has implemented further measures to bolster resource nationalism, including extending royalties on mining companies and enforcing more stringent environmental regulations to protect local com-munities. Critics of the move contend that these regulations could deter inter-national investment and make it more difficult for the country to attract the revenue needed to expand its mining industry. Proponents, however, counter that these steps are required to guarantee Zimbabwe optimizes the benefits of its natural resources (van Halm 2023).

Childs (2016) identifies a distinction between what he calls soft and hard resource nationalism. Soft resource nationalism involves regulatory changes, increases in corporate taxes, and export restrictions on natural resources. Hard resource nationalism, conversely, refers to government tactics such as the annulment of existing resource contracts, economic nationalization, or imposing strict demands for national participation in natural resource joint ventures. Hard strategies tend to be located in non–Organisation for Economic Co-operation and Development countries, particularly Africa, where they are often negatively framed as a threat. As Childs (2016) noted, resource nationalism in Africa is often met with skepticism and adverse judgment, in stark contrast to its reception in Western economies. For example, it is considered part of a valid, legitimate debate with merit on either side in Canada, Norway, and Australia. For instance, Norway's approach to imposing high taxes on petroleum activities is regarded as a measured success. At the same time, Canada has tightened its regulatory climate and has rejected takeovers from corporate giants Petronas and BHP Billiton in the last five years to the applause of Western countries. Similarly, Western Australia's Domestic Gas (Domgas) Policy ensures that a 15 percent proportion of produced liquefied natural gas is reserved for domestic use to ensure the state's long-term energy needs. This adoption of Australia's resource nationalism is viewed as a strategic defense against the possible effects of increasing Chinese investment. However, when the geographic focus shifts to African states, resource nationalism is often subsumed into a risk discourse and viewed as a barrier to growth and development. This risk is largely oriented to the imperatives of global investment flows; hence, those who see resource nationalism as state control or dominance of natural resources fear a country's resulting potential to use this power for political and economic purposes and view it as a threat to multinational interests (Childs 2016).

Regardless of the regional bias, the future of resource nationalism in Africa faces challenges. While it can lead to increased revenue and infrastructure development, it bears the risk of political instability, corruption, and economic inefficiency. Moreover, the global shift toward sustainable and environmentally friendly energy sources puts additional pressure on countries heavily reliant on non-renewable resources. Resource nationalism in Africa will likely involve a more nuanced approach to balancing national interests with the need for economic diversification and sustainable development.

RESOURCE LIBERALISM: EMBRACING THE GLOBAL MARKET IN AFRICAN RESOURCE GOVERNANCE

Contrasting with resource nationalism, resource liberalism advocates for a free market approach, emphasizing privatization, foreign investment, and minimal state intervention. Resource liberalism supports the engagement of private sector entities, foreign investments, and market dynamics in the extraction and production of resources (Wilson 2011). This is achieved by endorsing the creation of legal frameworks, institutions, and international regulations that guarantee responsible governance and equitable trade of natural resources. Proponents argue that it attracts foreign direct investment, introduces advanced technologies, and integrates local industries into the global economy. Countries like Botswana have successfully leveraged resource liberalism to manage diamond resources, ensuring economic stability and growth (Gapa 2013).

There is an acknowledgment of the economic benefits that mining companies bring to Africa via the transfer of skills and technology, greater innovation, more affordable financing, and higher-quality products and services through resource liberalism. African leaders have become increasingly aware of leveraging their natural resource wealth for socio-economic development. Across the continent, countries like Ghana, Botswana, and Namibia have embraced resource liberalism to attract foreign investment toward mining and oil and gas for the betterment of their populations. These regimes include privatization of mines (Negi 2011), deregulation within extractive industries, and increased mining and oil exploration incentives (Signé and Johnson 2021). In response to pressure from advocacy groups, host governments, and the international community, resource multinationals have become more aware of the positive community relations and the need for a "social license to operate" (McIntyre, Murphy, and Sirsly 2015). These discussions fall within the scope of corporate social responsibility, which emphasizes ethical business practices to foster accountable corporate behavior. In addition, there is a growing consensus that corporate social responsibility should extend beyond mere legal compliance to include funding social programs and establishing infrastructure to channel revenue into local initiatives that aim to improve the livelihoods of local populations in resource enclaves. Furthermore, mining companies are increasingly recognized as development partners and valuable stakeholders in maintaining environmental sustainability in mining areas (Besada and Martin 2015).

In Africa, perhaps the most successful instance of resource liberalism is the case of Botswana. In 1969, Botswana forged a joint venture with De Beers, a prominent diamond company, to establish Debswana. This collaboration granted Botswana a significant share in the diamond industry, including a 15 percent stake in De Beers, fostering shared decision-making and profit distribution with the industry titan. Botswana actively negotiated for substantial equity stakes in diamond mining operations, ensuring ownership and a share of the profits. Additionally, the government implemented royalties on diamond production, contributing to state revenues. Botswana prudently directed its diamond revenues toward critical infrastructure and education. This strategic allocation laid the groundwork for economic diversification and sustainable development, reducing dependence on diamond revenues. Demonstrating fiscal responsibility, Botswana's government avoided excessive spending or corruption. Instead, it established the Pula Fund, a sovereign wealth fund, to save and invest a portion of the diamond income to benefit future generations (Gapa 2016).

In 2011, Botswana reportedly exported twenty-five million carats of diamonds, making it the world's top diamond producer by value and the second-largest by volume, trailing only the Russian Federation. A significant policy shift occurred 2012 when Botswana, in collaboration with its partner De Beers, reduced its domestic rough diamond production by 18 to 20 percent and entered into a new marketing agreement. This agreement stipulated that all Botswana diamonds would be sold through the Diamond Trading Corporation Botswana by December 2012, with sorting now taking place in Gaborone instead of London (ECDPM 2013). The beneficiation of diamonds in Botswana is directly tied to the conditions for being a Diamond Trading Corporation Botswana sightholder, with a requirement for local processing. This policy compels rough diamond traders to engage in value addition activities if they seek access to rough diamonds. The implicit tax associated with this obligation, estimated at thirty-one US dollars per carat, is offset by the substantial access to rough diamonds, four times larger than the volume cut in Botswana. The economic rationale behind absorbing the beneficiation tax lies in the sufficient economic rent provided by access to rough diamonds, ensuring that production remains commercially viable. This approach has not faced severe objections from De Beers sightholders due to its economic viability, even though it is not strictly based on commercial advantage for the country (Gapa 2016).

The future of resource liberalism in Africa appears promising, but not without caveats. While it can spur economic growth and development, it also raises concerns about environmental degradation, social inequality, and the exploitation of local communities. Therefore, the sustainability of this model hinges on establishing robust regulatory frameworks that ensure responsible resource extraction, equitable wealth distribution, and environmental conservation.

RESOURCE DIPLOMACY: BALANCING ECONOMIC
NEEDS AND STRATEGIC INTERESTS

The third strategy for Africans to pursue in their bid to escape the resource curse, navigate the global resource political economy, and enhance their agency in resource governance is "resource diplomacy." Here, the term resource diplomacy reflects the strategic use of a country's natural resource wealth in its foreign policy (Gutman 1975). This would entail leveraging oil, natural gas, and mineral resources to achieve better political, economic, developmental, and strategic objectives. This is achieved by endorsing the creation of legal frameworks, institutions, and international regulations that guarantee responsible governance and equitable trade of natural resources.

According to Ashley (1982), two primary strategic frameworks are accessible to developing countries exercising resource diplomacy: non-alignment and regional cooperation. A natural resource development strategy oriented toward regional cooperation in resource diplomacy would pay due regard to the proven existence and availability of the resources and inputs necessary to undertake a proposed venture. This approach emphasizes a mutual goal or shared interest that, among other things, sees collective self-reliance through South-South cooperation as inherently beneficial. The approach views some close regional affinity among participants in a well-defined geographical area as preferable. On the other hand, African states guided by "non-alignment" necessitate geopolitical diversification of economic relations aimed at reducing vulnerability to unilateral action, greater flexibility in economic relations and interests, and moving away from traditional ties and parochial "national interest" calculations (Ashley 1982).

African countries have used regional harmonization to enhance bargaining power against multinational corporations and economically powerful states. This involves aligning policies, regulations, and strategies across multiple countries in the African region to create a more cohesive and integrated approach to economic and social development. One primary example is the partnership with mining titans and neighbors, the Democratic Republic of Congo and Zambia, with the European Union, to develop critical raw material value chains and improve regional rail transport connections. The European Union, Zambia, and the Democratic Republic of Congo agreed at the European Union's Global Gateway Forum to closer cooperation on integrating raw material value chains, funding for development infrastructure, sustainable and responsible raw material production, and research and development (Morris 2023).

Outside of Ashley's (1982) framework, another strategy of resource diplomacy is "friend-shoring" or "ally-shoring," which refers to the practice of manufacturing and sourcing goods from countries that are geopolitical allies, essentially functioning as a trade bloc. Resource multinational corporations and powerful governments adopt friend-shoring as a strategy to maintain access to global markets and supply chains while mitigating specific geopolitical risks. African nations can capitalize on existing structures within the international political economy, giving them an advantageous position. For instance, the thirty-five nations benefiting from duty-free access to the US market under the African Growth and Opportunity Act might incorporate providers of transition minerals that have undergone specific processing and refining (Usman and Csanadi 2023). This inclusion could be realized with the mutual support of the United States and African resource exporters, contingent upon endorsing specific policy facilitators and regulations. These facilitators have precedent and could be implemented through regulations formulated by the Departments of Treasury and Energy. Additionally, the African Growth and Opportunity Act could serve as the foundation for negotiating a Critical Minerals Agreement, akin to the agreement in place with Japan.

The US-Japan Critical Minerals Agreement builds on the 2019 US-Japan Trade Agreement to strengthen and diversify the supply chains of critical minerals and encourage the adoption of electric vehicle battery technologies (US Trade Representative 2023). Specifically, the agreement seeks to streamline trade, foster fair competition, establish market-oriented conditions for critical minerals trade, promote stringent labor and environmental standards, and encourage collaboration to ensure secure, transparent, sustainable, and equitable critical minerals supply chains.

The agreement introduces various new commitments and areas of collaborative efforts regarding electric vehicle battery critical minerals supply chains between the United States and Japan. These include provisions related to (a) non-imposition of export duties on critical minerals; (b) domestic measures to address non-market policies and practices of other countries affecting trade in critical minerals; (c) best practices regarding review of investments within their territories in the critical minerals sector by foreign entities; (d) measures that promote more resource efficient and circular economy approaches to reduce the demand for, and environmental impact of, virgin material extraction and related processes; (e) engagement, information-sharing, and enforcement actions related to labor rights in critical minerals extraction and processing; (f) remedying violations of labor rights at entities connected to critical minerals supply chains; and (g) promoting employer neutrality in union organizing and operations (US Trade Representative 2023).

Africa's approach to resource diplomacy has broadened to include alternative allies who do not have the baggage of slavery and colonialism and who do not impose conditions related to open markets and good governance. Therefore, it is unsurprising that China and Russia would be particularly attractive alternative development partners for sub-Saharan African resource exporters. Both China and Russia actively engage with autocratic African governments, especially when material interests dictate. The authoritarian Chinese Communist Party requires economic growth for its regime legitimization, leading to a "no questions asked" approach toward providers of vital natural resources underpinned by mercantilist principles. According to Carmody and Taylor (2010), China's resource and geo-economic strategy in Africa is embodied by clientelism with African state elites, proxy force, and other diplomatic elements. Moreover, Chinese actors adapt their strategy to suit the particular histories and geographies of the African states with which they engage. This contrasts with the United States' hegemonic vision for capitalist democracies in its grand strategy. Consequently, China negotiates resource access in Africa through collaboration with state elites, favoring a cooperative approach to a neo-colonial, realist strategy based on coercion (Carmody and Taylor 2010).

Africa's second potential partner is Russia, which is currently making inroads into the continent, especially in the Sahel region, by establishing protective, clientelistic alliances with coup leaders. The Sahel region, a region directly south of the Sahara Desert stretching from Senegal to Eritrea, has experienced several coups since 2020. Russia has historically seen instability and violent conflict in this region, dubbed the "coup belt," as opportunities to sell African combatant groups weapons, providing them with military training, military advisory, and mercenary services through the Wagner group. Russian weapons sales and transfers to African countries have expanded from around five hundred million dollars to over two billion dollars yearly within the last decade (Droin and Dolbaia 2023).

Russia now seeks broader and deeper interventions to influence African nations' conflicts, governance, economies, and security architectures to facilitate Russian commercial activities and seeks predatory profit by extracting natural resources (Marten 2019). Russia presents itself as an attractive partner to African countries in the Sahel region. Here, the Wagner Group has been a primary proxy, seeking trade deals from elites in exchange for security-related services. The Central African Republic has one of Africa's largest gold mines, the Ndassima mine, run by Midas Resources, which operates under the Wagner group (Doxsee, Bermudez, and Jun 2023). Part of what makes Niger geopolitically important globally is they are the seventh-largest producer of the world's uranium used in nuclear power and nuclear weapons (Reuters 2023). Niger also has minerals and oil reserves as well as a strategic role in the fight against Islamic militants. This makes them important to the United States, Europe, China, and Russia. Gold is the primary commodity in Mali's natural resource sector, ranking the country the fourth-biggest gold producer in Africa. In 2021, gold constituted over 80 percent of Mali's total export revenue (ITA 2022). Similarly, other parts of the Sahel region have economies dominated by copper, gold, diamond, and uranium mining and natural gas and oil extraction, all of strategic importance to Russia. Wagner's business model has included political backing and guidance, information campaigns, and logistical support for Sahelian clients, under which it receives rights to exploit the country's main gold mine and extract diamonds and timber (Sany 2023).

RESOURCE DECENTRALIZATION: EMPOWERING COMMUNITIES IN RESOURCE-RICH REGIONS

The final strategy this chapter outlines for enhancing African agency in developing natural resources is "resource decentralization." Resource decentralization expands the scope of resource agency from the centralized state lens of resource nationalism, liberalism, and diplomacy to instead ask the question "agency for whom?" This opens up the space to human agency, community agency, or regional agency.

Resource decentralization fosters autonomy among local entities, regions, and communities in resource-rich areas. It entails dispersing control and decision-making authority among local stakeholders in the interest of shared benefits and sustainable management. Farzanegana, Lessmannd, and Markwardt (2018) argue that while higher natural resource rents increase the risk of resource conflicts, this risk is moderated by political decentralization. Due to the arbitrary distribution of natural resources worldwide, the geography of subterranean resources has typically isolated from centers of power and commerce. As a result of this, many resource-rich areas such as Cabo Delgado, Cabinda, and the Niger Delta are resource enclaves and tend to be ethnically distinct from the rest of society. The resource-conflict nexus is contingent on a country's natural resource property rights regimes, as most conflict has been along ethnic and regional lines. The "grievance" theory suggests that the perceived deprivation experienced by resource-producing regions and specific social groups, or the indirect negative economic consequences of resource wealth, can generate grievances leading to violent uprisings (Collier and Hoeffler 2004). In such scenarios, resource wealth contributes to civil unrest as residents of resource-rich areas are economically motivated to seek greater autonomy for controlling natural resources in their regions or establishing a separate state. This dynamic is particularly evident when the distribution disproportionately impacts ethnically or geographically distinct regions that are typically marginalized. Instances of secessionist movements in regions like the natural gas–rich Aceh in Indonesia, the oil-rich enclave of Cabinda in Angola, oil-rich Biafra in Nigeria, and natural gas–rich southern Sudan align with this rationale (Gapa 2013). The goal of resource decentralization is thus to bring power closer to these marginalized communities in the extensive peripheries of Africa, enhancing accountability, service delivery, and development outcomes.

As a paradigm shift, resource decentralization focuses on devolving resource management to local authorities and communities. This model recognizes the importance of local knowledge, needs, and priorities in resource management. It, therefore, has the added benefit of promoting community engagement, transparency, and accountability, aiming to ensure that the benefits of resource exploitation directly reach the local population. One successful illustration of resource decentralization in Africa is the Royal Bafokeng Nation, which holds a stake in one of the most substantial community-based investment companies in South Africa. For decades the Royal Bafokeng Nation has directed profits from platinum deposits toward a diversified investment portfolio, supporting an active social development initiative that benefits 150,000 individuals across twenty-nine rural villages (Cook 2013). Recognized as a traditional authority, the community maintains patriarchal and hereditary modes of governance that coexist with and often surpass the political procedures of the state (Rajak 2008). The Royal Bafokeng Nation has undertaken a proactive corporatization endeavor, leveraging its platinum assets to secure the economic sustainability of the Bafokeng population in the anticipated period after the prominence of platinum, which is projected to occur around fifty years from the current time (Cook 2013). The Bafokeng leadership has implemented various measures, including corporate structures, stringent financial controls, and a meticulous commitment to corporate governance regulations. This strategic positioning aims to enable the community to effectively address future challenges while ensuring that current activities and interventions are optimized for effectiveness and transparency (Rajak 2008).

This model is a significant counterexample of approaches prioritizing extensive state involvement in allocating mineral wealth. In a context where the legal and political framework allows, local communities assume a prominent role in overseeing the distribution and utilization of their mineral dividends. Looking ahead, resource decentralization in Africa holds significant promise. It can lead to more equitable and sustainable resource management, fostering social cohesion and local economic development. However, the success of this model depends on the ability of local institutions to manage resources effectively, the establishment of clear legal frameworks, and the presence of mechanisms to prevent local-level corruption.

CONCLUSION—BALANCING THE PARADIGMS: TOWARD A CURSE-FREE FUTURE

The management of non-renewable natural resources in Africa is pivotal. The continent's future prosperity will significantly depend on how effectively it manages these resources, balancing economic growth, social development, and environmental sustainability imperatives. By critically evaluating and integrating the principles of resource nationalism, liberalism, diplomacy, and decentralization, African nations can harness their resource wealth to forge a path toward sustainable and inclusive development. In this endeavor, the role of robust governance structures, international cooperation, and a commitment to sustainable practices cannot be overstated. The journey is complex and fraught with challenges. Still, with strategic vision and collective action, Africa can unlock a future where its natural resources are a wellspring of prosperity for all its people.

The future of non-renewable natural resource management in Africa is not confined to a single approach. Instead, it requires a balanced and integrated strategy that combines the strengths of resource nationalism, liberalism, diplomacy, and decentralization. This entails creating synergistic policies that ensure resource revenues contribute to national development while promoting environmental sustainability and social equity. African nations must also navigate the complexities of the global economic and environmental landscape. This involves investing in technological innovation, diversifying their economies, and participating in global efforts to combat climate change. By doing so, they can mitigate the risks associated with overreliance on non-renewable resources and pave the way for a more sustainable and prosperous future.

REFERENCES

Alao, A. 2007. *Natural Resources and Conflict in Africa: The Tragedy of Endowment.* Rochester, NY: University of Rochester Press.

Alves, A. C. 2013. "China's 'Win-Win Cooperation': Unpacking the Impact of Infrastructure-for-Resources Deals in Africa." *South African Journal of International Affairs*, 20(2): 207–26.

Andreasson, S. 2015. "Varieties of Resource Nationalism in Sub-Saharan Africa's Energy and Minerals Markets." *The Extractive Industries and Society*, 2(2): 310–19.

Araji, S. M., and H. Mohtadi. 2018. "Natural Resources, Incentives and Human Capital: Reinterpreting the Curse." *Middle East Development Journal*, 10(1): 1–30.

Ashley, P. W. 1982. "Natural Resource Diplomacy: Non-Alignment versus Regional Co-operation." *Boletín de Estudios Latinoamericanos y del Caribe*, 33: 139–54.

Besada, H., and P. Martin, P. 2015. "Mining Codes in Africa: The Emergence of a 'Fourth-Generation'?" *Cambridge Review of International Affairs*, 28(2): 263–82.

Carmody, P., and I. Taylor, I. 2010. "Flexigemony and Force in China's Resource Diplomacy in Africa: Sudan and Zambia Compared." *Geopolitics*, 15(3): 496–515.

Childs, J. 2016. "Geography and Resource Nationalism: A Critical Review and Reframing." *The Extractive Industries and Society*, 3(2): 539–46.

Collier, Paul. 2007. *The Bottom Billion: Why are the Poorest Countries Failing, and What Can Be Done about It?* London, UK: Oxford University Press.

Collier, Paul, and A. Hoeffler. 2004. "Greed and Grievance in Civil War." *Oxford Economic Papers*, 56(4): 563–95.

Cook, E. 2013. "Community Management of Mineral Resources: The Case of the Royal Bafokeng Nation." *Journal of the Southern African Institute of Mining and Metallurgy*, (113): 61–66.

Cust, James, and Albert Zeufack. 2023. *Africa's Resource Future: Harnessing Natural Resources for Economic Transformation during the Low-Carbon Transition.* Washington, DC: International Bank for Reconstruction and Development/The World Bank.

Doxsee, Catrina, Joseph S. Bermudez Jr., and Jennifer Jun. 2023. "Central African Republic Mine Displays Stakes for Wagner Group's Future." Center for Strategic and International Studies. https://www.csis.org/analysis/central-african-republic -mine-displays-stakes-wagner-groups-future, accessed January 22, 2024.

Droin, Mathieu, and Tina Dolbaia. 2023. "Russia Is Still Progressing in Africa. What's the Limit?" Center for Strategic and International Studies. https://www .csis.org/analysis/russia-still-progressing-africa-whats-limit, accessed February 20, 2024.

ECDPM. 2013. "Diamond Beneficiation in Botswana." https://ecdpm.org/work/from -growth-to-transformation-what-role-for-the-extractive-sector-volume-2-issue-2 -feb-march-2013/diamond-beneficiation-in-botswana, accessed February 26, 2024.

Emel, J., M. T. Huber, and M. H. Makene. 2011. "Extracting Sovereignty: Capital, Territory, and Gold Mining in Tanzania." *Political Geography*, 30(2): 70–79.

Enders, K., and H. Herberg. 1983. "The Dutch Disease: Causes, Consequences, Cures, and Calmatives." *Weltwirtschaftliches Archiv*, (119): 473–97.

Farzanegan, M. R., C. Lessmann, and G. Markwardt. 2018. "Natural Resource Rents and Internal Conflicts: Can Decentralization Lift the Curse?" *Economic Systems*, 42(2): 186–205.

Gapa, A. 2016. "Strategic Partner or Shot Caller? The De Beers Factor in Botswana's Development." *Journal of Global South Studies*, 33(1): 49–82.

Gapa, Angela. 2013. "Escaping the Resource Curse: The Sources of Institutional Quality in Botswana." Florida International University. https://digitalcommons.fiu .edu/etd/1019/, accessed July 28, 2023.

Gutman, G. O. 1975. "Resources Diplomacy." *The Australian Quarterly*, 47(1): 36–50.

International Trade Administration (ITA). 2022. "Mali–Country Commercial Guide." https://www.trade.gov/country-commercial-guides/mali-mining, accessed May 22, 2024.

Lala, F. 2020. "Africa in the Changing Global Order: Does African Agency Matter in Global Politics?" *The Changing Global Order: Challenges and Prospects*, 127–43.

Le Billon, P. 2008. "Diamond Wars? Conflict Diamonds and Geographies of Resource Wars." *Annals of the Association of American Geographers*, 98(2): 345–72.

Le Billon, P. 2005. "Resources and Armed Conflicts." *The Adelphi Papers*, 45(373): 29–49.

Lemarchand, R. 1972. "Political Clientelism and Ethnicity in Tropical Africa: Competing Solidarities in Nation-building." *American Political Science Review*, 66(1): 68–90.

Marten, K. 2019. "Russia's Back in Africa: Is the Cold War Returning?" *The Washington Quarterly*, 42(4): 155–70.

McIntyre, M. L., S. A. Murphy, and C. A. T. Sirsly. 2015. "Do Firms Seek Social License to Operate when Stakeholders are Poor? Evidence from Africa." *Corporate Governance*, 15(3): 306–14.

Morris, Sian. 2023. "EU Signs Critical Minerals Partnership with DRC, Zambia." Argus Media, October 23. https://www.argusmedia.com/zh/news-and-insights/latest-market-news/2502953-eu-signs-critical-minerals-partnership-with-drc-zambia, accessed June 26, 2024.

Narizny, K. 2007. *The Political Economy of Grand Strategy*. Ithaca, NY: Cornell University Press.

Negi, R. 2011. "The Micropolitics of Mining and Development in Zambia: Insights from the Northwestern Province." *African Studies Quarterly*, 12(2): 27.

Okoh, A. S., and M. C. Onuoha. 2024. "Immediate and Future Challenges of using Electric Vehicles for Promoting Energy Efficiency in Africa's Clean Energy Transition." *Global Environmental Change*, 84: 102789.

Ostrowski, Wojciech. 2023. "The Twilight of Resource Nationalism: From Cyclicality to Singularity?" *Resources Policy* 83: 103599.

Pendergast, S. M., J. A. Clarke, and G. C. Van Kooten. 2011. "Corruption, Development and the Curse of Natural Resources." *Canadian Journal of Political Science/Revue Canadienne de science politique*, 44(2): 411–37.

Poelhekke, S., and R. van der Ploeg. 2007. "Volatility, Financial Development, and the Natural Resource Curse." CEPR Discussion Paper DP6513, Center for Economic and Policy Research, Washington, DC.

Rajak, D. 2008. "Uplift and Empower: The Market, the Gift and Corporate Responsibility on South Africa's Platinum Belt." *Research in Economic Anthropology*, 28: 297–324.

Reuters. 2023. "Niger Is Among the World's Biggest Uranium Producers." https://www.reuters.com/markets/commodities/uranium-mines-niger-worlds-7th-biggest-producer-2023-07-28/#:~:text=Niger%20is%20the%20world's%20seventh,propulsion%2C%20and%20in%20nuclear%20weapons, accessed December 29, 2023.

Roberts, M. 2023. "Resource Nationalism in West Africa." S&P Global Market Intelligence Blog. https://www.spglobal.com/marketintelligence/en/mi/research-analysis/resource-nationalism-in-west-africa.html, accessed February 26, 2024.

Sany, Joseph. 2023. "Great Power Competition Implications in Africa: The Russian Federation and its Proxies." US Institute for Peace. https://www.usip .org/publications/2023/07/great-power-competition-implications-africa-russian -federation-and-its-proxies, accessed February 5, 2024.

Signé, L., and C. Johnson. 2021. "Africa's Mining Potential: Trends, Opportunities, Challenges and Strategies." *Policy Center for the New South Brief*, 21: 10.

Singh, J., and E. Massi. 2016. *Resource Nationalism and Brazil's Post-Neoliberal Strategy*. New York: Palgrave Macmillan.

US Trade Representative. 2023. "United States and Japan Sign Critical Minerals Agreement." https://ustr.gov/about-us/policy-offices/press-office/press-releases /2023/march/united-states-and-japan-sign-critical-minerals-agreement, accessed January 25, 2024.

Usman, Zainab, and Alexander Csanadi. 2023. "How Can African Countries Participate in U.S. Clean Energy Supply Chains?" Carnegie Endowment for International Peace, Washington, DC.

van Halm, Isabeau. 2023. "Zimbabwe Joins the Wave of Resource Nationalism." *Mining Technology*. https://www.mining-technology.com/features/zimbabwe -critical-minerals-resource-nationalism/, accessed January 29, 2023.

Wilson, J. D. 2011. "Resource Nationalism or Resource Liberalism? Explaining Australia's approach to Chinese Investment in its Minerals Sector." *Australian Journal of International Affairs*, 65(3): 283–304.

Index

About the Contributors

Michael Ohene Aboagye holds a PhD in international relations from Florida International University. His research focuses on foreign policies of sub-Saharan African countries and international trade and energy policies. Currently, he works with the Government of Alberta, Canada. He coordinates the production and distribution of over 250 examinations used in the delivery of the apprenticeship program in Alberta and other jurisdictions in Canada.

Esther Leah Achandi holds a PhD in economics from the University of Dar es Salaam and has over eleven years of research experience in Eastern Africa.

Babere Kerata Chacha is a senior lecturer in African history in the Depart ment of Public Affairs and Environmental Studies at Laikipia University in Kenya.

Angela Zivo Gapa is an associate professor of international relations at California State University, Chico. She holds a PhD in international relations from Florida International University, an MA in international studies, and a graduate certificate in national security. She has published widely on African resource politics.

Antonetta Hamandishe is a PhD student in peace governance and develop-ment with UPEACE. She received an MA in international relations from the Department of Social Science at Oxford Brookes University; an MA in human rights, peace, and development from Africa University; a certificate in project monitoring and evaluation from the University of Zimbabwe; and a BA(Hons) in history and development studies from Midlands State University.

Charles Okongo Imbiakha is the head of teaching and curriculum at the National Defense University-Kenya and holds a PhD in diplomacy and international relations.

Cliff Ubba Kodero is an assistant professor in the political economy department at the College of Idaho. He earned his PhD from Florida International University's Steven J. Green School of International and Public Affairs, where he specialized in international relations, focusing on the international political economy.

Edward Lange is the senior research and advocacy officer at the Southern Africa Resource Watch. He has worked as the executive director of the Copper Belt Land Rights Centre. His areas of expertise include land rights, community mobilization, research, stakeholders' engagement and empowerment, human rights, and environment. His work involves coordinating, mobilizing, and monitoring community-driven initiatives with resource-host communities.

Fernand Guevara Mekongo-Mballa is a doctoral candidate in international law at the Catholic University of Central Africa. His research focuses on climate change, sustainable development, the rights of minorities, local populations, and the intersection of international law and international relations in the domains of security and development.

Arcade Ndoricimpa is an associate professor of Economics in the Faculty of Economics and Management at the University of Burundi. He obtained a PhD in economics from the University of Dar es Salaam (Tanzania).

Hassan Bashir Mohamed Nour is a professor of public economics at Al Nealain University, Sudan. He is the dean of the Faculty of Economic and Social Studies.

Kenneth O. Nyangena is a lecturer of sociology, leadership, gender, and governance at Laikipia University-Kenya. He is also the current chairperson of the Department of Public Affairs of Laikipia University.

Michael Ogbe is an advisor/data analyst at the Norwegian Institute of Public Health. He has a PhD in geographic information systems and natural resource management from the Norwegian University of Science and Technology. His research interests cover examining, mapping, and clarifying the spatiality of natural resources/environmental management; human livelihood adaptations and health; and sustainable energies at multiple spatial scales, using various qualitative, statistical, and geospatial tools. Additionally, he serves as an external examiner/visiting lecturer at the Department of Geography, Norwegian University of Science and Technology.

Parfait Oumba is an associate professor and vice department chair of the Department of Public Law at the Catholic University of Central Africa. His doctoral research centered on the international responsibility of the state and environmental risks.

Jacopo Resti is a development practitioner and researcher working on economic governance, taxation, food security, community stabilization, and migration. He has experience with international organizations and think tanks at HQ and field level on policies and projects covering Sudan, Eritrea, Ethiopia, and Cameroon. His latest professional and research endeavors focus on food systems transformation, the politics of taxation, and African Union-European Union cooperation on governance and migration. He is a PhD candidate in public policy at the Central European University (CEU), where he has researched tax morale and state-building in Sudan.

Dung Pam Sha is a professor of political economy and development studies in the Department of Political Science University of Jos, Nigeria. He received his PhD and MSc in political economy from the University of Jos, Nigeria, and a bachelor's degree in political science from the Ahmadu Bello University Zaria, Nigeria. His scholarly research straddles the subfields of political economy, public policy, and comparative politics. It focuses on the state and capital, trade unions, the politics of resource extraction, public policy, and minority rights, particularly in Africa.

Tinashe Sithole is a postdoctoral research fellow at SARChI Chair: African Diplomacy and Foreign Policy at the University of Johannesburg. His research interests focus on democracy, governance, and international political economy, focusing on challenges of development for African states in the global world, elections, human security, and peace and conflict. Sithole is interested in applying computational tools to his field. His main research projects utilize computational methods in topics such as the governance of extractive resources, social media, and democracy.

William John Walwa is a senior lecturer in the Department of Political Science at the University of Dar es Salaam. His areas of specialization include environmental security and governance, peace, conflict and strategic studies, politics, international relations, and governance.